Lawyers at Work

―――――――

Clare Cosslett

apress

Lawyers at Work

Copyright © 2012 by Clare Cosslett

This work is subject to copyright. All rights are reserved by the Publisher, whether the whole or part of the material is concerned, specifically the rights of translation, reprinting, reuse of illustrations, recitation, broadcasting, reproduction on microfilms or in any other physical way, and transmission or information storage and retrieval, electronic adaptation, computer software, or by similar or dissimilar methodology now known or hereafter developed. Exempted from this legal reservation are brief excerpts in connection with reviews or scholarly analysis or material supplied specifically for the purpose of being entered and executed on a computer system, for exclusive use by the purchaser of the work. Duplication of this publication or parts thereof is permitted only under the provisions of the Copyright Law of the Publisher's location, in its current version, and permission for use must always be obtained from Springer. Permissions for use may be obtained through RightsLink at the Copyright Clearance Center. Violations are liable to prosecution under the respective Copyright Law.

ISBN-13 (pbk): 978-1-4302-4503-2

ISBN-13 (electronic): 978-1-4302-4504-9

Trademarked names, logos, and images may appear in this book. Rather than use a trademark symbol with every occurrence of a trademarked name, logo, or image we use the names, logos, and images only in an editorial fashion and to the benefit of the trademark owner, with no intention of infringement of the trademark.

The use in this publication of trade names, trademarks, service marks, and similar terms, even if they are not identified as such, is not to be taken as an expression of opinion as to whether or not they are subject to proprietary rights.

While the advice and information in this book are believed to be true and accurate at the date of publication, neither the authors nor the editors nor the publisher can accept any legal responsibility for any errors or omissions that may be made. The publisher makes no warranty, express or implied, with respect to the material contained herein.

President and Publisher: Paul Manning
Lead Editor: Robert Hutchinson
Editorial Board: Steve Anglin, Mark Beckner, Ewan Buckingham, Gary Cornell, Louise Corrigan, Morgan Ertel, Jonathan Gennick, Jonathan Hassell, Robert Hutchinson, Michelle Lowman, James Markham, Matthew Moodie, Jeff Olson, Jeffrey Pepper, Douglas Pundick, Ben Renow-Clarke, Dominic Shakeshaft, Gwenan Spearing, Matt Wade, Tom Welsh
Coordinating Editor: Rita Fernando
Copy Editor: Kim Burton-Weisman
Compositor: SPi Global
Indexer: SPi Global
Cover Designer: Anna Ishchenko

Distributed to the book trade worldwide by Springer Science+Business Media New York, 233 Spring Street, 6th Floor, New York, NY 10013. Phone 1-800-SPRINGER, fax (201) 348-4505, e-mail orders-ny@springer-sbm.com, or visit www.springeronline.com. Apress Media, LLC is a California LLC and the sole member (owner) is Springer Science + Business Media Finance Inc (SSBM Finance Inc). SSBM Finance Inc is a Delaware corporation.

For information on translations, please e-mail rights@apress.com, or visit www.apress.com.

Apress and friends of ED books may be purchased in bulk for academic, corporate, or promotional use. eBook versions and licenses are also available for most titles. For more information, reference our Special Bulk Sales–eBook Licensing web page at www.apress.com/bulk-sales.

Any source code or other supplementary materials referenced by the author in this text is available to readers at www.apress.com. For detailed information about how to locate your book's source code, go to www.apress.com/source-code/.

To all the happy and unhappy lawyers I have come to know over the years.

Contents

Foreword vii

About the Author ix

Acknowledgments xi

Introduction xiii

Chapter 1.   Anne Vladeck, *Employment Law* 1

Chapter 2.   Jim Sanders, *Corporate Defense* 17

Chapter 3.   Jonathan Streeter, *Federal Prosecution* 37

Chapter 4.   Ken Kopelman, *Financial Services* 63

Chapter 5.   Nandan Nelivigi, *India Practice* 77

Chapter 6.   Jacalyn F. Barnett, *Family Law* 95

Chapter 7.   Peri Lynne Johnson, *International Law* 115

Chapter 8.   Kate Romain, *Cross-Border M&A* 133

Chapter 9.   Chris Sprigman, *Antitrust/Intellectual Property* 151

Chapter 10. Wayne Alexander, *Entertainment* 171

Chapter 11. Sean Delany, *Nonprofit* 193

Chapter 12. David Whedbee, *Civil Rights* 209

Chapter 13. Shane Kelley, *Trusts & Estates* 227

Chapter 14. Arthur Feldman, *Civil Litigation* 245

Chapter 15. Adam Nguyen, *Corporate/Legal Technology* 261

Index 281

Foreword

Lawyers at Work is a wonderful compilation of the eclectic and varied careers available to someone with a law degree. While perhaps most useful for those contemplating going to law school, or in law school, it is a fascinating read for anyone who is at all curious about what lawyers actually "do."

As a current federal judge who "did" criminal defense work as a lawyer, this was an eye-opener even for me. It's a real down-in-the-weeds look at what attorneys do every day: a family trust and estates lawyer in Florida who battles prolific fraud against the elderly; an entertainment lawyer who works with "hippie film makers like George Lucas" and helps creative authors bring their writings to fruition in a TV series or a movie; an entrepreneur who left legal practice to found a "profit-for-purpose" company that provided underprivileged kids with tutoring, test preparation, admissions advising, and mentoring; a law professor who studies stand-up comedy, the fashion industry, and cuisine in order to argue for more First Amendment freedom against prolific copyright laws; an American lawyer working in Paris, negotiating a multi-cross-cultural deal involving a Japanese-owned company headquartered in New Jersey buying a French-owned company in France; a director of a lawyer alliance in New York who in one year provided nearly 700 nonprofit groups with legal advice from a network of 1,400 volunteer lawyers.

Several of these attorneys knew even as children they wanted to be lawyers, while others meandered down accidental paths to law school, including one who admitted to being "completely clueless for about ten years" out of college before finding her way to law school. The author of this foreword sympathizes, having gone from college to working as a secretary, then to graduate journalism school, then to volunteering in civil rights, and then to law school—at which point her father began to despair if she would ever have a real job.

Some of these attorneys work in high-power regimented corporate offices with hundreds of other lawyers—while others operate in mom-and-pop outfits without a whole lot of rules. One attorney works in a firm specializing in police misconduct, wrongful incarceration, First Amendment claims, unlawful discrimination, and emphasizing a close relationship with each individual client—a holistic approach with empathy a foremost characteristic.

These lawyers also provide invaluable advice to those currently in law school: network with the school's alumni, even while in school. Get advice from them about legal and nonlegal careers. Also, cultivate and maintain friendships with

Foreword

your classmates. They become lifelong allies and resources as your career hits the inevitable twists and bumps in the road.

Other advice is more philosophical: "The biggest difficulty for students when they actually begin to work as a lawyer ... is transitioning from doing what they're told, which is how to excel in school, to doing what they want, which is how to excel in life and at a career... Chart your own path."

Some also provide terrific advice on good lawyering in the courtroom: "You want to tell a narrative, as opposed to just a bunch of little pieces of information. You want to teach. You want to simplify complicated concepts and make them understandable for the jury. And you want to keep the jury engaged and interested." The same attorney emphasizes establishing your "credibility" by knowing the evidence well, even to the point of memorizing exhibit numbers, and telling the story in a calm way that is supported by the evidence.

All in all, Lawyers at Work is a fascinating read. Among other things, I finally learned what a "derivative" is!

Helen G. Berrigan

United States District Judge

Eastern District of Louisiana

About the Author

Clare Cosslett is the principal and founder of Cosslett & Company, a New York legal search and placement firm. As a former practicing attorney and a legal recruiter with more than twenty years of experience, Clare has met and interviewed hundreds of lawyers. She works with top firms and a wide variety of in-house clients, placing lawyers at all seniority levels nationally and internationally. Before opening her own business in 2002, Clare was a senior recruiter with Lucas Group and a vice president and senior recruiter with its New York predecessor, London and Company. Clare practiced law as a corporate attorney in the New York offices of Skadden, Arps, Slate, Meagher & Flom LLP and Moses & Singer. She has a JD cum laude from Brooklyn Law School and a BA from Columbia University.

Acknowledgments

Many thanks to the lawyers who participated as interviewees and to friends who made introductions on my behalf.

Thanks to my family: my husband for encouraging me; Preston for reminding me how to work hard; Malcolm, without whose expertise, this book simply never would have happened; and Dante for keeping me company.

Thanks to Apress for the idea of this book; to Robert Hutchinson for trusting me to write it; to Rita Fernando for her endless patience; and to Kristen Ng for her perfect ear.

Introduction

The practice of law is not monolithic. Professional directories for the United States sort one million lawyers and 50,000 law firms into some 65 core practice areas. In *Lawyers at Work*, I interview fifteen lawyers in fifteen practice areas selected to be representative of the lawyering spectrum: employment law, corporate defense, criminal prosecution, financial services, international project finance, family law, international law, cross-border mergers and acquisitions, antitrust, intellectual property, entertainment, nonprofit, civil rights, trusts and estates, and civil litigation.

My interviewing method has been to elicit from this ensemble of lawyers their own stories in their own words. My aim has been to get at what makes them tick: why they went into law, how they matched their personal traits and values to their chosen practice areas, how they built their careers and developed their styles of practice, how they manage the tensions between their professional and private lives, and what drives them to lawyer on.

The lawyers I interviewed gave me a variety of reasons for becoming lawyers. About half of them became lawyers because of a strong family legacy in the law. One became a lawyer in spite of her family. Some found inspiring role models and others thought they would enjoy the intellectual rigor of the law. Some knew exactly what they wanted to do even before entering law school. Others stumbled into their area of expertise after leaving law school.

Some of the lawyers interviewed in this book are "true believers" whose practices reflect personal ethical imperatives to redress social inequities. Sean Delany, for example, has spent his career in the area of public service representing the indigent. David Whedbee has always reached out to protect the civil rights of the least affluent. Anne Vladeck never doubted that, as an employment lawyer in her family firm, she would represent unions and employee plaintiffs against big employers, just as her parents had done.

You can't imagine a "true-believer" representing the other side without a crisis of conscience. By contrast, a "shades-of-grey" lawyer such as Jon Streeter is equally at ease prosecuting or defending the same classes of litigants. And Jim Sanders, tongue firmly in cheek, avers that moving from a public defender role to a corporate defense role can still be considered indigent defense if your client doesn't pay.

Introduction

Some lawyers, such as Arthur Feldman, enjoy taking on a broad array of cases. Many others—like Ken Kopelman, Jacalyn Barnett, Wayne Alexander, and Shane Kelley—opt not to stray from their field of expertise. Some have taken their practice onto an international stage, like Nandan Nelivigi, Peri Lynne Johnson, and Kate Romain. Others have acquired their legal expertise in practice and then applied it to academia and authorship, like Chris Sprigman, or to entrepreneurship, like Adam Nguyen.

In interviewing these fifteen lawyers, I discovered that, despite the diversity of their practices, priorities, and personalities, they all shared one trait in common. Each had taken an aggressively proactive approach to his or her career. When they saw opportunities, either professional or personal, they went for them. They took risks and followed their instincts in selecting paths that were often neither straight nor continuous. Falling in love or raising a family can redefine a professional path without derailing it.

In twenty years of legal recruiting, I've seen the market seesaw back and forth between jobs looking for good lawyers in times of economic growth, and lawyers looking for good jobs in times of contraction. It is no secret that since 2008 law schools have been producing more lawyers than there are jobs and that the median salary for junior attorneys has dropped.

For those considering law school, it is always risky to predict what the job market will look like years down the road. What prospective lawyers do know is that a shrinking market swells the ranks of unemployed and underemployed lawyers, against whom they'll find themselves competing after law school.

In the face of a weak and highly competitive market, it is imperative for prospective lawyers to chart a realistic career plan before investing in a JD. Law is no longer a fallback profession for dilettantes and temporizers. If you understand what it means to practice law and you still want to do it—do it. If not, do something else. Being a lawyer is hard work for those who love it. It is not a life for those who do not.

The practitioners in this book all love their work, and all of them have weathered economic storms and market turmoil. Collectively, they prove two complementary propositions. First, lawyers can have exciting, remunerative, and personally satisfying careers. Second, before taking a shot at the first proposition, a prospective lawyer had better research deeply the practice areas that interest her, take brutally honest stock of her own temperament and abilities, and satisfy herself that the two are in perfect alignment.

So, if your passion is law, take what lessons of the head and heart you can from the words of these fifteen legal practitioners who honor the legal profession and love what they do.

CHAPTER 1

Anne Vladeck

Partner
Vladeck, Waldman, Elias & Engelhard, P.C.

If you believe in workers' rights and want to practice employment law, then you are going to be on the plaintiff's side. And if this is the path you choose, then prepare to embrace the fate of Sisyphus, condemned to push a boulder to the top of the mountain only to watch it inevitably roll back down. For there is an inequality of resources in plaintiff-side employment discrimination work, **Anne C. Vladeck** *warns, such that it's easier and more lucrative to do management-side defense. But if you are a true believer—like Vladeck, who has a strong family history of left-of-center politics and her name on the door—you would never consider representing a company that had wrongfully fired an employee. Never.*

Vladeck took her BA, magna cum laude, from the University of Pennsylvania and her JD from Columbia Law School. She is an adjunct faculty member at Columbia Law School and has taught at Fordham and Cardozo Law Schools. She is a trustee of the Federal Bar Foundation (secretary), a member of the Executive Committee of the Federal Bar Council Inn of Court (president-emeritus), a former member of the Association of the Bar of the City of New York Professional Discipline Committee, and a Fellow of the American College of Trial Lawyers. She has received numerous awards for her work and is a frequent speaker on employment law and litigation issues.

Clare Cosslett: When was the firm of Vladeck, Waldman, Elias & Engelhard founded?

Anne Vladeck: My parents started this firm together in the late 1940s for the purpose of representing unions and workers. They were on the ground floor of employment discrimination because the antidiscrimination laws began to develop in the sixties and thereafter. The firm's discrimination practice has been a natural outgrowth of the labor practice.

Cosslett: Did your parents have a particular political ideology that made labor law a natural area in which to practice?

Vladeck: I think that labor and employment law is one of the areas where you normally do have a political bent. If you are just interested in the subject matter but don't have a political leaning, you should do management-side work and represent companies, because you earn more and you're treated differently by some of the courts. If you believe in workers' rights, then you're going to be on the union side or the plaintiff side. And, more than just about any other area of law, it is political in the sense of which side you pick. There are some people who do both sides, but that's fairly rare. They tell you in law school that you can do either side and it doesn't matter, but I think with labor and employment law that's wrong.

Cosslett: When you say you're treated differently by the courts when you're representing the plaintiff side, what do you mean?

Vladeck: Many judges think that employment disputes are not really worthy of federal court because the plaintiffs are individuals. Some federal judges are more interested in antitrust or corporate cases. I'm not saying this is true of all judges, but certainly some judges think that employment cases should be dealt with by separate courts, like Social Security or immigration, they should be given a different designation. And it makes it more difficult when you have an employment case if you have a judge who, to some extent, thinks you're wasting his time. It's always been our belief that we have to put in papers that are better, and clearer, and more succinct, because we're going to lose the attention of the judge. It's not necessarily political, but some of it is also politics. Some judges really think that courts have gone too far in the antidiscrimination laws.

What's interesting, I think, is that judges are not happy to see certain claims in their courtroom, but if it becomes an issue for a friend or relative, then all of a sudden they're the best claims ever and we should go to the Supreme Court.

Cosslett: Why did you decide to go to University of Pennsylvania for college and did you know that you were going to go on to law school?

Vladeck: I grew up on the Upper West Side in Manhattan and went to PS 87. I then went to a very small high school and I wanted something that was big and urban. Penn just seemed to be perfect. And it was. I thought it was great. I actually didn't make the decision to go to law school until I walked in the door of Columbia Law School.

Cosslett: What other career paths were you considering?

Vladeck: When my mother was asked what I was going to do, she used to say I was going to be a doctor or a lawyer or do batik. If I had more talent, I would have been an artist. And if I could stand the sight of blood and been better at science, I would have been a doctor. Law school was a default position.

Cosslett: Once you had made the decision to go to law school, did you plan to join your parents' practice? Or did you say, "I'm going to do this, but I'm going to carve my own path"?

Vladeck: I don't think either. The first firm I went to right out of law school was an environmental law firm, and it was presented as a public interest firm, with clients like the Adirondack Council. There were issues relating to what they were going to do with Whiteface Mountain for the Olympics. I thought that was perfect.

They were then retained to defend a class action against a medical school. They thought I would be perfect for that. I didn't agree. I hated the work and so, while I still liked a lot of people who were there, I left after about a year to go to what was then Frankfurt Garbus Klein & Selz, which is a First Amendment entertainment firm. It is now Frankfurt Kurnit Klein & Selz.

Cosslett: So many lawyers start out in their career and they get to the first place, and they think, "Oh, this isn't what I thought. I don't like this." And then they feel stuck.

Vladeck: This was in 1979 and the market was very strong. I said to myself, "This isn't for me," did some exploratory work and had a job within a week.

When I was hired, I was the tenth lawyer at Frankfurt Kurnit. I think there are now about sixty lawyers. I did a lot of First Amendment work. I did some of the libel work for Viking/Penguin, which was a major client. Some of it was entertainment litigation, where a star was in a magazine and they airbrushed out her dress. Things like that.

Cosslett: You avoided the big-firm route, and I'm sure they were beating down your door.

Vladeck: It never occurred to me to do that. Even during the summer, I worked as an intern for the US Attorney's Office. I didn't want to work at a big firm. One summer in college, I worked at a big firm proofreading legal documents. It was mind numbing. I said, "Not for me."

Cosslett: You were with Frankfurt Kurnit for about three and a half years. Did you find that you took on a lot of responsibility fairly early on?

Vladeck: Yes. And it was a firm where there was some supervision, but there was also some, "Just go do it." There were a lot of very good lawyers there, so there were people you could ask questions of who were more senior and who would help. It was very collegial. It was a great place.

The firm was divided between entertainment and litigation, with litigation being the smaller practice. It was intense, but it was good intense because instead of having six layers, where I was an associate reporting to a more senior associate who reported to a more senior associate, it was one on one with the partner and the client. It was much more collaborative. So I thought it was great. There was no time or money for a small firm to do make-work—to say, "Do a memo on this that I'll never use."

Cosslett: Sounds as though you were pretty happy there. Why did you leave?

Vladeck: My father died in the late seventies. One of my older brothers is a lawyer, and he and I were thinking it was probably a good idea to have a family member join my parents' practice if we were going to maintain it as a family firm. We believed that our parents had created something valuable. My brother was firmly ensconced in DC. At the time, he was at Public Citizen Litigation Group and was about to argue before the Supreme Court. So it seemed to be a more natural move for me. I started here in 1982.

Cosslett: How big was the firm when you joined?

Vladeck: I think there were about ten to fifteen lawyers. About the same size as we are now. We had gotten to be a much larger firm doing more union-side labor work, but we don't do very much of that anymore. We find that the employment litigation practice is really our specialty. There are a few small firms in New York that do labor work, and they tend to have certain institutional clients.

Cosslett: When you joined Vladeck, you were a fifth-year associate. Your mom was a senior partner. How was it to walk in as a midlevel associate? Did your mom take you under her wing, or did she say, "You're on your own kiddo"?

Vladeck: It was very natural because she treated most of the young associates like her kids anyway. The one thing that we had a very hard time with was figuring out what I was going to call her. We had a major case when I was first here called *Whittlesey v. Union Carbide*. We represented an employee who sued Union Carbide under the age discrimination act. Union Carbide argued that he was a high-enough-level employee that they were able to mandatorily retire him. It's a case that went up to the Second Circuit. We were in court on an injunction motion and we were in one of those old federal court elevators. My mother, who had one speed, which was fast, was getting out of the elevator before it arrived at the floor, and all of a sudden, I screamed, "Mom!" And everybody in the elevator cracked up, even people we were just yelling at.

So I ended up just calling her "Mom." That was the only real issue we had to deal with.

Cosslett: How was the *Whittlesey* case decided?

Vladeck: We had a bench trial before Judge Pierre Leval, who's at the Second Circuit now. He found that our client was discriminated against. And he also, for the first time in this circuit, ordered front pay instead of reinstatement because, under the circumstances, reinstatement would have been difficult for both the plaintiff and the company. It became one of the cases that's cited all the time for the front-pay principle.

Cosslett: I'm very confused about mandatory retirement.

Vladeck: If there's a real partnership, you can have mandatory retirement. But if it's not and you have employees, then you can't because it's unlawful for age to be the motivating factor in a decision. Contrary to what a lot of people believe, there's no upper limit on the laws against age discrimination. You have to be over forty to be covered by the ADEA,[1] but you could be ninety and sue for discrimination. One of my partners had a sexual harassment case for someone who was in her late seventies. It was settled.

Cosslett: How have you built your reputation as a litigator?

Vladeck: We have a lot of contact at this firm with clients and potential clients. So I started meeting people and helping them. It's word of mouth. The one thing that can be very satisfying is that we get a lot of referrals from the other side—from our adversaries—and even from the courts. So we have the sense that if we had left money on the table in a settlement or had not done a good job, our adversaries would not be sending us their friends or their partners. So reputation is developed in part in that way and then also through speaking or teaching. There are a lot of opportunities for speaking, such as courses and events for the Practicing Law Institute, the American Law Institute Continuing Legal Education, and ABA and bar associations. I've also done adjunct teaching at Fordham, Columbia, and Cardozo.

In teaching, you find that you learn things that can be very useful in your practice that otherwise you wouldn't have focused on. You go back and read some of the early cases that you use but haven't really thought about in a long time. It can be very, very helpful.

Cosslett: Is your practice primarily national, or is it New York–oriented?

Vladeck: It's primarily New York area, but it is national in the sense that we do have cases in other states. If we have a lawsuit out of state, we have local counsel. We also have some lawyers who have membership in bars outside New York, but the firm's practice is generally local. The companies, on the other hand, can be national and now with people working remotely, it's like a law school exam: "They work in Canada, but their headquarters are in New York, but the act took place in Florida."

Cosslett: Where does jurisdiction lie?

Vladeck: Your guess is as good as mine.

Cosslett: Are you seeing more of a particular type of employment discrimination than you used to?

---

[1] The Age Discrimination in Employment Act of 1967.

Vladeck: The type of case that we have seen a lot of recently is employees who are fired after they inform their employer that they have cancer or some other debilitating disease. It's really hard to watch. Some of the employers are beyond callous. It's not uncommon for us to have cases where someone went in for chemotherapy and then all of a sudden they got a bad performance review. It's terrible.

Csslett: To what do you attribute the influx of these kinds of cases?

Vladeck: Companies are becoming more bottom-line-oriented. They're concerned about the cost of health insurance. Some of these companies are self-insured, and so they're concerned that having a sick employee is going to be an economic drain both in terms of having an employee out and the insurance costs for the treatment.

If the company is self-insured and is concerned that it is going to pay more it's brutal. They say things like, "You're fired, but we'll keep you on COBRA for two weeks." They actually have to offer you COBRA for eighteen months—it's now longer in New York State. It can be quite expensive. So they tell somebody who has a potentially fatal illness that they no longer have a paycheck and have no health insurance.

This is what I meant by "it's political." There are some people who could represent either side. I could never, ever represent a company who did that. I just couldn't do it.

Csslett: Are these are big companies?

Vladeck: One of my partners is working on a case where our client was fired from a very large and well-regarded company, and there were e-mails suggesting a total lack of sympathy for his illness. Our client died.

Csslett: Why do people believe that what they write in an e-mail is not discoverable?

Vladeck: You wonder. And you know that there are always more e-mails out there than what you see. Some of the stuff is just unbelievable. We had a case recently where there were e-mails that started out, "Guard this with your life. Don't show anybody." And we thought, "Oops!"

Csslett: Oops! Are there other areas in which you're seeing an influx of suits?

Vladeck: There are pregnancy cases: women who do great and then all of a sudden they're pregnant and they can't walk and chew gum. And we're finding it's even worse if you dare to have a second child. Employers might be very proud of themselves that they let an employee come back with the first—but if it's a second, they're not so happy. There are age cases, race cases . . . they run the gamut. There are always a large number of cases in these areas but there are definitely more cancer cases. People don't think that companies would fire an employee when he or she is sick, because in some ways it's the height of cruelty. They do.

Cosslett: You must want to take every case that comes in.

Vladeck: We do sometimes.

Cosslett: You have a finite amount of time, yet there seems to be an infinite amount of employment discrimination out there. How do you decide what cases you're going to take?

Vladeck: It's a little bit of an eye of newt. Some of it is your instinct, and sometimes your instinct is wrong. But you meet the person, you have a sense of whether they're credible, and you try and get a sense of what their expectations are. There are a number of people who really just want their jobs back. A lot of people who oppose discrimination laws say people just want money. That's not true. People just want to be treated fairly. People want their jobs. I think that there is a common misperception that you can only be fired for cause, which in New York is not true. Unless you have an employment contract or you're a member of a union, employment is at will.

Cosslett: You can be fired at will, but you can't be fired when it comes to certain protected areas, right?

Vladeck: Exactly. You can be fired for any reason or no reason. You can't be fired for discriminatory reasons, such as age or race, but you can be fired for totally arbitrary reasons, like you are wearing a white shirt today.

Cosslett: They can fire you for wearing a white shirt?

Vladeck: They could say, "Okay, anybody in a pink shirt today, you're fired. Anybody in a white shirt today, you're fired." And that would be totally lawful. Now, if everybody wearing a white shirt on a particular day happens to be an African-American woman, then there might be an issue, but that's the theory.

Cosslett: There was a case, *Ezold v. Wolf Block*, in which a female attorney was denied partnership at her firm and claimed that it was sexual discrimination. Could you talk about that case?

Vladeck: Ezold was a 1993 case that Debra Raskin and my mother tried. It was a bench trial because in those days, you didn't have a jury in sex discrimination cases. And the district court found that she had been discriminated against. The law firm said she was not analytical enough for partnership. And the court found that she should have been made partner. It went to the Third Circuit, and the Third Circuit said essentially: "We are not going to get involved in partnership decisions. They are subjective, and they're allowed to make whatever decision they want"—and they reversed. I think that it is true still that there are certain employers who are given more deference: educational institutions on tenure decisions, and partnerships on whether somebody's going to become a partner. Those are areas that I think courts are less willing to delve into. Subjective decision making is a way of masking discrimination, but a lot of judges believe that whether somebody should be admitted to partnership or be given tenure are subjective decisions.

Cosslett: When you take those sorts of cases, do you feel that the evidence of discrimination needs to be stronger because of that predisposition?

Vladeck: You never know what's going to happen. I had a case years ago that was a tenure case against Columbia. And we had two judges who supported the district court and affirmed summary judgment. And one judge who wrote a scathing dissent about how the courts were not doing what they should, and this person had been discriminated against, and that Columbia might win this decision, but at what cost? Our philosophy is that you have to take a case that you're willing to lose. If the principle is important—which it is—then you have to be willing to lose, even if it's subjective and even if it's harder.

Cosslett: What about discrimination issues relating to sexual orientation?

Vladeck: There is no federal statute that prohibits it, but there are state and city laws. And there are more cases than there used to be, because now it's protected. But we don't see a huge number. We see some. We see cases where if somebody had not been out when they were hired and then they come out, all of a sudden they can't do anything well. I think also with sexual orientation issues and with some of the illness issues, companies and managers in companies haven't really learned to be subtle in their comments and their e-mail communications.

Cosslett: Can you talk about defamation and how that fits into your practice?

Vladeck: You can have a self-standing defamation case where somebody is not an employee. But defamation cases also do arise within an employment context. For example, if a company wants to cover up its discrimination based on age, to suggest that an employee had done something either criminal or dishonest can become a defamation claim. There are different privileges that are available to employers in the defamation context with respect to an employee, but there are still cases where you win or you settle because what is said about an employee is not only false, but the employer knows it to be false. So you have self-standing defamation claims, but you also do have them in the context of employment. Or you might have a discrimination claim and also a defamation claim.

Cosslett: Do you find as a business that you take certain cases because you want them and you believe in them, and other cases because you also have to keep the lights on?

Vladeck: We've been very lucky that we've been able to keep the lights on with the cases that we want to take.

There's a saying that, "You can do well by doing right," and it's true. We're lucky that there are some equal-opportunity pigs out there who are very rich and just keep doing what comes naturally.

Cosslett: How does your firm work in terms of billing? Do you work on contingency?

Vladeck: It totally runs the gamut. We will occasionally work on a full contingency, but not normally. We will work on a hybrid, which is an hourly rate plus a percentage. It's all over the lot. We evaluate the case and the person, so while we have some general rules and general hourly rates, billing is more tailored to the particular person and the particular case.

Because of the way the laws have developed in discrimination cases, you're considered to be a private attorney-general in bringing a case that is supposed to have a public interest. Knowing that individuals couldn't afford to prosecute cases, discrimination laws provide for the award of attorney's fees to a successful plaintiff. So it's prevailing party, but if you lose, you don't automatically have to pay their fees. That has a different standard, which is that the case has to be frivolous. But there is a wrinkle: New York State law doesn't provide for attorney's fees, but New York City law does.

Cosslett: So you either have to have a federal cause of action or a city cause of action to have attorney's fees?

Vladeck: It's very convoluted. And some employers understand, even in settlement, that payment of attorney's fees is something that they're going to have to include because they would have to do it later. They are going to have to pay their own lawyers, too.

Cosslett: Do you see a lot of cases coming out of Wall Street?

Vladeck: There's always Wall Street, the bigger financial institutions, but in the past year or so, there have been a number of smaller hedge funds that have issues, generally involving bonuses. Somebody doesn't get their bonus. They're discrimination claims and retaliation if somebody complains. Retaliation is a big area.

If you have a reasonable basis to believe that you've been discriminated against and you assert a complaint, and then all of a sudden there's something done to you, like you're fired or demoted, that's unlawful. It's a separate claim. And that is where employers trip up a lot, because you can win a retaliation claim even if you don't win an underlying discrimination claim. So if you come to an employer and say, "He's sexually harassing me. He's done this, that, and the other,"—and then, all of a sudden, they start looking and seeing whether you've done anything with your expense account or they transfer you to Siberia: that's all a claim. They did it in reaction to the original claim, even if the sexual harassment claim is not enough under the law.

Cosslett: Aren't bonus cases just about breach-of-contract?

Vladeck: They are, but they're also potentially labor law claims. If you have earned a bonus but the company has these rules where they'll only pay you on an alternate Tuesday if the moon is in Arizona, then you end up having not only a contract claim, but a labor law claim, which gives you additional damages and attorney's fees, which contract claims do not. The issue is whether it is a discretionary bonus or something you've already earned. We have a fair number of those cases.

Cosslett: Do you tend to represent groups of people, or is it usually individuals?

Vladeck: We tend to represent groups for the wage and hour cases. But for the discrimination cases, we occasionally represent groups, but very often they are individuals or two or three people.

Cosslett: You've been involved in some very high-profile litigations, probably the most well-known of which was the 2007 lawsuit against the New York Knicks general manager Isiah Thomas and Madison Square Garden, in which you represented Anucha Browne Sanders in a sexual harassment action and secured an $11.6 million jury verdict on her behalf. How did you approach that case, and was there a moment in the courtroom when you realized, "Wow! All the stars are in alignment. I'm going to get a huge verdict for my client"?

Vladeck: I think a successful litigation starts well before you get into the courtroom. It really starts with the process of discovery and getting documents and knowing what they are and what they mean, and getting depositions. I think one thing that was critical in Anucha's case was that we had locked in testimony in video depositions of the decision maker saying he relied exclusively on his HR executive to learn that Anucha had done certain things that had led to firing her. And we had the HR executive on tape in his depositions say, "I never talked to him about her, ever." And we had the ability to show the jury the tape: "I just relied on him. That's where my knowledge comes from"—and then roll to the second tape: "I never talked to him about her, ever." So, as the judge said, one of them was lying, and they were lying about why she was fired, which was the ultimate issue, or at least part of the ultimate issue in that case.

So it really goes back to taking the discovery process extremely seriously, knowing your case, and not underestimating juries. Some lawyers assume that jurors are not smart and talk down to them. It's hard because there are certain things that you need jurors to understand, but you don't want to give them the impression that you think that they're not smart.

Cosslett: Do you find that the issues involved in a discrimination cases are interesting to and understood by jurors? Do you think there is more of a sense of empathy—"I could be that person in the plaintiff's chair next week"— than there might be in, say, a derivatives trade gone wrong?

Vladeck: I think jurors are interested in employment cases in the sense that everybody is either an employer, or an employee, or lives with somebody who's employed and so it's within their knowledge—which is very helpful in some ways, and in some ways it's not. People often have wrong ideas about what's protected, what's not, what's acceptable activity in the workplace, and what's not.

Cosslett: How different is a case that takes on front-page proportions from a case that's lower profile?

Vladeck: Even the judge was somewhat surprised by how much media attention the Anucha Brown Sanders case generated. When he did the voir dire—the jury selection—he had asked the potential jurors whether they could read the paper without reading the sports section during the trial. And then when the trial started, it was on the front page because you had Stephon Marbury and other high-profile individuals.

It can be daunting when you have so many people watching, many of whom are sure you're going to lose. You really have only two audiences: the jury and the judge—and not the people who are writing about the trial or reporting on it. But, obviously, that's something that you hear about and see. The number of people who predicted that we were going to lose was huge. To the extent that I could just talk to the jury, that's certainly what I tried to do.

Cosslett: How long did the case take from the day Anucha walked in to see you until the day you got the verdict?

Vladeck: It was quick: about a year and a half. The trial itself straddled three weeks, but it was also during the Jewish holidays, so there were weeks that only had two or three trial days. It felt like a long time, but it wasn't three weeks day-to-day-to-day of trial.

Cosslett: Do you like being in the courtroom?

Vladeck: I love being in the courtroom. I love trials, and I love the process of putting together a puzzle and having the jury understand it. When you talk to jury members afterward, it's amazing that they sometimes focus on things that none of the lawyers ever anticipated. Or they understand something in a way that you don't have a clue where they got it. But sometimes it's the opposite—where they really do understand what you have tried to do. We try to speak to the jurors after a trial to get their feedback and it is always interesting. Sometimes they'll say, "Why didn't you do this?" or "Why didn't you do that?" or "Why didn't they do this?"

Cosslett: Do you have a particular style when you walk into a courtroom?

Vladeck: I think it's a mistake for people to be different than who they are, because I think it shows. A lot of people are very dramatic and walk around and gesture. I'm not like that, and I don't do that normally, so I don't do that with a jury. I try and connect and look at jurors as I'm talking, but I don't think I have a particular style. It's just who I am.

Cosslett: I've talked to several other litigators and they said exactly that. You have to go in and be who you are. If you're flamboyant, be flamboyant. But if you're not, don't be.

Vladeck: There are people who would be critical if you're not flamboyant. I think if I tried to be flamboyant, I would look like a jerk, and I wouldn't even be credible to myself. So I think if there's a connection and you can try and talk to a juror as if you were talking to him or her the way we're talking, with coffee around the table—that's the way I am, and I think it would look hollow otherwise. There are some people who are very flamboyant who can be flamboyant in a courtroom. That's great.

Cosslett: Are there any "bells and whistles" that you use in the courtroom to keep the jury engaged?

Vladeck: One thing that has happened that is totally different today from the first trial I had, which was in the eighties, is that in those days, if you had a demonstrative, like on a big piece of white oak tag or cardboard, that was pretty special. Now you need pyrotechnics. You need videos of depositions. You need PowerPoints. You need timelines. You really need some kind of visual because, otherwise, I think a jury will get bored.

Cosslett: If the other side is introducing a stream of visuals, you don't want to look as though you're being outdone.

Vladeck: Exactly. So you have to have some of that. It used to be that we would read the deposition to the jury while another lawyer playing the part of the deponent was sitting in the witness chair. Half the time, the jury would fall asleep.

But now you can videotape depositions and one thing that can be very helpful is that high-level people often don't spend time being prepared for a deposition, so they can appear to be very, very smug and very, very cocky on their deposition video. They then come in trying to charm the jury. And the jury can see that these are two totally different people and think that they're being put on. So that can be very useful.

Now deponents are getting better because their lawyers are preparing them for their depositions. In the beginning, when the videos were new, you got a lot of inconsistency, which was very helpful.

Cosslett: Does it cost more to defend than to prosecute?

Vladeck: The amount of money that can be spent in the defense of one of these cases is frightening. Between the investigators, where they have people checking up on our clients going back to high school, with the jury consultants and so on, the money is astronomical.

You could spend the same to prosecute—but you don't, because first of all, we don't have it. What is remarkable is that companies will sometimes spend ten times the amount that they could have settled a case for. They want to prove something. They put their foot down.

Cosslett: These big companies are hiring big law firms. Do you enjoy going up against these firms? Is it a David and Goliath thing?

Vladeck: I do always have the sense that it's David and Goliath because of the amount of money that is spent by the defense. We had three lawyers on the Garden case and they had more than we could count, over twenty. They used Epstein Becker, Morgan Lewis, Berke-Weiss & Pechman, Eisenberg & Bogas, and Manatt. They had a number of lawyers.

But the one thing about employment is that you have the same adversaries very often, and you know them and they know you. There are some lawyers that we've litigated against in seven or eight trials.

My first trial in 1985 was against the same lawyer who represented the Garden more than twenty years later, Ron Green of Epstein Becker. It was an age discrimination case against ABC in the Southern District with Judge Weinfeld, who was something of a legend.

Our client had worked on a soap opera for thirty years, and he was fired. We said it was for age, and they said it was because he wasn't doing his job. And we were very lucky. Ron told me years later that he liked to try different strategies at different trials. In the ABC case, he was trying to show that our client's hearing had gone and so he couldn't do his job. When Ron started doing his cross, he did it in a very low voice. Unfortunately for Ron, the judge was over eighty years old, so when Ron was talking very quietly, the judge was yelling, "Speak up! I can't hear you!"

We won the case.

Cosslett: What is it about litigation that gives you the most satisfaction, and what's the most difficult?

Vladeck: The most satisfaction is that you have a client who needs to be heard and who is then believed. One of the things you get in these cases is that the client is a gold digger, or all they want is money, or they're making it up—so it's very satisfying to have that kind of affirmation. They were believed and can feel good about having done what they did. The hardest thing is when people that they thought were friends, and colleagues, and confidants all of a sudden are afraid to come forward, and, even at the last minute, will sometimes say, "I can't do it. I don't remember." These are very human situations, and so it runs the gamut of people who are, to some extent, heroic, because they are willing to do things that might cost them, to some people who, understandably or not, are either cowardly or want the jobs and the promotions that come with supporting the company.

Cosslett: You learn a lot about human nature in these cases, probably more than in other practice areas.

Vladeck: You do, which makes it interesting but hard. We have clients who do not believe that other people lie under oath, and we will have to tell them that people lie under oath all the time. I have to give them credit to some extent but they really think that that's not going to happen, and then they're open-mouthed when it does.

Cosslett: What continues to motivate you as a lawyer?

Vladeck: I like what I do. I think employment law is endlessly fascinating. You get to learn about a lot of different industries. You meet people at every level doing a lot of different jobs. You learn how widgets are made, which you would have otherwise never known. I think we're doing good things when people tell us that we've changed their lives by either getting their jobs back or getting them money so that they could have a bridge to another job. You can't beat that.

Cosslett: Are there issues of professional responsibility that come up for you in connection with your role as an employment litigator specifically, or in connection with your role as a litigator generally?

Vladeck: The one issue that comes up, and it comes up frequently, is that the people who believe they've been discriminated against are often human resources personnel or in-house counsel. And the question is, what can they show us? Or what is so privileged that they can't even show their own lawyers? So there are ethics issues that come up in those instances.

The other thing is that very often we will not see somebody because there's a potential conflict. For example, if somebody is an in-house lawyer or an in-house HR person and they want to have a consult with us, but we represent other employees of that company, legal and HR has access to what's going on with those employees, so we have to send them elsewhere. A lot of people have a hard time understanding that that's a potential conflict, even though we're not representing the company. It's our belief that that's a conflict or a potential conflict, but that's hard to explain. The people who seem to have the hardest time understanding the conflicts are the in-house lawyers.

Cosslett: Is there a skill set that's particularly useful for an employment litigator or a general litigator?

Vladeck: I think both for an employment lawyer and a litigator, one of the skill sets is intellectual curiosity and curiosity generally. You'll often follow down a path of either discovery or research, and while some of the paths may be fruitless, you may sometimes find amazing things. So I do think that curiosity is going to get you to the next step. It is also important to write well and be articulate. But I think the most important thing is to have interest in the area and to be willing to be like Sisyphus, where you continue to push the ball up when it comes down. There is an inequality of resources and reactions, so you have to be very committed.

The other thing about employment law is that very often you have cutting-edge evidentiary issues. And those are fabulous because they really help you realize that employment law is an interesting area of the law. For example, there's the equivalent of the rape shield law, where, in a sexual harassment case, you can no longer go back through a woman's history and find out information that really is not relevant to the case at hand. And you have issues related to evidence that are specifically for employment cases.

I think the most important characteristic for a lawyer and a litigator is that you have to learn to listen, and not just talk. People who just don't listen don't get the information that they really need.

Cosslett: Would you encourage lawyers who have that skill set to go into employment litigation? Is it a deep practice in terms of opportunities?

Vladeck: Yes, although I will come full circle. If you just like the area, go to the management firms or go to a government agency. If you have a political interest in workers' rights, then you come to a plaintiff's firm. And I think absolutely if somebody has an interest in it, they should try it.

CHAPTER 2

Jim Sanders

Partner

Neal & Harwell, PLC

Certain companies in America—some more frequently than others—find themselves in such high-profile, high-stakes litigations that they need to assemble a cadre of trial lawyers with the experience, the savvy, and the gut-set to defend what some would consider the indefensible. These are lawyers who take the "bet-the-ranch" cases: the cases that, if lost, would have severely negative financial and reputational consequences for their corporate clients. **James F. Sanders** is one of those lawyers. Trained by Jim Neal, one of the most highly-regarded corporate defense lawyers of his time, Sanders' most notorious client is likely Exxon Mobil Corporation, which he represented most publicly in the Valdez oil spill litigations and more recently in the 2006 Baltimore gasoline leak cases.

As a person and as a legal tactician, Sanders is not without contradiction. He is an avowed Yellow Dog Democrat and ex-hippie who enthusiastically defends big oil, big insurance, and big pharma. As a lawyer, he rues the increased tendency of litigants to settle cases without going to trial as a diminishment of the democratic process. Yet, as a corporate defense lawyer, he recognizes that he has to "redefine winning" when it comes to the challenge of persuading a jury of the plaintiff's peers to decide in favor of a "bloodless entity."

Sanders took his BA from Vanderbilt University and his JD from Vanderbilt University School of Law. He was a law clerk for the Honorable Judge William E. Miller of the US Court of Appeals for the Sixth Circuit and for the Honorable Judge Frank Gray, Jr., chief judge of the US District Court for the Middle District of Tennessee.

Chapter 2 | *Jim Sanders:* Corporate Defense

Clare Cosslett: I am with Jim Sanders in the elegant offices of Neal & Harwell in downtown Nashville, Tennessee. Looking out of the windows, I can see the Cumberland River meandering along in the foreground, and in the distance, through the rain, a cloud-covered mountain range. It is a beautiful view.

Jim Sanders: You did a good job pronouncing "Tennessee." You almost got it right.

Cosslett: Not bad for a New Yorker? Were you born and raised in Tennessee?

Sanders: I grew up in Johnson City, Tennessee, and what people find interesting about my family is that a couple of generations back, in the 1880s, my great-grandfather and my great-great-uncle were brothers, and they were both politically active. It was one of those parts of the South where politics divided within families: one was a Democrat, the other was a Republican. And they were both accomplished speakers. In 1886, they each secured the nomination of their party and ran against each other for the governorship of Tennessee. They didn't have much by way of funds, and so they traveled together throughout the state. There are wonderful stories about how they swiped each other's speeches.

Cosslett: Who won?

Sanders: The Democrat won, but the Republican, who was my great-grandfather, ultimately became governor of Tennessee in 1920. His brother, Bob, became governor, and then a US Senator. He was influential in the Progressive movement at the turn of the century. My great-grandfather had ten children and of those ten, two were lawyers: one was Bob Taylor, a federal judge in Knoxville. There was also a younger brother, Ben, who died young. Supposedly he was a better lawyer than Bob. That's the background of the family on my mother's side. My father got thoroughly sick of hearing all that. I would ask him about his people, and he would say, "They were horse thieves in Virginia."

Cosslett: What did your father do?

Sanders: He sold International Harvester farm equipment. Not many big farms in Johnson City, Tennessee. He had served in the Army in World War II and he did not like taking orders. So when he got out of the Army and was going into business, he didn't want anyone telling him what to do. He founded a business with a partner, and he chose that business more because he could be the boss than because he loved farm equipment.

Cosslett: When you were growing up, was it assumed that you would be a lawyer?

Sanders: Not at all. Uncle Bob, being a federal judge in Knoxville, had almost no influence on us. It might as well have been the moon from Johnson City to Knoxville in those days. He was very busy and very important, and I rarely ever saw him.

I decided to be a lawyer when I was in high school. I was lucky. I knew what I wanted to do pretty early on.

Cosslett: Why Vanderbilt Law School?

Sanders: As I mentioned, my father was not a business magnate, and I knew that if I was going to go to a good college, I would need to get a scholarship. I was an athlete in high school, and I was probably better at football than anything else. I had a wonderful teammate who became the Heisman Trophy winner at the University of Florida. He was the quarterback and I was the only kid on the team who could really catch the football, so we were a duo and I got several scholarship offers. I made a calculated choice and went to the best school that I could go to, regardless of the football team. That got me to Vanderbilt undergraduate.

When I got ready to go to law school, I was not flush. I was accepted at Vanderbilt. I could get a partial scholarship, plus I could be a resident advisor in a dormitory and get my room and board paid for. So it was a very easy choice for me. I was lucky to have Vanderbilt as an option, because it was considered a very good law school.

Cosslett: Did you enjoy law school?

Sanders: I liked law school as an intellectual exercise. What I didn't like was the preoccupation with grades and class standing. I was counterculture enough to not like that. Also, it was hard going to law school and being a dorm advisor. You're different from most of the people who go to an expensive private school. And law school was somewhat removed from what interested me about practicing law. I always wanted to be a trial lawyer and I was interested in learning how to try cases.

I was also very interested in the role of law in improving society. I grew up in a de facto segregated community—this was in the early sixties in Johnson City. There was no animus behind it. It just was what it was. We had a black high school and a white high school. The ballplayers were friendly with each other. We'd go to their games. They'd come to ours. We'd have sandlot games.

When I came to Vanderbilt, all of the issues of race that were on the nightly news suddenly came a little closer. It became an important issue for me as I went through undergraduate. I became cause-y.

Cosslett: If you weren't cause-y in the sixties you weren't paying attention.

Sanders: I viewed practicing law as an instrument of beneficial social change. One of the things that always fascinated me was criminal law. I believed that most people who were charged with offenses were innocent and I wanted to see justice done. When I was in law school, I volunteered to visit the prison and talk to prisoners. In the summers, I would help represent inmates with habeas corpus petitions. I was also interested in constitutional law.

Chapter 2 | Jim Sanders: Corporate Defense

Cosslett: You got caught up in the draft in the late sixties?

Sanders: My law school class was to graduate in '70. Around December of our first year, the Selective Service took away the 2S deferment for law students. So my whole class was presented with, "You are not going to get to finish law school on time because of the draft."

I got through the first semester of law school. My grades were pretty good, and then we get hit with this news. I ended up getting into the ROTC so that I could finish law school and not get drafted.

Cosslett: No wonder you didn't have fun in law school.

Sanders: It made a difference. And then of course, on top of that, we had all that was going on in Vietnam and Cambodia. It was a bad war for the wrong reasons. It made me very antiestablishment, naturally. Even the more conservative guys in the class got a little ticked off about what was happening.

Cosslett: When you were in Seattle with the ROTC, you worked at the public defender's office?

Sanders: My assignment in Seattle was with an induction center, an Armed Forces Entrance and Examination Center, known as AFEEC. It was a job that certainly didn't require a whole lot of work and thought. I still wanted to be a lawyer, representing criminal defendants, so I volunteered for work in the public defender's office while I was in the Army. I worked for free and I got involved in some interesting things, including a couple of small municipal court trials.

Cosslett: You also did a clerkship right out of law school?

Sanders: After law school and before going into the military, I clerked for about six months with a Sixth Circuit judge. It was an interesting coincidence. The law clerk he had selected avoided getting drafted by going into the National Guard. It turned out that part of his National Guard obligation was in the first half-year of his clerkship. So Judge Miller needed a law clerk for that time.

One of the reasons I got the clerkship was that Judge Miller was originally from Johnson City. He knew my family. He was a Republican appointee that they had sent down to Nashville, which did not sit well with a lot of Democrats. It turned out he was absolutely a great judge. And those who came to scoff stayed to praise.

I worked with Judge Miller in Nashville and Cincinnati, and then I had to go into the military. While I was in Seattle and volunteering for the public defender's office, another clerkship back here in Nashville came open. Judge Frank Gray was the chief judge at the time. He was a good old Democrat and was Estes Kefauver's confidant and political campaign manager. That's how he got to the judgeship. I got out of the Army a little bit early and I clerked for Judge Gray for three years.

Cosslett: That's a long clerkship.

Sanders: Yes, he had to run me off. I loved him. I was his only clerk, so I felt like I was the assistant judge. I wrote a bunch of opinions and I was drunk with power. It was a great experience. Nashville had an inordinate number of really fine trial lawyers, one of whom was Jim Neal. And I got to see some really good lawyers practice law, and that fanned the flame of what I wanted to do. But I decided that, "I don't want to stay where I am and network. I want to see how I will do practicing law where nobody knows me. And I'm going to represent indigent defendants." So I got a job back in the public defender's office in Seattle in the Felony Trial Section. My goal was to do something good for society and try cases, and I did. It was a great experience and I did that for two years before coming back to Nashville.

Cosslett: Why did you return to Nashville?

Sanders: I didn't see the caliber of trial lawyer doing the kinds of cases that I was seeing when I was clerking with Judge Gray. I wanted to learn to be a really good trial lawyer, and if I stayed in Seattle, I was only going to get as good as I could by pulling myself up by my own bootstraps. I wanted to be on a faster track. So I came back to Tennessee and, ultimately, Jim Neal and I got together in representing a defendant. I joined the firm in '78 and became a partner the following year.

Cosslett: What was the firm's practice when you joined?

Sanders: Our niche was big-time, white-collar criminal defense. We also had a significant local practice that was spearheaded by Aubrey Harwell. There was a lot of local work and also a lot of transactional work.

Cosslett: Did you do any soul searching when you moved from indigent defense to a white-collar criminal defense practice?

Sanders: I used to get made fun of by some of my adversaries, saying I sold out. My response was that some of our cases turned out to be representing people who didn't have enough money to pay.

Cosslett: So it was, in fact, indigent defense.

Sanders: I liked private practice better than public defense. It's necessary to have some control over your client, particularly in a criminal case, and the first thing you had to do as a public defender was to convince the client that you were, in fact, a real lawyer.

If you don't have respect, it's hard to get control, and I spent two years learning ways to get control so that I could adequately represent my clients and do the best job I could do. When somebody hires you, they give you credibility and you can only lose that. You don't have to gain it. So it was still the same sort of work, and it was still fighting against injustice. But public defense is a harder life, because when you lose, your client goes to jail. And that's terrible. If you cannot take that on a regular basis, it'll kill you.

Cosslett: Jim Neal, the founder of this firm, obviously had an extraordinary career.

Sanders: He was an extraordinary lawyer. He started his trial career on the Hoffa task force for Bobby Kennedy, and he prosecuted Jimmy Hoffa here in Nashville. Judge Gray and Judge Miller were on the bench at that time. It was a two-bit labor misdemeanor violation prosecution, a nitpick sort of thing. And Hoffa and his group tried to bribe the jury.

Cosslett: What was Hoffa doing in Tennessee?

Sanders: They bought into some trucking company here, in violation of the National Labor Relations Act provisions. Rather than admit they'd done wrong and take a misdemeanor settlement, they wanted to fight. Bobby and Jimmy were alike in that way.

Jim Neal had a couple of friends that promoted him to Bobby Kennedy, and Kennedy chose him as the trial lawyer in the case. So Jim tried that case, which resulted in felony charges for jury-tampering being brought against Hoffa and others. It was tried down in Chattanooga, in front of one of the great district judges of that generation, a guy named Frank Wilson, who was a fine judge, impeccably honest—as were the two up here. One of the problems Hoffa had was that he wanted to bribe the judge, but he couldn't find a single person in all of middle Tennessee who even would consider going to one of these judges to try to bribe him.

So, Jim Neal secured the conviction of Hoffa, and then went on to become a US Attorney. But his work as Special Deputy to Bobby Kennedy was the foundation for Archibald Cox and then Leon Jaworski to say, "This is the guy." Jim became part of the prosecutorial team during Watergate. And, of course, almost everything that Jim got from that point on was the same sort of thinking: "If it's important enough for us to get it done right regardless of what it costs, then Jim Neal's the guy we want to represent us."

Cosslett: It's interesting that "the powers that be" went outside the inner circle of Washington to find him.

Sanders: In those days, the inner circle didn't have geographic limits. The guys who were considered to be *the* trial lawyers—"If it's really important, you've got to go get this guy"—were in a certain circle, but it wasn't just on the East Coast.

Cosslett: Jim worked on some pretty high-profile cases. He defended Ford Motor in the criminal case relating to the Pinto design. He represented Dr. Nichopoulous, Elvis Presley's doctor in connection with overprescribing drugs. And there was a case that I understand you worked on with him extensively: the *Twilight Zone* case.

Sanders: Do you see that picture behind my desk? It is a scene from the pre-movie mockups. John Landis was the director of *Twilight Zone: The Movie*. There was a scene that called for a US helicopter to attack a small Vietnamese village. This racist, terrible character played by Vic Morrow, in his moment of redemption, was going to scoop up two Vietnamese children and carry them across a stream to save them from this helicopter attack. During the filming of the attack, the helicopter went down and beheaded Vic Morrow and the two children. So—and this was before OJ, but in typical Los Angeles style—the prosecutor decided to make a criminal case of it, a Hollywood trial. They charged John, his administrative guy, his producer, the helicopter pilot, and the stunt coordinator. The charges were homicide and two different theories of manslaughter. Jim was, at the time, trying the Edwin Edwards case, so I was doing most of the witness prep and preliminary work for *Twilight Zone* out in California while Jim was in New Orleans. Then we tried the case together. We started selecting a jury after the 4th of July in 1986. We ended the trial with a verdict in favor of all defendants on May 29, 1987. We were in LA on trial for almost a year. That was a hell of an experience.

Cosslett: Did you feel your background as a public defender and your clerkships prepared you well to join a firm with a rigorous corporate defense practice?

Sanders: There's nothing more strenuous, stressful, or demanding than representing criminal defendants in felony trials. And if you're doing a lot of that, then chances are you can do damned near anything.

Cosslett: What did you want to learn from Jim Neal when you first joined the firm?

Sanders: What I wanted to learn was how to practice law like Jim Neal—like one of the best trial lawyers in the country. I was hoping to try cases side by side with Jim and learn how it's done at the finest level. That's what I wanted. During the first few years, I got involved in as many of his cases as I could get involved in, and did as much as he would let me do. And he was wonderful to me in that respect, because he knew that I really wanted to do this and had some capacity to do it. And while he may not have had succession in mind, I do think he saw the need to have someone there to help as he went along. I became the guy who not only would help him get ready for trial, but also would participate in the trial, and then ultimately become his co-counsel. Indeed, we shared the closing argument in the *Twilight Zone* case. We shared the closing argument in two stages, the liability phase and the punitive phase, of the *Valdez* case. So I had a very unique opportunity. I think that's how you learn. You're not going to learn until you're actually doing it.

Cosslett: Can you talk about defending Exxon against charges resulting from the Exxon Valdez Alaskan oil spill?

Chapter 2 | Jim Sanders: Corporate Defense

Sanders: Let me start with my personal take on this situation. When the decision was made by Congress and the country that we wanted to have Alaskan oil and we wanted to have a pipeline, it is inevitable that if you do that, given the area you're dealing in—Alaska is one wild environment—and if you're going to transport that oil from the Port of Valdez in Prince William Sound out the Gulf, you're going to have some accidents. It's absolutely inevitable. But when an accident does happen—and it was an accident—everyone throws up their hands and says, "We've got to have a villain. They're going to have to pay."

Cosslett: If a tanker full of oil runs ashore or a pipeline ruptures, the consequences are devastating to people and to the environment. There may be fault, there may not be fault, but people look to those responsible to use superhuman efforts to prevent catastrophic accidents from happening in the first place.

Sanders: We want an easy answer, and we want not to accept responsibility for the decisions we make. And so rather than accepting responsibility and saying, "Okay, this is what we should do differently now that we've learned this lesson," we say, "But it wasn't our fault. It was Exxon's fault." And to me, that's the sad thing about it. We absolutely repeat all the mistakes of the past. Tell me what sense it is to go into Iraq, for a country that's gone through Vietnam? What are we learning? And ten years from now, I fear we'll probably do the same thing again.

Cosslett: Do you, as a self-proclaimed former hippie, ever think, "Am I on the right side of this thing?"

Sanders: I don't have moments in the middle of the night where I anguish over these things, but I do think about things like that, and the truth is I believe I am more effective at doing good with the power—whatever that is—as one of Exxon's lawyers to get things right than I would be if I were screaming in the darkness out on the barricades.

Cosslett: How did you establish a relationship with Exxon?

Sanders: I got into this because Exxon made the same decision on Jim Neal in the *Valdez* case that Leon Jaworski and Archibald Cox made in the Watergate prosecution, and Ford did in the Pinto case. They said, "We've got to have him." So I got to participate with him in those cases, and I got to participate in a meaningful way. I was trying the cases with him. So I then got to know their lawyers and they got to know me, and if you're in that kind of case, then the general counsel, and half the board, and all of the management committee knows who you are and know how the case is going. They're paying attention, and they certainly have a lot of questions. So if you get that opportunity and you meet their expectations, then when something really bad happens again, they think to call you.

Cosslett: Do they think of you for particular kinds of cases? They're not hiring you for employment discrimination cases or personal injury cases. They're hiring you for environmental disaster cases.

Sanders: It's the magnitude of the case as opposed to the type of case. I have worked with two or three generations of general counsel at ExxonMobil, and I believe that they think, "If you can try this kind of case, then if we give you enough help and support, you can try that kind of case and that other kind of case." So I've done everything from patents, to the Valdez disaster, to the two cases in Maryland in 2006 involving a gas spill into a residential neighborhood. We've had two huge trials relating to the gas spill outside of Baltimore—one for five-and-a-half months, one for six-and-a-half months. One turned out relatively well. The last one was an utter disaster. They are both on appeal in the Maryland state court system.

And then there are some other things I can't talk about. Some of your best work in this kind of practice nobody ever finds out about.

Cosslett: Is there a type of case that you like to litigate?

Sanders: I don't really care so much about the subject matter. Some subjects are harder to learn than others. Some cases take more work than others. Some are harder to try to explain to a jury than others. What I like is the trial work.

Cosslett: Your clients have included Exxon, General Motors, Morgan Stanley, Corrections Corporation of America, Mass Mutual, Ingram Industries, and Purdue Pharma. Big companies who come to you when they're faced with big litigations. There are a lot of other lawyers out there. Why are these companies coming to Nashville, and why are they coming specifically to you?

Sanders: They came to Nashville originally because of Jim Neal. Period. Let's call it the Archibald Cox–Leon Jaworski effect. And once they hired us, they came to understand that there are a number of lawyers in this firm who were trained either directly or indirectly by Jim Neal, who know how to do things the way Jim Neal did things.

So I think that's why we continue to get that business. Now, the problem with that is you're only as good as that last case. So you have to perform. And it's a pretty tough measuring stick. These guys are sophisticated. And they're paying attention. So if you don't deliver, then that's the end of it.

Cosslett: Can you estimate how many firms these huge companies utilize for litigation?

Sanders: It depends on the nature of the litigation. Let's say hypothetically that you are general counsel at Exxon, and you've got maybe a half a dozen firms that you generally go to for big cases. There may be a smaller subset of those firms that you go to in what's loosely called "bet-the-ranch" cases. Well, if you happen to have two bet-the-ranch cases going, then one of your go-to guys is unavailable.

Chapter 2 | Jim Sanders: Corporate Defense

Cosslett: How does a thirty-person firm handle a huge corporate litigation?

Sanders: These corporations, particularly Exxon, have a group of law firms around the country that have developed expertise over the years in the kind of business that Exxon does. There are a couple of firms that are literally experts across the board in underground storage systems. So if Exxon gets in a case involving the failure of an underground storage system, that firm is a resource for us. And, of course, you've got all the engineers and scientists that make ExxonMobil what it is. They generally can either give us the answer and explain it to us, or find somebody we can go to to get the answer. So we have all these resources. The thirty-person law firm doesn't do all that. We usually have two or three different firms working with us. We'll more than likely have a New York firm because you always need one of those. And then you want to have local lawyers. And then you've got the in-house lawyers.

What you're really doing, particularly in these big cases, is creating a new law firm. And you've got to run your side of the case as if it's one firm that's transparent. And it's seamless. So then the issue becomes—and this is an issue I had some trouble with—somebody's got to be in charge.

When I went to the first Baltimore trial, even as lead attorney, I was reluctant to be in charge of everything because I knew so little about some of the things I was supposed to be in charge of. As the trial went on, however, I realized it was my responsibility as lead attorney to be in charge and take charge. When it hits the fan, it won't matter that someone else was in charge of a particular part.

Cosslett: As the trial lawyer, are you making the decisions as to strategy and the way evidence is presented and what witnesses are brought in?

Sanders: If I'm doing my job right, I am the person who is deciding those things that the lawyer decides, and recommending on those things that the client decides. But I am listening to what everybody else has to say. And it's not an ego thing. It's my ultimate responsibility to make this call, but I've got to make the right call. And if it's somebody else's idea, then that's great.

Cosslett: So the bigger and more complex the case, the greater number of lawyers with different areas of expertise?

Sanders: Right. A high-profile case tends to be more complicated than a regular case, although there are huge areas of similarity. They all try about the same. But there are orders of magnitude of complication that have to be mastered and then boiled back down into a way that the case can be tried.

Most disasters involve something akin to that expression, "a perfect storm." It is never just one thing going wrong. That's why these are accidents and not designed. Just one thing going wrong will not produce a twenty-six-thousand-gallon gas spill into a residential neighborhood using well water. Nor can a ship hit a well-marked reef and leak all that oil with just one thing going wrong. You've got to understand all the complexities that led to what happened.

And then the consequences of what happened in the aftermath. You've got to master the life-cycle of a salmon. You've got to know something about carcinogenicity and what chemicals do what and at what levels. It gets very complicated.

Cosslett: You are working in an environment where there's a huge amount of anger, both from people who are personally affected by the accident, and from people who view you as the villain on a national stage. Your client has done something really bad, albeit accidentally. Does being in the spotlight add significant stress?

Sanders: You don't spend a hell of a lot of time worrying about how it's being taken by the media anymore. But you do have to take public opinion into account, because those jurors—as hard as they try, and they generally try hard, and generally do a good job—come in off the street just like everybody else and they have likely been exposed to what is in the media.

And ExxonMobil's not very popular. And juries are inclined to hit you: "You need to be punished. We don't like you. We don't like paying this much for gas. We don't like you screwing things up like this. You've got a lot of money, and we're going to try to make it hurt." So what you have—and what causes a lot of the stress—is not so much what the outside world is thinking about the case you're trying. It's the fact that you have no margin of error. You make one little mistake in the way you phrase something in a question or in an argument, and they will seize on it.

Discovery in these cases is particularly stressful for me. It seems the purpose of discovery is to have that ten-second sound bite. They will spend $5 million taking depositions to get a ten-second sound bite, and then they show that one in the argument.

Cosslett: How do you get a jury away from: "You are charging me too much for my gas," or "You're a big company—you're not going to feel it anyway," or "My neighbor can't fish down there because you polluted the water." How do you get the jury from that mindset into a more neutral place, where they can hear the facts without getting angry and necessarily deciding against you?

Sanders: What I do—sometimes with more success than others—is appeal to their character, to their responsibility as jurors: "You're not a person in a cocktail lounge listening to a story. You're a juror." You don't lecture them on what their job is, but you appeal to that sense that I think all of them have, that this is a higher calling, to be a juror in a civil trial or a criminal trial. And I think most jurors try to meet that obligation. I think they take it very seriously. I think in big cases, they do want to serve. Now, the reason they want to serve and how you can use that to make them behave right is a little tricky at times. There are two things I try to do. Number one is I try to appeal to their better side. And if they will do that, then that playing field gets leveled out some. The second thing I want them to do is to like me enough to give me a chance to earn their respect and to have credibility with them. So I've got to get them in the right mood as jurors.

Cosslett: How do you get them to like you?

Sanders: You shoot straight with them. In the first Jacksonville trial, the jury had to listen to—it felt like three days but was probably only a day and a half—of the plaintiffs' opening. Their lawyer was rather bombastic. When I stood up I said, "You know, there are an awful lot of things I could say in response to all that you've just heard, but the first thing I want to tell you is the most important thing. We're sorry."

Cosslett: You've put everything out there right at the beginning. If they don't believe you right then, then they're likely not going to believe anything that comes after that. But if they believe you then, you have a better shot of them believing your case.

Sanders: I think that's part of being a trial lawyer. You have to be willing to put it all out there and to not be thinking of ways to make excuses or to hold back. You have to get in the box with them. You have to put yourself on the line and be willing to do that. And then you shoot straight with them, and I think they appreciate that.

Cosslett: How many times in the course of the trial did you say, "I'm sorry"?

Sanders: In this case, it was fairly important to me to draw a distinction between those people that had suffered some damages that we caused and those that did not. So I apologized to those that I knew we had damaged. And then I apologized again in closing. And it stunned the plaintiffs' lawyers, and they spent a lot of time in helping me out by calling into question the sincerity of my apology and my client's apology. So they kept that apology at the forefront. That was not a great strategy for them.

Cosslett: Do you find in a lot of these big trials that separating the legitimate plaintiffs from the illegitimate plaintiffs is an issue?

Sanders: It is a huge issue, and I have to tell you, we haven't gotten there yet. We haven't figured out a way. We haven't gotten a jury to draw those distinctions in the Jacksonville case.

Cosslett: I think it's a hard distinction to draw. Once there's a wrong, I think juries would tend to sweep people into the class of injured parties.

Sanders: We try to delineate. "Here's the inner circle. Pretty sure we're responsible for those. And then you have this outer circle, and we're damned sure we're not responsible for those. And here's this gray area."

Cosslett: And you run the risk of alienating the jury if you start trying to pick off plaintiffs.

Sanders: It's risky.

Cosslett: What's the difference between a trial lawyer and a litigator?

Sanders: There are thousands of litigators. They take depositions. They file motions. And they help other lawyers who are doing nothing but taking depositions and filing motions. Trial lawyers go in there and stand in front of a jury and try the case.

Let me tell you what's happening. Part of this appeals to my conspiratorial side, and part of it is just my observations over the years. We are having fewer and fewer trials, and it's disturbing. And one of the reasons we're having fewer and fewer trials is that there are fewer and fewer lawyers and judges who want to try cases. The system is being stacked in many different ways to get cases settled. And there are now consequently fewer and fewer real trial lawyers.

There's a dynamic of fear that pervades trial practice, and how you deal with that fear often determines how well you do. There are many lawyers who are simply afraid to go in there and try cases. They want to be known as "trial lawyers." But they're really afraid to go in and put it on the line. They might lose badly. They might make a mistake.

This dynamic also affects judges, to a lesser extent. Judges in trials have to make decisions that get appealed. But if you settle them all, you never get appealed. Judges should not fear making mistakes. That is why we have appellate courts. But they should try to get it right.

Cosslett: Do they usually get it right?

Sanders: It depends on what judge you have. And how that person got chosen. We've now got these litmus tests. It seems that nobody cares anymore whether they know any law or not. It's how they come out on abortion.

Cosslett: Is going to trial always a good thing?

Sanders: If we could somehow turn this thing around and get more trials, the system would work better. I think jury trials have a lot to do with our concept of liberty. And the system ain't perfect—Lord knows, it's not perfect. But having juries decide issues is an important part of our legal system. So to have fewer trials should be alarming. We're losing something. And we're losing it from all perspectives, because a citizen who sits on a jury and does a good job goes out of that courtroom a good citizen and a believer in our system of justice. Even disappointed litigants, if they're honest with themselves, probably come out of a courtroom saying, "I got what I deserved. The system worked." And we all have an appreciation for justice. We're losing that with fewer jury trials and our system of justice is losing the respect that it needs from the citizenry.

Cosslett: So, settlements are simply about the economic cost of wrongdoing. Trials allow juries to decide the rightness and wrongness of a claim from both a societal and legal perspective. Juries then become the touchstone for what society values or will tolerate. There's something very grounding about juries.

Sanders: I've done this for a long time, and I've been in front of a lot of juries. And I'm satisfied that, by and large, they try to do the right thing and they generally get the right answer some way or another. They're not infallible. But if they fail, it's not because of the jurors.

Cosslett: It's because the information has not been presented effectively?

Sanders: Or because a judge doesn't do a very good job of keeping the gate closed so they don't get inundated with a bunch of junk.

Cosslett: What sorts of bells and whistles are you bringing into the courtroom?

Sanders: There are two categories of bells and whistles. One is the technology that goes along with every trial presentation now. I'm a firm believer that you have to do that. I am a dinosaur, but I have forced myself to learn those things that the audience demands. If you are sitting there with a twenty-seven-year-old juror, they don't want to see you walk up to a blackboard and write on it. They're used to getting information visually, electronically, digitally. So I'm a strong believer that you must do that. And I've had to become insistent on what I wanted in that respect, because everybody's idea is not the same as the guy who's going to have to present it to the jury.

The second category is jury consultants. I am a believer in jury research and jury consultants, but I have not liked the idea of a shadow jury. You've got enough trouble without dealing with what the shadow jury is doing. And the people who are running the shadow jury are going to the client, and then the client comes to you, "We've got a disaster over there."

In trial, I have enough to do dealing with the jury I have in the box.

But I want to emphasize that there are jury consultants, and there are jury consultants. What I want is somebody who thinks outside the box. I don't need somebody to come in here and tell me what's going to happen to me generally. I know I'm going to get hurt and the verdict could be awful. I want somebody to come in here and tell me how I can reach these jury members. What's going to resonate? What's not going to work? What should we say? What issues will hurt us?

Cosslett: Do jury consultants look at the composition of the particular jury that you're going to appear in front of?

Sanders: No. They'll look at the facts of the case and will have focus groups. And we will put on the plaintiff's case and try out various defenses.

We had a group of jury consultants called the American Jury Project that was willing to help us on the *Twilight Zone* case. They were located mainly in the San Francisco Bay Area, and they spent most of their time doing death penalty cases. They were very dedicated people—they weren't dilettantes. They really were serious about what they did. And they agreed to help us because we were representing an individual defendant, John Landis, in a big criminal case.

So we go into case preparation, and we're thinking that we will not subject the grieving parents to any intense questioning on the stand. Their children had been decapitated right in front of them. Well, these professionals from the American Jury Project did some focus groups, and they came up with the idea, "Let's see how the jury would really feel if you give them the facts." Jim and I said, "You're crazy."

Cosslett: You'd think on its face that's a bad idea. You'd be viewed as bullies.

Sanders: But they tried it, and the focus groups held the parents responsible. The parents were there when the accident happened. They could assess the danger as well or better than John Landis could and had more responsibility to the children. And so it turns out that my job was not to be sweet and kiss them on the forehead. Somebody thought outside the box, and they were exactly right. When we talked to the jurors after the case—it was nine months later—the jurors said, "I don't see that John had any more responsibility toward those children than their parents did."

And that's what I'm looking for. I'm looking for somebody that can think outside the box and somebody who's willing to fight with me on a day-to-day basis.

Cosslett: Can you outline the process of a typical case from beginning to verdict?

Sanders: That's hard for me because, the fact is, if you've tried one case, you've tried one case. Every case is different, and every situation is different. And the exciting thing about our practice is you're trying things all over the country—and it's really, truly different where you are, what kind of case you've got, who's on the other side. I don't know that I can give you a paradigm example of how it works.

And moreover, many of the big cases we've been in, including these Jacksonville cases and the *Exxon Valdez* cases, we get in because we're white-collar or criminal lawyers. We get in on the grand jury investigation, when the federal government is saying, "We may indict some of you guys from the company." That's how we got into *Valdez*. After we had resolved the criminal case, they asked us to help with the civil trial because we knew more about the liability part of it than anybody. So Jim and I were drafted—me willingly, Jim not so willingly—because Jim was smart enough to see the handwriting on the wall.

He knew what this was going to look like. We weren't in on the beginnings of the *Valdez* civil case. And there was two or three years' worth of depositions that we had no knowledge of until we got in the case, and then we had neither the staff nor the time to do all the depositions that were remaining to be done. It was the same thing in the Jacksonville case. I spent most of my time in the first six months after the Jacksonville spill working with the state in the criminal investigation.

Cosslett: Can you talk about trial preparation, depositions, and all the less glamorous jobs that need to be done in anticipation of a trial?

Sanders: I hate the discovery part of civil cases because, by and large, it's a perversion of what's being intended by the rules regarding discovery. What discovery really is in these big cases like *Valdez* and Jacksonville is plaintiffs' lawyers trying to get a couple of sound bites. They're not after discovery. They're after a fact to fit into their version of their alternate reality. And it just takes hours, and hours, and hours, and then you've got to review all the garbage. And the interrogatories and interrogatory answers. I just hate that stuff.

But the amount of preparation is incredible. It's the most tedious part, and you have to know everything. I think that's the difference between the guys that do well in court and the guys that don't do well in court—other than just courage and personality issues.

Cosslett: It's the preparedness and the familiarity with the material. For every hour in a courtroom, how many hours of preparation have been done?

Sanders: It's impossible to answer, but it's orders of magnitude. The truth is, in one of these big cases, it turns into twenty-four hours, seven days a week. If you're not looking at something, you're thinking about it. And the learning curve on some of the more esoteric issues is very steep.

Cosslett: Do you find there's still a big learning curve on the Exxon cases?

Sanders: Yes, every one is different. From what I read in the press, the next wave of cases will probably involve natural gas, because that's the new big thing and Exxon's heavily invested in it. And I think what can go wrong with that is different from what goes on in transporting crude oil.

Cosslett: What about wind turbines and solar power? Will they ever put you out of business?

Sanders: No, those things can go wrong, too. They're unintentionally, but inevitably, violating the Migratory Bird Treaty Act.

Cosslett: We talked a bit about what you like least about being a trial lawyer. What do you like most about it?

Sanders: I like the challenge of the competition on important matters in an important place: the excitement, the stress, the fear—all of that. And the need to perform and compete. That's what drives me. I love trials. If I could have one trial and get rid of a hundred conference calls, I'd trade in a minute.

Cosslett: Is your practice what you anticipated it to be when you were in law school?

Sanders: No. I thought that I was going to represent individual defendants in difficult circumstances with difficult trials and justice would be done. And maybe every once in a while they'd put my name in the paper as the guy who represented another guy and did a good job representing him. When I was in law school, the last thing I ever thought about was, "How much money will I make?" I didn't care. It was all about being involved in some important cases. And I thought representing an individual charged with a crime was as important as you can get. That's what I thought it would be.

Cosslett: And the money has been just a pleasant surprise?

Sanders: It's a gift. Of course, my attitude changed after I had children.

Cosslett: What is the nature of legal practice here in Nashville?

Sanders: When I joined the firm, Jim Neal was one of the best lawyers in America. Nashville had an inordinate number of good lawyers. Part of that I think was historical accident. And part of it was because the state capital is in Nashville, and much of the big-time constitutional civil rights issues were brought in federal court in Nashville. If you're going to sue the State of Tennessee, you sued them in federal court in Nashville.

There were a slew of good lawyers in this town, and there were a couple of criminal lawyers who preceded Jim who were fabulous lawyers. And the fact that you had two or three of those in one town probably had a lot to do with the quality both of the bench and of the bar in town. Those guys cast a wide shadow. They enhanced the quality of the practice. So Nashville was that kind of town. Is it evolving still? Yes. Are there as many of those kinds of lawyers? No. Nashville's becoming a city, and business predominates. And so the firms that are best known in this town, with the exception of ours and another two or three, are probably the bigger firms that have a lot of good business with the banks and the healthcare industry.

Cosslett: Are the firms here national or local?

Sanders: There are probably four or five large firms in Nashville that are regionally owned: they started here and they still have a pretty good influence. The merger and acquisition activity hasn't choked them into something other than they were. There's been a lot of that because this is an attractive market.

Cosslett: Are law firms here run as partnerships or as businesses?

Sanders: I regret to say I think that the trend is toward being run more like businesses. Indeed, I think the trend over my lifetime has been that the law is much less a profession than a business. I think we focus too much on the business of law and not enough on the profession of law.

Cosslett: What issues of professional responsibility can come up in connection with a trial practice?

Sanders: There are issues that come up on the professional responsibility side, the ethics side, that are difficult. I have watched lawyers get in trouble because it can be a tough practice. While I certainly do not condone it, I try not to be judgmental or hypocritical about some who fail to meet the legal and ethical standards.

Take a solo practitioner just scraping by in a given year. He's got a client who's got enough money to pay for legal services and that amount will enable that practitioner to pay the bills for that year. That client asks him to do something that, on a level playing surface, he'd say, "No, I'm not going to do that." But if he says no, then that client that he's counted on for the year may walk away and things get a little tighter for that lawyer.

I think it's a continuum. At the far end, unless you just have supreme confidence in yourself, you do get confronted with issues that make you ask, "Am I going to eat or am I going to do the right thing?" As you go along that continuum, it's still a tough call to make sure you're doing the right thing. And, to take this to the end of the continuum, what I have been surprised about and love about my practice now is that I represent corporations like ExxonMobil and General Motors, and I get to know their general counsel. And I don't ever have to worry about those kinds of issues. All I have to do when we confront legal and ethical questions is to say, "This would be wrong." They want to understand it, but if it's wrong, then it's decided. And they're straight. They are honest, and they don't want their lawyers or clients doing anything wrong. So these issues are wonderfully handled in this context. To have this kind of client is luck. In a large sense of the word, it's luck. It was an evolution.

Most of the issues that I do see in this area come up as a result of behavior on the other side. The question is always, "What should I do about this." And generally, the answer is, "You're an out-of-town lawyer. You represent a big, unpopular client. Shut up."

Cosslett: There's a reality to it.

Sanders: There is. Usually, I'll say, "Look, this is not my call. I think this particular conduct is horrendous. I think something ought to be done about it. You are the lawyer in this jurisdiction. I'm passing it to you. I'll support you if you want to do it."

Cosslett: Is there a skill set that's particularly useful for a trial lawyer?

Sanders: I think the answer is generally yes, but that skill set is probably a bit different for almost every trial lawyer, because I think what you have to be is true to whatever it is you are, to whatever your personality is. So the spin on the skill set is determinative because of your personality or your style. I think you have to love the battle. Now, that's not a skill set, but it is a mindset.

Cosslett: You pointed to your heart when you said "mindset."

Sanders: It's a soul set. It's a gut set.

You have to be the kind of person who wants to have your bat up, and there are men on base, and it's the final game of the World Series, and you get to hit. That's what the mindset is. The skill set is the ability to master a body of facts, however complex, and figure out what it is that will represent the truth in a way that will resonate with the jury. And you've got to be able to communicate to that jury. The other skill set is to be able to immerse yourself in the questions and the answers, and to enjoy doing it, and to adjust to the changes that inevitably occur in a trial.

You also have to learn to listen. You have to learn to listen to every single word. And you've got to pay attention not just to what you're doing, but to what the witness is doing or to what the other side's doing or to what the jury's doing. And I think that is a skill set, to be able to listen that closely, because most of us don't. Most of us listen to the first couple of words of a question and then we think we know what's coming. Most people don't even let you finish the question.

Cosslett: Well, you guys do talk slow down here. I'm just kidding!

Sanders: Guilty as charged.

Cosslett: What would you tell law students and practicing lawyers about being a trial lawyer and about doing corporate defense work?

Sanders: Number one: if you really want to do this, then you must make yourself do it. You've got to make yourself get the opportunities. You've got to push to get the experience, because the only way to become good at this is by doing it. And you have to do a lot of it to become good at it. And I think the hardest thing for young lawyers to get is trial experience.

Cosslett: So taking the path that you took, going into a not-for-profit role to get trial work is a good place to start.

Sanders: Absolutely. Or a good prosecutor's office that actually prosecutes and takes cases to trial, as opposed to finding these felony possession cases where they end up taking guilty pleas. Your stats look good, but you haven't done anything. If you can find a good prosecutor's office or good defender's office that actually gets trial work, then, yes, that's very good.

Cosslett: And what about doing corporate defense work?

Sanders: I am more than pleased for many, many reasons that I got to do this. It's harder than representing individuals in terms of results. Your chances of winning are much better if you represent an individual than a corporation. That's true civilly, and it's even more true criminally. It's hard to win if you're that bloodless entity as opposed to an individual. So it's not without its downside, but it is challenging work and you have the tools to do things right. I have had the kinds of clients that will allow me to do things honestly and right, so I'm not at all sorry at going from individual representation to corporate representation.

Cosslett: What I'm hearing is that you don't walk away as frequently with a sense of total success.

Sanders: You have to redefine winning.

Cosslett: And that I imagine takes a little getting used to.

Sanders: Oh, it does.

CHAPTER 3

Jonathan Streeter

Partner

Dechert LLP

"Greed and corruption. That's what this case is about." So intoned lead prosecutor **Jonathan R. Streeter** in his opening remarks to the jury in the largest insider trading case ever brought by the government, US v. Rajaratnam. Two months later, in May 2011, the conviction of the Galleon hedge funds manager on all 14 counts crowned Streeter's 11-year career as a prosecutor in the US Attorney's Office of the Southern District of New York. In successive positions in the Major Crimes Unit, as Assistant US Attorney on the Securities and Commodities Fraud Task Force, and as Deputy Chief of the Criminal Division, Streeter prosecuted 17 federal jury trials to verdict, losing only one. He secured convictions in complex white-collar criminal cases against lawyer Marc Dreier for swindling hedge funds, and trial victories against the CEO and CFO of Duane Reade for accounting fraud and against Ernst & Young partner James Gansman for insider trading. In 2010, Streeter received the Attorney General's John Marshall Award for Asset Forfeiture. Having put in his quota of 100-hour weeks as a federal prosecutor, he crossed over to white-collar criminal defense at Dechert LLP in 2012. Prior to joining the US Attorney's Office, he was an associate at Arnold & Porter in Washington DC representing Philip Morris during the mass tort litigation of the '90s. Streeter earned his AB cum laude from Colgate University and his JD cum laude from Northwestern University School of Law.

Clare Cosslett: Who inspired you to be a litigator?

Jonathan Streeter: My father was a corporate lawyer at a big law firm in Cleveland. My uncle was a lawyer in New York City when I was growing up and was kind of a well-known guy named Michael Armstrong, who did some high-profile things while I was a kid. He was chief counsel to the Knapp Commission, which investigated police corruption in New York City and gave rise to the book and the movie *Serpico*. He was the chief prosecutor and was on TV every day in the summer during the hearings in New York City. He was also a prosecutor in the US Attorney's Office, where I ultimately took a job. So, between my uncle and my father, I've always been inspired to be a lawyer, even when I was a kid.

I knew I wanted to be a litigator from the beginning. My father's corporate practice included taking companies public, and mergers and acquisitions, but I never understood what he did day to day. My uncle—my mother's brother—was a litigator, and that I understood. He was in the courtroom, he was trying cases, he was arguing—and that appealed to me. I always knew I wanted to do that. Also at a very early stage, I identified being a federal prosecutor as a way to combine my interest in doing public service work with being at the top of the profession—doing the hardest stuff and the most interesting stuff available.

Cosslett: The New York Observer reported that your brother remembers a time when you were in fourth grade and got into an argument about racism with older kids on the school bus. He said that you had "a very, very strong moral compass." Do you remember feeling that you were an advocate for justice even then, or did you just like to argue?

Streeter: I think a little bit of both. I've always loved to argue. I think the first job I ever wanted, after wanting to be a fireman or a cowboy or whatever a six-year-old kid wants to be, was to be a lawyer. I think I probably identified that when I was seven or eight years old. People used to joke about how I liked to argue a lot, so that was definitely a part of it. But, yes, I always had—and I'm flattered by my brother's comment—a strong sense of right and wrong.

I remember the argument on that bus. We grew up in a town called Chagrin Falls, which is on the east side of Cleveland. It was an upper middle-class town and it was almost all white, almost all Protestant, and almost all Republican. My family was one of the few families that were Democrats. I remember when I was a kid and Jimmy Carter was running against Ronald Reagan. In a middle school class, the teacher took a poll and it was twenty-six to two . . . twenty-six voting for Ronald Reagan versus me and, I think, the teacher, voting for Jimmy Carter. It was a conservative place, and I often found myself in the minority. That was the context in which that argument on the bus took place.

Cosslett: Was your father involved in local politics?

Streeter: He wasn't himself a politician, but he was always active in the community, serving on boards of charities and things like that, and that's probably part of where I got that moral compass my brother says I have. And my mother certainly is very politically active—just very interested in what was happening in the day, and talking to us about it. My mother is a psychotherapist. And my wife is also a psychotherapist.

I remember having a George McGovern sticker on my little car when I was a kid in 1972. There was a long string of Democrats that got destroyed in elections, including McGovern. But my parents talked to us about politics at a very young age, and they talked to us about moral issues, such as race. This was the early seventies, and issues of economic justice were important to them. Those were the causes they were involved in.

Cosslett: So on your way to law school, after college, you went to work in a national forest. What was your thinking in doing that?

Streeter: It's funny. I almost always knew I wanted to be a lawyer, but I had one brief period when I doubted that, and it was my senior year in college. I knew I wanted to do something public service-oriented, at least for part of my career, and I thought that lawyers just practice at big law firms. I worried that there wasn't enough opportunity to do public service work as a lawyer. I thought about becoming a journalist.

Since I was undecided, I didn't go to law school right out of college and I took a year off. During that year, I decided that I did want to go to law school and once I had made that decision, I wanted to do something interesting with the remainder of my time before I started. I applied for a bunch of jobs at national forests out west and ended up going to work at the Mount Hood National Forest as a wildlife biology assistant. I didn't know anything about biology other than what I had taken in eighth grade, but I went out there, and we did things like tag trees and build structures and streams to help fish. You know, I've never been that interested in environmental issues, but it was a summer of doing something interesting.

And I think it actually helped me get into Northwestern Law School. I was on the waitlist there and about two weeks before school was scheduled to start, I wrote them a letter saying, "Here's what I've been doing for the summer"—and a day or two later, I got in off the waitlist. So I think maybe they said, "Well, this isn't what our typical candidate is doing—chasing around spotted owls and tagging deer."

Cosslett: You also interned at the Department of Justice?

Streeter: I did. That was the summer after I finished law school, before I started my judicial clerkship. During that summer, I went to the Department of Justice and worked in the area of judicial appointments at the Office of Policy Development. The Office works with lawyers appointed to the federal bench, preparing them for their judicial confirmation hearings. There are two offices in the administration that work together to perform this function: the White House Counsel's Office and an arm of the Department of Justice.

The Office of Policy Development—now called the Office of Legal Policy—did research on candidates before they were picked to make sure that there were no problems in their background. It interviewed candidates. So a candidate for a federal judgeship would come in and someone from the department would interview them about their perspective on issues to make sure it was consistent with the president's goals in picking candidates. And then, once the president had nominated them, the Office prepared them for their Senate confirmation hearings.

The summer I worked there, Stephen Breyer, now Justice Stephen Breyer, was nominated to the Supreme Court. I worked on his judicial confirmation. I was responsible for reading anything he had written, an op-ed piece or anything like that, and writing a memo about it, which the folks from the White House and the folks from the Office of Policy Development would review and use in preparing him for his hearings. For instance, I became the point guy on Breyer's view of airline deregulation, one of the issues he was involved in when he worked for Senator Kennedy. So we did this background workup, wrote memos so that the people knew what the issues in the confirmation hearings would be, and then ultimately—just like prepping a witness for a trial—people at the Office of Policy Development would prepare the candidates for their hearing, give them mock questions about what they might be questioned about, and discuss ways to phrase their answers so as to not ruffle feathers.

For a long time I thought that this was the best job I ever had: meeting all these interesting people who were about to be nominated to the federal bench, from Stephen Breyer to Second Circuit judges to District Court judges. I was traveling between the Justice Department and the Hill to meet with Senate staffers, and I was reading about really interesting things and then watching the hearings happen, where I could see the candidates saying things that I knew I had refreshed their memory about or helped to prepare them for. It was a great experience right out of law school. I would have loved to have done that for a long time, but it was a summer job and I had a clerkship that I was going to.

Cosslett: You clerked in the Court of Appeals in the Ninth Circuit. Was that a one-year or a two-year clerkship?

Streeter: It was a one-year clerkship, and it was the Court of Appeals, so it was less interactive than the job I have just described. It was me, my two fellow co-clerks, and the judge, writing memos and opinions for the judge and sitting in chambers and having a very academic existence. The late Judge Brunetti was an incredibly warm, friendly person. He was a very pragmatic guy, so it wasn't as if we had to write a constitutional law treatise. He just wanted to make good decisions and write clear opinions. And that is what we did. We didn't seek to make his mark in any way. He had been on the bench for about ten years and was a Ronald Reagan appointee. I didn't try to find someone who was in my political vein—it didn't seem relevant for the job. I remember one case that had a very political feel to it in which the judges split on political lines, but my judge actually ended up joining the liberals to provide the deciding vote in an en banc decision, six to five.

Cosslett: So you then went to Arnold & Porter in DC and you joined them as a litigator. Why Arnold & Porter?

Streeter: I knew that eventually I wanted to work in the government, probably the Department of Justice, but I had student loans to pay. After law school and a clerkship, the easiest path is to go to a law firm for a couple of years and cut your teeth. So, not having any kind of geographic moorings anywhere—grew up in Cleveland, went to law school in Chicago, clerked out west on the Ninth Circuit—I thought, "Where's the place you go if you want to work in the government? Well, Washington, DC." And what are the best law firms in Washington, DC? Arnold & Porter was always one of those.

And Arnold & Porter had a strong tradition of people passing in and out of government, and it had a strong tradition of doing public service work. And so it was one of a couple of choices in DC that made sense, and that's the one that I picked.

Cosslett: How was your life as a junior litigator at Arnold & Porter?

Streeter: You know it was funny. Six months into it, I thought, "Wow, this is going to be awful." But after about a year, I loved it. During the first six months, I was working on a document production, which is incredibly grueling, and I thought, "I've entered the law firm associate nightmare world." But I got out of document production and moved on to other things and, for the next five years that I was there, I did incredibly interesting work. I got to take a lot of depositions. I got to argue motions in court. I got to write a lot of briefs on cutting-edge legal issues. I got to prepare expert witnesses. I got to work on a number of trials. I got to argue jury instructions at a trial. I was lucky enough to get on the right things and, I guess, skillful enough to do well enough at them to get more good work.

The work that I got initially that really gave me incredible experience—and you're going to be surprised by this—was working on tobacco litigation for Philip Morris. Philip Morris was a big client of Arnold & Porter. This was at the height of the tobacco wars, when the tobacco companies were being sued by fifty different states to recover Medicaid costs and their backs were against the wall. And there were issues about whether they were going to go bankrupt if they lost all these lawsuits. And there were really big issues about who was responsible for smoking? Is it the smokers? Is it the tobacco companies? Did the warnings get the tobacco companies off the hook? Lots of interesting questions about whether the states could or could not sue. So there were tons of cutting-edge legal issues that we were writing briefs about all the time.

There were fifty lawsuits. Most of the states in the country were suing, so there was tons of work and really interesting work that got pushed down to very low levels inside law firms. Ordinarily, you think that junior associates at law firms don't get to take depositions, but there were so many depositions to be taken, so many experts to prepare, so many trials to prepare, and so many motions to argue that if you were any good, good work got pushed down to you. I found myself, for four of those five years, running around taking depositions, meeting with experts, working on two different trials, and getting to argue motions and do jury instructions at those trials.

Cosslett: Did the nature of the work trouble you?

Streeter: My mother was very upset that I was working for tobacco companies. But to be honest, for me, the worst part about it was the losing. The tobacco companies had had an incredible string of success in litigation, and as soon as I started working on those cases, they started losing. I don't think I won a single thing, a single motion, a single anything. The tide had turned against the tobacco companies, and they were starting to settle. For four-and-a-half years, just about everything you did would have an unfavorable outcome. You would lose a motion or have to agree to a multi-billion-dollar settlement. And that was very hard. I believed in the positions that we were taking.

At the same time, I recognized that there were some public policy problems with the way that the tobacco companies had conducted themselves in years past, but they were also reforming themselves at the time. For the first time, while I was working on these tobacco cases, Philip Morris came out and said, "Smoking causes disease. Smoking is addictive." They had not said things like that before. I was okay with the positions that we were taking, but it was a challenge, out in the world, to tell people what I was doing. And, to people like my mother, it was awful. But in terms of the work I was doing and the briefs I was writing, and the arguments I was making, I believed in them.

Arnold & Porter had this great liberal tradition. And I think part of the reason why Philip Morris hired them was to say: "We can get these guys to argue for us and find the positions that are the good positions. We'll have a lot of credibility." When the firm first took the matter on, a long time before I got there, there was a lot of tension about that. There were associates in the firm who refused to work on those matters, and they were allowed to do that. I think the people working on the team liked what they did and thought it was really interesting. In fact, two of my best friends who were associates from that time at Arnold & Porter are now in-house at Altria, the successor of Philip Morris. And the partner who was my rabbi at the firm is the head of litigation there. So these are people who were like me, who were in the law firm working on this stuff, and now their entire careers are devoted to working for this company. And they seem to enjoy it. They're taking positions that they think are right and they believe in.

Cosslett: You make choices. And sometimes interesting law presents itself in unusual situations. It's not always easy to be the white knight. So you tore yourself away from Arnold & Porter and came to the US Attorney's Office for the Southern District of New York. Is it possible to go right out of law school into the US Attorney's Office?

Streeter: It's rare that people do that. There are some people who go, not straight from law school, but from a judicial clerkship, but it's one in a hundred. Often people will do a clerkship and then they'll work in a law firm for two, three, four years, and then they apply to the US Attorney's Office. That's the typical path, at least in the US Attorney's Office in Manhattan.

Cosslett: Let's talk about how you actually got the job at the US Attorney's Office. It's extremely competitive. It's extremely prestigious. You had a great background. But other people have great backgrounds, too. What separated you out in this case?

Streeter: This is another one of those instances where, I have to say, there's a little bit of luck and a little bit of skill. I had the credentials to get into the interviewing process, but there are a lot of people who have credentials like mine: went to a good law school, clerked, went to a good law firm, and got in the door. I don't know why I got the job. I think I interviewed well. A lot of people do in that situation. Later, I worked on the hiring process inside the office, and I learned there's a lot of luck to which day you come into the hiring committee.

I got in there and thought, "Wow, I never thought I'd get the job." I applied to ten different US Attorney's Offices, figuring that the Southern District was the Harvard of US Attorney's Offices. And I hadn't gotten into Harvard, so I didn't think I was going to get into the Southern District. And lo and behold! I got in. Now, it's very hard to get in there, but it's also a place where there's much more turnover than other US Attorney's Offices. People stay there for between five and ten years, whereas they make careers at other offices: they stay there for twenty years. So there are more jobs because people leave and new people have to come in. It's a place where you work incredibly hard for low pay in New York City. And you can only do that for so long if you have a family. You can only work law firm hours on government pay for so long. Frankly, the last three years there, I worked much more than law firm hours.

Cosslett: How can you do that?

Streeter: If you're on trial, you're working all the time. And, in New York City, it's particularly hard to live at the government pay level when you can go earn much more at a law firm. Especially if you have kids—you just can't afford it anymore. Also, I think it's the culture of the place. There's new blood and new energy and new people ready to work hard, and they're not jaded. I think people who stay there too long become a little bit jaded: you lose that fresh, ideal perspective. The experience helps, but the fresh energy helps as well. And the culture of the place is such that you go three, four years out of law school. Stay there for five, six, seven years, and then you go on to do something else. If you stay longer, well, all your colleagues have left and the people around you are all younger than you and are from a different generation than you. You start to feel out of place.

Cosslett: Could you tell me about the work of the Southern District?

Streeter: New York City is the only city in the country that has two US Attorney's Offices. The US Attorney's Office in the Southern District covers

Manhattan, the Bronx, Westchester, and other counties north of the city. The Eastern District covers Brooklyn, Queens, Staten Island, and Long Island. In terms of the staffing, there's a criminal division, which has about one hundred and sixty lawyers, and there's a civil division, which has about sixty lawyers. In terms of the subject matters that the offices cover, it's a big picture. I can't speak much to the civil division, but in the criminal division there's an organized crime unit, a violent gangs unit, a narcotics unit, a public corruption unit, a securities and commodities fraud unit, and a complex frauds unit, which covers all white-collar crime that's not securities fraud. And there's a general crimes unit, which is where everybody starts.

Cosslett: Where does the federal jurisdiction come in for something like a violent gangs unit?

Streeter: A couple of things. Number one, narcotics, because a lot of the violence in gangs is connected to narcotics. And number two, oftentimes we charge RICO[1] against an enterprise like that. You use RICO to prosecute organized crime, loan sharking, and murder for hire—those kinds of activities. When I was thinking about becoming a federal prosecutor, someone told me, "Go somewhere where there's good crime." And there's good crime in New York City.

Cosslett: Yes, we pride ourselves on the quality of our crime.

Streeter: I mean, there's everything. There's violent crime to organized crime to white-collar crime to terrorism work. Everything is there, and this office does everything, from the street crime stuff, which involves a lot of narcotics and guns and gangs, up through Bernie Madoff. That was one of the great things about working there: you could pick and choose.

How it works is that everyone starts out in the General Crimes Unit, which is a unit that handles a grab bag of simpler federal crimes: a felon in possession of a gun case, for example. If you've got a felony conviction, you can't possess a gun. That would be a case we would do. A simple credit card fraud case: a guy at a gas station steals the credit card numbers and runs up bills on them. A simple bank-fraud case: someone working inside a bank uses checks to steal money from the bank.

Cosslett: If something could be prosecuted at both a federal and a state level, how do you work in conjunction with other offices to decide who will have the pleasure of prosecuting the bank felon?

Streeter: At times there was tension between my office and the local prosecutors. The District Attorney's Office of New York, formerly headed for many years by Robert Morgenthau and now headed by Cyrus Vance, didn't particularly want us stealing their cases. For the most part, we would try and take the bigger, more complicated stuff, and they'd probably resent that. There was a lot of overlap

---

[1] Racketeer Influenced and Corrupt Organizations Act

and, to tell you the truth, a lot of it was happenstance: it could depend on which law enforcement agency was investigating it. If detectives in the NYPD were investigating it, for the most part it would go to the New York District Attorney's Office, although we worked a lot with the NYPD, too.

If the FBI or the Secret Service were investigating it, then they'd generally bring it to the US Attorney's Office. Now, there was overlap. The FBI works with the District Attorneys. The NYPD works with us. But generally, that's where the decision would start. If the DEA[2] is working on a major narcotics case involving multiple kilograms of heroin coming from Colombia, they're going to bring that to the US Attorney's Office. Small-scale narcotics organizations in the projects in the Bronx that NYPD detectives are working, they're going to bring that to the DA's office. So there are some natural lines that developed over time that would drive the process.

Everybody starts in General Crimes, grab-bag stuff. You learn. Because I had done no criminal work before this, I had to learn all that.

Cosslett: How quickly were you in court litigating a case?

Streeter: It might take nine months or a year before you actually get a trial, but you're in court right away. When a person is arrested, the first thing that happens is they show up in court and you argue about whether they're going to be detained or they're going to get bail. And then the person is indicted, you go to court and they make a motion to suppress some of your evidence. They say that you did an illegal search. So you're litigating about that right away: calling witnesses to a hearing, and saying, "No, this police officer did the right thing when he pulled over this car and searched the trunk." And you're putting witnesses on the stand. You're arguing the legal issues right away and during your first year, you're in and out of court all the time.

When I first started, I had probably done more in the courtroom and taken more depositions than the average assistant: in part because of the kind of work I had done at Arnold & Porter, and in part because I had been out of law school for six years. I was a little bit more senior coming in. So, right away you're going to court almost every day, or multiple times a day, to do all this other stuff that needs to be done in a criminal case. But it usually takes a while for one of your cases to make it to trial, and most of your cases plead out. For me, it wasn't until the end of my first year that I tried my first case.

Cosslett: Are you disappointed when they plead out and you don't get to go to trial?

Streeter: Yes, you are. I mean, sometimes you're not. If you think it's really a tough case and you might lose, you're happy when it pleads out. If you thought

---

[2]Drug Enforcement Administration

it was going to be a lot of fun to try the case and you had great evidence, then you're disappointed. But the problem is if you have great evidence, it's probably not going to go to trial. It's really the cases in between, where both sides think they have a good argument that are going to go to trial.

We used to say that there are three kinds of cases that go to trial at the US Attorney's Office. Number one: cases where the evidence is close and the defendant has a real reason to take it to trial. Number two: cases where the defendant is crazy. They're not making good decisions and so they go to trial. You usually get a longer sentence if you go to trial. Number three: cases where the stakes are exceptionally high, such as a drug dealer facing thirty years or forty-five years. The difference between the sentence they could plead to and the sentence that would come with a guilty verdict is not significant and they figure, "Why not go to trial?" So it takes a while to get your trials going, and then after your first year, you switch to the Narcotics Unit. And you do those kinds of narcotics cases I described earlier.

Narcotics cases can have a broader scope than the neighborhood-level, kilogram-quantity kind of narcotics cases. You work with the DEA, you do search warrants, wiretaps, and that kind of stuff.

Cosslett: Were you ever frustrated in those cases because you weren't going after the big guys?

Streeter: I didn't like the narcotics work very much. I always knew I wanted to do white-collar work because it interested me more. With the narcotics work, sometimes you end up prosecuting the low-level people, the "mopes"—the guy who got on an airplane in the Dominican Republic and carried two kilos of heroin into the country and got paid $5,000. This guy is not the bad guy at the top of the chain. You know that guy is in Colombia. Yes, the mopes were low-level—not street-level, but people with relatively minor roles inside a narcotics organization. But they carried a lot of drugs and we had to prosecute them.

We would always try to "cooperate up"—use a person to "flip up" in the organization. The US Attorney's Office gets a lot of high-level people in the organizations as well. It extradites people from Colombia and Mexico, and it does some really serious prosecutions of the high-level guys who are ordering the violence and are making tens of millions of dollars selling drugs. That's completely worthwhile stuff. I was only in that unit for a year and I had only a few cases reach that level because I knew I was going to go on to the white-collar practice. Some lawyers make a career out of narcotics at the US Attorney's Office, and they go down to Colombia and go after members of rebel organizations involved in drug trafficking, like FARC[3].

---

[3]*Fuerzas Armadas Revolucionarias de Colombia–Ejército del Pueblo*; in English, the Revolutionary Armed Forces of Colombia–People's Army

I liked the substance of the work I was doing because I got a lot of trials. I went from no trials at the end of my first year to five trials at the end of my second year. And I did some money-laundering cases, and I did some narcotics distribution cases. They tend to go to trial. They tend to have hearings. They tend to have interesting ways of gathering evidence, like wiretaps and search warrants and things like that, which are interesting to work on. So the substance of the work was great, but it wasn't where I wanted to end up.

Cosslett: Let's talk about the Securities Fraud Task Force. That was really what you had been chomping at the bit to get involved in. When did you go into that area?

Streeter: So, a year in General Crimes, a year in the Narcotics Unit, and then I spent a year and a half in something called the Major Crimes Unit, which is now called the Complex Frauds Unit. The unit covered white-collar crime—every kind of white-collar crime except securities fraud. So I spent a little more than a year doing that. That was great because I got to try four cases that were white-collar crime cases, but weren't quite as complicated as the securities fraud cases to come. And I got to learn the white-collar world a little bit before I went into the Securities Fraud Unit.

And so in May of 2004, about three-and-a-half years after I got to the US Attorney's Office, I went to the Securities Fraud Unit. And the Securities Fraud Unit at the time was prosecuting the Martha Stewart case. In my first year there, the Martha Stewart case, the Bernie Ebbers/WorldCom case, and the Rigas/Adelphia cable company accounting fraud case were happening. Accounting fraud was the crime of the day. This was right around the time when Enron had unraveled. Our office did not do that. A task force at the Justice Department did that, but that was one of the big crimes of the day. Enron and WorldCom and Adelphia. It was exciting. I was a junior person in the unit, making my way. The senior guys in the unit were doing those cases and I remember thinking, "Wow, I really want to do those big cases." Later, I was lucky enough to get to work on some big cases.

There were about twenty to twenty-five lawyers in the unit as well as a chief and a deputy chief who supervised the lawyers on a day-to-day basis. You worked on cases that come in the door mostly from the FBI and a few from the Postal Inspection Service. The FBI is working on these cases and you get your cases through your relationships with the agents: they know you and so they bring you a case. People viewed the FBI agents as their clients. They've investigated a case and they want you to now be their lawyer in the courtroom. Now, your role ends up being much more than that of client and lawyer because you become an investigator yourself.

One big difference between the DA's office and our office is that prosecutors get involved in the investigation at a much earlier stage. In fact, on those big accounting fraud–type cases and those big insider-trading cases, prosecutors are involved from day one. And we would be involved from day one with FBI agents. Sometimes the SEC[4] would refer cases to us. Sometimes a supervisor would come to you and say, "Are you busy? Why don't you work on this?" Sometimes the FBI would bring us our cases. And, as a junior person, you start out doing the less complicated stuff and you try to work your way up to the more complicated, high-profile cases.

Cosslett: You talk about doing the investigation. Could you elaborate on that?

Streeter: So, a case comes in the door. Either the SEC refers it, saying, "We saw something in a case we were working on that looks like it might be a criminal thing." Or a victim refers a case to you and says, "Hey, there's a Ponzi scheme going on here. I lost my money. Can you investigate this?" Or some cooperating witness tells you about insider trading that's happening. And what that means is interviewing witnesses—usually bringing the witnesses into the US Attorney's Office. Some of the interviews are done out in the field: an FBI agent goes and knocks on someone's door at six in the morning and interviews them and scares them, maybe.

But a lot of times, as federal prosecutors, we get involved in the interviews at a very early stage. Maybe the FBI does one interview and then we try to get that person into our office for an interview. So you're interviewing witnesses, reviewing documents, and reading e-mails to try to figure out what happened. In the white-collar context, you subpoena documents from banks, telephone companies, broker/dealers, and so on.

Cosslett: Are you investigating every case that is presented to you by your normal referral channels?

Streeter: No, there's an initial decision made either by the chief of the unit or by the chief of the unit in combination with what we call the "line assistant," which is one of the other assistant US attorneys in the group. Often they decide, "No, this case isn't worth us spending our resources on"—either because it's too small or not important enough and we've only got limited resources. Or it doesn't look like we're ever going to get the evidence. Or a crime never actually happened here. You try to make that judgment at the beginning and not work on the case at all.

Then, you might take a case in and it might be obvious right away. You're going to bring a case. And it might be fast-moving—you're going to have to write a complaint that afternoon and arrest someone the next day. Or you might investigate for three months and decide, "We don't have a case here."

Cosslett: There seem to be two issues: is there a case, and is there a winnable case?

---

[4]Securities and Exchange Commission

Streeter: If our view was that there was a crime that occurred, we'd try to get to the point of having a winnable case. It was pretty rare that we gave up on something simply because we didn't have the evidence, even though we thought there was a crime. If we thought there was a crime, we'd work really hard to try to uncover it. Oftentimes, what you conclude is there wasn't a crime, or sometimes, "We're never going to be able to prove it, or we're never going to figure it out." A lot of times you just don't ever figure it out. So you do an investigation, you review documents, you interview witnesses. You might search a place to get documents—if it's the kind of operation where you need to get documents in the context of a search—because you're afraid that if you serve a subpoena, documents will be destroyed.

Additionally, at the US Attorney's Office, we did wiretaps. That was relatively new to the white-collar world, at least in an insider-trading context. And you gather evidence any way you can, and you try to flip people, too. You try to use cooperators. You try to use someone who has criminal exposure. You convince them that it's in their interest to cooperate with you and they'll get a lower sentence. They agree to plead guilty and then you use them to record an undercover phone call to a person you're investigating. The FBI sets up the whole scenario and records the call and helps direct them in that process. These are all ways that you can gather evidence, and in the context of securities fraud cases at the federal level, the prosecutor is involved almost from the beginning, often before the FBI agents.

Sometimes we would go to the FBI and say, "Hey, we got a case and we want you to help us investigate." You work hand in glove with an FBI agent, decide what documents to subpoena, decide whether to use a cooperator to make an undercover phone call, decide which cooperators to try to convince to flip, and sometimes you're the one sitting in the room across from a person trying to convince them, "It's in your interest to flip."

Sometimes it's the FBI agent out in the field doing that at six in the morning on their doorstep. You make strategic calls with the FBI agent—what makes more sense, whether it's them or you. You work with the FBI closely to decide whether to do a search or whether a subpoena will do, decide what documents to get. They review the documents, you review the documents. You decide where the evidence is taking you. Sometimes you decide the evidence is taking you nowhere and you've got other things to do. Sometimes you decide, "We got a good case here," and you investigate further, and eventually you charge someone. It's very rare that the agents do all the work and just present you with something wrapped in a bow.

Cosslett: How many cases would you work on simultaneously?

Streeter: When I started in the Securities Fraud Unit, I probably worked on five to ten cases at once, and by the time I was leaving, I was working on one or two cases because the cases got bigger. If you're working on a big case that's going to trial, you don't have time to do anything other than that big case. And if it's an important case, you devote all your energy to it. As you become more senior and as the cases get bigger and more complicated, they demand more of your time. My last three years I essentially worked on only four different cases, toggling between them. I would think, "Okay, these three months I work on this case." And sometimes I'd be working on two at one time.

Cosslett: And some of these cases go on for a long time.

Streeter: They do. Look at the Raj Rajaratnam investigation from beginning to end at the US Attorney's Office. The office got involved in March of 2007. He was charged in October of 2009. He went to trial in March of 2011 and he was sentenced in October 2011. The case is still ongoing because of the appeal. It's not unusual for a case of that complexity to take that long. In fact, it was shorter than some others. I think a year and a half is getting toward the higher end, but it's not like that was an uncomfortably long time. We weren't thinking, "Boy, this thing is getting old and it's been kicking around forever." We were working that whole time and the defense was, too. It takes that long when you've got tons of documents, exhibits, wiretap calls, and witnesses.

Cosslett: Tell me about the momentum of your role on a case like the Raj case. At what point do you start thinking, "I haven't seen my wife. I haven't seen my dog. I haven't had a shower. I don't know what the weather is outside"? How long does that go on for? What do you do during that time?

Streeter: In the investigation stage of a white-collar case, you oftentimes don't have emergencies. You don't have hard deadlines unless someone is a flight risk: a person who is passing through the United States or someone who you think might take off at any moment. Then you have a rush, and you have to write a complaint and pull all-nighters to get the person arrested so they're in the system. For the most part, in the white-collar cases, you have the time to investigate at the pace you want. So in that investigation stage, you're seeing your wife, you're going home, you're coming into work every day, and you're working relatively manageable hours.

Now, you're working on other cases, too, and they may have you writing a brief or going into court to argue something. You have some late nights doing that, but the investigation in a typical white-collar case doesn't need to be frenetic.

Unlike a drug case—where the drugs are going to be gone, and the person's going to be gone, and you've got to do it now—most white-collar cases can be investigated fast, but not at breakneck speed, so you don't have to work crazy, all-nighter hours. So then you charge the person, and now you're in litigation. You're in front of a federal judge. You've got schedules that you've got to keep with the federal judge. You've got discovery. You've got to respond to motions. You have to start preparing for trial. You've got to try the case. The craziest time of all is the trial itself. But along the way you're going to have very busy periods. In a big white-collar case you're going to have very serious motions made by the other side that you have to respond to: a seventy-five-page brief that you have to write a similarly long brief to respond to.

Cosslett: The counsel for the defendant in these white-collar cases is often a big law firm capable of generating a lot of paper. You are not staffed that deeply in the US Attorney's Office, so how do you deal with that?

Streeter: To give you an example, in the Raj Rajaratnam case, we had three lawyers working on the case, never more. The other side, Akin Gump, a very prominent big law firm, had about thirty. And they had other law firms helping as well. So in that context, you can really be outmatched in terms of resources. We had three lawyers, two FBI agents, and two paralegals. That was our team up against a law firm that's got as many lawyers as they need and the client is willing to pay for. In that case, the client had the money to pay a law firm, paralegals, expert consultants, and so on. So, we would work really hard. In that motion stage, you're working very hard: you've got spans of a week or two where you're working around the clock.

Cosslett: Is part of the defense strategy to try to pull the legs out from under the prosecution team? To give them so many things to respond to that they're going to miss a deadline or they're going to get overwhelmed?

Streeter: I would think so, but I haven't been a defense lawyer long enough to know. There's no doubt that at the trial stage, we would suspect at times that the defense was burying us in paper—those were the words we'd use—so that we were distracted from focusing on the trial. Generally, the judges give you enough time to respond to things so that you can manage it in the pretrial stage. There's nothing artificial driving the deadlines then.

Cosslett: Do you think the judges are sympathetic to that imbalance?

Streeter: Not entirely. I think they view the government as having enormous resources. I think everybody does. They view the US Attorney's Office as having a whole lot of talented people. They view the FBI as having a whole lot of good people. So they think, "If you need more people, put more people on it." And on a big high-profile case, you would get as many resources as you needed, but there's a reality to how many people can work on something before you lose control of it.

Also, the defense has to be careful about generating too much paper because the judge doesn't want to get buried in it either. The judge is one person with some clerks. The judge has to read everything, so the defense has got to be careful not to alienate the judge by filing frivolous motions. So you have that stage of the litigation where it's a period punctuated by very hard work.

And then you might have a hearing after the briefs are filed: either an argument, where you go in and make an oral argument to the judge and you need some preparation for that, or you might have a couple of days of hearings, where you put on witnesses to prove that some part of the defense's motion isn't valid or they try to prove that it is. So you're putting on witnesses—it's a mini-trial before a judge having a hearing. And that happens. And then, the trial date is set some point in there. And you've got a trial. In these white-collar cases it might be a two-month-long trial. I worked on two, two-month-long trials at the end of my time there. I worked on the Raj Rajaratnam trial and the trial of the CEO of Duane Reade, an accounting fraud case. Those were both two-month-long trials separated by a year.

Cosslett: When you were on trial, were you were working day and night?

Streeter: Yes. Two to three months before the trial begins, you go into trial prep mode. Before that you're preparing and you're getting yourself into position, but really about two to three months before, you start working every day, all day, around the clock. So, in the Raj Rajaratnam case, for instance, we all took a little time off at Christmas. We came back and from January 2 until the day in May that the jury got the case, I worked every single day into the night, except for two days. So every single Saturday, Sunday, whatever, from January 2 to early May, I worked every single day, all day long, getting to work at 7 AM, leaving at 11 PM, going home, eating, going to sleep, getting up, going back to work. Round the clock, me and my two trial partners.

Cosslett: And did you love it?

Streeter: I can't say that I love the trial prep, which is why you really try to avoid preparing for a trial and not actually having it go. The trial itself I love. And being on trial is . . . is like the dream. If you're trying a case like that, you're in the courtroom every day. You're doing what you dreamed about doing when you set out to be a lawyer. You're doing an opening statement, thinking and responding to arguments on your feet, making a presentation to a jury, working with a witness on the stand to try to get the information out that you want and tell the story that you want to tell, and going back at night with your colleagues and figuring out strategically, "What do we do next?"

But for the two-and-a-half months leading up to the trial, you also work every day. And that's not fun. You're meeting with witnesses, you're reviewing documents, you're meeting with your team to make strategic calls: "What are we going to put on? What aren't we going to put on? What are we going to cut? What are we going to add? What are we going to investigate?" You never stop investigating as a prosecutor and, meanwhile, you're responding to motions and writing briefs. It's incredibly hard work.

Cosslett: And you're investigating because you're hoping for what—to get more information to substantiate your case? Or are you concerned that somehow your case is not in sync with reality?

Streeter: Your responsibility as a federal prosecutor is to put on the truth. So if you start finding out that the truth is inconsistent with your indictment, ultimately it is your responsibility to dismiss the indictment. Now maybe you find out that the truth is a little different than the way you described it in the indictment, so you have to file a new indictment or go to the grand jury and present new evidence and get them to file a new indictment. You might be changing your case a little bit because you find out the facts are a little different than you previously thought they were. And so you're constantly doing that. You're constantly interviewing new witnesses, looking at new documents, making new connections. As you look at the evidence that intensively before trial, you realize things you didn't realize before. You line a document up with a phone call, with something a witness said, and you see, "Oh, wow. This all clicks into place." It's like the pieces of the puzzle. You start out with a puzzle that's not finished. Even when you charge the case, you think you know what the picture looks like, but you're not positive. And it's in that intensive period leading up to the trial when you really, really figure out exactly what you know, what you can prove, and how it all fits together, and you have "Aha!" moments constantly—especially just before trial when all you're doing is thinking about the case. They come in the middle of the night, and it's all you're doing.

My wife went crazy when I had trials like this, and it was a real strain on us because my pattern is to wake up very early in the morning and start working. I would wake up at five in the morning, and I would go out into the living room and work, and then take a shower and go to work, and come back at midnight and go to bed. And I would forget to eat. I wasn't focused on her or what was happening with us.

And you do that for a couple of months and then the trial begins and now you're at least having more fun. Your spirits are lifted. The tension is incredible. The pressure on you is incredible. But at least you're doing fun, exhilarating things, like jury addresses, examining witnesses, arguing issues to the judge, and now everything's happening really fast: the defense files a motion at six o'clock at night, you've got to respond by ten o'clock so the judge can figure out what to do at nine the next morning. You're doing all that stuff, and that's where the fun is. When I decided to become a lawyer, that was what I wanted to do: get up and try cases and be in front of people and argue things and explain things.

Cosslett: Well, oddly enough, that's what people think all lawyers do—litigate. How crazy is that? I can imagine that the facts of the Raj case were incredibly complicated, as are some of the other high-profile securities cases. Your trials were long. What's your approach when it comes to juries? How do you break up a case for them to make it understandable and to engage them?

Streeter: A couple of things. We were lucky in the Raj case because the facts were really interesting. There were a lot of colorful characters and a lot of interesting facts. We had different kinds of evidence: wiretaps, cooperating witnesses, documents, company witnesses. One day Lloyd Blankfein, the CEO of Goldman Sachs, is testifying. The next day, we're playing a wiretap call. It was easier to keep the jury engaged when the facts were as interesting as they were in that case. That said, we made a real effort to make the case short and to only focus on the most important, understandable stuff.

So when I look at a trial, I think about a couple of things that you want to do. You want to tell a narrative, as opposed to just a bunch of little pieces of information. You want to teach. You want to simplify complicated concepts and make them understandable for the jury. And you want to keep the jury engaged and interested. And those are hard things to do, and it's harder in an accounting fraud case.

Honestly, the Duane Reade accounting fraud case, which I had done the year before, was much harder: facts weren't nearly as interesting, concepts were much more complicated, witnesses were accountants at Price Waterhouse Coopers, not Lloyd Blankfein. But regardless of the difficulty of the case, you're trying always to simplify.

In the Raj case, for example, we had thousands of wiretap calls to choose from. We ended up playing forty-five of them at the trial. We took what could have been a six-month-long trial and put in the government's case in one month. And then the defense put on a two-week-long case, and the jury deliberated for a couple of weeks and a juror was dismissed, and so the deliberations got extended. It ended up being a two-month-long trial: a month of that was the government's case, two weeks of it was the defense case, and two weeks of it was the deliberations.

Cosslett: That's a big strategic decision to take a case that has six months' worth of evidence and to shrink it to one month.

Streeter: There's a constant tension between making it simple and keeping the jury engaged, on one hand, and losing good pieces of evidence, on the other hand. Anytime you cut a witness call, you're losing a piece of evidence. We started out with six accomplices who'd signed up as cooperating witnesses to testify against Raj Rajaratnam, but we only called three of them. We had given the defense notice of somewhere between thirty-five and forty stocks that we would tell a story about, and each of those stocks is a different story. The Goldman Sachs story was different from the ATI Technology story, which was different from the Google story, which was different from the Hilton Hotels story. We told all those stories at the trial.

Cosslett: And just to clarify, we are talking about companies in whose stocks Raj was accused of making trades based on inside information?

Streeter: Exactly. We're talking about either a merger or a company financial performance report that was about to be announced. If you know about these things before they become public and you buy the stock, you can make a big profit when the announcement is made and the stock price runs up or down. And that's what Rajaratnam was accused of doing, and that's what he was convicted of doing: getting information from corporate insiders who weren't allowed to give it out and trading on it before it was public.

We had disclosed to the defense that we had allegations of insider trading with respect to thirty-five to forty stocks. We made strategic calls in the months leading up to trial and during the trial, and ended up cutting down the number of stocks whose stories we told roughly in half. We also cut the number of witnesses we called roughly in half. And we cut down the number of trading records that we were going to put on. So we made a judgment. We don't want to leave great stories on the cutting room floor, but sometimes we left a story on the cutting room floor because it just didn't fit in with the bigger chronological story.

You're making judgments along the way, for instance, about which witness to call first. We called around twenty witnesses in those four weeks. You've got to decide what order to call them in. And since they're telling different stories, you can't make it perfectly chronological. So we made the judgment, for instance, to call as our first witness of the trial a consultant from McKinsey who pled guilty to insider trading with Rajaratnam who could tell a chronological story, beginning at the beginning in 2003 when our allegations began and going to the end of the story, ending with some wiretap calls that he was on. He was also a witness who was very well-spoken and was able to teach the jury basic concepts. Like, what's a hedge fund? What's shorting a stock? What's private equity? And then later you have other witnesses who tell stories within that timeframe. You want the story to be a story. And your witnesses who come later build on what's happened earlier. And so the last witness we called was an FBI agent who summarized all the trading records and the phone records.

We had witnesses tell about the deal that was in play, and we'd played some wiretap calls and put up some e-mails and, at the end, we'd layer in: "Here are the records to show the trading Rajaratnam did. And look at this. He traded this stock right after this phone call. Here are the records to show his phone calls." We didn't have every phone call recorded because we were only wiretapping his cell phone, not his business line. And the last witness was what we call the "summary chart witness." He put in those kinds of brute facts such as here's when the phone calls happened, here's when the trades happened, here's when the deal was announced. Information like that wouldn't have made any sense if it had come first.

Sometimes you just have to accept the fact that the jury is not going to understand why you're doing certain things because you can't do two things at once. You can't put two different witnesses on the stand at the same time and have them alternate in telling parts of the same story. You wish you could do it like a movie, so you have one character talk, and then you have another character talk, and then you have the first character come back and talk again. At a jury trial, you put your witness on just once, and then they're done. What is hard is sequencing your witnesses to tell a somewhat interesting story that is simple enough so the jury understands, but not so simple that you give up evidence.

Cosslett: Was this was the largest insider-trading case ever?

Streeter: It depends on how you measure it. At the end of the day, at the sentencing, we sought to prove that Raj Rajaratnam made about $75 million in profits as a result of his insider trading. I don't know how that compares to Michael Millken and Ivan Boesky, and those cases had other elements besides insider trading. I don't know how you decide whether it's by number of defendants, number of stocks, dollar amounts. It was big.

Cosslett: What about personal style? The New York Observer has said that you are "calm and laid-back." You're not a "showboater" or "a typical buttoned-down prosecutor." Do you think that makes a difference?

Streeter: What I'm going for in the courtroom is credibility. I want the jury and the judge to think they can believe everything I say and everything I'm doing. So what I'm going for is: "That guy, I can trust him. I can believe him." And I do that any number of ways. I do in part by always telling a story that's fully supported by the evidence. I do it in part by just presenting that kind of calm: "I'm not emotionally attached to this or biased. You can trust me because my life isn't on the line here, so I've haven't got to win at all costs."

And I do it, in part, by constantly proving that I have incredible knowledge of the facts: I have exhibit numbers memorized and can just call them out. "Wow, that guy has a mastery of the facts, and therefore I can trust him when he tells me what the facts are." So that's what I go for. I also want to be likeable to the jury. I don't want to bore them. I want them to like me and respect me. That's what I'm going for in the courtroom.

Cosslett: And is that who you are anyway, or is this something you have consciously adopted for the persona in the courtroom?

Streeter: I think you try to work with what you have. Going back to my brother's comment about me, that's what I like to think I am in the real world, and so I try to act like myself in the courtroom. And another person is more of a showman or showwoman. If that's what they are in the real world, then it works. My trial partner was a more demonstrative kind of character and was much more dramatic in his approach. That was natural and authentic for him. I think the jury can pick up on when you're not being authentic. I try to be authentic in the courtroom. And if I was more of a showboater, then it would be authentic for me to showboat.

Cosslett: Well, whatever you're doing has been extraordinarily successful. The New York Observer reports that you have been involved with roughly one hundred and thirty cases to date, you've personally tried thirteen to trial, and supervised four jury trials to verdict. You have only lost one of the cases you personally tried, so I have to ask you about that one.

Streeter: The one that I lost was a drug case. It was my third trial and it was a very sympathetic defendant. The drug dealer was a guy in New York who sent his girlfriend and her best friend to Aruba to pick up some drugs, which they packed in their suitcases. The defendant was pretty far removed from the real culpable character: she was the friend of the girlfriend of the drug dealer. She testified at the trial, and I think the jury just decided we didn't have it on her. The judge said to her afterwards, after the jury was dismissed, "You're very lucky. Don't do it again." I think everybody knew she had done it. But, look, she was not the kind of dangerous person that you would really want to be in jail.

And I will tell you another thing about losing. The former US Attorney in the Southern District of New York had something he called the "Chickenshit Club." And the Chickenshit Club was made up of people who had never lost a trial. And that meant you'd never taken a risk. What he wanted us to do was, if you know the person's guilty, go get the evidence and bring them to trial. And tolerate the possibility of losing. You can't just try the easy ones. And if you only try the easy ones, he said you're in the Chickenshit Club. So, I got out of the Chickenshit Club on my third try.

Cosslett: What about the other cases in which you were part of what Business Insider called the "prosecutorial dream team?" In 2009, you secured the Marc Dreier conviction for a $700 million fraud. You secured the conviction of a former Ernst & Young partner for insider trading, and then in 2010, the CEO and CFO of Duane Reade for securities fraud. Did those cases garner the same level of attention as the Raj case?

Streeter: The Raj case got the most attention. It had a lot of features the media focused on. It had a lot of money, and it happened to happen right after the financial crisis, so people were focused on white-collar crime generally. It had colorful characters. It had Goldman Sachs, and Google, and Hilton Hotels, and all these household names. It had interesting people. Danielle Chiesi, one of his co-defendants, who pled guilty, was a very colorful character who said a lot of off-color things. Raj Rajaratnam himself was a larger-than-life figure. So all that added up to a lot of media attention and a lot of attention from the US Attorney himself. I don't mean this as a criticism in any way—that's what the highest levels in the office are going to pay attention to. It's a statement case. It's a case where the office says, "You're not going to get away with X." And so the office is issuing press releases: it's part of the mission. If you publicize your cases, people hear about them, they know they can't do that thing.

The Marc Dreier case got a lot of attention, too. Lawyers focused on that case because he was a lawyer. He did some totally bizarre things, and it was a lot of money. Now, I think the attention on the Marc Dreier case got overwhelmed by the attention on the Bernie Madoff case. Marc Dreier was arrested five days before Bernie Madoff, and both of those cases came about because of the financial crisis: they were really connected to the financial crisis because when all the money dried up, the Ponzi schemes got exposed. They couldn't find new investors to pay off the old investors when the money disappeared.

Cosslett: As Warren Buffet said, "When the tide goes out, you learn who's been swimming naked," right?

Streeter: That's exactly what Ponzi schemes are. That's what Bernie Madoff is. If the financial crisis doesn't happen and the economy keeps going gangbusters, Bernie Madoff probably dies and no one ever knows. And Marc Dreier's the same way. It was also a Ponzi scheme case. It was a big deal in the legal community. He got a lot of attention because he did some very strange things. There was a *60 Minutes* episode about Mark Dreier and that case also had colorful characters and interesting facts. The Marc Dreier case was incredibly fun to work on because the facts were so interesting. He pled guilty. There were a lot of interesting proceedings along the way, but it wasn't a trial. Great facts and great fun going up against Gerry Shargel, a very prominent trial lawyer in town. The US Attorney was focused on that case as well.

The Duane Reade case was, of all my cases, the hardest one in terms of the complexity of the facts, trying to take boring facts and bring them to life for the jury. The US Attorney was aware of it and focused on it when he needed to be, but it didn't have the same level of media attention. It didn't have the same level of impact. It was an accounting fraud case—and accounting fraud cases, at that time, weren't the crime of the day. The defendant didn't, like WorldCom or Enron, destroy a whole company, ruin tens of thousands of people's pensions, and put all kinds of people out of work. The company goes on. There are Duane Reades on every corner.

And it wasn't as important a case in the grand scheme of things, as those cases were. But it was the hardest case that I tried because the facts were really complicated, and it was very hard trying to explain it to a jury. I remember trying that case, and my strategy there was to keep on retelling the story a different way because you never would get it the first time—I didn't get it the first time I went through the story. It was more like the third time through that you have those "Aha!" lightbulb-going-off moments. And I can remember during the trial when our last witness was testifying, looking at some of the jurors and thinking, "They're finally getting it."

Cosslett: There can't be a worse feeling than being a litigator looking at the jury, thinking, "I've just lost them." Accounting fraud is interesting to lawyers and accountants, but sometimes a juror is thinking, "I need to go home and feed the cat." It's not compelling.

Streeter: It happens, and you feel awful, and you try to adjust. You try to back up. In the Duane Reade case I felt finally, the third time through the story, that they were getting it: I put on a witness, they got a little of it, put on another witness, they got a little. You figure out excuses to retell the story and then tell it again in your closing argument. That one was hard, though, because that one was dry, complicated, and not nearly as momentous as some of these other stories.

Cosslett: In your time in the US Attorney's Office, there was a succession of five different US Attorneys in the Southern District. This meant you had a new boss about every two years. Did your job change as each new US Attorney came in with their personal vision of what they wanted to accomplish for the office and themselves?

Streeter: Only in ways at the margin. The office is able to accomplish what it does because it's such a great institution and it has really talented people, and you're imbued with the tradition of the place from the day you walk in the door. You have responsibilities to do the right thing, to be a public servant, and always to pursue the ends of justice. While the kinds of cases that we do didn't change much, it's true that the emphasis of different US Attorneys was different at different times, depending on what was happening.

So, for instance, I was there on September 11. Not surprisingly, the emphasis became investigating terrorism. Just after that, the US Attorney was a person named James Comey, who had been more of an organized crime and terrorism prosecutor, and so that was his emphasis. We still did white-collar cases, but that was the emphasis. His successor was a guy by the name of Dave Kelly, who also had that same background. He focused on the same thing. Then, as you know, the immediacy of that declined and we went back to doing more financial fraud cases, but everybody was still doing the same kinds of cases, so the core of what the office was doing remained the same during the eleven years I was there.

The ways in which it makes a difference who the US Attorney was is at the margins. So more terrorism cases under one US Attorney than another, more insider-trading cases under Preet Bharara because that got a lot of momentum and he realized that was an area that he could really focus on and make an impact. I don't know that he decided before he came in that he was going to go after insider trading. I think he got there, it was happening, he realized he could really make a mark in that area, so he pushed it. And he did a good job of publicizing it and also making it a place where he put resources. So, maybe emphasis changes a little bit, but not as much as you think.

In terms of the message to you as a prosecutor, the message remains the same: we're here to do the right thing. Whether it's a Republican appointee or a Democratic appointee, it was the same.

In my time there, as I became more and more senior, I had more of a relationship with the US Attorney. Every US Attorney tries to focus on what everybody's doing. They try to focus on the minor drug case that you're doing your second year there and they certainly come around and congratulate you and watch you in the courtroom. But that's a far cry from the Raj Rajaratnam case, where the US Attorney Bharara was in the courtroom many days during the trial, giving us his thoughts. We were supervised directly by the highest levels of the office, including the US Attorney, the Deputy US Attorney, and the Chief of the Criminal Division. We had regular meetings with them to talk about, "What are we doing? What's our plan? What order are we going to put the witnesses on? What evidence are we going to present? What's going to be our opening statement?" The highest levels of the office were directly involved in those things. It was in the newspapers every day, and the US Attorney wanted to know what's happening on a regular basis.

Cosslett: Speaking of the current US Attorney in the Southern District, Preet Bharara, I understand he is rumored to be the successor to Eric Holder. Do you have any thoughts on that?

Streeter: I only have heard the rumors myself. I really like him. I think he's a really capable guy. We're all ambitious, but he seems to be a very ambitious guy, so I'd be surprised if this is his last stop. I don't have any insight into that other than that it seems realistic. He has a high profile. He's done a good job with the things he's done. Often people do the Attorney General job for four years and move on. If Obama gets reelected, he may be looking for a new Attorney General. And Preet is a guy who's distinguished himself, so maybe he will get the job.

Cosslett: You joined Dechert six weeks ago as a partner in their white-collar and securities litigation practice. What motivated you to leave the US Attorney's Office after eleven-and-a-half years?

Streeter: Part of it was what I said in the beginning about how the US Attorney's Office in the Southern District of New York is a young person's place. The US Attorney himself is only a year older than me, I think. Also, the biggest single thing for me is I had done everything that I set out to do. I really lived my dream. When I was sitting in the courtroom during the Raj Rajaratnam trial and Lloyd Blankfein is on the stand testifying about Warren Buffett's $5 billion investment in Goldman Sachs on September 23 in the middle of the depths of the financial crisis, I had to pinch myself. "These are our facts. These are our facts for the trial. This is what I dreamed of doing: trying a complicated white-collar case in the media spotlight on incredibly interesting facts. And I got to do it, and so where am I going to go from here? It's not going to get any better than this."

I had tried a complicated accounting-fraud case. I had done a high-profile Ponzi scheme case. I had had an incredible time, so I had done everything that I had set out to do. I tried three cases in my last three years, two of which were two months long. I did a huge hearing about the wiretaps in the Raj case. I did a hearing about the sentencing in the Duane Reade case. I tried the partner in that Ernst & Young case involving insider trading. I worked incredibly hard. It was three years where I had worked around the clock, and I just couldn't keep on going at that pace.

I'm sure I'm going to work very hard in private practice, and I'll have periods where I'll work like that, but I just couldn't keep going at that pace. My wife would have divorced me. And so it was the combination of having done everything I wanted to do, feeling like I couldn't do any better than what I'd done there and having worked so hard. And I had liked private practice at Arnold & Porter. A lot of people don't like private practice. I liked it. I had gotten to do great stuff, so I wasn't upset about the prospect of turning the page and starting a new chapter in my life, trying something else. I've been at Dechert for six weeks. It's been great so far. I like the people. I find the cases I'm working on interesting. It's a little bit different role now.

Cosslett: You've spent over eleven years doing prosecution work and from one day to the next, you're going to turn around and do defense work. That must be a huge mental adjustment, just in terms of approaching your clients.

Streeter: Well, for some people I think it's more than others. In the US Attorney's Office and in the defense bar, we talk about "true believers." They're people who either are just true-believer prosecutors, and that's all they can do, or they're true-believer defense lawyers, and that's all they can do. But I was always a "shades of gray" guy. Even when I was a prosecutor, I understood the defense perspective, and I think defense lawyers liked me for that because I wasn't too much of a true believer as a prosecutor. I always got that the world was complicated and life was complicated.

Cosslett: You didn't see yourself on the white horse with the banner for truth and justice?

Streeter: No, I definitely felt like truth and justice were the objective, but I didn't have any misconception that the world wasn't a complicated place. I was able to see the shades of gray. And I think when you're a defense lawyer you've got to be able to manage the shades of gray. And so far it hasn't been that hard a transition. I'm not yet representing a defendant who's charged in a case, and that will present new challenges. But, as a prosecutor, I understood the defense perspective, and I think it made me a better prosecutor in front of the judge, in front of the jury.

If you're taking into account the other side's perspective, you're going to be more credible. I think it will also make it easier for me to make the transition. It won't be as big a move. If you go from being a true-believer prosecutor to a true-believer defense lawyer, that's a big leap. If you're in the shades of gray and you just move a little to the other side of the shades of gray, it's a little easier. Look, it remains to be seen, but so far it hasn't been a glass of cold water in the face. It's been manageable.

Cosslett: Lastly, do you have any advice that you might give to undergraduates and law school students about being a lawyer for the government? Not everyone can go work for the Southern District. What about other governmental roles?

Streeter: I wanted to get any good job in government that I could find, either a local prosecutor's office or at the Justice Department in Washington, DC, or working at the Securities and Exchange Commission, or anything. There are a lot of reasons to do it. First, you get a lot more responsibility. I tried thirteen cases as a relatively young man, got to try some incredibly high-profile cases against lawyers who were fifteen to twenty years senior to me and much more experienced than me. You don't get to do that in the private sector. You get to do that in the public sector. You get to run your own cases and do your own thing. It's one of the greatest things about the US Attorney's Office: I was supervised, but I was essentially my own boss.

Another reason to do it is that your job is just more interesting. The third reason to do it is the public service component. I don't know where my career is going to take me from here, and I'm sure I'll do a significant amount of pro bono work here in the future, but I always thought it was important to have a part of my career be public service. And so I think if a young lawyer has that desire, that's a way to make your job all about public service. If you're working for the government, your objective is to serve the public. And you've got to make sure you don't lose sight of that when you're in the job.

I would have worked for the government somewhere, somehow. If I didn't get into the Southern District, I would have gone to another US Attorney's Office. And if I didn't get into another US Attorney's Office, I would have gone to the Justice Department in Washington, DC or the Securities and Exchange Commission. I was doing it unless I just couldn't find what I wanted.

Cosslett: What's going to continue to motivate you as a litigator?

Streeter: I do want to continue to try cases. It's exhilarating and you feel like "Wow! I'm a real lawyer!" when you're in there trying a case. But also, I found, even in the short period of time that I've been here at Dechert, that it's interesting to give people advice and to have them take your advice, to be on the phone with a client and say, "Here's what I think you should do and here's why," and they appreciate that and do what you suggested. So, I hope to do some trial work and build up my practice. This is a great place and there are a lot of people here who are very busy. So I'm planning to strike a balance between doing some of the work that's already here and going out, getting my own clients and making my own way.

Cosslett: I think you'll do okay.

Streeter: I hope you're right.

CHAPTER 4

Ken Kopelman
Partner
Bingham McCutchen LLP

Kenneth A. Kopelman's *practice as a financial services lawyer would have looked completely different had he worked in any city other than New York or at any time other than the two decades leading up to 2008. Kopelman is an expert on derivatives and their applications in trading, structured products, and capital markets, as well as on broker-dealer, securities, and futures regulation.*

Raised in Yonkers, he did his undergraduate work at SUNY Binghamton and got his law degree from Brooklyn Law School. He began his career as a corporate associate at Baer Marks & Upham in 1985 and moved to Bear Stearns as in-house counsel in 1993, where he served for 15 years, rising to the position of senior managing director and head of the Fixed Income and Derivatives Legal Groups. Since 2008, he has been a partner with Bingham McCutchen in its New York office, where he provides cross-product legal advice and solutions to banks, broker-dealers, hedge funds, and other financial institutions. Few on Wall Street have had a more continuous or more privileged view of the meteoric rise of complex structured instruments and their impact on the financial markets.

Kopelman recounts the making of a corporate legal career in New York over a turbulent period. He tells how law firm life looked to a corporate associate in the '80s, working 13 hour days, often seven days week. He describes the work of in-house counsel during a period of corporate growth ending in crisis. Kopelman explores what it means to be a law firm partner in the post-crash era, when client expectations are high and the old models of associate training and partner loyalty are changing. Are mid-sized full-service law firms a thing of the past? Is partner portability undermining trust and collaboration in today's firms? What exactly are derivatives good for today?

Clare Cosslett: Where in New York did you grow up?

Ken Kopelman: I grew up in the suburbs of New York: Yonkers, New York—gateway to Westchester or gateway to the Bronx, depending on which direction you're facing. Solid middle-class background. My father was a teacher who became the principal of the Bronx High School of Science. I went to a public school in Yonkers. When it came time for college, the state schools made a lot of sense and the best state school at the time was Binghamton, so that's where I went.

Cosslett: And when did you decide you wanted to be a lawyer?

Kopelman: I'm not sure. I was always told, "You should go to law school." And I think you'll find traditionally with people who become lawyers that they're verbal. They may be good or bad at math, but it's not their first love. And they're somewhat argumentative.

Cosslett: So that's what you were hearing?

Kopelman: That's what I was hearing, but that's not what led me to law school and I don't know that I can to this day pinpoint what did. I spent three years working between college and law school, and I'd recommend it for a lot of people. First of all, it gave me time to appreciate school because I had had it with school by the time I graduated as an undergraduate. There was no path that was so appealing to me that I wanted to go straight in for more education. So I did something else for a little while, and when I came back to law school, I was motivated. I recognized I'd be working hard, and I appreciated it.

For those three years between college and law school I taught high school English in the Bronx, in the New York City school system. It was a great experience. I found that I loved getting in front of people. I loved the kids. I loved the idea of learning something so well that you could teach it to others. I hated the pay and I hated the prospects, however. So I said: "I like using words. I like working with other people. I need something with better pay and prospects." Law school became one of the obvious choices.

Cosslett: Why Brooklyn Law School?

Kopelman: Brooklyn appealed to me as well-suited to what I was trying to do. It had a good record of people who went on to do well and the professors were practical and well-regarded in their field.

Cosslett: When you got there, did you feel that you had made a good decision? Did you enjoy law school?

Kopelman: As it turns out, I really liked law school. I really liked what we learned, the way we learned, and the people I was learning with. But the deal with Brooklyn, and the deal with all law schools at that tier, is that you need to do well in school to have more opportunity. You have to understand the deal going in to make it work.

Cosslett: Did you do internships?

Kopelman: I did, and wish I had done more. I did very few clinics. The student internship that I found the most valuable was during the school year with a federal court judge, Judge Morris Lasker in the Southern District of New York. Judge Lasker was best known for forcing New York City to clean up its overcrowded jails and ordering the city to release some prisoners from Rikers Island. He was highly controversial and known as being a very liberal judge. He was a wonderful man with wonderful clerks, and I learned how to write and research in a different and more practical way than one learns in law school.

Cosslett: When it came time to take your first job, what opportunities were presented to you coming out of Brooklyn Law School, and what was the most appealing to you?

Kopelman: One of the reasons I went into the law in the first place was for the chance of better opportunities, and better compensation—and summer associates at New York firms were paid a fair amount at the time, as is still the case. I did well the first year; I had written on to law review, so I had a choice of law firms. I would read the law firm brochures and they all looked exactly the same, but it turns out that when you speak to a number of people at a firm, you see that the firms are really quite different. Firms have different cultures. They have different approaches. Some have more jerks, some have fewer jerks. And the personality of a firm really comes across when you meet with three or four associates and three or four partners. I remember sitting in one office at a big firm and the guy said, "I do municipal bonds. I'm trapped. I can't get out of doing this." He had a very long, narrow office. It was scary.

So I had a choice of firms, and I chose an eighty-lawyer firm that is no more, Baer Marks & Upham. And it's no more both as a firm and as a type of firm. There used to be eighty-lawyer firms that did sophisticated, diversified work. Today an eighty-lawyer firm is more or less a boutique, specializing in a few specific areas. It might do some other things, but it's a boutique. Back then, there were about twelve firms in New York with under one hundred lawyers which were full-practice firms. Every firm claimed, "You'll get great hands-on experience"—and at Baer Marks, I believed it. I did the summer there and it was a great summer. I got to see so many things up close: litigation, the way a firm worked, and what corporate transactional lawyers did—all of which, frankly, I had no idea about.

What do you know in law school? You know appellate arguments, so everyone wants to be an appellate attorney, arguing in front of the Supreme Court or the Second Circuit. And while that all sounded appealing, I realized that before you argue appellate cases, you've got to read a lot of cases, you've got to brief a lot of cases, you've got to do a lot of document production. Those were not the things I wanted to do full time. I liked the idea of getting up in front of a panel of judges, and I wanted to get right to that. It's like not wanting to train or work out, but wanting to be a professional athlete.

But corporate law was very appealing to me—it had everything I wanted to do. Some writing. A lot of talking and thinking about things, which I really liked. And analyzing and understanding the transactions and the people, which was a skill set I think many of us who end up going into law have, but don't realize that a corporate practice is a good place to apply it. It was eye-opening to me, and after the second year I decided, "That's what I want to do. I want to be a corporate lawyer."

Cosslett: Your relationship with your clients as a corporate lawyer at an eighty-lawyer firm was probably different than it would have been at a bigger firm.

Kopelman: Yes. Case in point: I was working with a partner on an application for funding for a municipal bond deal. I had worked with the client and had meetings with him. Client contact, by the way, is a two-edged sword for junior associates and some clients are better to deal with than others. So this is in the middle of the summer, as summer associate jobs tend to be, and the partner and I are working together on this application. He calls me into his office, and I, of course, am nervous. He says, "I'm going to Europe for three weeks. Here it is. It's yours to fuck up." Those were his very words to his summer associate. I said, "That's great." It was sink or swim.

So I worked with the client and we developed a very good rapport. I did have people I could go to. The partner had said, "Speak to this other partner if there's any problem." And it's actually very important, because if you're going to be a lawyer handling complex matters, you have to know when you need help and you've got to be able to deal with it when you don't. That was one of the things I learned there, because I did have people I could call on and people were happy to help. And he was just a very distant phone call away. It was hilarious.

Cosslett: You've been in-house and you've been in two firms. What is the best part of firm life for you?

Kopelman: I think the best part of firm life is the work itself—working with clients and colleagues on varied matters, and continually learning.

Law school grads know virtually nothing of real practice, unless they have worked as a paralegal. Some have the capability to learn quickly, and some do not. That's the big breakpoint. If you're able to learn quickly, you need to be willing to immerse yourself in it. Working at a law firm—and I think working in most areas of the law—requires total immersion and total commitment.

As an associate, I enjoyed the commitment and what I accomplished with the commitment. I enjoyed getting better. The learning curve is very steep for a junior attorney. It starts to plateau after a while, and then it steepens again, and then plateaus again. I always worried about it going in the other direction at some point, but that clearly doesn't happen. So I enjoy the entire experience although I will readily concede it is consuming. Working in the right way in a law firm is an absolutely consuming life. I have a family, and ironically I felt terrible for junior associates who didn't, because I didn't know how they were going to find one.

Cosslett: What was the lifestyle?

Kopelman: At the start, I was not working with traders. I later became a lawyer who worked with traders and investment bankers. Before that, as an associate, I worked in a standard corporate lawyer lifestyle: get in at nine or nine-thirty in the morning, go home around eleven o'clock at night. We'd order meals in at the desk. Occasionally we got to go out to lunch if we were entertaining the next class of summer associates. That was one of the fancy perks: you got to take the associates out to lunch. Now, as a partner, I work every weekend, but I don't come into the office every weekend, which is a real pickup in lifestyle. On the other hand, it's a negative, of course, because you're working from wherever you are.

Cosslett: That's technology.

Kopelman: Another two-edged sword.

Cosslett: What is it like to be a law firm partner?

Kopelman: Being a partner in a firm is a multifaceted job. There's the work itself, which I find challenging and love. Clients want us to have experience. They want us to have thought about the questions and to know the market, to know the answers and to be able to explain all of that in a cogent, concise way. The demands are high and the work is every bit as consuming as it was when I was an associate, it's just on a different level.

There's also working with the associates. The best associates are valuable from the beginning, and training and working with them is a pleasure.

And then there is working with my colleagues, whose particular expertise help me in my practice and mine often helps them. Again, finding the right firm is really important, because it's not a solo practice at this level.

Cosslett: In the past couple of years, there has been a lot of movement amongst law firm partners.

Kopelman: I don't know how radically different that is from investment banking, where I saw a lot of people jumping and some people staying loyal. Going back to the eighty-lawyer firm that used to exist, I think partner portability actually killed those firms. The ability of a partner to take a portable book of business and go somewhere else threatens the fabric of a firm. It also can make partners suspicious of other partners. We don't have that issue here at Bingham where the culture is open and collegial, but there are other firms where partners are looking over their shoulders at their partners.

Cosslett: That's unpleasant to be in that kind of an environment and it's a disservice to the client. If you have a guy down the hall who has expertise in an area that your client needs, you should be able to bring that partner in without worrying that he's going to elope with your client.

Kopelman: Absolutely. I think in the best firms, clients are shared and it's collaborative and a pleasure. It gives better service and enables us to provide more to the client.

Cosslett: Do you have any insight into why so many top firms have run into trouble recently?

Kopelman: Not really; the most I can say is when you see a financial firm or a law firm go down there are probably things that are wrong at the heart of the business model or management and it leads to people losing confidence. Lawyers, more than a lot of other businesspeople, tend to be risk-averse. The thought of being the one to turn the lights off at a law firm is scary. When they see people leave, they say, "That's scary. I should leave while I can." I think it's very hard to reverse the process once it has started.

Cosslett: Were you a corporate generalist at Baer Marks & Upham?

Kopelman: I was, and I still consider myself something of a financial services generalist. There's a real need for core competencies in the market. You need to develop core in-depth competencies around which you build your practice. You can't really be a generalist—well, you can if you hang your shingle in a small town upstate, but that's a different practice.

Cosslett: You joined Bear Stearns in 1993. Why did you leave the firm if you were happy? What were you looking for in a move to Bear?

Kopelman: In 1986 Baer Marks was approached by a Wall Street bank who said, "We'd like you to do our derivatives work." Derivatives were a brand-new thing, a new area of law (to the extent it's even an area of law as opposed to a conglomeration of other areas of law). So we started doing the derivatives work and I found it to be interesting and challenging. The lawyer was important to it. The contract is the product, and that's what lawyers do: draft contracts. I got to deal with businesspeople and traders, whom I found to be very smart, very thoughtful and very creative. We were their partners in putting together products and getting trades and deals done.

So derivatives were a natural fit for me. I just loved it. Working with derivatives guys, I thought about the business in a whole different way. I'm not a mathematician, but as a result of my work in derivatives, I understand the math concepts a lot better, which I think is important for business lawyers.

Cosslett: To be an effective business lawyer, you can't just deal with the law. You have to understand the business, especially in financial services.

Kopelman: It's critical. I started doing derivatives at Baer Marks, and instead of having one client, it turned out we had three derivatives clients because business people move around. Our individual client contacts moved to different swaps dealers, started doing very well, and gave us their legal work. The derivatives business grew. At that time, it was still in the early stages. I knew that, by necessity, the relationship I had with traders, salesmen and businesspeople was one step removed. I was being asked, "Write this provision, help me with this contract," but I wasn't in the room. I began to realize that, for derivatives work at least, being in-house was a better place to be than a law firm. Now, in-house had historically been viewed as a second-tier place for lawyers to be.

Cosslett: It's changed certainly.

Kopelman: It's changed radically, and I think financial services lawyers helped lead the way. In-house actually became the place to be, and outside became a place to help the people who were doing the in-house day-to-day thinking and work. I got a very nice offer from Bear Stearns in '93. Former clients had come to Bear Stearns to start a derivatives business. This made the offer very attractive to me; more attractive at the time than staying in a law firm.

Cosslett: How did you find the transition from a firm to in-house?

Kopelman: It's interesting. Everybody thinks not doing timesheets would be the most wonderful thing in the world, and for about forty minutes you think, "Boy, this is fun. I don't have to do timesheets." But that's not the real difference. I describe it to my partners now: "Imagine on the floor above you and the floor below you are all of your biggest clients, and they pay you a fixed fee per year." What happens is they come to recognize you're essentially a fixed resource in terms of cost, and they use you as much as they can. So that's one difference—nobody thinks twice about using you. The second big difference is the rhythm and the nature of the day. At a law firm, I would get in at nine to nine-thirty. Once I started working at a bank, I was in at seven-thirty, eight o'clock, maybe eight-thirty, and my stomach would start to hurt if I was in at eight-thirty. Nine o'clock, forget it.

Cosslett: And that's because of the market opening? Because it's an investment bank?

Kopelman: It's the market and it's the hours of the trading desk. So on the trading side of a bank, the day starts early and it ends early-ish. When I was an associate at a law firm, I never made dinner arrangements. I didn't feel like I had sufficient control of my day to do that. In-house, I could make dinner appointments. Now, occasionally, it would blow up. Occasionally, I would work late into the evening or on weekends. The tradeoff is that the day is incredibly intense. It's nonstop. In-house I would look up and say, "I only have two more hours before people start going home, but not me, maybe. I can stay around and do a little more work."

Key characteristics of in-house work are the intensity of the day and the collaborative nature of the work. A law firm is a little more isolated. You're working more with lawyers. You're often one step removed from the business. It's not a relaxed day, but it's a more thoughtful day. In-house, you're reacting all the time. You're in the middle of the mix and you never know when you're going to get a call from someone or another: "Come on up, we have a problem right now."

Cosslett: Now, is that all the more so because you're dealing with financial products affected by the market? Were these business issues or were they market issues?

Kopelman: They were always legal issues, first of all. And they were legal issues that were triggered by any number of things: a misunderstanding by a client, maybe a regulatory issue that had come in, a question someone very senior had raised about a transaction, or a transaction that needed to get done very quickly. But there would usually be some immediacy.

Cosslett: You might be working on a derivative at a law firm and you might be working on that same derivative once you get in-house, but the experience in-house is different: interfacing with the trading operation and the back-office, reacting to the exigencies of the market, et cetera, are realities of the business and can, I imagine, be overwhelming to a lawyer transitioning from a law firm.

Kopelman: People usually get it. It's just a question of how quickly; although, some people never get it, never like it. You come to realize that at a bank there are different groups and each of them is critical to the bank's functioning.

You mention operations. I spent a lot of time in operations because that's what drove a lot of the structuring: "Can operations do it?" I spent a lot of time with credit and risk management. "What's the effect from a risk management and credit perspective if we do this?" That mattered to the firm and to its basic overall well-being. After a while—and it does take some time to recognize it—you realize that while the issues are going to be different trade to trade, you really need to understand how the bank functions overall so you don't go ninety percent down the way and the guy from operations says, "We can't book that," or a guy from regulatory capital says, "That's going to blow things up."

Cosslett: How many lawyers were at Bear when you started?

Kopelman: When I started there must have been about thirty. When I left in 2008, there were over one hundred. Bear was not known as having the biggest legal department of the banks, nor did it have the smallest. Bear felt that if the lawyers were involved, the chance of issues being spotted and problems being cut off was higher.

We had lawyers seeking out and supporting business groups, and the general counsel was very supportive of this. He said, "We shouldn't have areas where there's no lawyer involved at all." I think that's typical in the street now, where lawyers are, for better or worse and I think it's better, involved in virtually every business in the firm. I think most risk management people, most regulators, and most lawyers think this is a good structure. There might be a few businesspeople out there who disagree.

Cosslett: Let's talk about how your role as in-house counsel changed over time.

Kopelman: I think the role of in-house lawyers generally is very important, especially in financial services. It's cost-effective and you get a different type of coverage than you get from outside counsel. Outside counsel is critical to all these businesses but having good in-house counsel to work as the liaison between the business and the outside counsel is a very important function.

In my own career at Bear, I began to get more responsibility as I worked on more things. That's how you move forward in an in-house department: you find yourself dealing with more issues and more parts of the firm. So I started as the derivatives lawyer, the derivatives business grew, and I had to grow with it and build a team. Then I was given the role of overseeing the fixed-income business as well, which was a big business at Bear, and that was a lot more responsibility and a much wider coverage area. So, again, my team grew and my areas of coverage grew. I think it's the same as in any other business: if you do a good job, I like to think you get rewarded with, among other things, more responsibility.

Cosslett: And, hopefully, higher compensation. As in-house counsel, is equity part of your compensation package?

Kopelman: Banks, investment banks, and other companies as well, will often include attorneys in whatever equity program they have, whether it's a restricted stock program or an options program. With respect to compensation, many investment banks tended to treat most people, both front and back office, as very bonus-based: their compensation had a small base component and a high bonus component. Now, in a banking world, it really matters if an investment banker or trader has a good year or a bad year because his overall compensation is based on his performance. There can be a big difference in a banker's compensation in a good year versus a bad year.

On the other hand, lawyers and control people, didn't experience that volatility in compensation because what they do doesn't change that much year to year. They have good years and bad years I suppose, like any human being does, but our performance isn't measurable in the same way as a trader's is. Bonus was generally paid in a combination of cash and whatever the equity incentive pay was, just as it was for the business people. That's still the case at banks, but what they've done is make the base compensation a larger portion of the total compensation, which I think is probably a smart idea.

Cosslett: And they've tended to pay more of the bonus in equity.

Kopelman: They've done that for everybody. And they've done that for a couple of reasons. One is they want to retain people because a lot of it vests over time, so it's a way to maintain loyalty. Also, it puts people in alignment with the company, and they like that. And there may be some financial reasons why it's easier and better than paying in cash up front.

Cosslett: And usually it works out nicely, depending on where the stock moves.

Kopelman: It always works out nicely, except when it doesn't.

Cosslett: Tell me about the role of in-house counsel during a crisis.

Kopelman: I've always believed and I've always told people who've worked with me that a time of crisis is when a lawyer's supposed to be front and center. Typically lawyers have a supporting role, especially in-house. During a crisis, the lawyer has to be front and center because the legal issues are going to be critical. How things get handled will matter from a legal perspective and will have ramifications later. When you're an outside lawyer, if your client has a problem, call them up and say, "How can I help?" I believe the same principle applies in-house; if there's a trading problem, go to the trading desk. It's important to volunteer your services and be visible.

Cosslett: Is there a role or are there issues specific to in-house counsel that you need to communicate to the businesspeople if there is a stress in the company?

Kopelman: There are a lot of constituencies when any company is in a crisis mode. One of them is obviously senior management. Another one, in a regulated business, would be the regulators. In terms of where the conflicts come in, it's important for in-house counsel to explain to executives that counsel's representation is of the company and not of the individuals. It can be hard to separate it out. It's not exactly a dancer from the dance type of thing, but it's a little difficult.

Sometimes it's less difficult to say, "Your interests and the company's interests are not aligned." But it's very important to recognize that the privilege that's so important to lawyers is a privilege that belongs to the company and not to an individual. While this can be an abstract concept, it's an important one for lawyers because representing the company can mean different things in different circumstances.

Cosslett: And that conflict could come up not only in regard to senior management, but in regard to board members, for example.

Kopelman: And, in fact, down to most all employees. It goes all over—it's really a general truism. More and more, in-house lawyers find themselves saying, "Just remember, I represent the company. I don't represent any individual."

Cosslett: Unfortunately, you're often not in a position to make that sort of statement until there's a problem.

Kopelman: In a bank, a regulated business, there are enough regulatory inquiries that, for better or worse, you do have opportunities to say it, so I think that's a place where firms will ordinarily say it in an ordinary course.

Cosslett: You're an expert in derivatives, the application of derivatives in trading, structured products, and capital markets. You're also an expert in broker-dealer, securities, and futures regulation. In an annual report to shareholders for 2002 Warren Buffett called derivatives "financial weapons of mass destruction." What he was looking at in 2002 is probably completely different than the derivatives that we're looking at now.

Kopelman: I think he was looking at his own portfolio at the time. He happened to have an extensive number of derivatives he had written over the years.

Cosslett: What's a derivative?

Kopelman: First of all, a derivative is a contract. It's an agreement between two parties that has one party paying or receiving amounts based on the performance of an underlying asset, rate, index or event. I'll give you two simple examples.

First, a total return swap: we have an institutional client who wants to get exposure to a particular asset, but he can't or chooses not to buy it (for some reason), but he can take it in derivative form. He doesn't want to own the asset. He wants to have financial exposure to the asset. Let's say it's a bond. So he can go to a bank and say, "I'd like to get exposure. I'd like to receive performance on this bond that I can't/won't buy (for some reason)." And, of course, if you're a bank and someone comes to you and asks you that, you have to think about whether there's a legal issue. But let's assume there's not.

We do the analysis and it's a legitimate transaction that he's looking to do. So you write a contract that says, "Currently, the bond is trading at $90. We, the bank, will pay you any appreciation above $90 over the course of the next year when the trade terminates. You will pay us any depreciation, so if it goes to $80, you'll pay us $10. If it goes to $100, I'll pay you $10. And as part of that bargain, because it's basically a trade where I'm funding you, I'm providing you exposure to an asset that would cost $90 in this example, I will charge you, in addition to your paying depreciation, an interest rate on $90."

So we write up a contract. There are forms to do these contracts. And that's a derivative. You don't have an actual bond. You don't have the right to vote the bond. If there's a consent on the bond, you don't get the consent. You don't have any indicia of owning the bond other than through a contract with the bank.

Cosslett: Now, if these derivatives are issued on a one-off basis, we must be talking about significant amounts of money to make this worth the time of the bank.

Kopelman: Well, banks have trading desks that trade derivatives, and they do these with a lot of hedge funds and institutional investors over time, so you have a desk set up already. You do a fair amount of business with the same people again and again, and it doesn't have to be a gigantic trade.

The market has changed, and Dodd-Frank will change the world fairly dramatically. The idea is that derivatives will start to be traded on swap execution facilities, exchange-like trading platforms for swaps, and the trades will be cleared. Once the clearinghouse accepts the transaction, it becomes counterparty to each side of the transaction. So, once a trade clears, the two parties will no longer be facing each other's credit. This is a big change because now, in the example I gave you on the total return swap, if the bond goes down and you owe the bank money and you go into bankruptcy, the bank's lost money. It has credit exposure to you, and vice versa. If the bond goes up and the bank goes into bankruptcy, you've lost money. Collateral reduces but doesn't eliminate the risk.

Another type of derivative trade is an asset or liability hedging trade. For example, a company that makes widgets needs to borrow money. They do a floating-rate bond issuance because that's the best funding they can get. So they have a bond issuance outstanding and are paying a floating-rate plus a spread.

And the corporate treasurer might say, that he doesn't want to pay floating. He is worried about rates going up. And so a bank may enter into an interest-rate swap with the widget company. It will agree with the widget company that it can pay a fixed interest rate on its debt issuance through the interest rate swap.

So the widget company and the bank enter into a contract. This contract will specify an amount—a notional amount—let's say the amount of the bond issuance. The bank will pay floating rate, the widget company will pay a fixed rate, and the result is that the widget company has now swapped its floating rate payment to a fixed rate payment.

Cosslett: So the risk of interest rates going up becomes the risk of the bank as opposed to the risk of the issuer.

Kopelman: Correct, and the bank could hedge that risk. And that's a derivative that serves a hedging purpose and makes a lot of sense. Now, it so happens that a lot of companies got burned because rates didn't go up. Rates went down, and they ended up owing the bank a lot of money. But they got the protection they were looking for—it turned out they just didn't need it.

Cosslett: I think of derivatives, and hybrid products, and complex financial instruments as tools used amongst the banks. The example you gave is a company that made widgets. Are derivatives part of their balance-sheet planning?

Kopelman: Very much so. Companies' asset and liability management groups often use derivatives. It's a very accepted tool. You can't believe everything you read in the popular press.

Cosslett: So a company out in Omaha making widgets is using derivatives as a way to hedge risk.

Kopelman: During Dodd-Frank, when Dodd-Frank legislation was moving forward, there were very few constituencies that got a hearing. Certainly, banks didn't go near the Hill. Individual companies did very well. Individual companies said, "Here's what we need. We like this type of trade, not this type of trade"—because industrial companies use derivatives all the time to manage their assets and liabilities. Of course there are also financial derivatives that are used not for hedging purposes but for investment purposes, to get a different type of exposure to a different types of asset, sometimes on a leveraged basis.

Cosslett: In your role as a derivatives lawyer, does the client come to you and say, "What kind of a product might help us to achieve these goals?" Or do they come and say, "We have this product, prepare the documents."

Kopelman: We represent financial sell-side and buy-side and corporate-end users. Their requests will be different. So a bank might say, "We're developing a new product. Here's what we think it's going to look like. Here's what we want to do. What are the regulatory and legal issues you see? How should we disclose it? What sort of documentation do we need?"

A buy-side participant might say, "I'm being offered this. How should we change what they're doing? How would it work better if what we're trying to achieve is X and Y? How can we change the document to make it work better? And what do you think the regulatory and legal issues are?"

Corporate-end users might just want an explanation, and they might come to us and say, "How can we do this differently? Does this make sense to you? What do you see in the market?" So different counter parties, different clients will have different questions and requests for us.

Cosslett: This is such a highly specialized area. As a lawyer, does this get your juices flowing in the morning? Do you find this to be intellectually challenging?

Kopelman: I really like it and what I like about being in the derivatives area is that it's creative and novel because you start with a blank piece of paper and you and I can write anything in a contract within the bounds of good taste. You can write a contract with any number of permutations.

Once you start thinking about the variations, you realize how boundless the creativity can be, which can also be a negative, and there were some examples of that leading up to 2008. And it can be a positive, such as enabling corporations to manage the risk of price fluctuations in their assets or in the supplies they need.

Cosslett: I read something the other day about regulators looking at some of these derivatives and saying, "There's no financial basis for some of these products. They're just gambling."

Kopelman: Well, I know the theory. I had a friend who worked in a derivatives desk of a bank, and he said, "What could be a bigger gamble than buying a share of Google?" But that's investing in a company, so that's a good thing. I described to you the total return swap on a bond. You could say that's just betting on the value of the bond going up or down. But you could also take that view of buying a bond. There are certain derivatives that people object to as a matter of public policy—structuring derivatives around election results, for example.

Cosslett: Did your experience at Bear Stearns make you a better lawyer?

Kopelman: Absolutely. Working in an intense atmosphere, with a lot of smart people, trying to think of new products and figure out ways to work in a very competitive environment was very helpful. In any crisis, such as the one in 2008, you learn a lot about the law, about how people react, about high-pressure situations and how to deal with them—you learn a lot of non-legal stuff.

Cosslett: What continues to motivate you as a lawyer? What do you get excited about in the morning, coming to work?

Kopelman: I love new business and I love new business ideas. I enjoy being able to take something that someone sees as a difficult problem and help them work it through very quickly and efficiently, which is not what outside lawyers often are known for. But I try to get answers to clients quickly, if the questions are susceptible to quick answers. Some of the questions in the areas that we work in are not susceptible to easy answers. I think Einstein said, "Make everything as simple as possible, but not simpler." We can only make it so simple.

The other thing I really like, going back to my teaching days, is working with smart, motivated junior associates. You have to be ready for their questions. Part of your job is to make them better, and part of their job—whether they know it or not—is actually to make us better.

Cosslett: What would you tell law students or undergraduates considering law school about being a financial services lawyer?

Kopelman: I would simply express my view of it, what I find good about it, what I find difficult about it. I wouldn't recommend anything to anyone. The most I can do is to give people information. Right now it's a tough market and it's a tough business to be entering.

Cosslett: It is. But for kids who are thinking about law school now, it is impossible to know what the market is going to look like in three years. It is so cyclical.

Kopelman: You're right. Because the market is unpredictable, if they want to do it, they should do it. And if they don't, they shouldn't.

CHAPTER 5

Nandan Nelivigi

Partner

White & Case LLP

As the head of the highly experienced India practice at White & Case, **Nandan Nelivigi** enjoys walking a tightrope. As a dual-qualified India-US lawyer intimately familiar with the Indian legal system and equally expert at executing transactions in a sophisticated Wall Street style, Nelivigi is acutely sensitive to the dynamic tension between constructing deals that are perfect for New York vs. constructing cross-border deals that are perfect for an emerging market, where risk and potential ROI are highly accentuated and need to be delicately balanced.

To mitigate risk exposure in India for foreign investors such as private equity funds, hedge funds, investment banks, and commercial lenders, Nelivigi excels at fine-tuning his energy and infrastructure project deals to protect his clients against unfamiliar hazards such as fraud, corruption, "creeping expropriation," retroactive taxation, unstable political commitment, and massive infrastructure failure. Nelivigi also represents banks, export credit agencies, and underwriters in the financing of conventional and renewable energy projects in other parts of the world, including the United States, the Middle East, East Asia, and Latin America. His deals have involved some of the world's largest wind energy farms and conventional power plants.

Nelivigi earned his BA/LLB with honors from the National Law School of India University, Bangalore, and his LLM from Harvard Law School. He is a member of the New York State Bar and the Bar Council of Karnataka, India. He is a member of the adjunct faculty of Columbia Law School.

Clare Cosslett: Where did you grow up?

Nandan Nelivigi: I grew up in South India in a small town about two hundred miles north of Bangalore. Bangalore is the Silicon Valley of India and is where the Indian IT industry originated and is presently located. Bangalore is home to Infosys, one of the biggest outsourcing companies in India.

Cosslett: What is the school structure in India?

Nelivigi: I went through twelve years of schooling and then went directly to law school for five years. No college in between. My law school was the first to implement a five-year program and I enrolled in the first group of students. We graduated in 1993. Since then, a number of law schools have implemented five-year programs. There is also a parallel system in which students go through twelve years of schooling, three years of undergraduate, and then three years of law school.

Cosslett: You can opt for either system?

Nelivigi: You can but the five-year course has more credibility these days. Medicine and engineering are both five-year programs. Many students who were rejected from these more popular professions would go to law school as a fallback. It was decided that if they made students choose law school right out of high school, they would get students who were more seriously inclined towards the law, and ultimately better lawyers.

The practice of law was once very prestigious in India. The first prime minister of the country, Jawaharlal Nehru, was a lawyer. Mahatma Gandhi was also a lawyer. It is beginning to regain some of that prestige now, although there is a divide between corporate lawyers and the cadre of solo practitioners who go to courts.

Cosslett: In 1961, the India's Advocates Act banned foreign law firms from practicing law in India.

Nelivigi: To fully articulate their outward position, many Indian lawyers say law is a noble profession in India, whereas law is a business in countries like the United States. They say, "we don't want to pollute the noble profession with business practitioners." I do not subscribe to this view. There is some element of protectionism. India will need to decide what is best for its legal system as a whole.

Cosslett: Are there well-trained corporate attorneys in India who represent the other side of the transactions that you are on?

Nelivigi: There are. A number of lawyers have gone back to India after having been trained in the US or UK. There are also very good lawyers graduating from the better law schools in India, and they now have fifteen to twenty years of experience. Other than a handful of lawyers, they do not have many thirty- or forty-year veterans in this business yet, because corporate law practice itself is still very new in India. India only opened up in 1993, so many of the most senior and experienced lawyers are relatively young.

Cosslett: Do you expect that India will open its doors to foreign lawyers in the foreseeable future?

Nelivigi: Early on, many people hoped that the market in India would open up but that hope has been completely destroyed. There is so much internal Indian opposition that the probability of the market opening up to foreign lawyers is quite far away.

Cosslett: There were three international firms that had liaison offices in India: White & Case, Ashurt, and Chadbourne Parke?

Nelivigi: Yes, in 1994 we were granted permission by India's central bank, called the Reserve Bank of India, to open up a liaison office. The Bank regulates the entry of any foreign company into India, because it regulates the inflow and outflow of foreign exchange. The Reserve Bank was not the regulator of the legal profession, and the courts have now ruled that it didn't have the power to give these kinds of licenses to legal professionals. It's only the Bar Council of India which has that power.

Cosslett: Why did you decide to go to law school?

Nelivigi: I grew up thinking and reading about public figures who were also lawyers. Also, my father is a leading trial lawyer in India.

I also looked up to a number of "senior advocates." While India is supposed to have a single class of lawyers called "advocates," in practice, there are various distinctions among lawyers. High courts, the highest courts in each state, and the Supreme Court of India, designate certain advocates as "senior advocates." Like barristers in England, senior advocates are not allowed to interact directly with clients. Clients brief solicitors. Solicitors brief the senior advocates. Some lawyers designated as senior advocates hold very senior positions in the government. I looked at them, and I said, "I want to be one of those senior lawyers" and a litigator.

I also knew that having a legal education was going to be useful on several different levels. Most of the people who were in senior political positions were lawyers, and I had an interest in politics as well as law. That is why I went to law school. I also got into engineering and medical school. Law was not a fallback profession for me.

Cosslett: The National Law School of India University at Bangalore. Is this the Harvard of India?

Nelivigi: They think of themselves that way. And, in fact, when we started, they sold us the school by saying, "This is going to be the Harvard of the East." Not just of India ... the entire Eastern world. And the school is highly regarded by many South Asian countries: Sri Lanka, Bangladesh, Pakistan, Nepal, Bhutan.

Cosslett: How big is the law school?

Nelivigi: When I started, I was one of fifty-five students, so there were about two hundred seventy-five to three hundred students in the whole school at the end of the fifth year. Tiny. I've heard they've increased class size to about eighty or ninety students every year, so there are about four hundred and fifty students now. It's still very small.

It was supposed to be a model school for the other law schools in India. There are about ten schools like it now, which is good news, but they are still an oasis in the middle of a large number of very mediocre law schools in the country. Ten schools make very little difference. I am glad though that there are good schools in India like Jindal Global Law School, a pioneering law school with whom White & Case has a cooperation agreement. We are doing our part to support and promote legal education in India.

Cosslett: Why did you decide to go to Harvard for your LLM?

Nelivigi: India just started opening up when I was graduating in '93. Many leaders of the independence movement in India had gone overseas and studied. I'm not one of the elites at all, but a lot of the political elites went overseas and came back. A lot of the senior advocates had gone overseas, to Cambridge and Oxford mostly, and come back to India. And the people with high standing were those people. Of course there were others who had not gone overseas.

Cosslett: There was not a history of Indian intellectuals coming to the United States to be educated.

Nelivigi: It has changed quite a bit in the last twenty years or so, especially with the information technology revolution. That's really being driven by the US. We've suddenly discovered each other.

My thinking was twofold: "If I want to model myself after some of these more respected lawyers, then I need training at an international school, Oxford or Cambridge." And then the Indian economy started opening up and I said, "Well, if I come back, I'll at least have learned the tricks of the new trade that is going to take root in India going forward." We had no idea what corporate finance was in India at that point in time. The stock market was nonexistent in any meaningful way.

I wanted to learn, "What does all this mean? How do you finance a big infrastructure project? What does it mean to do an M&A deal or an IPO?" All of these things were just words that I didn't really understand. I hadn't studied them in law school, even though I supposedly went to the best school. Law wasn't taught in that fashion. So I planned to get that experience and then go back to India.

Cosslett: And why did you go to America and not to England?

Nelivigi: I applied to both US and UK schools, and I was admitted in both places. I chose to go to Harvard. I thought that the way law was taught in the US was more progressive and probably comparable to the way I had studied in National Law School. We had a number of professors from the US, one of whom was from Berkeley. He offered me a fellowship in the US after I finished my LLM. I figured it was easier to do my LLM in the US and then do the fellowship for three months in California

Cosslett: What did your dad say about it?

Nelivigi: He really pushed me to go overseas. He had wanted to go to Harvard himself but never had the opportunity. I was born to my father when he was much older. He's eighty-three years old now, and he's still practicing. He goes to court every day. He modeled himself after the old-time lawyers with high ethical standards. He came to visit me when I was at Harvard. He loved it and was living vicariously through me when I was there. He was very proud.

Cosslett: When did you decide not to go back to India?

Nelivigi: At the end of doing the LLM program, I thought, "Wouldn't it be nice to gain some experience in a law firm?" I had decided that I wanted to do corporate law more than litigation, as it was more relevant to what was going on in India. I thought, "I've got to work in a corporate law firm." I planned to learn whatever I could in one year and then go back to India.

I got a job with White & Case for nine months in an international lawyers' program that the firm used to have then. It was for foreign lawyers who were going to be at the firm for a few months and then go back to their home jurisdiction.

White & Case said, "We're going to be opening an office in India very soon, so you can go back and join our office there." But that didn't happen.

Cosslett: White & Case at one point did a lot of domestic law work. They exploded internationally in the mid-eighties.

Nelivigi: Under the leadership of Jim Hurlock, the firm dramatically expanded its overseas practice by doing a lot of sovereign debt restructuring. By the time I joined, it was one of the few international law firms that we heard of in law school. And for me, it was an obvious choice, with my international background and my desire to go back to India. White & Case was one of the pioneers in doing deals in India. It was a natural fit for me.

Cosslett: What happened at the end of nine months?

Nelivigi: At the end of nine months, they hadn't yet opened their office in India, and they said, "Maybe it will take one more year. Why don't you stay another year?" The other thing that happened that was life-changing was that on the first day I walked into the office, White & Case was working on the biggest foreign investment in India at that time: the Dabhol Power Project. The Dabhol Power Project was one hundred–percent owned by Enron, GE, and Bechtel. These three were the flag-bearers of the US independent power sector at that point in time. They had gone to India to set up this massive power project when India was opening up the economy and the market for it. And White & Case had been hired to represent all the lenders for that project, both Indian and international.

I walked in and was staffed on that transaction. This was the most high-profile deal in India in the nineties. And people still talk about it.

Ultimately, the project didn't go well. It was built. And then there was a change of government and the new government cancelled it. The new government said, "We'll throw the Dabhol Project into the Arabian Sea." There were allegations of corruption in the award of the project and when it was cancelled, India became a pariah for international investors during the mid-nineties.

An arbitration petition was filed in London. The state government came back to the negotiating table and the project got renegotiated. Concessions were made on the electricity price, and the project got back on track and was expanded from approximately fourteen hundred megawatts to about twenty five hundred megawatts. In 1999, there was another change of government followed by another cancellation of the project. There was another big international outcry and another international arbitration. Around 2001, Enron collapsed and went into bankruptcy. Then the deal collapsed. Yet another restructuring followed. The international investors got out. They sold their stake to Indian lenders. Finally in 2004, the project was transferred to Indian lenders.

Unfortunately, the power problems haven't been solved, but this is a gold-plated twenty five hundred megawatt power-project sitting in India that was built by international developers. The government kept cancelling it because it didn't make sense economically.

Cosslett: Was this the first big foray of foreign investment into the country?

Nelivigi: The first of the first. It's unfortunate that we're talking about the Dabhol Power Project 15 years later when this project is not running up to its full capacity, and the country is having a ten-percent shortfall in power.

Cosslett: Why is Dabhol not running at capacity?

Nelivigi: The fuel needed to run the plant is not easily available. The plant is capable of operating on natural gas, naphtha, and diesel. And prices of each of those fuel sources keep varying. Enron had negotiated twenty-year supply contracts with Oman and Abu Dhabi, where natural gas was going to be liquefied and shipped to India from there, re-gasified, and put into the power plant to run the turbines. When they cancelled the project, they cancelled those twenty-year contracts too. And when they all woke up and tried to find gas around the world, there was not enough gas available.

Ten years ago, when this was being restructured, 1999 through 2002, gas prices were very high. There was not enough capacity in any of the gas terminals around the world, even in Qatar or Australia. Everybody was in need of gas, and India just couldn't find the gas to supply it on a reliable basis. It's a tragedy.

Cosslett: How long were you involved in this transaction?

Nelivigi: With some interruptions in between for a period spanning about ten years. I worked on it the very first year and I was flying in and out of India. The deal was setting precedents and was on the front pages of all the newspapers. I said,

"Wow! This is fascinating. Why would I want to go back to India? I'm dealing with India. I'm looking at it from the perspective of an outsider, but I'm still an insider." I was able to make a unique contribution when it came to dealing with issues from both perspectives.

Cosslett: The best first-year associate they ever had.

Nelivigi: It was perfect for me. In the mid-nineties, we did about twenty power project financings in India. We were representing all the big international financing corporations, Asian Development Bank, International Finance Corporation, all the commercial banks, and some Indian and international developers as well. It was very exciting. I had some good mentors. And so I changed my mind about going back to India.

Cosslett: It sounds like you walked into the firm and hit the ground running. You didn't go through the normal transition of junior associate to mid-level associate.

Nelivigi: I hit the ground running and I got a lot of responsibility very quickly. And, as luck would have it, the first time the project was cancelled, it was reconfigured and expanded into Phase 2. I was the senior associate running Phase 2 when I was in my fourth or fifth year. Pretty soon, I was the associate with the longest history in the transaction.

Cosslett: Was there a designated India practice at the firm?

Nelivigi: There was a thriving India practice out of the Singapore office at that point in time with about five to eight lawyers. I wasn't part of the core India practice group then. I was part of the project finance group. The only reason I was doing the Dabhol deal was that I thought it was the largest project finance deal the New York office was handling at that time. It was a classic international emerging market project financing. It was one of the best runs we have had because the infrastructure practice was so big in India. And that dried up when Dabhol collapsed. International lenders exited the Indian power sector.

They said, "Forget it!" to India. "There is too much political risk." And so that work collapsed. In between the restructurings, I was doing a bunch of non-Indian deals, and in the late nineties when the Indian infrastructure scene collapsed, I started doing US project financing.

Cosslett: Project financing isn't always just in the energy sector.

Nelivigi: You can build a sports stadium on a project-financing basis. You could build toll roads or telecom networks, but the power sector is particularly well suited for project financing because of long-term contracts for sale of power on a fixed-price basis. That makes it ideal for project financing.

Cosslett: Because you have a stream of revenue to show the investors?

Nelivigi: Fixed streams of revenues—that's what the lenders in project financing want: stability of the stream of revenues. And long-term fixed-price contracts are the most financeable contracts.

Cosslett: I know I'm going to be sorry I asked this question. Will the firm create a structured security based on a stream of revenue from a project finance deal?

Nelivigi: Some firms do it. The principles are similar, but in project financing, you usually have a single asset. Or, if you have multiple projects in one company, it's a single portfolio financing. Lenders have much more direct linkage to the security—to the asset—when the lenders are financing it. In a collateralized finance, lenders take security a couple of levels up.

Cosslett: Corporate America has created a seamless web of product that doesn't appear to have a beginning or end.

Nelivigi: That's what makes the capital markets efficient.

Cosslett: Until they go awry.

Nelivigi: The fact that everything is very interlinked also makes them very risk-prone.

Cosslett: What firms do you see on the other side of the table in project finance deals?

Nelivigi: We see Milbank Tweed, Latham & Watkins, Sherman & Sterling and a few others. When we were growing internationally, we reduced our involvement in the US project finance market for a few years. And so the major players in the US market were Milbank, Latham and Shearman & Sterling—not White & Case. We have now gone back in the US market in a big way and are on par with those firms on domestic project financings.

Cosslett: You were an associate at the firm for nine years and were made partner in January of 2004. Did you ever have doubts that you were going to make partner? Did you have a Plan B?

Nelivigi: I thought about a Plan B frequently. We've all been there.

Cosslett: A lot of people don't make it, but some people do. I think everyone has that moment of panic because so much is out of your control. You could have done the best work ever for nine years, and the firm could decide they don't want to take the practice that way.

Nelivigi: If Dabhol had not been cancelled, if Enron hadn't gone bankrupt, if the Indian infrastructure story hadn't gone down, I might have become a partner several years earlier purely on the back of India practice. But that was not the case, and the India practice had pretty much receded into the background by the time I was up for partnership. So I became a partner as a member of our global project financing practice.

Cosslett: I hope your recruiter didn't say this, but the market for people with your expertise is not huge. Project finance is a practice that is fairly unique to sophisticated law firms. You can't really go to Dunkin Donuts with that background.

Nelivigi: You're absolutely right. You can't go in-house. Most of the project finance work gets done by outside counsel. In-house lawyers don't specialize in project finance. They oversee it. A lot of the big corporate firms don't even do project financing or do very little of it. Now it's become a little bit more fashionable.

Cosslett: And specialty area is something to think about when you plan a career path. You might be putting all your eggs into one basket. Obviously, for you, it was an excellent choice. But certain practices can limit your mobility.

Nelivigi: As a junior lawyer, project financing is very sexy. You're dealing with emerging markets, political risk, economic risk. You are not just dealing with the documents. You're dealing with macro political and economic factors. You've got to look at the big picture. The project finance practice in White & Case is the most sought-after practice by the summer associates and first-year associates. They don't realize what is in store for them. Lawyers in other practice groups, like M&A, are much more transportable.

Most students understand what M&A is. Most students don't fully understand what project finance is. People who have an analytical aptitude and some interest in public policy and international relations tend to get drawn towards this specialty.

Cosslett: Your practice falls into three areas: representing lenders and developers in complex energy infrastructure, real estate, and project finance transactions around the world. Advising Indian companies in connection with their investments and capital-raising activities outside of India. And, advising foreign investors and commercial lenders in connection with their investments in India and loans to companies in India.

What sort of project finance work are you doing in the United States?

Nelivigi: With regard to US project financings, one of my favorite transactions was the financing of wind farms. In 2003 and 2004 we represented the initial purchasers—the underwriters—who financed wind farms by selling bonds issued by these wind farms. We helped to finance two groups of ten separate wind farms that were developed by one of the world's largest developers of wind farms. The wind farms were located all over the country, in some seventeen states.

Last year I worked on a solar project in Austin, Texas. I also took the lead on two natural gas-fired power projects in California. These projects were all very exciting. Many renewable energy projects were being done largely because of the incentives that were being provided by the federal government. There was a cash grant of thirty percent of the value of the project being given by the federal government.

Cosslett: And, at the end of the day, we got wind farms, which is excellent.

Nelivigi: In the last two or three years, most of our project financing activity in the United States has been around renewable energy. Last year the cash-grant program expired for most projects and there is something called the Production Tax Credit. For every kilowatt-hour of power that you generate, you get a credit in your tax obligations of about 2.2 cents per each kilowatt-hour of electricity in 2012. So if you have taxable income, you can reduce your tax liability by generating wind or solar power. Big corporations do it. Farmers do it and bring a wind turbine onto the farm, onto their house, at the top of a hill, or they create a solar farm.

A lot of the projects in the United States now have become quite standardized, so the work doesn't always have the kind of complexities that international projects have—although we did have big political risks in California in the early 2000s when California had a power crisis. A big electric utility in California went bankrupt and was restructured. The Department of Water Resources cancelled a whole host of power purchase agreements [PPAs] from independent power suppliers, because they were too expensive.

Déjà vu for me. California was cancelling PPAs. We restructured and refinanced a lot of the projects.

Cosslett: Let's talk about the second part of your practice: Indian investment out of the country.

Nelivigi: There were a number of Indian companies that went overseas and started buying up companies. For example, the Tata company out of India bought Jaguar Motors. They also bought Corus Steel, which was the biggest European steel company. Now I understand the biggest employer in the United Kingdom is Tata. This is something of a role reversal.

Cosslett: Is there any industry segment that's particularly interesting to India in terms of financing?

Nelivigi: Natural resources, mines and metals, oil and gas. A lot of Indian companies have been going overseas trying to buy up natural resources. For example, we represented a client in India that bought a stake in a Canadian publicly traded company that had coal mines in South Africa. We represented a company that bought a fifty-percent stake in an international power generating company, which had assets in the US, Mexico, Philippines, Australia, United Kingdom, and the Netherlands. The stake cost in excess of $1.3 billion.

That was one of the deals I led. It was perfect for us, perfect for the firm, perfect for my power background, perfect for India. All things came together for that deal. And then the client turned around and sold it to a Chinese state-owned buyer. It was fascinating. The management of the target was in Boston. It was incorporated in the Netherlands. The assets were all over the world. The seller was Indian. The buyer was Chinese. And most of the negotiations were happening in Hong Kong.

We also represented an Indian company that was buying oil and gas assets in Brazil and Argentina that were owned by an Italian company. We looked at those assets and did a lot of diligence. Ultimately, the client decided not to go forward with it because the Chinese companies came in and bid more. There is a lot of international competition in this area.

Cosslett: Were you working 24/7 during these deals?

Nelivigi: I was in Hong Kong every other week. The trend I was trying to ride was this wave of Indian companies going overseas and buying. Of course, the bigger trend is the Chinese companies going overseas and buying, which is unfortunately not part of my practice.

Cosslett: Your practice seems to blend private and public international law.

Nelivigi: The Dabhol project illustrates how a private international transaction can involve public international law. When the project was cancelled and the disputes arose, the government started cancelling licenses. The investors made the argument that this was essentially expropriation—not a classic expropriation, but a constructive expropriation, also called a "creeping expropriation."

Cosslett: Did they make that up?

Nelivigi: It's become a term of art. And there was a political risk insurance policy that was obtained by the equity investors from the Overseas Private Investment Corporation [OPIC]. A political risk insurance policy says essentially, "If there is an expropriation, the insurance company will pay the insured." And OPIC said, "This is not expropriation." The definition of what constitutes an insurable claim in connection with expropriation depended on whether the relevant government action was in violation of public international law.

The parties went into arbitration, and the arbitration panel had to consider whether this was a violation of public international law. So this transaction transitioned from private international law to public international law.

It happens all the time, especially when the bilateral investment treaty claims come up

Cosslett: Let's talk about the third part of your practice: international companies investing in India.

Nelivigi: In 2005, India opened up its real estate sector to foreign investment in a limited way, and now I have significant experience advising investors in that sector. A lot of the real estate private equity investors entered the Indian real estate market at that point of time. And I rode that wave.

Cosslett: What sort of real estate were your clients investing in?

Nelivigi: All types. Residential, office, malls, storage, warehouses, logistics. Any type of real estate you can turn into a rental stream or sale proceeds. Hotels, tourism facilities, convention centers. We advised clients on a lot of those transactions with help from Indian counsel.

In areas other than real estate, we represented a number of US corporations buying stakes in India. We represented a large Internet company when they bought a stake in one of the Internet companies in India. We represented a big pharmaceutical company when they did a joint venture with a company in India. We had a client who was looking to invest in the oil and gas and power sectors in India. So I have worked with a lot of inbound investors going into India.

Cosslett: How do you best protect the interests of your clients when they are investing in an emerging market?

Nelivigi: The law is always changing and evolving. Recently, there was a big controversy in India when legislation was enacted that imposed taxes retrospectively on deals that were done ten years ago. That's the kind of stuff our clients worry about all the time. Now, you can't protect them against arbitrary changes in law. But what you need to do is think about the possibility of things like that happening, and see if you can mitigate the risk by passing it onto the right party. You can't always do that, and quite often the answer remains only in a risk-and-reward analysis. If people are investing in India, they have to be prepared for that risk, but they do count on a much higher reward than in a more developed market.

I think about my role here as being a lawyer who is intimately familiar with the Indian legal system: knowing what can work and what can go wrong, and bringing that knowledge into the mix of doing deals in a sophisticated New York Wall Street style. But, at the same time, not always trying to prescribe the Wall Street model for an emerging market. It's a constant struggle to balance the two: having a perfect deal versus a deal that works for the situation, for the reality that we're dealing with. The tendency for a lot of people is to go one way or the other, and my role is to be able to balance, by having that perspective from both sides.

And how do you best protect your client? Quite often, there are unique areas in which things do go wrong, and you've got to have your finger on those and figure out the right clauses to put in your documents. Let me give you an example. In these investment deals, we always insist on offshore arbitration provisions: if there's a dispute, we don't go to Indian courts.

Cosslett: If you sue or are sued, will you ever find a remedy in the Indian courts?

Nelivigi: Indian courts are very, very slow so you don't have much of a remedy if things go wrong. The laws generally exist on the books, but it's very hard to enforce them because nobody has the time, patience, or resources to go through the process.

We would rather not be in that situation, so quite often we insist on offshore arbitration. We also build provisions into our documents, which disincentivize parties from getting into a litigation. Certain contracts provide for change of economic control if certain bad things happen. Then they never do the bad things.

Having started off wanting to be a litigator, I do everything possible to avoid Indian courts now.

Cosslett: What you're saying is that there are certain things that you can protect against—there are certain ways to draft documents to minimize exposure—but, in the long run, you can't protect against everything because India is an emerging market. Your role is to advise the client as to the risk and allow them to decide if it's worth the ultimate reward.

Nelivigi: We tell them to avoid litigation. They can't always do that, so that's why we put in the arbitration language. We tell them to avoid expropriation. That's not in their control, but that's why we tell them to choose the right jurisdiction from which to make the investment: a jurisdiction where you have the protection of a bilateral investment treaty.

Cosslett: Does a fraudulent business in India look like a fraudulent business in the US?

Nelivigi: It takes an emerging markets lawyer to really worry about fraud. We really don't worry too much about corruption in the vast majority of our deals here in the US—not in corporate deals. When you do deals in India, your first thought is, "Where can risks arise if, for example, some rogue employee is caught in a bribery scandal?" What if we get caught up in the Foreign Corrupt Practices Act? These sorts of issues are common in the emerging markets practice.

Cosslett: There are requirements in India that foreign investments in certain industry sectors involve a significant portion of local manufacturers. What effect do these requirements have on foreign investments?

Nelivigi: There is a trend all over the world these days to try to promote local goods and local employment. And it's true for the US as well. In India, you see this in the retail sales sector. There is a lot of opposition to foreigners setting up stores in India—like by Walmart, for example. The government is saying that they will allow a limited number of foreign retailers into India, provided they procure thirty percent of what they sell from within India. So, for example, when IKEA comes into India, they have to indigenize thirty percent of the products they sell in India.

There are some sectors that are just not open to foreign investors, like casinos or any other form of gambling. The insurance sector, for example, is one where there are limits on how much foreign investors can own. You can't have more than twenty-six-percent foreign ownership. In real estate, a foreign investor just can't go and buy a built-up office space. They can only invest in a new construction. The government wants new capital. They don't want people coming in and speculating.

Cosslett: Let's talk about what's been going on in India with 9.5 percent of the world's population without power for three full days. Six hundred and seventy million people. How will the inadequacy and unreliability of the public power grid affect foreign and domestic investment, and will it hobble growth prospects?

Nelivigi: One of the biggest constraints for India's growth is lack of adequate infrastructure of all types: whether it is adequate roads for transporting goods and people, whether it's railway lines or airports or seaports. But the most critical of these issues is the power. There is not enough power. And this has been a problem that was identified a long time ago, and they've tried to solve it for the last twenty years. Unfortunately, they have taken one step forward and two steps backwards every time they've tried to solve this. And I think what has happened recently—the national blackout—simply reflects the lack of any serious efforts to solve the fundamental problems.

Growth has already been affected in India. The growth projections have come down from eight and nine percent to five and six percent. The US would love to have five-percent growth, but the US is starting from a much higher base. It's not really comparing apples to apples. In terms of how it affects international investment, it's not like the problem is unknown. Everybody knows the problems with the Indian power sector. But it is not good to see them on the front page of *The New York Times*.

If somebody is looking to make investments in India, it's going to be very difficult to defend that in a board meeting if someone asks "Why are we putting $100 million in this country, where you have these big risks?" But if you're going to invest in the power sector in India, maybe they'll stand up and say, "Hey, there's an opportunity there."

Cosslett: The power sector has been privatized in India?

Nelivigi: Oh, definitely—but when you're trying to restructure and reform a sector like the power sector, it cannot be done overnight. It's a big problem because you can't turn the switch on and say, "We've privatized it." What the government really needs to do is dismantle these state-owned distribution companies and make them healthy, or sell them off to the private sector and put regulations in place to ensure that the private sector does not overcharge people. You've got to transition properly and India hasn't been doing it. The policy objective has already been set but getting there in a chaotic democracy like India's is going to take a while.

Cosslett: Looking at your crystal ball, when do you think they'll have a completely reliable power supply in India?

Nelivigi: I think it will take at least fifteen to twenty years. If I'm wearing my optimistic hat, I would say ten years. Pessimistic hat, thirty years or more.

Cosslett: The other big issue for foreign investors in India is corruption. Can you talk about that?

Nelivigi: It's a pervasive problem in India. But the good news is that there is a lot more awareness of the fact that it is bad. For a long time, it was simply accepted as a way of life, of doing business in India. A positive side effect of globalization and economic reform and growth is that it has turned the growing middle class into a constituency for good governance and for continuing economic reforms.

As part of that, many people in the middle class are not willing to tolerate some of the older problems, such as the electricity supply issues and corruption issues. They are coming to the surface. There is a lot of internal strife, opposition, and pressure being brought to bear on the government to recognize and solve the corruption issues. But it's a big structural problem. And a lot of people who are benefiting from and dependent on corruption on a day-to-day basis are those who have been charged with eradicating it. It becomes a big problem for India to attract foreign investors who do not want to have to deal with these kinds of issues.

Cosslett: Foreign investors who don't want to deal with them? Or don't know how to deal with them?

Nelivigi: There are some companies that will say, "We know that the problem exists, but we are not going to get involved in it. So we'll go in and invest. We have a very strong compliance culture, and we'll deal with it. We're going to turn away some types of businesses where we are being asked to bribe people." There are other companies that go in there and say, "Well, this is part of life. We are generally clean, but sometimes we have to compromise." And then there are other people who will say, "There is no way to do this business, and we are just not going to enter this country because of this problem."

I think India is losing a lot of investments because of that third class of people, who are not going in there. And US businesses are not as competitive as they could be, because they don't have a level playing field. There are a number of the players who are taking advantage of the broken system, which US companies, rightly, are not taking advantage of. We would advocate that they not try to take advantage of it. But until India fixes the problem, we will continue to be on a weak footing. Not only is India losing people who don't want to enter the country because of its problems, but those who don't have the same competitive footing are not doing as much business as they could be doing otherwise in India.

Cosslett: How has your practice been affected by the recent economic downturn and by the current economic situation in Europe?

Nelivigi: For a period of time, India was seemingly immune from it. When everything was falling apart, India seemed to be standing upright, in large part because it is very underleveraged. Most of Europe's problems are due to it being overleveraged. Most of the problem in the US was overleverage.

The Indian mentality is very conservative when it comes to borrowing money. Most people don't want to borrow money. Indian regulators are very conservative. India's central bank didn't allow banks to lend to certain types of borrowers and certain types of assets. So Indian regulators have been patting their own backs. But the reality is: yes, they're conservative. Yes, India's financial problems were not as bad as Europe's—but it's like being proud that your son, whom you have never let out of your house, has never had an injury.

I'm not a big fan of that regulatory model but at the end of the day in bad times like we had in 2008 and 2009, India looked great. Deals were happening. We were busy. But now it has caught up. A lot of the growth in India in the last five years was foreign investment-driven. And as the European and US investors had problems at home, they've pulled back from emerging markets. As risk aversion to emerging markets has increased, they have pulled back from India, and therefore new investment has gone down. Private equity investors, in particular, who are looking at a four- to six-year horizon for exit from a business, have stepped back big-time because that time frame for exit is no longer realistic in India.

Generally speaking, people are getting out. Therefore, the prices are coming down. There are some people with more risk appetite still going in—but not in a big way and certainly not at the levels that we saw before 2009. There are a few of them, sophisticated ones, who are getting in now. If the problems get solved in the next three years and the prices start going up, that would be great for them.

Cosslett: What secular trends do you perceive as being the most important, worrisome, or promising when projected to the future of your practice area?

Nelivigi: India is going to be a growth economy no matter what. It's going to be an emerging market with ups and downs. The way I look at it—and what I tell my clients—is: when times were good, the good things were being exaggerated. When times are bad, the bad things are being exaggerated. To my mind, the secular trend is a growth trend. And so this practice, in the long run, can only grow. There may be another year of slow down, or another year of extraordinary growth. But when you average it all out, it's a healthy growth trend.

Indian companies also have become a lot more sophisticated. They have international ambitions. And while the macro-growth rates have fallen, there is still a tremendous domestic demand in India. There's a growing middle-class population. The cultural norms are changing dramatically. The joint Hindu family structure where uncles, aunts, nephews, nieces, fathers, and grandfathers all lived under one roof, is breaking up. The family unit is becoming more nuclear. In many households both husband and wife are now working, so income levels are rising. Consumer demands are also rising because of this change in the extended family structure. People need their own apartments, and their consumption has gone up. That's a huge social and economic shift and that trend will continue.

There are a number of companies that are still growing at an enormous pace in India—especially those that are driven by consumption such as restaurants and businesses specializing in consumer goods such as textiles, clothing, and jewelry. Construction, infrastructure, and cement. Wood, coal, and fuel. All these sorts of things. There is a tremendous demand that will continue to grow. And so these companies will continue to do their international deals and will need to continue to raise capital internationally. All of those trends only help my practice.

Cosslett: Are there issues of professional responsibility that come up specific to an India practice?

Nelivigi: As we discussed, India now prohibits foreign lawyers from practicing in India. The contours of what is permitted and what is prohibited are still being defined and remain very unclear.

A recent dispute has arisen about whether flying in and out of India on a temporary basis as we do for meetings—where we don't advise on Indian law, but advise only on New York law—constitutes practicing law in India. The Indian government, when it is selling off its stakes in government companies to foreign investors, needs advice on US securities laws. They invite us to visit India. Certain Indian lawyers are arguing that this is practicing law in India in violation of the Indian law. If you step foot in India and practice any form of law, they're saying that. So you've got to really be conscious about the boundaries of what you can and cannot do generally in an international practice, and certainly in India.

Cosslett: In terms of your US practice, are there any professional responsibility issues that come up?

Nelivigi: A US attorney needs to be conscious about not practicing the law of states in which he or she is not admitted. If you are not admitted in California, for example, it is not appropriate to advise on California law. In the US, issues about ethical behavior in a corporate practice generally revolve around conflicts and issues of good faith. Are you fully disclosing everything when you have a hard-fought negotiation? Is this fair play or not? The line between negotiations and ethics sometimes raises issues, but those are generally gray areas.

The lines are sometimes starker in an international context because different legal cultures view ethics differently. The enforcement of ethics in India is not at the level it should be. Ethics rules are certainly on the books. The rules are there but the enforcement is not there, and therefore there is a tendency and temptation for lawyers to take advantage of the lack of supervision. There are a lot of good ethical lawyers, but you can't assume they are all above reproach. So, unfortunately, you always start from a position of figuring out the bona fides of the person on the other side of the table. This can be a real obstacle in establishing relationships and doing business. Thankfully, we don't worry about it too much with most of the lawyers we deal with.

Cosslett: Isn't it a good thing for a lawyer to have that degree of skepticism?

Nelivigi: Sometimes, in an emerging market like India, we come across as being naïve. When I say "we," I'm wearing my New York lawyer hat. Indian lawyers are so savvy, they will always figure out the angle. New York lawyers are savvy—too, in a different way. We assume some basic canvas that we're playing on. But in India, there is no canvas. It's a rough turf.

Cosslett: What advice can you give law students or practicing lawyers considering a career change about how to best position themselves for practicing as an international lawyer?

Nelivigi: I think you need to start by being a good lawyer. Period. You can't start out by being an international lawyer. All good international lawyers are first and foremost good, basic commercial lawyers. I have had the best training by learning to be a good New York lawyer. And then add on to that the international component. My advice to law students and anybody else starting out in this career is that you've got to master the fundamental technical skills—the basic analytical, writing, drafting, negotiating, and presentation skills. It's easy to add the building blocks on top of that foundation.

I also think you have to have the aptitude. You have to have that interest in looking at diverse cultures. You can't get too spoiled by growing up in the New York culture. That's the only caveat. First, go be a good New York lawyer, but don't get too comfortable in how well the system works. You've got to have the ability to really appreciate the imperfect systems—and actually enjoy them. I thoroughly enjoy how challenging some of these systems are, because quite often the New York practice becomes standardized. Everyone in our practice knows what everyone else is talking about.

Cosslett: Everyone is sophisticated.

Nelivigi: Everyone is sophisticated. There are no unexpected issues. There are difficult negotiations, yes, but the same issues comes up. In an emerging markets practice, we're talking about, "Are they going to expropriate?" You've got to be alert for really crazy problems—even for just outright fraud. How do you deal with it? And you have to factor all of that into your documents. When you come back to your New York practice from that angle, you'll be that much better prepared to think about how things could really go wrong in a bad situation. No matter how good the New York practice is, things still go wrong. There is fraud here. Remember Madoff?

Being an international lawyer has helped me become a better New York lawyer, and being a good New York lawyer helped me become a good international lawyer. So, hopefully it makes for an all-around good lawyer!

Cosslett: A perfect conclusion.

CHAPTER 6

Jacalyn F. Barnett

Principal

Law Offices of Jacalyn F. Barnett, P.C.

"All marriages end. Either someone walks out or is carried out. The good ones are when you're carried out. That's a successful marriage."

This is the credo of **Jacalyn F. Barnett**, a.k.a. The Love Lawyer. Across three decades of representing unhappy spouses in New York City, Barnett has looked steadily on the bright side of marital dissolution. She champions the view that divorce is a wonderful exception to the rule that life rarely gives you a second (much less a third) chance to get things right. Divorce is the portal to a radical do-over, and crossing that threshold to a new beginning requires courage, composure, smarts, and sound legal advice. Barnett tested and refined this heart-and-head approach in her family law practice through two brilliantly happy and successful divorces of her own.

Barnett earned a BA from the University of Wisconsin at Madison, studied at the University of London, and received a JD degree from Brooklyn Law School. Prior to starting her own firm, she was the head of the matrimonial department at the New York law firm of Shea & Gould.

Clare Cosslett: Where did you grow up?

Jacalyn Barnett: I had a wonderful, middle-class childhood growing up with two sisters in Long Island. Neither of my parents was college-educated and there were no lawyers in the family. But I was *always* this kid who was fascinated by law and by justice.

My parents didn't really want me to be a lawyer. Quite frankly, they were very against the idea, especially for a girl. When I was young, my mother used to say, "Don't run so fast. Don't do this, don't do that." You had to lose games to the boys, you should not look too smart and that was the mentality of a young mother with three daughters. However, that was never a mentality to which I subscribed. They really thought I should have become a nursery school or kindergarten teacher.

My father especially was not someone who respected the law. In fact, he used to ask me legal questions, and when I would tell him the answer, he'd say, "No, don't tell me that I can't do it. Tell me *how* I can do it." To him, being a lawyer wasn't something to aspire to; he did not respect lawyers in general. Since no one in my family came to my college graduation, I was thrilled to have my family celebrating my graduation from law school. We went to Tavern on the Green's Crystal Room, a then magical restaurant in Central Park, which had just opened up. My maternal grandmother, who was kosher, came to the luncheon. She never would have gone to a non-kosher restaurant for any other occasion. I felt so honored by her presence at this moment about which I had fantasized since childhood, but at the end of the celebration, even she said, "The only thing better would have been if you were a grandson." And she meant it.

Cosslett: Well, there's no pleasing some people.

Barnett: I was always involved in student government and was always organizing things in the community. My mother remembers me telling my third-grade teacher that I was going to be a lawyer and would sit on the United States Supreme Court. I think that was a pretty good aspiration at eight years old.

When I was a senior in high school I was determined to get my pilot's license, so I taught piano lessons to young children in their homes as a way to earn money to pay for flying lessons. My first student was a six-year-old neighbor. Within less than two weeks I had ten students. That was a tipping point in my life. What I learned from the experience was that even in these upscale Great Neck households, where I was the wallpaper—when you're a senior in high school giving piano lessons, nobody pays attention to you—I witnessed the reality of these children in these picture perfect homes. In that moment, I decided, "I want to represent and protect children." I always knew I wanted to be a lawyer, and in that year, watching the incredible differences in families, I decided to do family law. Most high school students don't think, "Oh, gee, I want to be a divorce lawyer." Having known since third grade that I wanted to become a lawyer, I discovered from that pivotal experience that I wanted to become a divorce lawyer. My parents were in an intact marriage and nobody in my family at the time was divorced. I was just always interested in children and their rights and their voices. The only deviation from that commitment was the month after my sixth grade class went on a field trip to the UN, I thought about being a UN tour guide, it was a very cute uniform, but that was only a one-month deviation from my dream path of law.

Cosslett: You didn't go into child advocacy?

Barnett: I thought the grownups were really in charge and what interested me was being an advocate for children in the context of their families. I was always fascinated by family relationships and changing family dynamics. In fact, I represented my mother against my father in their divorce after they were married for more than four decades, so I appreciate how relationships change over time. I still believe my parents had a successful marriage, just not for the last 25 years of it. They each would have been happier if they had their opportunity for a do-over earlier in their lives. So many people get divorced later in life. And people do live longer. I believe that a divorce is an act of courage: a statement that, "I believe there's a better life for me and that there's only a limited amount of time." If you've really worked on a marriage and it's not going to work, just to be there for the sake of an endurance contest is, to me, not the way you should live your life. I think the message that I got from children who didn't have a voice is that you really need to get involved in a timely and meaningful manner to solve the problems of family situations and to recognize that sometimes staying together is not in anyone's interest. It really is never the same thing because every family has a different dynamic and each family's dynamic needs to be respected as unique and not approached in a cookie cutter style. Children are sacred and deserve more respect than that.

Cosslett: To quote Tolstoy: "Happy families are all alike: every unhappy family is unhappy in its own way."

Barnett: Exactly. What always intrigues me is how people turn around something that's adverse. Being successful and becoming more successful to me is not fascinating. When I was in law school in the mid-seventies, I had the opportunity to be in a clinic with Judge John J. Galgay, who was then a bankruptcy judge in the Southern District of New York. There was a wave of bankruptcies, and I was an eyewitness to the positive impact that a financial restructuring could have on people.

I remember when REA Express filed its petition. I saw people sitting in the courtroom who had been affected dramatically by the company's financial disaster. Restructuring, however, allowed companies to emerge and, in cases like a Toys R Us, to flourish. While you saw the human stories of the sadness, you also realized that if somebody got a chance to restructure things, there could be a happy ending. It may not be the happy ending that they had planned when they started the company, just as it's not the happy ending people planned when they called the caterer and set up the wedding.

Cosslett: It's interesting to analogize divorce law to bankruptcy law.

Barnett: Judge Galgay was a wonderful man with seven children. He was a delicious, warm human being, who demystified judges for me. I remember saying to him, "I should make a sampler to hang above your desk that says, 'Your rupture is our rapture.'" I really started to understand how people sometimes need to have a do-over—another chance.

My life has been based on a do-over. I have been very happily married for almost 24 years, but it's my third marriage—and, in fact, I represented my first husband in his third divorce. I was my first husband's second wife, my second husband's second wife, and my third husband's third wife. I had to give up the dream of being anybody's first wife.

Cosslett: Well, at least it's almost symmetrical.

Barnett: As a family lawyer I get a front-row seat watching how people can transform their lives. I want to know what my clients have done with their second or third chances at happiness. I have been blessed by staying in contact with many of my former clients. I can tell you a really romantic story. Twenty-three years ago, a woman came to see me. She had signed a divorce agreement in which she agreed to give her ex-husband parental access with his two children three weekends a month. She then fell in love with the president of a subsidiary of Lloyd's of London and wanted to relocate to London with the children. The children were about seven and five at the time. For me, relocation cases are the most emotionally wrenching cases because it's one thing if someone pays X or Y to their spouse, or a client gets to live in this house or that apartment, but whether a parent gets to live and be near their child and whether or not the child is in the best environment is a life-altering decision. I can see it from both points of view and have handled relocation matters from each side. It is exquisitely fact-specific. We were very lucky. We prevailed, and the mother got to move to London with their children, and we were upheld on appeal.

Through the years, she sent me Christmas cards, and I have heard from her periodically and seen her occasionally. About six years ago I got a call. The little girl was now twenty-one. She was in New York City for the summer and wanted to come and say hi. She and her mother came by and sat in my office. This little girl, who I had last seen in front of a vending machine in the courthouse, was now a sensational young woman. She was going into her last year at Brown University. I impulsively picked up the phone and called my husband's nephew, who I've known since he was ten years old. I said, "This lovely girl's going to be in New York for the summer. Would you just take her out for a drink?" Well, they got married three years ago. So now, suddenly, the man who had had his children relocate to London almost twenty years earlier was now going to be the father-in-law of my nephew, and we're all family. The last time I had seen the father, I was cross-examining him at trial. When I saw him at my nephew's wedding, he was graciously charming, happily remarried with a wonderful family. My client is happily remarried. Everybody gets along and, most importantly, everybody did what was right by the kids. I am proud to have my former client and her former husband as part of my extended family.

Cosslett: That's a great story. You chose University of Wisconsin for undergraduate?

Barnett: Yes, I wanted to go to a big university. It was an exciting time at the University of Wisconsin. It was a fabulous education, but my junior year I purposely chose to spend in London because the roots of American law derive from England. I went to the University of London for a year. It was a turning point in my life and perspective of life choices. I loved the whole structure of their legal system, with barristers and solicitors. It really made you think about how things are done and how they could be done differently. As an undergraduate, I was a history major. And one of the things that made sense to me, and I think is so applicable in law, is that you have to go to the core research. You have to go to the heart of everything. All too often you read newspaper headlines and think, "Oh, well, this is true." I don't mean something factual—like Michael Phelps winning a race in the Olympics—but the impression the headline alone creates, and how the attendant photograph suggests the direction of the piece, even before reading it. If it's Hillary with a bad haircut, then you know right away that the piece will likely be negative for her. One of the things that I learned in studying history is how important it is to form your own opinion and not to rely on secondary information, which ultimately is nothing more than hearsay.

Cosslett: Did you have an opportunity to work in a law firm before committing to law school?

Barnett: To prove to my parents that I was serious about pursuing a legal career and to confirm to myself that it was a real fit, during college, I worked every summer in a law firm. I loved the environment. I loved the culture, the sight, the smell, the touch—just everything about being in a law firm. The summer between college and law school, the firm had added an incredibly cute lawyer named Michael Barnett. We were married after my first year of law school. And I was very lucky because he's a fabulous man and he's a very dear friend. In fact, I did his third divorce a few years ago. He always tells people I'm his favorite ex-wife.

Cosslett: You joined the bankruptcy practice at Shea & Gould after law school?

Barnett: I had gotten experience in bankruptcy from my clinic with Judge Galgay, and I fell into the bankruptcy area after law school because that's what became available. I started working at Shea & Gould in my third year after law school as a bankruptcy lawyer.

Cosslett: They had a big bankruptcy practice?

Barnett: They did have a big bankruptcy practice, and because there were few women in the field at the time I was asked to do speaking engagements to some women's groups on bankruptcy law, which had been dramatically revamped at the time.

When I was asked to speak, however, I talked about the interrelationship between bankruptcy and divorce, and ended up developing a successful divorce practice for the firm. When I was thirty-three, they made me partner of the matrimonial department. I wasn't doing bankruptcy anymore, but my background in the area was invaluable. As a bankruptcy practice makes you think about all the things that can go wrong with money, a divorce practice makes you think about all the things that can go wrong in a marriage. I am a fervent believer in prenuptial agreements and co-habitation agreements. Similarly, when you are preparing a separation agreement you have to think about what can go wrong with it—issues such as enforceability. I am much more sensitive to those sorts of issues because of my background in bankruptcy.

People tend to think that bankruptcy is just about money, but that is too simplistic. If people lose their jobs and people lose their homes, they have to change more than their Facebook status, they have to change their vision of their future and of their family's future, including all too often, the educational plans they had for their children. Take Bernie Madoff. There are countless people who could have had an intact marriage but for his bankruptcy and the shadow it cast on so many people, directly and indirectly. When law firms implode and the media reports that "X numbers of lawyers are out of work," I don't focus on the lawfirms breaking up, I think about the individuals that are affected by the trickling effect—the cab drivers, the service people, the childcare people, the receptionists and how their loss of employment and their loss of faith in the institution of their employer makes them challenge the institution of their own marriages. So to me, whether the disaster is a bankruptcy, a divorce, or an earthquake, what we really need to do is to create a plan to defeat the problem, not some other person. When people get married, they become a family. They're not just going to be husband and wife—or husband and husband or wife and wife, because now we're doing gay divorces, too. They are always going to be a family.

Cosslett: Can a lawyer maintain expertise in more than one practice area?

Barnett: I find it absolutely stunning for a lawyer to say they're a general practitioner capable of doing anything and everything. I don't know how anybody could feel that they know every area of practice and are willing to have people rely on them to protect their interests in almost all areas. That is very frightening to me as a lawyer. A lot of young lawyers just hang out a shingle and say they'll do anything, whereas I won't even write a real estate contract. I won't do anything other than what my area is, because I think that's what a reasonable professional should do.

Cosslett: What about a small town where a person needs to have a will drawn, or sells a house, or falls down, or gets into a car accident? Isn't a less-than-perfect will better than no will?

Barnett: As long as you're not dead, the will won't matter, but if you were to die, you would have problems. My husband—my final husband, the love-of-my-life husband, the father-of-my-child husband—he's an internist, and he's smart enough to know when to call a specialist for different issues. I believe that, especially in such a dense-information world, it is impossible for someone to keep up in all the different areas of law. The landscape shifts so much.

Cosslett: Speaking of shifting landscape . . . in New York, do you need to have grounds for divorce?

Barnett: Prior to October 2010, you had to have fault grounds in New York to get divorced. The only alternative was if two people signed a separation agreement and the spouses lived separate and apart pursuant to the agreement for twelve months. That was the only no-fault ground. New York was the last state to change its law. As a result if your spouse contested grounds, prior to 2010, you had to engage in mudslinging simply in order to get divorced. Grounds included adultery, cruelty, imprisonment for more than three years and constructive abandonment, meaning you had to prove that you didn't have sex with your spouse for a year and that you wanted to have sex with him or her.

Cosslett: You had to prove it?

Barnett: That would be if somebody challenged it. You're entitled to sex once a year. May I add, I always have to qualify that the sex is "with your spouse." There was a client who once actually asked me, "Does sex in New Jersey count? And what if I am having sex with someone else?" And I'm thinking, "Where in the statute does it say anything about New Jersey?" and "Obviously committing adultery does not fulfill your obligation to have sex once a year—it is sex with your spouse!" One fault ground, cruel and inhuman treatment, was interpreted to mean that the longer you were married, the more cruelty you were expected to endure. People were denied divorces when they were married for twenty years because it was determined it was neither unsafe nor improper to live together since the couple had done so for so long. When this aspect of the law changed in October of 2010 in New York, the Legislature added a new ground called "irretrievable breakdown for six months," which effectively permits no-fault divorce in New York State.

Cosslett: Was there a reason that the law was so difficult before 2010? It seems so archaic.

Barnett: A lot of things in the law derive from either religious origins or protective instincts. In the "olden days," people were concerned about women in long-term marriages being abandoned by their husbands. All they were entitled to was alimony and the assets in their own names. Only wives were entitled to receive alimony then. Alimony comes from the French word *alimentaire*, meaning food or sustenance. Since equitable distribution went into effect in July of 1980, support became gender neutral and was called "maintenance." Since that time spousal support can be paid from a husband to a wife or a wife to a husband, and it's more rehabilitative in nature than alimony was, meaning that it may be set to a period of years based on the reasonable expectation of how long it should take for the supported spouse to become self-supporting. And since you're dividing marital properties equitably, there is a very different perception of marriage than before 1980. Marriage truly is an economic partnership. I always remind clients that there is no romance without finance.

By my definition, when you get married, you enter into a ménage-à-trois among you, your spouse, and the State. Unless you have a prenuptial agreement, you're now governed by the laws of the state that you live in at the time you break up or when one of you dies. So, on the day you get married, not only do you not know if divorce is going to happen, when it's going to happen, or where it's going to happen—but you also don't know what the laws will be at that point in time. If somebody had whispered "equitable distribution" to my parents when they got married in 1947, they wouldn't have understood what the term meant. They would have thought maybe someone was taking too much of the wedding cake, whereas it really did make a difference to them four decades later, when they broke up.

Cosslett: And it's the same point with a prenuptial agreement: you are agreeing to settle for some percentage of some unknown quantity in the future.

Barnett: That is not necessarily true. There are some people who write prenups where they completely waive any interest in the assets or income of their intended spouse. There are people who write prenups that divide property in a myriad of different ways. Some people's prenups just deal with rights of inheritance, because when you get married under present law in New York, you automatically are entitled to one-third of someone's estate unless you waive it. It's called a right of election. So there's an entanglement that's created by the law when you say "I do" and death actually does part you. Going down the aisle you are engaged, going back up you are a potential heir to one-third of your new spouse's estate. Each state has different laws which continually change.

When most people get married, they don't really think about marriage as being a legal contract among the husband, the wife, and the state. When most women get married, they think about the all important dress and shoes—and I'm not minimizing their significance—especially the shoes. But to me, if your wedding day is the best day of your life, it's a very sad statement. You have to think about what it truly means to get married. The key question you should be asking yourself before you walk down the color-coordinated aisle, is whether you are prepared to identify that person as your primary family? If somebody asks you, "Who is your family?" and your response is your mother, your father, and your siblings, and not your spouse, I think it is a very revealing statement and should give you pause about entering into the union. I see so many divorces where the family of origin remains the person's family, and the spouse is just a companion. That emotional definition of family can be fatal to a marriage's success.

Cosslett: Can you explain equitable distribution?

Barnett: Equitable distribution is how property is divided in many states. On July 19, 1980, New York changed the law of marriage to equitable distribution. Until that time, everything was based on how title was held. If it was in his name, it was his. If it was in your name, it was yours. My mother raised me with the belief that, "If he loves you, he'll put the house in your name." And while that may be a nice Hallmark sentiment and while that legally would have been true in those days, it's not so under equitable distribution. Title isn't dispositive of that issue in a divorce, so my mother would have been wrong on that, but if you outlived him it would not be in his estate in determining your right of election.

Cosslett: Is equitable distribution fifty-fifty?

Barnett: No, that's why it's called "equitable." Community property is a fifty-fifty split. In changing the law in 1980, New York said, "What matters is when property was acquired and how was it acquired." So what you do is a process where you are "ICED": *identify* all of the assets, *classify* them as marital or separate, *evaluate* them and *distribute* them. Marital property is anything acquired after you say, "I do," which is the day you get married until the day you say, "I don't," which is the day either you file a summons or sign a separation agreement. There are exceptions, of course, within that timeframe which actually make sense.

First, you identify the assets and liabilities. You put together a statement of net worth listing every possible asset and liability, bank accounts, houses, pension funds. In fact, the definition of property has been expanded in many ways: a law degree, or even a celebrity career can be evaluated and its value distributed. You then classify the assets as being either "marital" or "separate." If you owned the asset before the marriage, generally speaking, it's separate property, but there are variations. For example, property inherited before or during the marriage remains separate property because the person gave it to you because of who you are to them, not because of who you're married to.

A damage award for personal injury will also remain separate property, because that's intended to make the injured party whole. But if separate property appreciates or becomes comingled with marital property, then it becomes marital. So, for instance, if my grandmother left me a tea set and I polished it every day, and it just happened to go up in value because it was a Paul Revere set and that became popular, the appreciation had nothing to do with anything as a result of the marriage so it would remain completely separate property. It didn't get comingled. But if my grandmother left me an apartment building, and the day she left it to me, it was worth a million dollars, and it was managed by us during the marriage and we collected rents and its appreciation was not due to market value changes, but due to our labors, the appreciation would be potential marital property.

How you acquire money is critically important. When young couples want to purchase an apartment, often their parents want to help them and they give the down payment for the home. The parents think, "Oh, isn't this wonderful? Here's a check for $30,000." They write out the check to the husband and wife jointly. Well, they just gave separate property of $15,000 to each spouse and they may have to buy their child's spouse's share of the house back in a divorce. People don't understand that *how* you do something can transform the end result. Let's say a person has a million dollars in separate property and he or she never touches the separate property account during the marriage and it simply grows. However, during the marriage if the couple accumulates a million dollars in another account which consists solely of marital property, whether it's in individual names or joint names doesn't matter because title is irrelevant. If they use the marital funds, and at the time of the divorce there's only $100,000 left in the marital account, that's all the property that would be available for equitable distribution. The person who had never touched his or her separate property account would retain the separate property. Most people don't think about which account they use and why they use it, much less keep the paper trail.

You need to gather all of the records to understand what you each own, and what you each owe, and what your respective income is. It is stunning to me how many people have not a clue what their spouse earns, even though they sign joint tax returns. So many people do not look and right above their signatures on the tax return it says, "Subject to penalties of perjury." So if they want to claim their spouse is not reporting his or her income fully, they have to recognize their exposure to perjury. And many spouses often have no idea about liabilities: it can be very dangerous to marry someone who has really bad credit, or during the marriage accrues huge debts, or has a gambling or addiction problem. That problem becomes your spouse's problem because not only is the spender not able to contribute, but the non-spender might then end up losing the home and many of the meaningful aspects of their life due to their spouse's spending habits. Get a credit report, not only to keep your credit in good shape, but to understand what factors are considered. Divorce frequently impacts someone's credit because someone doesn't pay the bills on a timely basis. Late bill payment can be as serious a problem as filing a bankruptcy can be to your credit.

So after you have identified the assets and liabilities, you classify the assets and liabilities, and then you evaluate them. An appraisal is something that can be subjective in some situations and objective in others. You can look up the value of shares of stock, but there can be a range of values for any number of things. What's the value of a house if you're not selling it at that moment?

What's the value of a degree? There was a case, *O'Brien v. O'Brien*, where the husband went from being a college graduate to becoming a doctor during their marriage. The wife wanted the enhanced value of becoming Mrs. Doctor. They had gone to Guadalajara so the husband could attend medical school. The wife had made all of these sacrifices and investments for their future, allowing the husband to enhance his earning capacity. That enhanced earning capacity can be evaluated. The difference in the earning potential of the degree owner's working lifetime as a result of the advanced education versus what the degree owner's projected earnings would have been without the advanced degree can be calculated through actuarial tables, and then a court can determine what would be equitable for the non-degree holding spouse to be awarded as part of a property settlement, if anything. A factor to consider is what if the doctor wanted to do public medicine or became disabled, how can a court impute that into the calculation?

Timing is a big factor too. When you value something, what date do you use? Consider 2008, when the financial market collapsed. If you looked at a house in Quogue in January of 2008, valued at $3 million, it was significantly less by December of 2008. So when you get into evaluations, you also have to look at the valuation date as well as how it's valued, and its liquidity. Valuation has become more difficult in recent years because of the economic challenges we all face. There have been major fluctuations, not only in the valuation of goods, but in people's predictable patterns of earning.

Cosslett: So let's say in high school you married a bricklayer who was a high-school dropout. You were supportive, you did all the right things, and he graduates business school and is now a highly-paid investment banker. When you are getting divorced, do you look at his future earning power or do you actually try and evaluate the contributions made during the time you were married, or are the two inextricable?

Barnett: You do everything. There are different types of intangibles. If somebody gets an MBA during the marriage, sometimes the student spouse is not earning during that one- or two-year period when he or she was in school, but undoubtedly their earning ability has escalated. A spouse may have invested in the other spouse, whether it's through student loans or supporting their spouse while he or she is in school, so in a sense what a court is doing is valuing the couple's investment into one person as if the person was a business investment by the couple.

Every marriage is as different as each snowflake. If someone says, "Let's judge the contributions you made," the first question should be "By what method?" or "What was the agreement that the two of you made?" This question can be difficult to answer if you didn't write it down or actually articulate it. If a spouse says, "I'll pick up and relocate so you can go to graduate school," or "We'll put you through school and then I'll go to school," how will that be judged years later? Even if people did have that conversation in the beginning, a lot of people probably wouldn't even agree as to what their understanding had been.

Let's assume we don't know each other and you agree to meet me at Grand Central Station. If I told you I have red hair, you might think I have bright red Little Orphan Annie hair, but I might actually have auburn hair. People are not lying to each other. There is simply a misunderstanding or miscommunication because the meaning of the words is unclear. Let's say you have two people who are getting married: one is widowed and one is divorced. The husband says to the wife, "We're going to treat all of the children the same," and the wife thinks, "Oh that's great. So they're all going to have the same education." What the husband actually meant was that they'll all go to college, but his children would go to private college and hers would go to community college. You have to clearly say what you mean and mean what you say.

In a divorce, all the information gets presented to the court. It will look at statistical tables to assess future earning power. It will also look at the contributions made by the spouse during marriage. If, during the time one party was in business school, the other party gave birth to three children and left the work force or ran the home and typed the other party's papers, the judge would look at that level of contribution which had been made to the family. It would be different if a spouse was wealthy and had been unaffected by his or her spouse going to school.

Contributions can be financial or non-financial. Someone could be taking care of their in-laws. Someone could be taking care of their kids. Someone could be providing emotional support or employment advice. It really depends on what the facts are, what you want to highlight, and what side of the equation you're on.

You can't guarantee an outcome with equitable distribution: it depends on what other assets exist and what someone's ability is. I think in many ways the system punishes people who are productive, because if somebody is very successful, they're not going to be a candidate for spousal support. Rather, they potentially could be a candidate to pay spousal support.

When my daughter, Jamie, left for college, I was sad but so proud and happy for her. I realized then that if you've successfully raised your child, they're independent and they will leave home. One day I not so kiddingly said to her, "Wait, if I'm a good mother, I am going to get punished. If I'm a bad mother, you'll stay with us. Right?" There's something wrong with the whole karma of this system, I deeply miss her but rejoice in her independence.

The same thing is true in terms of divorce in that spenders are rewarded and savers are punished. Think about this concept. If you spend freely, then you can show a need for more spousal support. If you're frugal and save, then you have created a lower standard of living, so you would qualify for less support, if any. These are all the little things that strike me as endlessly fascinating.

Cosslett: Do you find you have more clients coming out of a given profession? And has the recent turmoil in the financial markets affected your practice?

Barnett: Because I'm in New York, a lot of clients are doctors, lawyers, Wall Streeters, entrepreneurs, that sort of thing—more than you probably would see in certain other areas of the country. It's a terrific mix of occupations, and one of the greatest parts of my work is getting to understand the inner workings of how someone practices a particular trade and how they do certain things. Dramatic changes in financial markets affect bankruptcies because in a good market, people gobble up or expand their businesses, and in a down market, some of these businesses fail or downsize. Great economic change, either positive or negative, also directly impacts divorce because when people experience dramatic change, they ask, "Is this person truly on my team? Are we rowing the oars together?" And if you're going through rough times, which is an inherent part of "for better or worse," and you're rowing in the same direction, you can succeed. But if you're going through rough times and you don't pull in conjunction with one another, it simply won't work and you may have to leave the sinking ship. Marriage needs to be your sanctuary, not your prison.

Cosslett: I can understand why economic strains stress marriages.

Barnett: Marriage or any intimate relationship is difficult under any circumstance. Any real change can be stressful. A spouse with a chronic disease or a child with serious learning issues can force a couple to assess whether they are on the same page, if they agree on how to address the issue, or even if they both accept that there's an issue. The Kodak commercials are wonderful, but they're simply not realistic. Nobody actually gives birth to the Gerber Baby. There may be one in the ad, but as wonderful as it is to be a parent, there are going to be challenges which can torpedo the romance which led to the child's conception.

Similarly, when times are fabulously successful it can be equally challenging for a relationship because people can become grandiose and fail to appreciate certain values. Often people say, "We were happiest when things were simple, when we were just starting out." And I think there's something to that. One of the lessons I learn every day from going to the office and watching what goes on in relationships is that simple courtesies to one another, simple thoughtfulness to your partner in life, can make all the difference in whether your marriage succeeds or not. If you, just for that moment, think about what you could do every day that would make the other person's day better, and if you did that on a regular basis, how many divorces would be prevented? Too many people wait until their problems are too big. It's like the person that ignores the root canal. You've got to deal with the fundamental problem while you can create a meaningful solution. Loving maintenance of a spouse now can prevent paying future spousal maintenance to a former spouse.

Maybe if you've been divorced before, you've learned that lesson, I certainly have. And maybe one of the biggest issues, too, is when people get married just because they think that's the next step in their relationship, or because all of their friends are getting married, and then it does not end up working out. I've had so many people come to me and say, "I knew as I was walking down the aisle that it was a mistake but the invitations were done, the dress was ordered—I felt like Princess Di, like a lamb to the slaughter."

Cosslett: Do you encourage people going through a divorce to seek therapy?

Barnett: I'm a very, very strong believer that people going through any major life crisis should be in therapy. It's really important to have the objective insight of a mental health professional, and it makes sense from an economic point of view because they're more qualified and cost-efficient than lawyers. It's also burdensome to solicit advice from friends, who cannot in any case give proper judgment. I think that a lot of times people impulsively jump to a conclusion simply to go forward. When people walk into my office, I always tell them, "You're not on a conveyor belt to divorce. All you're doing the first time is coming in for information. Knowledge is power. I can tell you what your rights and responsibilities are, but you really have to think about how your life will be different and decide what you want to do with the power of that knowledge."

It is important to realize, however, that sometimes a therapist's advice can have significant negative legal consequences. For instance, a therapist could say, "You should move out and give each other space." But that could have a dramatic impact in terms of custody and support. So while you're telling somebody that they need to be in therapy, you also have to caution them that, if there are children involved, it won't necessarily be a privileged communication if there's a custody battle. But I think people should have as much information as possible, legal and psychological, to make the best decision for their families and themselves. In order to be able to go through that challenging transformation of your life, you need to be as introspective and as realistic as possible.

Cosslett: Is the idea of culpability relevant to a divorce?

Barnett: What a great question. That's a perfect example of the eye of the beholder. When you say culpable, to some people, it means someone is having an affair. Some people really don't care whether their spouse has an affair or not as long as they don't bother them and make them have sex with them or if they are discreet about the trysts. To some people, culpable means that the spouse is not earning what he or she could be earning. If somebody doesn't meet their earning potential, if someone doesn't take out the garbage or do a fair share of the household responsibilities are they culpable? Divorce is not the morality play that people think it is.

Culpability is fact-specific. It depends what the issue is. If somebody is fighting about custody and their spouse is having sex in a room while the children are present—those things happen, believe it or not—then that would clearly be a factor about someone's judgment and about parenting, and custody, and decision making. Does that necessarily tie to money? Well, it could tie to finances in the sense that if you're not the custodial parent, you won't get child support, you may end up being the one that pays child support. In terms of property division, it's really not an issue. The percentage of people who have affairs is astronomical. I assume the courtroom is filled with active daters.

I think it would be an error to make a generalization that culpability is always applicable or isn't always. It really depends on the issue at stake and what you mean by culpability. Let's take a Bernie Madoff. Did Bernie Madoff wastefully dissipate assets? Yes. Does it really have to reach that level? No, but you really have to look at the situation, and what's involved. Judges are sophisticated people. They've seen and heard everything, so what's going to shock their conscience about something? If somebody unsuccessfully hired a contract killer to eliminate their spouse, that will affect equitable distribution. But the fact that somebody had an affair with his or her dentist will likely not have the same impact, nor should it.

Cosslett: I'm thinking about the perception of the person who comes to your office who is sufficiently offended or disappointed in the conduct of their spouse that they've come to see you.

Barnett: Everybody who comes into a divorce lawyer's office is unhappy, either because they want out, they think their spouse wants out, or they both want out. They don't come to show me the wedding album. That's not the reason.

They discover that divorce is multilayered. How will it affect their present lives and future? Frequently, people focus on property and forget there are also liabilities. So we don't just think about assets. You consider liabilities too. If you signed joint tax returns, if you have overdraft loans or contingent liabilities—any of those things—must be discussed.

Support is a separate issue. There's spousal support and child support to consider. And then the most important issue, custody, legal and physical, is a whole other arena. A lot of people don't really understand what custody is about. "Where do you put your head down on a pillow?" is physical custody. Legal custody is what school do you go to? What religion will your children practice? What extracurricular activities? The decision making: that's what legal custody is about. In New York, the obligation to pay child support goes until the age of twenty-one, although custody only goes to the age of eighteen.

Cosslett: Does joint custody mean that a child's time is divided evenly between the parents?

Barnett: It depends on the situation. If someone says joint custody, you also have to look at how the term is defined. Some say, "The parties will have joint legal custody, but if they disagree, then so-and-so is the final decision maker." Well, is that really joint? And sometimes there are zones of responsibility.

Sometimes they'll say, "Okay, the two of you have to meaningfully discuss this area, but if you don't agree, then the mother will decide as to, say, education, and the father will decide as to medical." There are as many variations in custody as in a Bach fugue.

Cosslett: What if your client is behaving in a way that's not necessarily in his own best interests because he is hurt or angry?

Barnett: That's something that you try to address as a lawyer. My role is to be a counselor, not a decider. It is a challenge to work with people who are going through deeply emotional and stressful situations. Sometimes people are self-destructive, whether it's intentional or not. I think one of the things that is really interesting to me is that some people are into revenge, and that's clearly intentional. Whereas other people simply can't get out of their own way.

There also are stages to the process. If one side hires a lawyer and says, "I want it to be about revenge," then what does the other side do? That's one of the thorny problems. Sometimes people claim that the issue is about children when it really is not about the children. Sometimes it's about power and control or hurt feelings because their spouse wants to leave them. I see it from both sides of the equation, which I think is one of the advantages of representing men and women.

Cosslett: Secret gathering of information about spouses seems to be fairly prevalent. Could you talk about that?

Barnett: I was "Quote of the Day" in *The New York Times* on that issue: "No one cares more about the things you do than the person who used to be married to you." The quote was about how EZ Passes are used or intentionally not used in certain circumstances. When you live in Manhattan, EZ Pass will record when you go in and out of the Island. I always look at the cash line at the toll and think, "Those are the adulterers because they don't want to have a record of when they're coming in or out of Manhattan."

Similarly, ATM receipts are evidentiary. The receipt doesn't just say how much you took out. It tells you from what branch. Most people go to the machine by their office or by their home. If they're suddenly in a different neighborhood, that's the neighborhood where they're using cash because they don't want to have a record of what they're doing there. It's really quite easy to find these things out.

It's not difficult to gather information in a very legal way because so many people are careless about their use of cell phones and laptops, forgetting that their use will be discoverable later. A lot of people think if they delete a text message, that it is gone. It is not. It's written in ink, it's not pencil. Text and e-mails are all discoverable. Also, many people leave their computers open and just mindlessly go to all kinds of sites and leave revealing information in open view. It's as if you had an open file cabinet.

A big "tell" is if your spouse suddenly changes his or her behavior. When you have a child, you don't need to take her temperature to know if she is sick—you know it. If all of a sudden your spouse goes to the gym, suddenly starts to lose weight, and buys new underwear, there is an issue. Generally, if you think someone's having an affair, they are. And then you have to decide what you're going to do about it—if anything, because that could be just a warning bell, it doesn't have to be the end of a marriage. Marriage can survive affairs.

People have different rules for their marriage. In my marriage, my husband knows how I feel about adultery. We discussed it thoroughly before we were married. I saw it firsthand with my father. For me it's a deal-breaker. But I'm not judgmental about other people's choices. I clearly told my husband, "Don't ever stay with me for one extra day that you don't want to." But other people don't feel that way. They say, "It's comfortable. It's not that important."

And what might be more important to some people is whether their spouse is not living up to his or her earning potential, or whether someone's not being a responsible parent, or if someone simply is tuned out and is just a couch potato and not engaged in life.

Cosslett: What advice would you give either law students or practicing lawyers considering a career change about how best to position themselves for practicing in the field of matrimonial law?

Barnett: I don't think you should practice matrimonial law unless you consider it a calling, because it doesn't have an off button. It's 24/7. I've had sleepless nights worrying about children and clients and their well-being. It can be difficult and emotionally exhausting. I get calls, texts, e-mails most every weekend, every night, all the time. There are emergency situations and sometimes people just need to vent to me so that they don't do something that would be destructive to their life or to the case. And you have to not resent that if you choose to practice family law. You have to understand that that's part of being supportive. I think if you look at it as a job, you should practice in another field. If you look at it as a privilege and you are inherently curious about people, problem solving, and love and its many mysteries, then it is a good fit. I know so many matrimonial lawyers who don't enjoy the field at all. I feel blessed to do this work.

Cosslett: Why do they call you "The Love Lawyer"? Whenever I have mentioned that I'm going to go meet "The Love Lawyer," people say, "But isn't she an out-of-love lawyer if she's a divorce lawyer?"

Barnett: Absolutely not. I think there are stages of love. I think divorce is just another stage of love.

Cosslett: For some people, it appears to be the stage of intense dislike.

Barnett: There are different stages and ages where a different life partner makes more sense, just like the people who were your best friends in high school. You go to the high school reunion, and you realize that you still have a lot in common with some of your former classmates—but others you think, "What on earth?" So when people end up marrying their high school sweethearts, I wonder what are the possibilities of picking a life partner at a time when you can barely pick a major in college?

People get upset when I say it, but all marriages end. Either someone walks out or is carried out. And the good ones are when you're carried out. That's a successful marriage.

Cosslett: Unless the remaining spouse is instrumental in the other one getting carried out.

Barnett: Everything in my work deals with love and sex. What can be better?

Cosslett: Can a divorce have a happy ending?

Barnett: What is a happy ending? There's no such thing as an ending. That's really the difference. If you think of the phrase "happy ending," then you're thinking about the wedding day. If you think about a happy ending, then you're thinking about the day your child graduates college. When we went to my daughter's college graduation in May, my husband said something that resonated: "Now I understand why today he gave a commencement speech. It's not the end: it's a commencement."

I think when someone gets divorced, it's a commencement of the next chapter of their life. So happy ending to me is not what it is about. I want to know what happens to them later. There are people whose divorce I handled ten or twenty years ago, with whom I still stay in touch. I hear what happens and I hear how their children are and how they're doing. And it truly matters to me. If that's not the kind of person you are, you shouldn't be doing matrimonial law. You really shouldn't.

Cosslett: On a purely pragmatic level, do divorce lawyers bill per transaction?

Barnett: No, you bill by the hour. That's why you tell people that they've got to be cost-efficient in working with professionals. You say to them, "Organize yourself and try to pull records together." And when people come in, I say the most cost-efficient way to present information to me is to "Sit down and write your life story. Tell me how you got to this place." Just like you're doing this interview: "Tell me how you got to this place in your life. How did you get to be a matrimonial lawyer sitting in New York on Madison Avenue." So I'm saying to them: "How did you end up sitting in a matrimonial lawyer's office when that was the last thing you planned when you sent the wedding invitations?" And some of people find it very cathartic to write it out. And it crystallizes what they're thinking. The more information they give, the better of a job I can do for them, because then I can see themes that they don't understand or articulate.

Cosslett: Is there anything that you want to add?

Barnett: When people talk about lawyers, they always make jokes, bad jokes. When I was a little girl, I looked up to policemen, I looked up to doctors, I looked up to teachers, I looked up to judges, and I looked up to lawyers. I think that it's very sad today that people do not assume that choosing to be a lawyer is the calling that I thought it was when I came to the profession and that I wanted it to be when I went into practice. When you said to somebody in high school, "I'm going to be a lawyer," every teacher would smile, "Wow, that's great." It was a valued profession.

The reality of it is that people don't have that feeling now. When a young person comes to me and says, "Should I go to law school and take out student loans and all of that?" If it's not something that they feel absolutely passionate about, I don't think that they should do it. Since the job market is so different, I don't think that anybody should go to law school if it's not their passion, because then I think that they're not using their talents properly, and they will have to reconfigure their lives later. A lot of people used to think of law as a safety career, but if somebody nowadays is thinking of law as a fallback or as a safe profession, I think that's a huge mistake.

Cosslett: I agree completely.

CHAPTER 7

Peri Lynne Johnson

Director, Office of Legal Affairs
International Atomic Energy Agency

Michelle Bachelet, the executive director of UN Women, charged women to "make gender parity a lived reality, not just a mantra." **Peri Lynne Johnson** has done just that in her own career at the United Nations, becoming the first woman legal advisor for both the United Nations Development Program (UNDP) and the International Atomic Energy Agency (IAEA). Johnson's life-long belief that there are no limits to what professional women can accomplish was instilled in her from childhood by her father, an attorney active in the civil rights movement.

Johnson also believes that women must have the freedom to choose what is right for them, both personally and professionally, and she acknowledges the influence of motherhood on her own career choices. She resigned her position as an associate with Arnold & Porter in Washington, DC, in order to join her then husband in Guinea, where she worked for the United Nations High Commissioner for Refugees (UNHCR). Remaining in the United States upon the birth of her son, Johnson continued to build her UN career in New York, eventually rising to director of UNDP's Legal Support Office. In January 2011, her son lodged happily in boarding school, Johnson chose to relocate to Vienna, Austria, to serve as director of IAEA's Office of Legal Affairs. She earned her JD from Harvard Law School and her BA from Cornell University.

Clare Cosslett: Why did you decide to become a lawyer?

Peri Lynne Johnson: I grew up in Jacksonville, Florida. My father graduated law school in 1957 and began his career in the early days of the civil rights movement working with the NAACP and with Dr. Martin Luther King. He was very involved in the St. Augustine march in the early 60s. Later in his career, he established his own general practice and became a local politician. In the seventies, my father became the first black president of the Jacksonville City Council and acting mayor of Jacksonville. So the law is in the family and that's the origin of my interest in everything legal.

Cosslett: Do you have brothers and sisters?

Johnson: Yes. I have an older sister who is a psychiatrist in Atlanta and an older brother who is a practicing lawyer in Jacksonville. His practice is a lot like my father's: a general practice in his own firm. I obviously have a very different practice than my father and my brother. I have another brother who is in television production in California and I had a younger brother who is deceased. We were originally five in the family.

Cosslett: How did you choose Cornell for undergraduate?

Johnson: My mother strongly encouraged us to go Ivy League. My sister went to Harvard College. I really liked Cornell and we had a close family friend who had gone there and had raved about it. It was definitely the right choice for me and I loved my college experience.

Cosslett: When you thought about law school, were you intending to be a civil rights lawyer like your dad?

Johnson: I knew I was interested in international work even from my days at Cornell. I also knew I was going to go to law school and I talked to my dad about my interest in international work. I studied French when I was in high school and fell in love with the French language and French culture. In addition to the importance of an Ivy League education, my mother's other contribution to my résumé is that she loved everything international herself. We often had students visit us for about a month over the summer as part of the international exchange program. We had a Japanese student, a Swiss student, a French student, a Mexican student. I don't think that's a typical American experience. In college, I signed up for the exchange program that my mother had had us participate in for so many years and I lived with a French family in Nantes. I also studied abroad in France.

While I was at Cornell as a French literature major, I took a lot of coursework in international law, international relations, and government. I knew where I was headed. I wanted to balance my interest in foreign affairs with my interest in the law. I knew I wanted to blend both.

Cosslett: You made that decision very early on in your career.

Johnson: Very early. But even in law school I wasn't exactly clear how it would all come into play. I was thinking that I would work in a private law firm and that I would be able to blend law and international work there, but it turned out not to be at all like that. I ended up joining the United Nations very early on in my career.

Cosslett: Did you continue with the international focus when you were at Harvard? Were there lots of courses that were available to you?

Johnson: In your first year at an American law school, you have to take a number of core requirements: civil procedure, criminal law, property law, and the usual. You don't have a lot of choices. It's really in your second and third years that you have more options and that's when I took international law, international human rights, and a clinic. At Harvard we had the option of taking clinics as well as standard coursework. One of the best things about being at Harvard was having so many options. You have access to the best professors and so many resources.

I had a very diverse law school profile. I did all of the standard requirements, including a lot of corporate work. I did a clinic in family law and although I knew I wasn't going to have a family law practice, it was really exciting as a law student to have clients and to be working in the Boston courts. I worked with the Legal Aid clinic helping indigent families and women who were in abusive relationships trying to get divorced. It stands out as one of the important experiences of law school: the idea that with my legal training I could make a difference in people's lives.

Cosslett: I've spoken with a number of attorneys who early in their careers had an opportunity to get into the courtroom through working with social services agencies, and that experience invariably is a powerful one.

You graduated Harvard Law School in the Class of 1991. Was Barack Obama in any of your classes?"

Johnson: Yes, we were classmates, although I was in a different section. He was really good friends, and still is, with one of my very good friends during law school. Through her, I got to know him. He was brilliant in law school—you know already that he was the first Black president of the Harvard Law Review. So even then he stood apart. More than his intelligence, I remember him as down to earth, and basically a really nice guy. So I've told people when they ask, that although he is "more polished now," he is largely the same as he was in law school—what you see is really how he is—good values, thoughtful, smart. At the Harvard party during the inauguration celebrations, there were jokes about how many students and professors claimed to have him in their classes. So then Dean Clark, now Justice Clark, said, he must have taken more classes than anyone in the history of Harvard!

Cosslett: When you graduated, why did you choose Arnold & Porter?

Chapter 7 | Peri Lynne Johnson: *International Law*

Johnson: After my second year, I split the summer between the DC offices of Arnold & Porter and Debevoise & Plimpton. I wanted to be in Washington. I really liked both firms and had a fabulous summer, but ultimately I chose Arnold & Porter because it was a large and very well-respected DC-based firm, and I thought I would get a wider variety of work than I would at the DC office of a New York–based firm.

Cosslett: And when you were at Arnold & Porter, you did both litigation and international work?

Johnson: I was really in the litigation practice, and the most interesting international work was the pro bono work. Because Arnold & Porter was a large firm with really good values, they strongly supported pro bono work. To give you an example, one project involved research for the Washington Lawyers' Committee that was being used to facilitate the CODESA[1] negotiations in South Africa. That was the process of transition to majority government. So, as a junior associate at the firm, I was being paid to do research on what kinds of precedents existed for this event. What is out there that might be relevant to this process of transitioning?

I remember that we were looking at the Native Americans here in the States and we were looking at the French colonial period. That was a fun and exciting project and they were really happy with our research. Another project involved reviewing and advising on the Togo Constitution. Togo is a country in West Africa. That was also very interesting, and so I had really good international projects that were pro bono. The firm's for-profit international work was generally more commercial, and the international aspect was that you were dealing with parties in different countries.

Cosslett: What is the distinction between public international law and private/commercial international law?

Johnson: For the most part, private international law is commercial law involving entities within different countries. Public international law deals with states, international organizations, and treaties that impact states and international actors as opposed to just private companies and business. When I was in law school, I didn't anticipate that an international practice in a major law firm, like Arnold & Porter, is essentially a corporate practice with international players. While there were exciting opportunities to travel, I was dealing essentially with commercial transactions.

Cosslett: What triggered your move to the United Nations?

Johnson: I got married during my third year of law school and my now ex-husband was joining the United Nations Development Program. He was assigned to

---

[1] Convention for a Democratic South Africa

Guinea, West Africa. We were newlyweds and I was in Washington with Arnold & Porter, and he was in Conakry with UNDP. We needed to figure out how we could be together, so I left the firm and joined the United Nations High Commissioner for Refugees as a junior professional officer. I was recruited through the State Department.

The United Nations had a program whereby governments cover the costs of young professionals from their countries in order to afford them the experience of working in an international organization. That's the idea of the Junior Professional Officers Program. I interviewed with State and was selected, and I moved to Conakry, Guinea. I was replacing another Harvard-trained American lawyer who had been the attorney at UNHCR and was finishing her two-year term. It just so happened that the timing was right. People are surprised to hear this because there are very few positions that the US government finances as junior professional officer posts, and that was one of very few globally that they financed.

The position involved working with political refugees from Liberia and Sierra Leone, so I assume the US had an interest in supporting those activities of the UN. The office in Conakry was quite small: there were only about four or five international staff, and the rest were national staff.

Cosslett: What did the work involve?

Johnson: It was human rights work, refugee law. It was very different from the work I had been doing at Arnold & Porter. I had some background from my international coursework at Harvard, but you don't really understand the work of UNHCR until you're on the ground doing it. I was an associate protection officer, which means that I was the lawyer for the refugees. My mandate was to protect them and their right to asylum, which included getting them to an asylum country. There wasn't an issue in terms of access because Guinea had pretty much opened its borders to the refugees from Liberia and Sierra Leone. Conakry was sensitive because that's where the political refugees were: the family of Samuel Doe, the assassinated president of Liberia, the military, senior officials in the government who couldn't, for security reasons, be in the border areas where ninety-five percent of the refugees were.

Cosslett: Was Guinea the refugee country or were people in transit to another place?

Johnson: Guinea was where ninety-nine percent of the refugees stayed, and many of them are possibly still there because the conflict went on for so many years that some may have remained permanently. Don't forget that the boundaries in Africa are, in some respects, artificial, so there are the same tribes and ethnic groups on both sides of these boundaries. That made it easier for Guinea to open the borders. There were some language issues—Guinea is French-speaking, whereas Liberia and Sierra Leone are English-speaking—and there were some cultural issues, but one advantage was that some of the same ethnic groups are in these border areas.

Cosslett: What did your days look like?

Johnson: In 1993 to '94, the refugee population throughout the country totaled several hundred thousand. In Conakry, the capital, there were about twenty thousand or thirty thousand. It was a much smaller number of refugees. The day-to-day work was making sure these refugees were getting the benefits they needed to live: housing, food, and so on. To the extent possible, we also wanted to support them with education and training. I was involved in facilitating these things as much as possible, liaising with our NGO[2] partners, who were primarily responsible for the distribution of food and benefits. I remember the Evangelical Protestant Church of Guinea was one of our partners. The Red Cross was another partner. So the work in the field of a protection officer involves a lot of social services as well.

Cosslett: Was your background as a lawyer relevant to the work you were doing there?

Johnson: On a day-to-day basis, I would say it wasn't. There was an incident, however, when a Cuban refugee defected and walked into our office saying, "I need protection." I had to make the case as to why this person was a refugee, why he needed legal protection, and why, if he left our office, he would be vulnerable. I had to liaise with our offices in Geneva to get him out of the country. He lived in our office for seven months, and then finally, we were able to get him resettled in Venezuela. So that was the one case where I really had to use legal skills. The other skills necessary for the position were good management and administrative skills and just common sense.

Cosslett: You were there for almost two years. Was that the term of your posting?

Johnson: No, I came back early because I conceived my son there, and I had a high-risk pregnancy. The medical facilities in Conakry at the time were really not great for a high-risk pregnancy, so I ended up being evacuated and delivering in the US. After my son was born, I decided to stay in the States. When he was still an infant, I moved to New York, and started in the UN Office of Legal Affairs as an associate legal officer.

As you can see, as a woman, many of the career choices I made were around family issues. I moved to Guinea because my husband was there and we needed to be together. I wanted a job in the UN because he was there in the UN. And then once I had my son here, it did not make sense to take an infant to Conakry at the time. So there are personal family reasons that have really shaped my career.

It's unrealistic to think that women, in any profession, can make career choices without regard to family matters, unless you choose just not to marry or have

---

[2]non-governmental organization

kids, and many women do that. I'm not dogmatic. I think every woman has to have the choice and, for me, as long as that woman is choosing what's right for her and her personal circumstance, that's what's important.

Cosslett: You went in to the UN via the State Department to fill a role in the UNHCR. Once you finished that role, were you able to go into any arm of the United Nations? Are you now part of the club?

Johnson: There's no guarantee. The contract with UNHCR ended. Conakry had been exciting and important and was a way into the UN organization but being back in the UN Office for Legal Affairs was really coming home. I started out as a consultant for about six months. I then took the National Competitive Exam, which was the career entry exam for the UN. It was offered to different countries in different subject areas, so I took it as an American in legal.

Cosslett: If someone now wants to go work for the UN as an attorney, do they still offer those examinations?

Johnson: Yes, there is still an exam for young professionals who are interested in a career track at the UN, like the Foreign Service Exam for the US government. I think you have to take it before the age of thirty-two. It's offered by country and subject, so if your country is overrepresented in a certain subject area, you wouldn't be eligible to take it. That is the way the UN recruits staff for junior career track positions.

Cosslett: Can you outline the organization of the UN Legal Department?

Johnson: The Office of Legal Affairs has several different divisions. There's the Office of Legal Counsel, which focuses on pure public international law, the rules and procedures of the governing bodies of the UN. There's also the General Legal Division, which is the in-house counseling division. Much of the work in the General Legal Division is exactly what you would think an in-house counsel does in a US corporation: you're dealing with personnel issues. You're dealing with contractual issues.

We also dealt with institutional issues, which are more in the public international law area—issues of mandates and authorities of the governing bodies. Institutional work would include, for example, an analysis of the mandate of UNDP in terms of either a certain development assistance program or a developmental modality, meaning the way in which they would work with a government to provide assistance. The institutional work is about understanding what the basis of an organization's mandate is, and whether a proposed action is within that mandate, or whether they have to go back to the General Assembly or to the Executive Board for an additional mandate. It's really the internal institutional work of the UN.

Cosslett: It's like looking at a corporation and asking, "Is this activity within the scope of its charter?"

Johnson: Exactly. And in the UN context, you're looking at General Assembly resolutions and Executive Board resolutions and tracing things through history. In fact, I have published an article about this very topic—UNDP's national execution modality. The article looks at the issue in a historical context. In the seventies, the member states said that UNDP should be working with its national partners in providing development assistance rather than just having international experts come in. Using a historical analysis, we considered the evolution of modalities for providing development assistance and whether the then current approaches were consistent with the mandate as articulated in General Assembly resolutions and Executive Board decisions.

Cosslett: This work sounds so interesting and unique to the UN.

Johnson: I think you would see it in another international organization, but I have to say—and I'm biased, obviously—that it's really exciting to be with the UN. The work has been really interesting. I have shared notes with friends and colleagues who have taken different tracks and they weren't all excited about their work. You must have heard lawyers say things like their work was boring, that they were just doing it for the money. That has not been my experience at all since I joined the UN. I have really liked the work here and am lucky that, for family reasons, my career took a different direction early on.

Cosslett: Do UN salaries stack up against salaries at Wall Street firms?

Johnson: Absolutely not. The salaries are good and we have nice benefits. We have the tax benefit and a nice package, but there's no comparison to partners in New York who are making a million-dollars plus. The secretary-general makes around $350,000 to $400,000, just to give you an idea. These are not million-dollar salaries. They are government salaries. In fact, there's a formula: they benchmark against several government salaries. So that's really the comparison, not private sector.

Cosslett: How does the UN reward seniority?

Johnson: Of course, you have much more authority. You make the decisions. As a junior lawyer, I was researching important questions, I was drafting important documents, I was involved in important issues, and I was in important meetings—but I couldn't make the decision. Of course, since I was doing the research and the drafting, I could contribute, but at the end of the day, decisions are made that take into account many factors that I wasn't always privy to.

As a junior lawyer, I had the best mentors—great UN lawyers who had started in the seventies and who were the second generation of UN lawyers. They were the decision makers. The difference now is that I have lawyers whom I can guide in terms of the research and the original drafting—although I always tell my staff, "I'm a working director." So even now I often do my own research and drafting, especially if it's a very sensitive project. I've always been a hard worker and I think that's why I got more projects and interesting projects. And I've always been excited to be part of the organization and excited to do my best work. Even today, legal is one input to a decision and is not the only consideration. I can't say today that everything the Legal Office recommends is adopted as the final approach in a given case, but, as director, what comes out of the Legal Office is absolutely a recommendation that I agree with.

Cosslett: Where does the Office of Legal Affairs fit within the UN structure?

Johnson: The Office of Legal Affairs is an independent office within the United Nations, as is the IAEA. I'm the legal advisor to the Office of Legal Affairs here at the IAEA. We're independent of the United Nations secretary-general, and I report directly to the director-general. Each UN organization—and there are many—has its own legal advisor. Sometimes they are called legal counsel or general counsel. And most of the structures have the legal counsel reporting directly to the executive head, which is what it should be, in my view. People assume you have the legal counsel reporting to the management, and I don't think that's the right approach. You advise management but you report to the head of management? I think it's got to be an independent function.

Cosslett: Tell me about your move to UNDP.

Johnson: As part of my position with the Office of Legal Affairs, I was involved with a lot of UNDP- and UNICEF-type work, which is the work of the funds and programs. I had been advising and writing on UNDP's development framework, so I knew quite a lot about UNDP. They asked me to come and expand their legal office. While I am sometimes credited today with having created the legal office, there was a small office when I arrived in 2000. Two or three lawyers. I was responsible for corporate law and built up that team. I was promoted to senior legal advisor, and in 2007, I was asked to be officer in charge. I was confirmed shortly thereafter as director, so I was then responsible for the entire office, which included an administrative law section dealing with personnel issues, amongst other things, as well as a corporate section.

Cosslett: What's the mission of UNDP?

Johnson: UNDP is the largest organ of the UN. It's a multi-billion dollar organization. It has offices in one hundred sixty-six countries and it has eight thousand staff. UNDP is very, very large, and it is the face of the UN in the field. The head of the UNDP office is always the head of the UN on a country level, unless there's a peacekeeping mission and there's a representative from the secretary-general's office there.

UNDP's mission is to eradicate poverty. It's a really huge mission: working in partnership with people and institutions to eradicate poverty. One of the things that UNDP has always struggled with is the brand. You hear, "UNICEF," and you know what it's about, right? Children. UNDP has a broad mandate, but it's not one you put a face to—like women and children. It's about poverty. It's about crisis intervention. It's about governance. It's about working with institutions to have institutional policies that support growth in a transparent and democratic way.

Cosslett: How big was the legal department by the time you left?

Johnson: I think we were close to thirteen lawyers when I left to join the IAEA and we had a few additional lawyers out-posted to regions, which gave greater support for those regions. So it was a proper legal office with full teams on both the administrative and corporate sides. I was very happy to leave a full team. In the UN, everybody is from somewhere else and I don't remember the number of nationalities, but typically there were a few American lawyers. There is a practice in the UN overall that the number of posts that a country is allocated is based on the amount of money it can contribute.

Cosslett: Tell me about your experiences practicing with attorneys trained in other countries. Do you find that their methodology and their intentions are generally the same as US-trained attorneys, or are they completely different?

Johnson: I've been impressed that the UN has attracted, in general, really smart lawyers—lawyers who were top in their countries and in their systems. I've worked with great Russian lawyers. My mentor was a Chinese lawyer in the General Legal Division. I've worked with great African lawyers. But, of course, if you're coming from common law training, you find that common law lawyers have a different approach than do civil law lawyers. Common law lawyers are looking for precedents. It's just the way we're trained, and civil law lawyers are looking for what the statutes say. So, yes, you do notice these different traditions.

Cosslett: I do think lawyers are trained differently in different countries. US lawyers often pride themselves on their role as dealmakers rather than drafts people.

Johnson: I agree with you that there are some differences, and then, at the same time, when you come into the UN, there's a UN practice. There's a UN approach. So lawyers coming in try to blend in. If you get a file, you are thinking, "Okay, what's been done before on this?" Nothing is ever for the first time in the UN. As a junior lawyer, I loved to get the file. I loved reading the file to figure out, "Okay, how was this question answered before? What was considered before?" It was a lot of that work. So no matter your tradition, no matter where you're coming from, no matter what your training, what you're going to be doing as a junior lawyer is to get the file, to see what the precedents are, to understand how it was handled before, and then you're formulating advice that's pretty much in line with past practice unless there's some reason to depart now.

In most cases, the question has been asked before. It's hard when it's the first time, and there's a lot to learn. It doesn't mean you always do what was done before, but our decisions are informed by history.

Cosslett: It must be nice, as a lawyer, to have that body of past practice to advise you.

Johnson: Oh, absolutely. My most important resources are my files from the past twenty years that are with me now in Vienna. I have kept them always because I've worked on so many matters, and they are an invaluable resource. I have so much knowledge about the history of why things have been decided a certain way at the UN. It's really important.

Cosslett: You joined the IAEA in January of 2011. How did you make that transition and was it a big decision for you to move to Austria?

Johnson: I was invited to apply to this position. It had been advertised twice, and I hadn't noticed it, but they sent me an e-mail and I thought about it, decided to apply, and then was successful in getting the position. It was a big change from the development side of the UN, but I was ready to make the change. I had been in UNDP for ten years and had done everything I could possibly do there, so there wasn't really any more growth for me in that position.

I think when you get to a point where you can do your job in your sleep, it's time to move on. The timing was perfect because my son was in boarding school and, although I wasn't actively looking, inside I was feeling: "If I'm going to make a change, this is the time." So, yes, it was a big move, but I was really ready for something new and I really wanted a challenge. I wanted to keep growing and learning. I wanted to continue to be stimulated. I didn't want to become "dead wood," where I just lost my motivation because, so what, I've done it for ten years.

Cosslett: What is the relationship between the IAEA and the UN?

Johnson: The IAEA is established as an independent organization, but in autonomous association with the UN. The director-general of the IAEA does not report to the secretary-general. My boss at UNDP, on the other hand, does report to the secretary-general because UNDP is a fund of the UN. The IAEA is a completely separate international organization.

Cosslett: What is their mandate?

Johnson: The IAEA was established as a result of the vision of President Eisenhower in the early fifties. The mandate of the organization is (1) to facilitate the use of nuclear material for peaceful purposes and (2) to make sure that nuclear material is safeguarded. Implementation of safeguards is the work that has made the agency famous. It's the work you read about in the news. Safeguarding includes the verification activities of inspectors to ensure that we know where the nuclear material is located in a country and to confirm that it's not being used for military purposes. For this reason, the IAEA is known as the nuclear watchdog.

But the IAEA has a huge development function as well: there are many uses of nuclear energy that benefit developing countries. The focus this year is food and how we're using nuclear technologies for food production. Last year the focus was water, how we can use nuclear technologies in connection with water—even how to find water in dry areas. The year before that it was nuclear technologies and cancer therapies.

So there is a whole development side of our work, which doesn't get the kind of attention that the safeguards and nonproliferation work does, but the current director-general has wanted to highlight that we're not just the nuclear watchdog. I think my being selected, coming from the UNDP, has a lot to do with that: I'm a lawyer from the development arm of the UN, and now I'm the lawyer for the IAEA.

Cosslett: Was the IAEA established as the enforcement agency for the Nuclear Nonproliferation Treaty?

Johnson: Based on the NPT, parties to the NPT agree that they will have their nuclear material under IAEA safeguards. That is how we come in. The NPT specifically provides that parties should have a safeguards agreement with the IAEA. We have over one hundred and seventy such comprehensive safeguards agreements and this is the agreement by which we verify the use of nuclear material in a country. They have to report what they have, they have to report what they're using it for, and we have a number of provisions that allow us to determine that the material is being used for the purposes declared and we can then verify that. We have a number of procedures and tools under the agreement that we can use to give assurance to the international community that the nuclear material in the relevant country is being used as intended. That is essentially the concept of the safeguards agreement.

Cosslett: Let's talk about Fukushima. Did the IAEA have a role in disaster relief?

Johnson: We have an action plan on implementation and follow-up for Fukushima, but the short of it is: immediately after the incident, we were notified and our emergency machinery kicked in. Under an agreed framework with member states, we notified our members that there had been an accident. So our immediate role is getting the information out there to the international community.

The other role, of course, is where states request assistance, we facilitate that assistance. The main conventions are the Early Notification Convention and the Assistance Convention. Assistance can also be offered and provided bilaterally outside of the convention. In the case of Fukushima, such arrangements were made including with the United States government. And the agency offered to provide whatever Japan needed. Since the accident, there have been a number of expert missions looking at different technical issues. There are lots of different aspects to this accident and the agency's role is far-reaching.

Cosslett: So the role of the agency is that of prime responder in terms of coordinating an international response to a nuclear disaster?

Johnson: That is the specific role for the agency that you will see in the Assistance Convention, when requested. We also have the responsibility of notifying member states as described under the Early Notification Convention. And then outside of these two conventions, our General Conference has adopted resolutions that have expanded the role of the agency in these areas. For example, relating to support for an accident in a nonmember state. We have a primary role in safety, security, and safeguards. So in a nuclear accident, that kicks in in terms of immediate support upon request of a state concerned and, at the same time, we keep the member states and the international community informed because there is the obvious risk that when there is a nuclear accident, there could be impact beyond borders. The system is very much also focused on information sharing.

The IAEA has a secretariat, but we're an organization of member states just like the UN is an organization of member states. We have one hundred fifty-four member states. We can't provide assistance if states don't want assistance. But of course, we offer. And so we have been able to work directly, in this case with Japan, and there are other states that have had accidents over the years—much smaller ones of course. But it's not just the agency. Don't forget there's a lot of bilateral assistance. What we saw play out in Japan is that they had a number of bilateral relationships—with the US, for example. The US and Japan have worked closely together, and very soon after the accident, the US was sending in all kinds of equipment, support, etc. The IAEA is not the only actor. We have a prime role as reflected in the treaties and the General Conference resolutions when it relates to nuclear, but we are not the only actor.

Cosslett: The IAEA has issued a formal rebuke with regard to Iran and their nuclear program. What does that mean? What's the sanctioning authority of the IAEA?

Johnson: I'm not talking about Iran, but in general terms. Under Article 12C of our statute, there's a provision saying that if there's a finding of noncompliance with the state's safeguards obligations, this information is reported to the board of governors, which is our executive board comprised of thirty-five states. If the board actually finds noncompliance, then, under the statute, there are a number of measures the board can take, including referral to the Security Council. So that is the gist of it.

There are a few other possible actions as well, such as curtailing assistance on technical assistance projects. What you read about with regard to the Democratic People's Republic of Korea and Iran have included referrals to the Security Council. Once things are referred to the Security Council, depending on the action taken, it could lead to Security Council sanctions. So the secretariat's role under the Safeguards Agreement is to report to member states about compliance with safeguards obligations. If the secretariat finds that there is noncompliance or that there is concern about whether nuclear material is being used for the purposes declared, this is information that we have to raise with the member states, and then they decide under Article 12C of the statute, what action is required. So there are different tools.

Cosslett: Germany has said that they no longer want to have nuclear power within the country for any purposes after Fukushima. Do you see more countries wanting to move towards a non-nuclear future?

Johnson: What I can say is the agency was itself created to promote the use of nuclear energy. After the atomic bomb, President Eisenhower wanted to use this power in a productive way, for the benefit of humanity. It is powerful. It can be dangerous, and at the same time, you can provide energy that's used to provide electricity. It's allowing us to develop technologies in terms of medical treatments and cancer therapies. Our statute is about the promotion of the peaceful use of nuclear energy. That's what we're here to do.

I think the sight of those nuclear reactors at Fukushima that couldn't be immediately controlled was very scary for our citizens. But from what I understand, and this is not my area as legal advisor, while some states are scaling back or phasing out nuclear power generation, like Germany, many others are moving ahead, like China and other countries in Asia. Perhaps the increase in the number of nuclear reactors won't be as high as it was before Fukushima, but it is still growing.

Cosslett: I live within ten miles of a nuclear reactor, and I have difficulty in reconciling the claims that it is "safe, secure, and vital" with the constant testing of the emergency evacuation siren.

Johnson: If I were not supportive of nuclear energy, I couldn't be the legal advisor of the IAEA. I'm not opposed to nuclear energy, but I am for safe use of nuclear energy. And because it is a potentially hazardous source, then we have to impose the highest standards. I think there's zero tolerance for safety lapses or security lapses, and this is the work of the agency. Safety, security, safeguards. I feel good to be a part of the agency that's charged with that mandate. Since nuclear energy is here and it doesn't appear to be going away anytime soon, and I don't think that it will, at least not in terms of peaceful purposes of nuclear energy, let's work together to make sure it's the safest, it's the most secure, and it's safeguarded.

Cosslett: Where do you see yourself in ten years?

Johnson: I'm forty-five years old, and legal advisor of the IAEA. For many, this is the height of a career. For now, I'm happy in this position. I still have my links with my position in New York City, as I have a permanent contract in UNDP. And then who knows down the road.

But obviously, at this point my career is very much UN, so I do see myself staying within the UN world. I don't see myself going out and going into the private sector at this point. I have a mandatory retirement age of sixty-two. For those who entered before 1994, it's sixty and they are currently thinking about extending it to sixty-five.

Cosslett: I'm just thinking that's a great age to go into a law firm in a counsel position, where you can, at an exorbitant salary, advise people on all of these issues upon which you are now an expert.

Johnson: I'll have to keep that in mind.

Cosslett: Within the UN, who do you actually represent?

Johnson: In the UN, we have many stakeholders. If you look at the mission statement of the Office of Legal Affairs, I am the director-general's lawyer. That's first. Second, I also provide technical support to member states because this is their organization. So member states ask questions, we give technical inputs, and provide legislative assistance on their nuclear laws. It's a big part of the work that we do in the Legal Office.

Cosslett: Is there a code of conduct specific to lawyers within the UN?

Johnson: The UN has rules and regulations and a code of conduct applicable to all staff, including lawyers. In recent years, there has been a focus on ethics and ethical standards for all UN staff. There's mandatory training. There have been some high-profile harassment cases that you may have read about. So from the UN perspective, these issues of professional responsibility have been about that. It's also been about ensuring that we follow the code of conduct. We are an organization of many states, so you see this play out in terms of procurement. We want to make sure it's a transparent process, that no one state has a favored access to another state. We can't take gifts from states, and as for other gifts, these can't have more than nominal value. We have to ensure there's no pressure or favoritism or anything like that. Also, staff at a certain level have to disclose if they have any investments or any other outside activities that would infringe on their independence.

Cosslett: What advice can you give to law students or practicing attorneys about jobs at the UN or other international agencies that might provide attractive career opportunities?

Johnson: I think the UN is the best and the broadest. And the UN is huge. It is not one organization. If you go to the UN.org web site, I think there are more than thirty different UN organizations. But other than UN, you could look at the banks. Don't forget the World Bank and the regional development banks. There's the African Development Bank, there's the European Regional Development Bank. These are international institutions as well. They're focused on financial issues, but they're international organizations. There's the OSCE[3]. There's the OECD[4]. There are many international organizations.

---

[3]Organization for Security and Cooperation in Europe
[4]Organization for Economic Cooperation and Development

Cosslett: If it's an acronym, apply! What advice would you give law students about positioning themselves as attractive candidates for an international career?

Johnson: Everybody wants to talk about careers in international law, and I've spoken and written on this. I have been hiring lawyers for many years now in the UN. I look for someone who has international experience, someone who speaks a foreign language, someone who I can see really has some kind of interest and awareness of things international. You get so many applicants for these positions that this is a threshold determination.

An American candidate, for example, who doesn't have a foreign language and has never lived abroad is not an interesting candidate for the UN. You want folks who are acclimatized to working in an international environment. They've lived abroad or they have had some international experience—even volunteering, like Peace Corps or working for an NGO, even sometimes teaching international law. One of my lawyers in the IAEA is a professor of public international law, so he's a respected public international lawyer, but from an academic background. And, at a junior level, I'm really looking for someone who demonstrates that they can speak a foreign language.

The UN has six official languages, and in many duty stations you work in more than English. At the IAEA we work in English, but we still have six official languages. As you know, I studied French, I studied Spanish. I am now learning German, being here in Austria. And it's important because you're working in a multicultural environment, so a candidate that is from a different country or that speaks a different language or has lived abroad is interesting.

Cosslett: If you have someone who's been a litigator or a corporate lawyer but who happens to have a strong international background and languages, then that would be an attractive candidate?

Johnson: I came from Arnold & Porter and that's an American law firm, but I could tell the UN that much of what I did was international. We want the best lawyers, and I think the training that you get in law firms is top training. So a law firm background could be interesting if you can demonstrate some kind of an international link as well. Now, at the same time, don't forget we have special needs for lawyers in certain areas of expertise, so at the UN in New York, we hired a number of lawyers out of firms who had experience in international arbitration. Don't forget that the UN spends millions in procurement, so we do have claims and we do have arbitration.

Cosslett: Have you encountered issues specific to being a female attorney?

Johnson: You see greater gender parity at the UN. In my office at the IAEA, for example, we're almost fifty-fifty female/male. I think legal is a field where you see more equity. Harvard was definitely about fifty-fifty. Within the UN, UNDP is one of the leaders in terms of gender equity: Helen Clark, the former prime minister of New Zealand is the administrator and the deputy, Rebecca

Grynspan, former vice president of Costa Rica, is also a woman. Half of the assistant secretary-generals are women. As an organization focusing on development, women at UNDP are well represented.

The IAEA, on the other hand, is traditionally male given it is a technical organization. I work with physicists and engineers and, for whatever reason, there are many fewer women going into that field. But, as I said, the Legal Office is just about 50/50. I have never personally experienced any discrimination because of gender. I was the first woman legal advisor in the UNDP and I am the first woman legal advisor in the IAEA. I asked my staff whether it meant anything that I'm woman versus a man, and I couldn't really get a concrete answer.

At a recent event held by the IAEA, there was a focus on how to recruit women in the agency. There was a lot said about a women's style: that we're more collaborative. That if there were more women leaders there'd be less war. I think no one really knows for sure exactly how it would really play out, but one of my favorite quotes about women came from Michelle Bachelet, the executive director of UN Women. She said let's "make gender parity a lived reality, not just a mantra."

Women can be who we want to be. We can be physicists, engineers, lawyers. I am a lawyer because of my dad's influence. I grew up knowing I could be whatever I wanted to be. I never grew up thinking there were limits.

CHAPTER 8

Kate Romain

Partner

Bredin Prat

When people think of successful lawyers, they may think of wingtip shoes and a stern demeanor, a pinstripe suit and a pedantic mindset. They may not have an image of a person raised by an avant-garde family in 1970s Houston, a young lawyer conducting multimillion-dollar acquisitions in her bare feet, or a person who would move to Paris for love. Most people wouldn't have an image of **Kate Romain**. She is not your traditional buttoned-up lawyer and has not followed a traditional path to becoming a partner at Bredin Prat, one of the most prestigious law firms in Paris, where she specializes in the representation of French and non-French clients in cross-border mergers and acquisitions.

Opting out of the safe path of biglaw in Texas and following her heart to France, Romain embarked on a life adventure that validates the notion that the combination of being very smart, being ready to work hard, and being true to who you are and what you believe in will ultimately lead to success—even if, early on, you are not quite sure what all that means.

Prior to joining Bredin Prat in 2006, Romain was an associate with the Paris offices of Hogan & Hartson and Paul Weiss. She began her career at the Federal Trade Commission's Bureau of Consumer Practices in Washington DC. A graduate of the University of Texas School of Law (JD, with honors), Romain was admitted to the Bar of the State of Texas in 1991 and the Paris Bar in 2004. Her native language is English and she is fluent in French.

Clare Cosslett: By way of providing a mise-en-scène for this interview, Kate and I are in a conference room in the extraordinary mansion that houses the law firm of Bredin Prat on one of Paris' most fashionable streets, rue du Faubourg Saint-Honoré. We are sitting on vintage leather chairs, having had a delicious lunch served to us in elegant navy-blue boxes. It's a delight to come and visit you here, Kate. Tell me about yourself.

Kate Romain: I grew up in Houston, Texas, one of four kids. Houston is a very conservative place politically, and both my parents were Democrats. My mother was a first-generation German immigrant and my grandparents, Omi and Opi, spoke only German. My parents were very involved in the arts: with the opera, with the ballet. Every year, we had young opera singers who were singing with the Houston Opera stay with us. We had gay friends, which for Houston was very avant-garde.

My father was a very good cook and was always trying cuisines from different cultures. When my friends came over, they would think they had gone to some exotic country. My family was not like any other family in Houston, so I grew up being different, and I knew that when I could, I would leave and go somewhere far from Houston.

Cosslett: Were both your parents professionals?

Romain: At the time, women didn't work much outside the home, but my mom did a lot of volunteer work. She volunteered as president of the Houston YWCA for about ten years. She woke up every morning, put on a suit, and went to work. She was also president of the UN Allocations Committee for Houston. She had very visible, high-level volunteer jobs and every year she would win an award with a terrible name: "The Most Beautiful Volunteer of Houston."

My dad was a lawyer who had a small, one-man practice. He did divorces, he did litigation, and he worked with real estate developers. He usually had two or three clients at a time. A very small practice.

Cosslett: Did you know that you were going to follow in his footsteps?

Romain: I knew that it made sense for me to follow in his footsteps, but I never really thought a lot about it. My dad said, "Go to law school. Even if you don't want to be a lawyer, you will love law school. You can put that degree in your pocket and then do whatever you like." My mother gave me great advice too. She said, "Learn to type, because you never know what life has in store for you, and if you know how to type, you can always support yourself." I thought that was pretty good advice.

Cosslett: Where did you do your undergrad?

Romain: I started at Vanderbilt, which was a terrible choice for me. My parents were so afraid of being too hands-on that they were too hands-off. I arrived at Vanderbilt and said, "What have I done? I'm here at this super-conservative, white, privileged university in the South." It was a total mismatch. I immediately transferred to the University of Colorado in Boulder. And that was a much better match. I did a year abroad in France and went to Grenoble, which was also a good time.

Cosslett: Did you think about any career paths other than becoming a lawyer?

Romain: Right after college, I worked as a waitress for a couple of years and I wasn't really thinking of anything. It took me five years of working as a lawyer in Paris to earn as much as I earned waitressing between college and law school. I was happy then. I was going out every night, and dancing, and waiting tables, and making tons of money. I really wasn't worrying much about the future. I think when you have a mother who doesn't work as a professional, you think that your life is going to be exactly the same. I didn't really know what I wanted from law school or from being a lawyer. When I came to France, I still didn't have much of an idea as to what I wanted to do. I didn't even really know what I had done. I was completely clueless for about ten years, seriously.

I went to the University of Texas Law School, which was like going back home. I had a great time in law school, and I did really well. I thought, "Wow, maybe I'm supposed to be a lawyer." Because, in fact, it came very easily to me and I wasn't necessarily trying very hard. My dad had told me before I went to law school, "All you have to do to do well in law school is be smart." You have to work hard, but mainly you have to be able to synthesize information. If you can do that, you can be a successful lawyer.

Cosslett: Of the courses you took in law school, was there anything that you particularly enjoyed or anything you found particularly challenging?

Romain: The more challenging courses were things that you had to take that I wasn't necessarily interested in. I also think—and I tell my kids this now as they're going to college—that a good professor can make a course that you're not interested in fascinating. A bad professor can make a course that you're interested in the worst thing in the world.

So I tried to always choose the good professors and, because of that, I took a wide variety of courses. One of the most interesting courses that I took—and it was a seminar so it was meant to be interesting—was a course on prominent women in the legal profession. We had women partners of law firms come and talk to us. I wrote a paper on challenges that young women lawyers were experiencing. It was very interesting, but it wasn't very legal.

Probably the course I enjoyed the most in law school, bizarrely, was first-year contracts—maybe because the professor, David Sokolow, was fantastic, but for me, the law of contracts was really the basis of law, and that's what I do now. I also really enjoyed the Socratic method of teaching. I remember I got called on to discuss the rule against perpetuities. And the teacher asked me a question, and I said, "That's so funny because I was going to ask you the same thing." That was my big moment in law school.

Cosslett: "A life in being plus twenty-one years." It's like pornography, you can't define it, but you know it when you see it. Did you take any internships or any clerkships?

Romain: I had to fund my own studies and was employed during all three years of law school. I worked as a clerk during my first and second years at a law firm in Austin, Texas. The firm was handling a huge litigation and I did a lot of deposition summaries. I went to the firm, picked up a couple of three-inch-thick depositions and a Dictaphone, and read the depositions and made summaries sitting by the pool. I was paid by the hour for my work. So it wasn't a full-time job. It was as many hours as I wanted to work. In my last year, I taught legal research and writing to first-years.

Cosslett: You didn't find reading all those depositions to be boring?

Romain: It was fantastic. It was a take-or-pay oil and gas case. Take-or-pay is an oil and gas contract where you undertake to buy a certain minimum volume that you have to pay for even if you don't take it. So I was working there during my first year and hadn't made any plans for the summer. I was very clueless and asked my classmates, "What are you supposed to do after your first year of law school?" They said, "You haven't been interviewing for internships or summer clerkships?" I said, "No, I haven't."

I saw a poster in school that said, "Study abroad in France," and at the bottom it said, "A limited number of clerkships available." It was the University of Iowa School of Law. So I went home, called the guy, and he said, "I'd be thrilled if you came, and I'll give you a bottle of French wine for every student from the University of Texas you can bring with you."

I came to Arcachon, which is near Bordeaux, on the coast, and it was great. We had six weeks of classes, for which I got law school credit. We all lived together in this old house right on the sea and rode our bikes to classes. Then I had a six-week clerkship at Donovan Leisure right here in this building where we are sitting. It was during that clerkship that I met my husband, and that is why I'm here now.

Cosslett: But you had to tear yourself away to return to law school?

Romain: I tore myself away and moved back to Texas for my second year of law school. In my third year, my husband came to the University of Texas and did an LLM. When he graduated in '91, he could not find a job in the United States. None of the US law firms were running their foreign intern programs due to the economic crisis. He had to come back to France.

Cosslett: And you moved to the Federal Trade Commission. Why?

Romain: When I graduated from law school in 1991, the market was terrible, but since I didn't really know what I wanted to do, I didn't really have any expectations. I interviewed at some of the big firms in Texas because that's what everyone else was doing, but I knew that I really didn't want to do that.

I don't remember why I thought of applying to the FTC but I did, and I applied remotely—no interview—and got the job. I didn't even know what the FTC did.

My other job offer was at a firm in New Orleans that specialized in admiralty law. I thought admiralty law sounded very international, but when I flew out there to interview, the culture of the city was very racist, and I decided I could never live in a city with a culture like that. So I went to the FTC. I had a very good friend living in Washington at the time and it just made sense.

Cosslett: What type of work did you do at the FTC?

Romain: The FTC has a Bureau of Consumer Practices, and that's where I was. It was a fascinating job. It was litigation, but I didn't even know it was litigation until I got there. I realized, "Wow, I'm doing litigation. This is fantastic." When I first arrived, I was given about two dozen letters from people complaining about a bad investment that had been marketed to them over the phone from a place in Florida: First American Trading House, FATH. We read the letters, called the people who had written them, and began to gather information. We subpoenaed the FedEx records of the boiler room selling the investments, found and contacted people to whom they had sent solicitations, found other people who had invested, and, little by little, started writing affidavits.

We would go to Florida and interview former salespeople on the playground of an elementary school, or in the back of Denny's. We had some weird meetings. It was fun. We made a request to get either a temporary restraining order or an emergency injunction, and we got to put on official Broward County jackets and go in and shut them down. After we closed them down, we realized they were just one of many boiler rooms selling bad investments for a bigger company called Unimet Trading Corporation, so we started to shut them all down—an operation in Arizona, an operation in California.

Cosslett: Could you get anyone's money back?

Romain: No. The money was all spent, but at least we were able to close up the businesses. It was a very interesting job. The people I worked with at the government were all top-notch: very smart and very dedicated. They were there because they believed in what they were doing, not because they wanted to make a ton of money. The job did have a lot of perks, one of which was the hours. There was a lot of flexibility. I worked nine to six for eight days in a row, nine to five on the ninth day, and then had the tenth day off. So you had every other Friday off. And you could work whatever hours you wanted to. Some people dropped their kids off at school at seven and started working at seven thirty. Now, you had the salary that went with it, but I worked with very smart and very dedicated people.

I would recommend the FTC or other similar government agencies for people who are having trouble finding a job in the private sector. I think it's probably better than working in a small, no-name firm. The training was hands-on. I got to argue a motion in court and nearly died of a heart attack. I realized I didn't want to do litigation in the end, and I was lucky to leave before they all knew that I didn't want to do litigation.

After a year with the FTC, my husband and I decided to get married. While the market in 1992 was a bit better than it had been the year before, it was still much easier for me to find a job in France than it was for him to find a job in the States. So I moved to Paris for love.

Cosslett: Let's talk about the practice of law in France generally. How big are most French firms?

Romain: As a general rule, French firms are smaller than US firms. At Bredin Prat, we have one hundred thirty-six lawyers, and we're a pretty big firm. We're not full service in that we don't do IP and we don't do real estate, but we cover most of the other practice areas. We have about seventy lawyers in our corporate department, which makes us probably the biggest corporate practice in Paris. One of our closest competitors is Darrois Villey, which is another French firm that's very much like ours but much smaller.

Cosslett: How many of the one hundred thirty-six at Bredin Prat are partners and how many are associates?

Romain: There are forty-two partners and the rest are associates, so we have leverage of two-to-one. We currently have nine female partners and in the fairly recent past, let's say eight to ten years, we've made more women partners than men partners. If résumés were gender-blind, we would hire all women because their résumés are so much better. We have to engage in affirmative action to hire men. In the US, you want your son or daughter to be a doctor or a lawyer, or maybe a banker, although perhaps less so now. In France, you want your son to be an engineer. One of my nephews was not doing that well in school and my father-in-law, who is an engineer, said dejectedly, "Well, I don't know. I guess he can be a lawyer."

Cosslett: So for a boy, it's not the first thing the parents are aiming for—it's a fallback. For a girl, it's an acceptable profession.

Romain: That's how I explain the fact that there are so many women lawyers and so many good women candidates.

Cosslett: Are there distinct practice area groups within the firm?

Romain: A peculiarity of the practice in France is that you have a lot more people who do both corporate and litigation, even in big firms. So, of our corporate partners, we have probably five or six who regularly litigate. And the junior associates coming up are hired for both corporate and litigation. While market forces are definitely pulling lawyers toward more specialization, we're trying to keep junior associates in the courtroom in order to give them a more generalized experience. This is the old-school way of doing things.

Cosslett: Are you the only US-trained attorney in the practice?

Romain: No. We have a partner from Tennessee. She's the smartest person in the firm and has been a partner here for many years, and we also have an

American attorney who's a senior counsel. We have a number of associates who have done LLMs in the US, because today if you want to work in a firm that's doing cross-border work, it's one of the pieces of the puzzle that you need to fill in.

Cosslett: Can you explain the structure of US firms that are in France?

Romain: There are two models for US firms practicing in France. There are US firms that are real competitors of ours, because they practice French law. Cleary Gottlieb and Linklaters are probably the firms that we see the most on the types of deals that we're working on. Cleary and Linklaters have both American and English partners, and they have a very strong French practice. Cleary has been here forever. Linklaters established themselves here during the 1970s. Sullivan & Cromwell picked up a strong French practice and then added American lawyers, which, I think, works well for American clients. The firms that have done the best have a real French practice, with real French lawyers.

In addition, there are a number of US firms with more general practices that maintain small offices here with about ten or fifteen lawyers. These offices are usually staffed with some French lawyers experienced in working for US firms and a small group of US lawyers.

Cosslett: Paul Weiss decided to not stay in France?

Romain: Paul Weiss established their office in Paris in the late 1970s. Nobody knew then whether Paris or London was going to become the financial capital of Europe. Paul Weiss bet on the wrong city and opened their office in Paris. In 1996, Steve Wolfram, the partner with whom I worked at the Paris office of Hogan & Hartson, and I were brought into Paul Weiss in order to help integrate the office with New York. That was before the Internet in France, so communications were difficult. That was when you had modems and dial up. People would stand around the computer . . . *dee-dee-dee-dee-dee-dee*. And they would send the billable hours by modem once a month. That was their only communication with New York. We were hired to Americanize the office. Paul Weiss opened its London office in 2001, and it made sense to close the Paris office after that.

Cosslett: Do US firms tend to have either London or Paris offices?

Romain: It's usually London and maybe also Paris. I don't know that there are very many US firms that have only Paris and not London.

Cosslett: What was the culture at Hogan & Hartson?

Romain: When I joined Hogan in Paris, I was a baby. Steve Wolfram was a wonderful mentor. He had a very small and informal office, and we usually walked around the office barefoot. Our main client was Thales, the French electronics defense company, which at the time was called Thomson CSF. They were doing acquisition after acquisition in the US.

There was one other young lawyer in the office and we got involved in everything. We took a plane to the US, we did the due diligence, we wrote the due diligence report, we came back, we wrote the contract, and we negotiated the contract. And we made the coffee. I got to do everything from being a paralegal to being an eighth-year associate—good and bad. And it was fantastic.

Steve Wolfram was a very well-trained New York lawyer and he rewrote much of my work, even down to a cover sheet that read, "Please see attached." I mean, he rewrote everything and you know what? Little by little, I became a very good draftsman by learning to adopt his style. Steve is really an excellent lawyer.

Cosslett: How different was the culture at Paul Weiss?

Romain: Very different—I had to wear shoes. At my very first Paul Weiss dinner, a partner asked me, "So now you've been with us for six months, how do you find the culture?" I said, "The main difference is that Hogan is based in Washington, DC, and in Washington, people are much more chatty."

When I dealt with people in Washington, I knew how many kids they had, what other matters they were working on, and what they were doing that weekend. Paul Weiss was all business. The partner from Paul Weiss said, "That's very interesting because in Washington, information is power. And people in Washington are just naturally trained to keep you talking because they never know when you're going to say something that could be useful." I thought that was kind of interesting.

Cosslett: Knowledge is power.

Romain: As far as the practice, I found that working with a Washington law firm was more loosey-goosey in style than working with a New York law firm—which was more bing-bing-bing, getting business done, much more serious, much more structured. There was the New York way of approaching and doing something, and it was all very serious.

I didn't come from that culture growing up. I didn't come from a culture with a lot of rules and regulations at home. We had no rules at home. We could do whatever we wanted, but we were responsible and did well in school. Obviously, at Hogan & Hartson we had no shoes and very few rules even though we worked very hard. So I've always been the one in the room that's a little more informal than everybody else, and that's always served me fine.

Cosslett: Is the French salary structure comparable to the US?

Romain: No. Salaries are just a lot lower. Also, French lawyers are considered independent contractors: *profession libérale*. The way it works is this: even if you're a first-year associate, you have to get a number, and you are, from the administration's point of view, your own business. Every month you send an invoice to the firm. If you invoice your firm $100, you pay social charges of about twenty-five to thirty percent on that. That leaves you $70, and then you're taxed on $70. So on the $100 that you've invoiced, you probably take home $50.

This treatment of lawyers as independent contractors developed from the noble principle that lawyers should be independent and should not be beholden to anyone except to their clients. So in the olden days, you could not be a salaried lawyer. In 1991, the law was changed and they said, "You can be a salaried lawyer," and everybody changed all their lawyers to being salaried lawyers, which had two benefits. One was they could work the lawyers harder. Secondly, they didn't have to permit them to have their own clients. Everyone thought it was great. Then somebody started looking at the math and realized it was cheaper for firms if their associates were independent lawyers. So everybody has gone back.

The other thing in France is that it's very difficult and expensive to fire salaried employees. If a firm wants to separate from an independent lawyer, it's just a three-month notice period. That's it. Legally, no amounts are required to be paid. An advantage to being independent, though, is that young lawyers all are permitted to have independent clients. You're supposed to leave them time to develop their own business. A lot of associates significantly increase their salary by having independent clients.

Cosslett: In the States, the model at some big firms is to encourage associates to develop their own book of business, but the reality is, when you're billing long hours, there's not a lot of time for that. Also there's not always an interest in smaller clients, because a smaller client may struggle with big firm billing rates.

Romain: When people come to me for very small things, I say, "Do you want me to find a very good senior associate who will take this on as a personal matter?" And they usually say, "Yes," and then they get the senior associate at Bredin Prat who is completely capable of handling their small matter, who charges half and who has all the resources of the firm available.

Cosslett: How long does it take to make partner at a firm such as Bredin Prat?

Romain: Well, as in the US, the track is getting longer. It used to take seven or eight years, but now it is closer to ten years as a general rule.

Cosslett: Given what you have described, there is likely not a service partner structure here. Over ten years, it seems that lawyers would have developed their own books of business.

Romain: It depends on the firm and the structure of compensation of the firm. Bredin Prat is very fortunate to have a lot of institutional clients, so that when people are up for partner, their individual book of business is not really considered. The question is do we like this person? Is she a good person? Do we want to be partners with him? And then, of course, there's their practice area. Do we take another partner in financing, or labor law, or M&A?

Cosslett: How has your practice been affected by the financial downturn in 2008 and by the current economic crisis in Europe?

Chapter 8 | Kate Romain: Cross-Border M&A

Romain: I think that the US is rebounding a little bit now. I had lunch with a partner from a leading New York firm a couple of days ago, who said, "Of course, this is not going to be a stellar year for us. It won't be the best year ever, obviously. But, crossing our fingers, we're not expecting a real catastrophe."

But here, with the problem in Greece and the euro potentially coming apart, and the recent presidential and legislative elections in France, things are slow. We're fortunate here at Bredin Prat in that we are probably like many top firms. We're saying, "Well, we're not going to disappear. It's not going to be the best year, but it's not going to be horrible."

There are a lot of firms out there, however, that over the past few years have been de-equitizing partners, firing partners, not hiring and letting go associates. A lot of partners are moving from one firm to another and a lot of firms are really, really downsizing. It's in the press every day. It has gotten very bad over the last two years. The downturn took a little longer to hit here than in the States, and we're paralyzed. We're all waking up in the morning, brushing our teeth, going to work, and not knowing what's going to happen. At some point, something's gotta give.

Europe had a lot of advantages, but I'm not sure people thought too hard about the disadvantages of a common currency. One of the disadvantages is that the strong are going to have to bail out the weak, and I think you've got a lot of votes that have to be collected for that to happen. The governments are also doing a Band-Aid approach with funding countries on the verge of bankruptcy.

Cosslett: Do the French approach the practice of law differently than Americans?

Romain: I am an M&A lawyer, so I will talk about the different approaches to that practice. Maybe I'm a bit biased, but I think good French lawyers tend to be a lot more flexible and nimble in getting the deal done, in cutting through what's important and what's not important. A good French M&A lawyer is not afraid to sign a big deal with a fifteen-page contract.

On the other hand, I'm doing a four-million-euro deal with New York lawyers. It is a teeny-weeny deal, and the huge American company has just sent across their seventy-page contract. And I want to say, "Do you know what you're buying? If you want us to give you reps and warranties that we have no elephants in our garden, we will give you reps and warranties that we have no elephants in our garden. But is that really relevant?"

The lawyers that we're talking to on the other side said, "This is our standard contract." I think on the French side, we're a lot more adept at cutting through what's important and not important, and a lot less scared to deviate and take a chance. It means we can get the deal done, which I like. To many American lawyers, the French approach might look fast and loose, but as I work more with senior American lawyers, I see that they get it.

Cosslett: Maybe they get it, but they still want that rep that "there are no elephants in the garden," because there's just no comfort unless everyone has checked behind every bush.

Romain: There's a lot of heavy-handed American ticking of the boxes. We frequently work hand in hand with US firms, and there is one big difference—we don't bill by the hour. Fees are discussed at the end of a matter and agreed to by the client at that time. That has a huge impact on how you work. If I've got something to do and it's six at night and I can do it in two hours, I'm going to do it in two hours because I want to go home and I don't bill by the hour. An American lawyer now is trained to believe that the same thing that might take me two hours is going to take him four-and-a-half hours. I don't think they make this decision consciously. I think it is the way they are trained. My work product might have two typos. Theirs is going to have no typos. Does the client want to pay two-and-a-half more hours for no typos?

In our firm, probably because we don't bill by the hour, everybody just wants to be as efficient as possible. For any given task, if there is someone in the firm who has done it already or can do it better than me, I'm going to call him or her immediately. We all want to work as efficiently as possible and as quickly as possible. We don't keep timesheets. No one's going to evaluate me on how many hours I billed this year. And so we're very, very efficient.

Cosslett: If French attorneys are characterized by their ability to cut through complex legal issues with laser-like sharpness, and American attorneys are characterized by their fear of elephants and love of mountains of paper, how do you characterize British attorneys?

Romain: Of course, these are just generalizations! In England, we work most often with Slaughter & May, which is a very elite, very good UK firm. They're very hard workers. They're very thoughtful. They are very similar to New York lawyers. On both ends you get this very methodical thinking through of everything they do—there's very little shooting from the hip. Everything is very serious, very considered. So I put them in the same category.

I must admit that sometimes we may make fun of them here in the firm, because we say, "You have to know the code." So when they say, "We've received your markup. It was very useful, very insightful," it means it was crap and they threw it in the bin. You have to know the code to work with them. I'd say culturally the French are probably closer to the US than we are to the UK. It's a whole other culture. But as far as working with lawyers from the UK, I've always had very good experiences.

Cosslett: What are your days like?

Romain: I'm at the office at nine thirty. I'm probably one of the first lawyers to get here. Most lawyers arrive around ten o'clock. I usually get home around eight thirty and, when I'm really busy, between nine o'clock and ten thirty, at the latest.

Cosslett: What about the two-hour lunch? I have to ask.

Romain: As I am American, I don't do it as much as the others, but three times a week I eat a regular hot, sit-down lunch. Once a week it's business development. Twice a week it's with friends from the office, and then a couple times a week I usually get something quick to eat and then bring it back in.

Cosslett: Okay, so the lawyers arrive at ten o'clock, they go to lunch from twelve thirty to two thirty and then go home at eight o'clock. US firms tend to have a late start and go later in the evening, but a two-hour lunch is just not part of the culture.

Romain: Here it's perfectly normal to say, "I'm going to lunch." The other thing that's different in the culture is vacation. Vacation is very important to French people, and you don't hide the fact that you're going to take a few weeks of vacation. Around this time of the year, you are in meetings, sitting around, having lunch, talking with clients or counsel on the other side, or people on a deal, and somebody will start, "Hey, so where are you going on vacation this year?" And people say, "I'm going three weeks to Greece and then two weeks to our country house in the south of France." And you talk about it and you find out where other people are going. People take real vacations.

Cosslett: Is it difficult for female attorneys to balance family life and work life?

Romain: We are trying to make the older male partners in the firm a little bit more sensitive to this issue, but fortunately, we have a lot of young male partners who have kids. And that, I think, helps a lot. In today's world, men are more involved in bringing up their kids. They will say, "I was late this morning because I went to give the bottle to my twins." People say, "Oh, that's so cute!" Women, on the other hand, can't say that. It's different.

Balancing long hours with raising kids can be difficult for some of the younger female associates, but women are having babies later. They are having babies at thirty instead of twenty-five. So at thirty, they've already worked for five years and are a little more established, a little more comfortable than before. We have a lot of women partners who had their kids either before they joined the firm or after they became partner. I'm one of them. Everybody's very comfortable talking about their kids and that makes for a good culture.

Also, weekend work is not as prevalent here as in the US, and we do have all that vacation time. We are not that strict with vacation days. While, it's supposed to be five weeks, if you're working very hard and you happen to take six weeks in a year, it's okay. It doesn't matter. Nobody's counting it. I've always worked quite hard, but I took a lot of vacation. My kids are pretty normal. We also have lots of good help available. Everyone has got nannies and there's a very good daycare system and network of help. Also, school starts at age three, so the guilt factor is not overwhelming.

Cosslett: Tell me about your practice.

Romain: My practice is "cross-border M&A," which means somebody buying a company in another jurisdiction or creating a joint venture with someone in another jurisdiction. I started off representing French companies making acquisitions in the US. Viewed from the French point of view, that's outbound work. Then I went through a period of time at Paul Weiss when we were doing inbound work—so Time Warner investing in cable activities in France and things like that.

The constant in these cross-border deals is that you have two different cultures. Usually, you have oral negotiations in English, and the contract is usually written in English, which is why somebody like me can be helpful on any deal. Even Franco-French transactions often are in English these days because when you start out, you don't know who you're going to sell to, so you do everything in English. And then maybe you end up with a French buyer and you've got this strange situation where two French people negotiate English-language documents.

I've represented Crédit Mutuel, the French bank, in deals in Spain and Germany. I'm an American lawyer, but the secret of M&A is that there's very little law in M&A. So what's M&A? Once you learn the basics, it's drafting. You have to be a very good draftsman. It's issue spotting. It's knowing when you need to call upon a specialist. A specialist for me could be a French corporate lawyer. I'm admitted in France, but I'm not a specialist in French law. The same way a French corporate lawyer is not a specialist in environmental law. I always say it's like doctors. You wouldn't call upon a heart surgeon to operate on your brain, but brain surgeons and heart surgeons are both doctors. We're very specialized.

Cosslett: Let's say your client is buying a company in Germany. How do you know what issues might be specific to a company in that industry in Germany?

Romain: The last deal I did in Germany was representing Crédit Mutuel buying Citibank's retail banking operations in Germany. I did that deal with another partner at Bredin Prat, and, of course, we had a German law firm that was on the ground advising us as far as what authorizations we needed to get, and what the banking and regulatory issues were. They also did the due diligence. So what did we do? We negotiated the contract, which took their due diligence report that said, "Here are the issues we need to be careful about." We drafted and negotiated the contract, always keeping them in the loop and always calling upon them as necessary. But the client relationship was ours. We knew the client—we've represented them on a lot of transactions—and they're comfortable working with us. That's my favorite kind of deal to do.

With regard to inbound work, I just represented Berlitz on a transaction where they bought a company in France. I had a French law firm on the other side. Berlitz is actually a Japanese-owned company. Their headquarters are in Princeton, New Jersey, and so I'm dealing with the Japanese and American clients doing the deal in France. I was the main lawyer in France. I had a team of young lawyers doing the due diligence, and there were things that came up where I had to call one of my partners and say, "Should I be worried about this?" in the same way I would if it were real estate or IP or something like that. You call upon specialists.

Drafting, negotiating, communication, good organization, good deal management skills, good delegation skills. Those are the talents that you need to be a good M&A lawyer. None of that has anything to do with law.

Cosslett: How would you assess the role of in-house counsel in a French company as compared to a law firm?

Romain: I mentioned earlier that French parents don't want their sons to go to law school. The same prejudice exists in French companies historically. It's starting to change, but historically the French general counsel usually reports to the financial director of a company. Already that gives you an idea. The French in-house lawyer traditionally does not have a very important role. They're viewed in France the way that human resources professionals are viewed in the US. The French general counsel is usually not the right-hand man to the president. The French general counsel is probably not on the executive committee. The French general counsel is just a whole different role.

We are often hired by the president of the company, the financial director, and maybe the general counsel. It depends on the company. Now, the role of in-house counsel is changing as the legal element has become more and more important for companies in France—but the general rule still holds. When I was first practicing, it led to awkward situations because you had the financial director asking you for your advice on something, and you could see that the in-house legal guy was furious that he wasn't being asked his opinion. And you had to manage the relationship.

Cosslett: That could be tough. It is very different in the States where, in some cases, in-house legal departments can resemble law firms.

Romain: There's been a lot more internalization of law firm talent in the States than in France, although I did read an article just yesterday that the French are starting to internalize a little bit more.

Cosslett: It can be a lot less expensive to pay a salary than to retain a law firm.

Romain: Except in France the salaried workers are very protected, as we discussed. So you think ten times before hiring somebody because it's very costly to get rid of them.

Cosslett: Tell me about the process of being admitted to the French bar.

Romain: It almost killed me. The way it works here is that if you're admitted in another jurisdiction outside of the EU, you take a special bar exam for non-EU lawyers called Article 100.

There was a bar review course held three nights a week and all day Saturday. I started the course in mid-October and the bar exam was scheduled for early April. As we got closer to April, class was also held on Sunday. It was a huge undertaking. I was still working at Paul Weiss and it was a very long and very tiring process, but my family was really supportive and proud.

It was fantastic because for the first time—and remember I had been in France for eleven years—I had to write in French. My oral French was much more developed than my written French. I would speak to somebody in French on the phone, hang up, and write an e-mail in English or write a fax in English because we weren't permitted to make any mistakes and my written French wasn't perfect. But for the first time I was reading and writing in French. I also learned French law. I had to take commercial law, civil law, civil procedure, and ethics. So I really learned all of the areas I had touched upon, but barely knew about before. I was so proud.

The exams here are both oral and written. In the oral exams, you walk in and, literally, you pull a subject out of a hat. You have a certain amount of time to write a short outline. You are permitted to have your statutes with you. And you write an outline in a very specific format. There's this very regimented way to give your answer. You have to sit in a certain way and have a certain posture. And you have to present your answer *en trois parties*, in three parts—so, whatever the subject is, you have to think of a way to divide your answer into three areas.

Cosslett: This is in front of a panel?

Romain: Yes, you present yourself and then they ask you questions for what seemed like an eternity, but was probably about sixty to ninety minutes. And then there's a written portion as well. Civil law and commercial law were written, and civil procedure and ethics were oral.

Cosslett: Is it an issue for a lawyer trained in a common law system to practice law in a civil law country?

Romain: It depends on the type of law that you're practicing. In M&A, it is not an issue. There are some practice areas that can cross a border, and some that are more difficult. Arbitration you can do. Financing you can do. It is easy to transfer most contract-based practices, and it takes about a year to understand the particularities of the new jurisdiction.

Being a litigator would be more difficult, not only because of the differences between the civilian and common law systems, but because you wouldn't know how to address the court and all the particularities. There are a lot of unwritten codes of practice. I don't really litigate, but I do work on some litigations—brief-writing and things like that. And it's very interesting because just the manner of writing briefs here is very unlike the States. Here you can say something just totally outrageous and the other party in their brief will say,

"That's so outrageous. You said the opposite thing in an e-mail." And then you say, "Oh well, whatever"—and move on. The rules are different. I think you tend to be more reasonable in the US.

Cosslett: Where do you see your practice in ten years?

Romain: I hope, because I'm so happy here, that I'll be right here, a little bit further along in my practice. One of the things I'm trying to do now is to build my recognition in the legal community. I have the privilege of working in a very visible law firm, and that brings with it a lot of opportunity. My professional goals are to do more business development.

Bredin Prat has something of a best friends network, where we're best friends with Slaughter & May in the UK, Bonelli Erede Pappalardo in Italy, Uria Menendez in Spain, De Brauw Blackstone Westbroek in the Netherlands, and HengelerMueller in Germany. We also have very good friends all over the world. So I'm part of an informal international group who are often working on cross-border matters. We travel all around the world. About twice a week I meet with lawyers from different jurisdictions. Last week, I had dinner with lawyers from Brazil. So, I'm constantly trying to increase my own visibility, and the firm is very interested in helping me to do that.

Cosslett: It is great to be with a firm where you can leverage their footprint in your own practice.

Romain: I've never been ambitious in that I've never had a business plan. I've always stumbled into things by accident. I feel very lucky to be here because I didn't really plan any of it.

Cosslett: From a professional responsibility perspective, what is the difference between practicing in France and practicing in the US?

Romain: There is one very important difference that comes up every single day. In France, when a lawyer has a communication with another lawyer on a matter, which we do constantly, you're not permitted under the French bar rules to tell your client about that exchange. All communications between lawyers are deemed to be confidential unless you have both agreed otherwise. So, what you do is establish a practice at the beginning of a matter: "Let's say that everything is nonconfidential unless we provide otherwise." That's how we usually start out. If you don't establish nonconfidentiality at the outset, communications look like this: "Here's the draft contract with our comments." The other lawyer writes back, "Am I permitted to share this with my client?" You write back, "Of course." If another lawyer writes you an e-mail, you must ask, "Can I share this with my client?" Even if the other lawyer says yes, you would never just forward the e-mail, nor would you cut and paste. You always put it in your own words, just because there's that sensitivity about what a lawyer tells another lawyer.

A good thing about this emphasis on confidentiality between lawyers is that you can say, "I want to have a confidential conversation with you," and you tell the lawyer on the other side of a matter something that maybe as a US lawyer would say is "between you and me," if you know the lawyer very well. You can tell him things, and it permits the other lawyer to understand what you're going through on your side and helps him to help you to get the deal done, which is, in the end, what the clients want. And you can say, "Listen, let me tell you, confidentially between us, Joe on our side—he's not the one. He's having to make these difficult decisions, and it's because his boss, Steve, is really worried about such and such." You say it in a confidential way. He's not permitted to share that with his client. And people take that very seriously here. We have to remind French lawyers here, "Be careful when you're conversing with your American lawyers because they don't understand this concept of confidential versus nonconfidential."

Cosslett: You've practiced in France for a number of years now. How have you seen the practice change over time?

Romain: French lawyers have become much more—I hate to use this word because it's a little bit pejorative—sophisticated and as good as or better than New York lawyers at their own game. When I arrived in France, a New York lawyer could come here and he could outtalk and out-negotiate most French lawyers, and the sophistication of the documents was overwhelming. The French lawyers would receive these eighty-page contracts and just not even know what the words meant. Actually, a lot of New York lawyers didn't even know what the words meant in the contracts that they were sending. But the French were overwhelmed.

Now the young French lawyers—they're smart, they're savvy, many have done LLMs at Harvard or NYU or Columbia. And they speak good English and they're no longer intimidated or certainly less intimidated by the New York lawyers. Both sides are now equals from the very first moment and you can see the mutual respect. Ten years ago, you saw the New York lawyer thinking, "I'm just going to roll over these French lawyers." So that's the main difference. And you also see French lawyers saying, "Sorry guys. To get this deal done, we're not going to do this on a sixty-page contract. We're going to do it French-style. We're going to use a twenty-five-page contract that covers all the main points. If we can say something in one sentence, we're going to use one sentence. We're not going to use six sentences." And it's working.

Cosslett: While the practice of law has certainly become internationalized, ultimately, a contract's a contract.

Romain: A contract is a contract is a contract. Also, the crop of lawyers who are doing cross-border work has become a lot more homogeneous. While you're working with lawyers in different countries at top-notch firms, they're all very similar. They've all done LLMs and they all speak excellent English.

Cosslett: Have you felt that being a woman has been a relevant factor in your practice, either positively or negatively?

Romain: I think being an American woman has been a positive. In my early years, I was always the only woman and the only American on the team, and there was always a special place for me in the team, but positively. In work and at the negotiating table, I've never felt that if I were a man I would have had a different treatment or a different amount of respect. I think France may be a bit ahead of the US as far as seeing and accepting women lawyers and working women. Even when I first came here, a French working mom was not at all as strange as it was in the US.

Cosslett: What advice would you give law students or practicing lawyers considering a career change about how best to position themselves for practicing as a lawyer overseas?

Romain: It's harder now than it was before to work overseas, because your competition is no longer just other American lawyers wanting to work overseas. Your competition becomes these young star French lawyers as well. It's not as easy as it used to be. But as far as coming to France, you have to speak French. You have to have some nexus with France. Hiring somebody is an investment, and we would hesitate to hire someone unless they had a French husband, French wife, some reason to come to France. Because otherwise, you know they're going to stay two and a half years and then they're going to want to go back. If somebody shows up on this doorstep today and says, "I'm a fifth-year associate at a very good US law firm. I speak French. My wife or my husband or my mother was French"—some nexus to France—"and I want to come here," I think we would consider hiring him or her because well-trained American lawyers are useful. Just the fact that an American attorney has English as a mother tongue makes him very useful.

Another piece of advice I would give to law students is to meet with as many lawyers as you can informally—your parents' friends, your doctor's wife. Meet with as many people as you can because that's a great way to listen and learn. Just listen and ask questions because you'll realize you don't know as much as you think you do. The same thing is true for somebody wanting to come to France. I meet people all the time who just have a little seed of an idea that they want to come to France, and I tell them the advantages and the disadvantages of practicing here.

I think you also need to understand the legal market wherever you're seeking to go. Do your homework. Call people up. What does that market need? For example, I'm sure right now any firm in Paris would hire a French-speaking associate doing energy law. There's a lot of energy work going on in French-speaking Africa. So a lot of the companies most naturally call the Paris firms, yet we don't have big energy practices in France. We have some big energy companies, such as Total, but it's not traditionally been a huge practice area for French lawyers. So you're a US-trained, fifth-year associate in energy law and you speak French and you have a reason to come to France: that would be something that the market needs right now.

CHAPTER 9

Chris Sprigman

Professor
University of Virginia School of Law

Imagine a job where you spend your days teaching, writing, and thinking about the legal issues posed by red-soled shoes, stand-up comedy routines, and football plays. **Christopher Jon Sprigman**—*a law professor specializing in the study of the effects of legal rules on innovation and the deployment of new technologies—has that enviable job. He finds that creativity in such intensely innovative and imitative industries as fashion, music, sports, entertainment, cuisine, and open-source software tends to thrive best where intellectual property protection is least stringent.*

Sprigman's own career exemplifies the creative freedom he studies. As he moved from the United States to South Africa and back, and from law firm associate to high-flying law firm partner to basement-dwelling junior legal scholar to tenured professor at one of the country's most prestigious law schools, he kept in mind the advice from a federal judge about the false allure of biglaw and the importance of charting his own path. To this career advice, Sprigman added his own self-admonitions: resist getting carried along with a tide that might cough you up on the rocks; and never invest so much of yourself in tokens of high status as to be unwilling to throw them away in order to pursue a more intellectually challenging direction.

Sprigman is the Class of 1963 Research Professor in Honor of Graham C. Lilly and Peter W. Low at the University of Virginia School of Law. After receiving his BA from the University of Pennsylvania and his JD from the University of Chicago Law School, he clerked for Judge Stephen Reinhardt of the US Court of Appeals for the Ninth Circuit. He spent three years working on antitrust cases for Davis Polk in New York before moving to South Africa to become a visiting professor at the University of the Witwatersrand School of Law—while at the same time clerking for Justice Lourens H. W. Ackermann of the Constitutional Court of South Africa.

Sprigman served as appellate counsel in the Antitrust Division of the Department of Justice, where he worked on US v. Microsoft. After he was promoted to partner at the King & Spalding office in Washington, DC, he left practice to become a residential fellow at the Center for Internet and Society at Stanford Law School. He has published extensively in the area of popular culture and intellectual property, including a book, The Knockoff Economy: How Imitation Sparks Innovation (Oxford University Press, 2012), coauthored with Kal Raustiala.

Clare Cosslett: Why did you go to law school?

Chris Sprigman: When I graduated from the University of Pennsylvania, I considered a couple of things. I thought of getting a PhD in history and I thought of going to work for a newspaper. I had worked on the school newspaper at Penn and liked it a lot. While there were different ways that I was thinking about starting my career, it boiled down to the fact that Chicago gave me money and it wouldn't cost much to go to law school. It actually cost very, very little. So I thought, "Well, I'm interested in this. It's not clear that it's exactly the right thing for me, but it's pretty close to free."

Cosslett: For most students, law school is such a big financial commitment that it's tough to say, "Well, I'll try it and see what it's like. Maybe it will work, maybe not."

Sprigman: Things have changed so much. The financial hit that students take these days is gigantic. It's a different world. Students can't afford to be casual in their thinking about law school unless their parents are very wealthy and willing to underwrite them. Just editorially, Mitt Romney said the other day that young people should take risks and they should borrow money from their parents if they want to. I wanted to laugh because that is ridiculous. Not everybody has parents who can shell out thousands of dollars.

My parents were public school teachers. They spent a lot of money putting me through college. They were incredibly generous. But I thought, "If I go to law school, and it doesn't cost them that much, that's good, right? I'm not going to put them in the poorhouse. They'll have a decent retirement." As teachers, they made a respectable salary, but certainly nothing fantastic. And they were getting older. It turns out their retirement's fine, but not having to spend fifty thousand bucks a year to send me to law school was certainly helpful. And I was very glad that that was the case.

Cosslett: Once you got to Chicago, did you like it?

Sprigman: I suspect it's changed a bit, but when I was at Chicago, it was very old-school, very formal. You knew you were someplace special. It was a tremendously talented, exciting faculty. The giants of the legal academy were teaching there at the time: Richard Posner, Richard Epstein, Cass Sunstein. And I felt like I got a great education. It was very demanding. It wasn't always pleasant, but in retrospect, I'm very glad I went there. It helped to shape my intellect in a way that I think has served me well. It made me a bit more skeptical than I was. It made me very open to other people's points of view. Chicago is known as a place where a huge diversity of viewpoints are actually listened to, paid attention to, engaged with. I thought intellectually it was a great place.

Cosslett: I've noticed that students coming out of University of Chicago have a strong business and economics orientation.

Sprigman: Starting in the late 1960s, Chicago began to stand out as a place where law and economics was very strong, and when I was there, they had a wonderfully deep pool of people who were leaders in this field. I was very interested in that. I felt that it was a valuable way of looking at the law. It made sense of some things that were otherwise very hard to understand. It wasn't useful in every area of the law, but in the areas that I was most interested in, antitrust law and intellectual property law, it was extremely useful. With that set of tools, a person who comes out of the University of Chicago is very well equipped to be a valuable lawyer in areas where law and economics thinking can be helpful. That's why I think you see that orientation. It has nothing to do with an explicit law and business orientation. It has more to do with the law and economics discipline overall.

Cosslett: Do you approach your teaching and writing from that same perspective?

Sprigman: I know law and economics has been a valuable tool for me, but a lot of my current work is skeptical of the classical law and economics approach. Much of my current work involves what's called "behavioral economics." I do experiments to examine how people actually behave when they transact in intellectual property, for example. And what you observe when you simulate human behavior in the lab is often quite different from what the theory tells you to expect if you design your experiments carefully, which I hope we've done, my coauthor Chris Buccafusco and I.

We have provided some reasons to think that the law and economics account of intellectual property is a little bit off. And I think at this point in my career, I'm in a position to test some of its foundations and to some degree, criticize it. I'm not an acolyte of law and economics. I'm both an intelligent consumer and a skeptic of law and economics, just like Chicago taught me to be a skeptic of everything else.

Cosslett: So you're coming full circle and beginning to challenge the premises of their curriculum.

Sprigman: As wonderful as I feel the place is, they don't have the final wisdom on anything. That is, it remains to be seen. But I have benefited enormously from having gone there.

Cosslett: After you graduated, you clerked for a year with the Ninth Circuit Court of Appeals.

Sprigman: I clerked for a very interesting judge named Stephen Reinhardt. He's one of the giants of the Ninth Circuit and very much a liberal stalwart on that court. He was a fascinating person to clerk for, in part because he's just an incredibly talented legal technician. He is someone who really knows what he's doing, understands the craft of judging at a very deep level. But aside from that, he also—and this was something I found out as we went along—invested a lot in his clerks in the sense that we got to see up close a lot of what he was doing.

We got to learn through example how to make an argument and how to write that argument as effectively as possible. In a million different ways during that year, I was exposed to his talent at doing those things. I hope that some of it was absorbed in the process. At the same time, it was a lot of work. I worked very hard, and there were times where I felt overwhelmed. Looking back on that experience, it was great. I was very fortunate to do that clerkship.

Cosslett: When you joined Davis Polk's New York office after the clerkship, did you know what practice area you wanted to get into?

Sprigman: I had a couple of ideas about things I might want to do—and this is where the hard part of my career started. I knew I wanted to do litigation. While a summer associate, I had done some corporate work and thought, "Well, this isn't really what I want to do." So I knew that. And I had done a little bit of antitrust, and was really interested in it. I had done a little white-collar criminal work, and had a good time.

I had also done some intellectual property work. I thought, "Let me start doing some work in these areas and see what I think." At the time, Davis Polk didn't have a lot of IP work, and so most of my exposure to IP came through antitrust cases, where there were IP issues mixed in. I started doing a bunch of white-collar criminal stuff, too. And what I learned over time was, for my taste, while the white-collar criminal work often had very interesting facts, after a few weeks they became mundane. And it seemed to me, the legal issues in the white-collar area had mostly been decided in favor of the government, and so the real trick was positioning yourself to negotiate a favorable deal. That wasn't really what I was either interested in or good at.

On the other hand, antitrust is often much less glamorous, but theoretically much deeper. There are many more open legal questions where analysis and creative argument could actually make a difference. It fit with my law and economics training, so eventually I thought, "Well, that's what I want to do," and I started to focus more and more on antitrust and did a lot of different antitrust work. I did some merger work, some governmental representation, both the Federal Trade Commission and the Department of Justice. I did some civil nonmerger stuff, including a big franchising case. I got involved in a lot of different antitrust work at Davis Polk.

Cosslett: Did you ever see yourself going for partnership?

Sprigman: Not really. I liked the job a lot and there were some Davis Polk lifers I liked a lot, too, but many of the people that I admired the most had done other things. They had worked in government, for example. And I thought, "I'm not ready to settle down." There seemed to be a lot of opportunities, and I thought, "Let me just see what comes along." I was not in a rush to settle down into the rest of my life.

Cosslett: After three years at Davis Polk, you went to South Africa?

Sprigman: The woman I was with at the time was in a PhD program at Columbia. She got funded to do dissertation research in South Africa. And, somewhat oddly, I'd been doing some pro bono work for a South African newspaper, the *Pretoria News*, in cooperation with some South African lawyers. The newspaper had been sued for defamation. They had run a bunch of stories about this reclusive rich guy, the South African version of Howard Hughes, who'd been using his private air charter service, the paper alleged, to run weapons to the UNITA[1] rebels in Angola, which was against South African law.

So this man turned around and sued the *Pretoria News* for defamation. Defamation law in South Africa had been a strict liability rule, much like in the UK, only without much of the UK's protection—like strict liability run amok. The South African lawyers wanted American advice on whether they could make arguments that, by virtue of the free speech provisions of the new constitution, defamation law in South Africa had been limited by free speech interests the way it had been in the States, and whether this meant that the strict liability regime now had to be scrapped. So I had been working on that with the lawyers, and talking with the South Africans a lot, and crafting, as it turned out, a brief to try to convince the constitutional court that defamation law could no longer be a strict liability rule in South Africa.

Cosslett: That sounds like a big undertaking. Were there a number of lawyers working on this in New York?

Sprigman: No, there was a South African guy who was a good friend of mine by the name of Michael Osborne, who had a lot of connections in South Africa and who had pulled me into this. So it was Michael and me, and that was a great deal of fun. When the possibility came up for this move to South Africa, I made a few phone calls, and Michael made a few phone calls, and I was interviewed by a justice of the Constitutional Court, Lourens Ackermann, who hired me to be his

---

[1] National Union for the Total Independence of Angola.

clerk. Then I talked to the dean of the University of Witwatersrand Law School in Johannesburg, and she hired me to be a visiting lecturer. This all just came together in a couple of weeks.

Cosslett: This is pretty heady stuff for a fairly junior associate. You had four years under your belt at that point: a clerkship and three years at Davis Polk. You were pretty fearless.

Sprigman: You can apply for things and you can ask for things, and the worst thing that can happen is that people say no. If you don't push for things, you never get anything. A lot of bright and wonderful people go into law, including many of my students, but they're just too polite and they're too coy. Fortune favors the bold. That's just the way it is.

Cosslett: The most successful people do seem to be the ones who take chances.

Sprigman: You identify something that you think might be good, where you might learn something and that might be fun, and you just try to make it happen. And, surprisingly, sometimes it does. I applied for this clerkship and was hired. I applied for the teaching position and was hired. And it was great because the court and the university were a five-minute walk away from one another, so I had two offices. I essentially was working two full-time jobs. It was wonderful. I had a great year. I wrote an academic article with Michael Osborne, and then I wrote a follow-up a little bit later. Those were really interesting and fun to write. They sparked a little bit of controversy.

Cosslett: Ultimately, how was the case against the newspaper resolved?

Sprigman: Michael and I had worked on the First Amendment question, but the case ended up being dismissed because the Constitutional Court ruled that the constitution did not apply to a purely private dispute like a lawsuit between this Howard Hughes figure and the newspaper.

And Michael and I took a look at that and we said, "That's incredibly interesting." Our client didn't win the case, but a very different state action doctrine has developed in South Africa starting in that case, *Du Plessis v. de Klerk*, compared with what had developed in the US—to simplify a lot, the decision of the Constitutional Court in the Du Plessis case meant that the South African Constitution would not govern private disputes, at least not directly. That isn't what a lot of people expected would happen. Michael and I wrote an article describing that new South African state action doctrine and saying we thought it was a good idea and giving reasons why. That article got published in the *South African Journal on Human Rights*. We published a follow-up somewhat later in the *South African Law Review*.

Those articles did very well. People read them and some people liked them. Some people really didn't. That was my first taste of academic success because I had written something with Michael that was interesting and creative and made people react, and made, at least for me, the beginnings of an academic reputation. The university offered to hire me full-time, and I seriously considered it, but eventually decided to return to the States, and it was the DOJ job that convinced me to return.

Cosslett: Had you taken a leave of absence from Davis Polk?

Sprigman: I left. I knew whatever happened, I wanted to do some work in government. I had spoken to a bunch of friends in DC about wanting to do that. While I was in South Africa, I remember sitting in my office at the court when I received an e-mail from a friend of mine, Mark Popofsky, a lawyer with whom I'd clerked on the Ninth Circuit. We hadn't clerked for the same judge, but he had been clerking when I was clerking for Reinhardt.

He was at DOJ at the Antitrust Division working on Microsoft, and he e-mailed me and said they needed more people: "They want to hire someone at the appellate level. Are you interested?" I said, "Hell, yeah."

I sent him a CV, and that day he started showing it to the relevant people. I had an interview a week later and was offered the job shortly after that. Again, it was just happenstance that probably the thing I was most interested in doing, DOJ needed someone to do, and I had a friend who alerted me to that fact. So the whole thing happened in the way that these things often do.

Cosslett: Was it particularly the Microsoft case that was appealing to you? Or was it working in antitrust generally?

Sprigman: I wanted to go to the Antitrust Division or to the Federal Trade Commission to do antitrust work for the federal government, but remember that at the time Microsoft was a case that meant a lot. It is hard to remember, but before 9/11, this was a huge thing. It was in the paper every day and the case was just chock-full of interesting and new antitrust questions. For anyone in the antitrust world, that's what you wanted to be doing.

Cosslett: What was the level of your involvement?

Sprigman: When I got to the Antitrust Division, it was in the early stages of the Microsoft trial. I was an appellate lawyer, so I wasn't working on the trial team, but one of my responsibilities was to watch as much of the trial as I could. Along with several other appellate lawyers, I started working with the trial team to deal with the legal questions that would come up during the trial.

We won in the district court, but we knew that there was going to be an appeal. One of the first things I did was to help write the brief requesting expedited appeal to the Supreme Court. The Supreme Court turned that down and we ended up going to the DC Circuit. I was one of five appellate lawyers working on this more or less full-time, and I was one of the lawyers who drafted the appeal brief that went to the Solicitor General's office. The Solicitor General's office is responsible for U.S. government briefs and oral arguments in the Supreme

Court, but they were called in specially in the D.C. Circuit appeal in Microsoft because of the importance of the case. We prepped the SG guys for oral argument on a huge set of issues. There were lots of lawyers who got involved from the SG's office and from the Attorney General's office.

It was a great education because I was present to participate in the case. And a great privilege to watch the best lawyers and economists doing antitrust at that time.

Cosslett: It sounds like an exciting time to be in the Antitrust Division

Sprigman: It was. The Antitrust Division was at the center of policy at that time. When Joel Klein was the Assistant Attorney General in charge of Antitrust, it was a great place to be. I don't think it's been that way ever since. Things changed in 2001 when Bush took office, and it became clear that he was going to settle the Microsoft case on terms that the Clinton people would never have accepted.

Cosslett: Did a lot of people leave after George Bush was elected?

Sprigman: Yes, a lot left. I stayed for some months into the Bush Administration because I had stuff I needed to finish, but it was very clear that the Antitrust Division would be a very different place. And it was after the Bush people fully took control of it.

The Antitrust Division didn't entirely go to sleep, but it was nothing like what it had been. The civil nonmerger docket just disappeared. That's what Microsoft was—a civil nonmerger case. It wasn't a criminal price-fixing case. It wasn't a merger case. It was a Sherman Act civil case not involving a merger. In some ways, that's the most interesting field of antitrust for people who are really interested in the analytics, although mergers are very interesting, too.

Civil nonmergers just went away. That's where I had spent the bulk of my time. I had also done a bunch of mergers. In the Clinton Administration, there was a chance that if you investigated a merger, you would try to stop it. Under the Bush Administration, the habit was to investigate the hell out of things and then say, "Okay." And that's by way of making a show.

So I thought, "Well, it's going to be a very different place. My learning curve is going to flatten out. My ambitions to do better and better work are going to be stymied. So let me see what else I can do." And just to be clear: I have really liked being a lawyer. I liked what I was doing at Davis Polk. I liked my clerkships. I loved being at DOJ. It was really challenging and great. I have never faced the problem of, on a day-to-day basis, thinking, "Why the hell am I doing this?" I've always felt that what I've been doing is good for me to be doing. And that is a tremendous pleasure.

Cosslett: After the DOJ, you joined King & Spalding's DC office as a counsel, and pretty soon after you were made partner. Tell me about your practice there.

Sprigman: I started working on a very interesting patent antitrust case involving both IP and antitrust issues. Our client was being sued in the International Trade Commission as well as in district court, so it was both an ITC proceeding and a federal litigation. It involved a whole lot of parties. It involved a lot of patents. There were some very interesting antitrust issues. I felt that, while I had moved from DOJ to a private firm, I had kept the level of work very high. I felt lucky to be doing this. I was working with smart people. I had a lot of substantive responsibility. They felt that they could make use of my DOJ experience. They felt that I had something to add rather than just billable hours. It was a really good setup.

Cosslett: Had you gone back to Davis Polk in a role as a counsel or eventually as a partner, do you think you would have had that same experience?

Sprigman: King & Spalding is a very different firm from Davis Polk. Davis Polk is one of those charmed firms in New York that has an incredible client list. Their culture is very egalitarian among the partners. Partners are paid according to their seniority. King & Spalding was more subject to the hurly-burly of the business. That said, I think for me there was, at the time at least, more interesting antitrust work to be done at King & Spalding. I don't know what it's like now, but then, the work was interesting and their antitrust practice was a DC-based practice, and I wanted to be in DC. And they were big enough in DC to be a credible player.

It was an interesting time. Making partner at the firm set off a bunch of thoughts about, "Is this it? Is this what I'm going to do for the rest of my life?" Be a law firm partner? A big law firm partner?

Also, there was, of course, the knowledge that I needed to develop a book of business, and that's very challenging for young partners, at least it was for me. I encountered a lot of conflict issues at the firm. If I brought in a client, there was bound to be a conflict of some sort.

And I thought, "This is a tough situation. On the one hand, I've got to build my own book of business if I expect to do the sort of work that interests me. On the other hand, this firm, like any big firm, produces a lot of conflicts, and conflicts are hard to work around."

Cosslett: And am I wrong in thinking, particularly in the antitrust area, the clients that you'd be looking to bring in are going to be pretty large companies?

Sprigman: That's true. I was also doing IP work and had some smaller technology companies that were interested in working with me. And there were conflicts. Some of the conflicts were with major media companies that the firm represented. Were they willing were they willing to ask the current client for a waiver? Sometimes yes, sometimes no. But it just seemed to me that there would be a struggle, and it was not a struggle I was fully in control of, and one which, when it boiled down to it, I wasn't really prepared to engage in. I wasn't prepared to bet my career on being able to navigate that relatively narrow passage. Also, I was in DC. The center of gravity of the firm was in Atlanta. Culturally, I was not a perfectly comfortable fit with the firm. I felt that I had limited ability to control my own career, and I didn't like it.

Cosslett: How did the opportunity at Stanford present itself?

Sprigman: There was a professor who had taught me in Chicago named Larry Lessig who had moved to Harvard and then to Stanford. I had stayed in touch with him, and I gave him a call and said, "I'm thinking about making a move into academia." He said, "Oh, that's interesting because when I came to Stanford, I negotiated funding for this center—the Center for Internet and Society—and I have a couple of residential fellows that I can hire: people who come here and get paid to write and to do a little bit of work on the center's litigation. Would you be interested in that?" I said, "Well, yes. Let me come out and see you."

So I flew out there, and I talked to Larry. I said, "This is a big move for me and I'd like to give this a shot because this would serve for me as a transition into academic life, but I'm at the stage of my career where I have a lot to lose. If I do this, I will show up in September. And I want to have a draft of an article by the new year and I want to know that you're going to take a very close look at this and give me comments and help me to turn this into a good article, because I need you to know that I'm going to need help from you." And Larry said, "Yes, absolutely. I'm on board."

And I think the key was that I asked for something and I got it. And that made me feel comfortable enough that I would leave the partnership I had been given, that I would leave all the great things at King & Spalding and go sit in some tiny office in the basement of Stanford Law School and write. The plan was to go there, write a couple of articles, and then go on the market for academic jobs, which is what I ended up doing.

Cosslett: Did you have any moments of doubt when you got to Stanford?

Sprigman: Well, I went from young partner at King & Spalding to basement dweller. I spent my first day at Stanford trying very hard to get a wastepaper basket for my office. And I remember thinking, "This had better work out. People are going to wonder whether I have lost my mind."

Cosslett: Why did you want to have your article done by the new year?

Sprigman: Because I wanted to get a first draft quickly so that I would then have time to make it better. The idea was I would have a draft by January. I would have until March to collect comments and implement them. I would submit it to law reviews in March, and I would go on the market in August.

Cosslett: And so this article was your entrée into being a professor?

Sprigman: Yes, this was the infamous job talk piece. And this is one of the most important things that a budding academic has to do. They have to write a paper that is going to get them a job. These days, an academic job is not just based on your pedigree. It's really based on what you write. It used to be that law schools hired Supreme Court clerks because they thought, "Oh, these people are smart." It turns out that a lot of very smart people aren't really great at being academics because being a good academic involves a lot of creativity. Being a Supreme Court clerk may or may not.

Cosslett: And they might be great at writing, but not so great at teaching.

Sprigman: It's typically the other way around. They tend to be great at teaching but not great always at writing. If you know the law and you're pretty decent at conveying it, you're probably going to be a good teacher. But being a good writer depends on being able to see interesting problems, being able to see interesting solutions. It involves creativity more than merely academic pedigree.

Cosslett: What was the subject of your article?

Sprigman: I wrote about something that I was interested in and talked about a little bit with Larry, which was the formalities system in copyright. There was a very big change in copyright in 1976 when they put the current copyright law into place. It used to be that to get a copyright, you had to claim it. You had to publish something with notice of your copyright. You had to register your copyright. You had to renew your registration after a relatively short period of time. And if you didn't do all that, your work went into the public domain.

After 1976, you didn't have to do any of that. If you fixed a creative work in a tangible medium, that is, you doodled something on a cocktail napkin, the minute you lifted your pen, it got a copyright, automatically, indiscriminately.

The point of the article was to figure out how that affected the copyright system. How did that change people's incentives to create? How did that change the cost of licensing? Was that on the whole a good change or a bad change? That was the first article. And it ended up in the *Stanford Law Review*. It ended up getting me a job.

Cosslett: That transition from being a practicing lawyer to becoming an academic is a big one.

Sprigman: Well, the magnitude of the transition depends a lot on what you've done as an attorney. Even for practitioners, antitrust is a field in particular that is driven by scholarship. Scholarship is woven into what antitrust practitioners do much more intimately than in almost any other practice that I've ever seen. So for me, it wasn't as much of a leap as it would be for others because so much of the thinking that you need to do in an antitrust case to be an effective practitioner is based on having a very good understanding of the current state of both the legal and the economic literature.

Let me give you an example. You're an antitrust lawyer, and you're helping an economist prepare expert testimony in a merger case. Now in order to be effective, you have to be a savvy consumer of the economics literature because you need to be able to help structure this testimony to present it to a judge or a jury. And you have to be able to understand it. If you're the lawyer on the other side, you have to be able to critique it. The wonderful thing about antitrust practice is just how smart a lot of antitrust lawyers are and how involved they are in advancing the state of the art in the practice.

Cosslett: So tell me a little more about the Center for Internet and Society. What was Lawrence Lessig's mission there?

Sprigman: Larry had been one of the architects of the *Eldred v. Ashcroft* case, the case that ended up in the Supreme Court challenging Congress's twenty-year extension of existing copyrights. That case went against the petitioners. The twenty-year extension was upheld. When I got to the Center for Internet and Society, we were thinking about ways to capitalize on what we thought was good language in the case in terms of the ways in which the First Amendment would discipline or limit Congress's copyright lawmaking power. We launched and litigated a couple of cases that were attempting to take advantage of some of the opportunities the Eldred case opened up.

Cosslett: Does the Center take the position that intellectual property laws should be curtailed because they somehow restrict creativity?

Sprigman: Intellectual property rights can be beneficial. They might help to induce investment in creative labor. So that's good. They also have costs. To the extent that we overdo copyright, it inhibits others from building on what's come before. So much creativity involves people building on stuff that is already there, and overenthusiastic copyright interferes with that. It also interferes with speech.

Prokofiev's *Peter and the Wolf,* for example, has been in the public domain for a long time. Orchestras all around the country can entertain kids with *Peter and the Wolf*. Congress then comes along, takes *Peter and the Wolf* and millions of other works out of the public domain, and puts them back under copyright. So orchestras now can't perform *Peter and the Wolf* without paying for the rights to do so.

Cosslett: Congress did this when? And why?

Sprigman: Congress did this in the late nineties. And so the question is whether there is any incentive effect? Is anyone, any creator, encouraged to create by the re-propertization or re-copyrighting of *Peter and the Wolf*? No, *Peter and the Wolf* has already been created. You can't incentivize Prokofiev again.

Congress did this in order to accede to a trade agreement. They thought that foreign governments would treat American copyrights more favorably if they took this action. Now whether or not this is true is a long debate, but when Congress does something like this, it has First Amendment effects. It inhibits speech. Before, you could play Prokofiev's *Peter and the Wolf*. Now you can't without paying. That's a burden on speech. It's not as if Congress can't burden speech, but when they do burden speech in this way, the First Amendment requires that a court take a look to see if the burden is proportionate to the benefit.

That was the simple point we were trying to make in a case called *Golan v. Holder*, which was one of our attempts to expand some good language in the Eldred case. We won in the Tenth Circuit and then we lost in the Supreme Court. So the bottom line is the courts are not going to take on the job of enforcing sensible First Amendment limits to Congress's copyright lawmaking power. But what Larry has done is launch a much broader movement, one which I'm hopeful will ultimately lead IP law back in a more sensible direction, and will do so better and more durably than any judicial decision could.

The most important point is that people's thinking about intellectual property has shifted tremendously. It used to be that people thought about intellectual property as a one-way street: it was all good. But there are good and bad parts of intellectual property. It can be both beneficial and harmful, like virtually anything. It can be great if you do it right. It can be terrible if you overdo it. And that consciousness about the costs and benefits, the tradeoffs in intellectual property, has really taken root.

You saw that just a few months ago in the online protests against those proposed IP laws, SOPA[2] and PIPA[3], which totally shut them down. You now have a whole generation of people who are aware that copyright can stimulate creativity and speech or inhibit them, depending on context.

Cosslett: Can you talk about what is going on now with regard to people downloading and sharing music?

Sprigman: Content owners are engaged in a process where they're trying continually to make IP laws stronger in an effort to stop this. My view is the law is not going to stop illegal downloading—ever. What's going to happen over time, and is already happening, is that the way that people make money from creative goods like music is just going to change. It's going to be harder and harder to make money from the recording. You're going to make money instead from the live show. And you're going to make money from social networks that deal in this stuff. There's a lot of ways other than the recording to make money off music.

The major record labels in the last decade have shrunk, adjusted for inflation, by about sixty percent. That said, while the record labels may be wounded, music is doing great. It's a golden age for pop music in the midst of the record labels' decline. The reason is that the music business isn't dying; it's just shifting away

---

[2]Stop Online Piracy Act
[3]PROTECT IP Act (Preventing Real Online Threats to Economic Creativity and Theft of Intellectual Property Act)

from the labels. And the calls for stronger intellectual property enforcement in the music industry aren't really about saving music. They're about saving the major record labels, which is a totally different proposition. So the connection between strong IP laws and strong creativity is weaker and more contestable than people think.

A book I coauthored with Kal Raustiala—*The Knockoff Economy: How Imitation Sparks Innovation*—makes just this point. We look at the fashion industry, cuisine, stand-up comedy, football plays, open-source software, financial innovations, and other areas in which there's lots of creativity, but no or very little intellectual property. And for each of these areas we tell the story of how creativity thrives without intellectual property. We hope the payoff of the book is not just to understand these important areas of creativity, but to understand how industries like music or film—that have long relied on intellectual property, but find it more and more difficult in the internet era to do so—might restructure themselves to take a page out of the playbook of these low-IP industries like fashion or food or finance.

Cosslett: Can you talk about intellectual property issues in the area of fashion?

Sprigman: Kal Raustiala is a childhood friend of mine and teaches at UCLA Law School. He and I wrote an article together on the fashion industry. The point of the article was pretty simple. There's a theory of intellectual property that says, "IP law, which controls copying, is there to incentivize people to invest in the creation of new things." So if people are free to copy, then, the theory goes, originators will stop investing in the creation of new things. Well, that, in theory, makes a lot of sense. But take a look out there at how the world actually works—the fashion industry is huge: about a trillion and a half dollars worldwide per year. Two hundred billion or so in the States. It's a very big industry. Much bigger than movies or books or music.

This creative endeavor—the making of new fashion designs—is not protected in the United States by copyright law because fashion designs are useful articles, and copyright doesn't protect useful articles. So there's no IP protection for the designs, and what you get in the fashion industry is what you might anticipate, which is lots and lots of copying. You get tons of knockoffs. More so than knockoffs, you get clothes that look similar—that are responding to and recognizably appropriating some particular popular design theme, but with their own take on it.

The point of our paper is not only does this copying not hurt the fashion industry, it helps the fashion industry. People buy clothes to stay on trend. What is a trend but a design that is copied, right? We know trends because there are lots and lots of versions of a particular favorite design. Copying helps create trends, and copying helps kill trends. When the copying goes too far, the fashionistas jump off and find the next trend. Fashion depends on copying.

Cosslett: What is the issue with the Christian Louboutin red-soled shoes?

Sprigman: That's different. That's trademark. Louboutin is arguing that that red sole serves as a source identifier, so that when people see that red sole, they identify that as a Christian Louboutin. It's like the Nike "swoosh." But Yves St. Laurent—that's who's being sued here—is saying, "We used a red sole on a red shoe, and when we use a red sole on a red shoe, it's aesthetically functional. That is, it preserves the shoe's all-redness, and so we cannot be held liable for trademark infringement."

I think Yves St. Laurent is correct about this. Red soles on a red shoe are functional—they are necessary for the shoe to be red. And functional things are outside the domain of both trademark and copyright. Functional things are the domain of patent. I filed a brief to that effect with several other academics. Of course, by now you can't patent a red shoe sole because it's not novel in the way that patent requires.

Cosslett: That's great. I love the idea of academics writing about red-soled shoes.

Sprigman: Someone said to me once that my career as an academic has involved more things that people like and think are fun than most other people's careers. I spend my time thinking and writing about the fashion industry, and about cuisine, the stand-up comedy world, open-source software—which is actually really fascinating—financial innovations, and that kind of thing. All of the areas I study are areas where there's a lot of creativity, but for one reason or another, not a lot of intellectual property. How did that happen? And do these areas have lessons for industries like the music industry, where there's lots of IP, but it's not really doing them a whole heck of a lot of good?

Cosslett: Can you talk a little bit about stand-up comedy?

Sprigman: Copyright, at least at the theoretical level, covers jokes. But for a variety of reasons, it's actually very difficult to protect your joke against appropriation by a rival comic using IP law. One reason is copyright covers expression, but it doesn't cover ideas. So anyone can take the idea behind the funny joke and just express it a little bit differently, and escape copyright. So, what do comedians do? Well, my UVA colleague Dotan Oliar and I interviewed a lot of comedians, and we wrote a paper in which those comedians describe their own private IP systems. They have a system of norms that stand in for the law and they have a community project that detects and punishes joke stealers. This isn't legal punishment. It's group sanctions, private sanctions. It's the comedians' version of *Lord of the Flies*, although a lot less violent.

Cosslett: What's a comedic sanction?

Sprigman: Badmouthing. That's where it starts. A lot of people respond to badmouthing. If you're a comedian and you're working in the clubs, you've got to be around other comedians five nights a week. You don't want to be around a lot of people badmouthing you and giving you dirty looks. So that kind of social pressure keeps people honest. And then if it goes beyond that, you'll get group boycotts. You'll get refusals to appear on the same comedy bill as someone who steals jokes. And for comedians who are not huge stars who can call the shots, that can be a very painful sanction.

And then, very occasionally, you have comedians beating other comedians up. That's the last resort. The last resort can be someone gets punched in the mouth. That's not great, but it doesn't happen very often. Really, the norm system, without beating people up, keeps most comedians very honest. It provides enough protection against comedians taking their colleagues' jokes that comedians have a perfectly adequate incentive to invest in the creation of new material without copyright law playing any new role.

Cosslett: So if you have a peer group that can exert sufficient pressure, then the absence of law is not going to make a difference?

Sprigman: Let me give you another example of the relevance of community norms to inhibiting piracy. The music industry is going through a phase now where there's so much different music being produced and there's so much easy communication between bands and their fans that the market is changing in ways that make governance by norms more possible. It's disaggregating into smaller and smaller groups that are yet more and more connected. It looks like there will always be a few big stars. But because the cost of creating and marketing a record and the cost of communicating with your fans has fallen so enormously, there will probably be more of a music middle class where artists have an audience substantial enough to make a career. They're in communication with this audience.

It's precisely under these kinds of circumstances where norms can actually do some work. If there's a community built up around a musical group, you might get norms about copying having some effect. Take all the bands like the Grateful Dead that make up the jam band genre. Most of these bands deal with their fans in much the same way. They have studio albums that they copyright, but they allow fans to make live recordings of their shows and to share those freely. What you get is fans feeling that there's a set of norms that are reciprocal. The bands have given them access to the live shows. On the other hand, they reserve copyright on the studio recordings. Because there's reciprocity, the jam band community polices piracy for themselves. So you can imagine the music industry becoming more like the jam band genre and more like stand-up comedians. They would be more reliant on norms than on law.

Cosslett: What are the intellectual property issues specific to open source software?

Sprigman: Open source software doesn't depend on the IP system. Programmers who work on open source projects do so for a variety of reasons. But one thing these projects have in common is that everyone expects that they will not use a copyright on the software to deny access to others. Open source software code is distributed via a license that allows the user to freely copy, modify, and re-distribute the code. But only if the user agrees that any changes he makes will be available on the same basis. These licenses turn copyright on its head, encouraging copying and blocking ownership. And yet, there is great creativity in the open source world. Mozilla Firefox, the world's second largest browser with over 150 million users, is open source. So is the Linux operating system, which is running on about 25 % of all corporate servers. Over half of corporate servers run Apache, the open-source Web server software. And these are just a few of the many thousands of open-source projects.

Cosslett: Your students must love this

Sprigman: I teach copyright and trademark. I don't spend a huge amount of time talking about my research because, unfortunately, the amount of material I need to get through in a semester is so unbelievably huge that it's a struggle just to get them acquainted with the black-letter rules of copyright and trademark.

Cosslett: Maybe after class you should have coffee and get them thinking about the stuff that's probably much more relevant to their lives and is certainly more fun. Do you love teaching? Do you ever see yourself going back into private practice?

Sprigman: Being an academic is only partly about teaching. What I try to do is to advance knowledge. That's my job, right? My research is at the center of what I do. That said, I also care a lot about teaching. I want to be a good teacher. I want my students to benefit from law school as much as possible.

As a whole, my job is great. It's about the best job I could imagine. I have a tremendous amount of freedom to think about the things that interest me. It's a real privilege to be able to have control over my own life, over my own day-to-day. I can have a voice on some issues that matter to me. Getting into academia is really difficult—so, if you do it, typically it's because you really want it. I liked lawyering, but at the moment I can't imagine doing it again full-time.

Cosslett: What would you give by way of career advice to law students or practicing attorneys?

Sprigman: The biggest thing I learned really doesn't have anything to do with getting into teaching. It just has to do with your attitude about your career. All the smart people I knew who did really well in school, and then did really well in college, and then did really well in law school, they were all alike in a way. And how where they alike? Well, you do well in school by doing what you're told. But, that is not how you do well in life.

The biggest difficulty for students when they actually begin to work as a lawyer or really work as anything is transitioning from doing what they're told, which is how to excel in school, to doing what they want, which is how to excel in life and at a career. That involves learning how to tell people, "No, I don't want that.

I want this." It's easier to do if you have some clear idea of what you want. And part of understanding what you want is having a questing disposition. Not just taking what comes along, but being open to things and reaching out for things that you think might be interesting, and then being hardheaded. Asking yourself, "Did I enjoy this?" Really paying some attention to what it is you like and what you don't like, and acting on it.

What leads to success between the ages of five and twenty-five for people who go to law school? You have assignments, you're organized, you do the assignments the best you can. That leads to success. In school, you never say to the professor, "I don't want that assignment. I want some different assignment." But when you get to a law firm, it's very important to be able to say to your employer: "I don't like that assignment. I want a different assignment. I just spent a month in a windowless conference room doing a document review. I don't want to do another one. In fact, I'm not going to do another one for the next six months. I'm going to do something else."

Cosslett: That takes a very bold associate to do that

Sprigman: Well, then nut up. Seriously, because if you don't do that, you are going to get carried along with the tide. And getting carried along with the tide might cough you up on a really nice place, or it might cough you up on the rocks.

Cosslett: Lawyers who have identified success with acceptance by a series of institutions may have difficulty in thinking outside the box when it comes to careers.

Sprigman: I went to public school through high school—there were very good public schools in Smithtown, Long Island, where I grew up. I went to Penn for undergraduate and I really loved it, but I don't have a Penn sticker on my car. I don't identify with institutions in that way. Most of my family were working-class immigrants. Not my parents, but my grandparents' generation.

I have this one memory that I think is so illustrative of why I am the way I am. I was in law school and I had gotten this clerkship on the Ninth Circuit, and I was extremely excited. I was at a family gathering in New York, and my Uncle Mike was there. You have to understand my Uncle Mike was a World War II veteran. He's passed away now, but he was the salt of the earth. The loveliest, most genuine guy. And he said, "So, have you decided what you're doing after law school yet?"

And I said, "Yeah, it's really great. I've got this federal clerkship. I'll go to Los Angeles and I'll work for this federal judge for a year. I'm really excited about it."

And he was puzzled by this—I don't think he understood why I'd want to take a job that lasted only a year. I think he thought I was desperate. He put his arm around me and he said, "Don't worry. You'll get a job."

What I was doing, in his mind, was making the best of a bad situation—trying to be excited about some non-job. And I thought, "I love my Uncle Mike, and if that's what he thinks about it, then it's not the end-all and be-all of my life to jump through these hoops. What he wants for me is for me to have a good job so I can raise a family and so that I can pay the bills. That's what he wants for me—and frankly, what I want for me. And all this other stuff: yeah, it is great, but it's not me."

I would add that there are a couple of traps that people fall into, and these are things that limit people's ability to follow their instincts and to take chances that make for an exciting, fulfilling career. They are probably pretty obvious. One is money. I didn't come from a lot of money and I like money. But I didn't like it enough that I was going to make important career decisions based primarily on money. I make a lot less now than I would have made had I stayed at a law firm, but that doesn't really matter too much to me. I make a perfectly adequate living. I never wanted expensive things enough to suffer for them. So that's one very significant and very basic thing.

And then the other thing is authority. Young lawyers often tend to take instructions. My judge, Judge Reinhardt, said something to me when I was leaving chambers. He said, "These people in law firms are not your family. There might be people at the law firm who tell you that the firm is a family, and you're part of it. They're not your family. You're in business with them. And they have their own agenda, which may not coincide with yours. You've got to be really mindful of what they want you to do and whether doing it produces some long-term gain for you or whether it's just wasted time."

And I remember thinking, "That's absolutely right." I always had this voice in the back of my head. It was Stephen Reinhardt's voice saying to me, "Chart your own path." And this was someone I respected enormously, and he'd done exactly that with his life. It struck me that here was a guy who had been in a law firm, who'd had his own law firm, and who was a federal judge. He had been around the block, and I thought, "He's telling me this for a reason." He called me in specially to tell me this and it wasn't as though he was sending me out in the world saying, "Go get them, Tiger." It was more like, "Watch out."

Cosslett: Well, it sounds like he gave you some really good advice and you were smart enough to listen.

CHAPTER 10

Wayne Alexander

Partner

Alexander, Lawrence, Frumes & Labowitz, LLP

You have written a bestselling book. Now imagine sitting at your desk working on the sequel, Lawyers at Play. Your phone rings. It is a big Hollywood producer saying they want to option Lawyers at Work for a movie or TV series. Your next call is to **Wayne Alexander.**

As a senior entertainment lawyer in Los Angeles, Alexander has significant experience in publishing, television, motion pictures, and related industries. He can explain everything you need to know about how the entertainment business operates. This might feel like a fall down a rabbit hole. Nothing is quite straightforward: books are not books—they are brands, video games and theme park attractions; contracts are reinvented at each new negotiation; directors are directors—except when they are producers; and, if you are lucky, you might see a man in a tie enjoying his life.

Alexander has practiced in the entertainment industry since the 1970s and is a founding partner of Alexander, Lawrence, Frumes & Labowitz, LLP. He has significant experience with the development, financing, production, and distribution of independent and studio films, and television movies and series. Clients include writers such as Charles Frazier and James Ellroy, directors such as Bill Condon and Stuart Gordon, producers, visual effects supervisors, executives, and production/distribution companies.

Alexander graduated Phi Beta Kappa with a BA in psychology from the University of California, Berkeley, and earned his JD from Yale Law School. He is a member of the California State University Entertainment Industry Advisory Council and plays guitar in a classic rock band called the Greyhounds.

Chapter 10 | Wayne Alexander: Entertainment

Clare Cosslett: Was your family involved in the entertainment industry?

Wayne Alexander: I didn't have even a remote contact with the entertainment industry growing up. I was born in East Texas, and my father was an aerospace engineer. He was one of the early rocket scientists working on the civilian side. We went from government contract to government contract when I was a kid. We moved from Texas to California, to Utah, to Colorado, and then back to California when my dad got a job at Jet Propulsion Labs. I went to junior high school and high school in La Crescenta.

Being the child of a rocket engineer means you have a very suburban life. La Crescenta was a small town and there was nothing to do there except go to the bowling alley. I was in a rock band. We would play a fair amount at high school and college dances and we played on and off during college at dances and clubs. I'm still in bands now.

Cosslett: The band you are with now is called the Greyhounds?

Alexander: It's the Greyhounds because we're all old. We tend to play boomer-type rock stuff from the sixties and seventies mostly.

Cosslett: You went to Berkeley for undergrad?

Alexander: I started at Occidental College right after high school and was there for two years. It was a really small school and it all got very claustrophobic, so I tested Berkeley out in summer school after sophomore year. It was nowhere near as small and personal as Occidental, and as far as education, a big school like that is like going to the movies. You'd go into class with three and four hundred people. But Berkeley was beautiful and an interesting place to be.

Cosslett: Then you went on to Yale Law School?

Alexander: When I got out of Berkeley, I had no real career plans. I wasn't exactly a hippie, but I hadn't ever really thought about what I wanted to do after college. At one point, I thought I would be in a band but it didn't really seem like a valid career path, so I just always kept it as a hobby. I thought, "Well, now what do I want to do?" So I just took a temporary job working for Xerox.

In those days, they would hire people as management trainees and pay you enough to live on. I wasn't really thinking about law school, but one of my friends bet me $200 he'd beat me on the LSAT. There was not a lot of planning in my early life. I did really well. I always had good grades, so I thought, "Well, okay, I guess I should be applying to law school."

People nowadays will often decide they want to go to law school, and if they don't have an aptitude for law school admission tests, they take practice tests and get coached. People that I knew in those days were using these tests more as an aptitude test. If you scored well, you thought, "Huh, that's a clue. Maybe I'd be good at this sort of thing." I applied to a handful of schools, and I thought, "If I get into Harvard or Yale, I'll go there"—because otherwise I wanted to go to Berkeley.

Well, I didn't get into Berkeley, which shocked me. I had a 3.9 grade-point average. So I went over and asked them why, and they explained that they wanted to be a national school and only took a limited number of people from California and an even more limited number—only about twenty-five—from Berkeley. So why didn't I make the cut? Test scores?—passed that one. Recommendations?—passed that one. Thought of coming here before last week?—[Buzzer Sound]

Cosslett: Didn't take the LSAT just to win a bet?—[Buzzer Sound]

Alexander: I clearly hadn't thought about it because people who had thought of it would have gone over to the law school, maybe as a sophomore, and said, "What do you like to see?" They might have taken constitutional law, and I hadn't done any of that. I was technically a psychology major—a classical liberal arts guy. I clearly had not thought of law school. So then, shockingly, I didn't get into Harvard, and then I didn't get into Yale. Well, actually, I was admitted to Yale but I didn't know.

Cosslett: They forgot to tell you?

Alexander: They didn't notify people who were on the waitlist until very late in the summer, and by then I had moved to UC Davis for law school. The post office didn't forward the letter from Yale. So I went to Davis for a year, and it just happened that the people I was sitting next to took it very, very seriously. I had been a good student, but I'd never been as focused as some of these people were. The people sitting to the left and right of me in the first class I was in were the people who were going to run the *Law Review* and go on to be famous lawyers. I would be at school for my first class in the morning around eight and I would stay in school until eleven at night because the people I was around did that. There were people who did it another way, but I didn't know that.

Cosslett: So your future would have been different had you had a different seating assignment?

Alexander: Probably, yes. There was a professor named Carol Bruch who taught our contracts class, and she had been the first female clerk for Justice William O. Douglas. At one point, she said, "You're good at this. You should consider teaching." I said maybe I would, because when you don't have a career aspiration and law school seems interesting, you think, "Hey, maybe I'll teach."

She said, "Well, if you're thinking of doing that, you can't get there from here. You have to work for the Supreme Court. You need a place with an old boys' club. If you're thinking about teaching, go to Yale." Carol had graduated from Boalt, which did have Supreme Court connections. Davis didn't, at that time.

So, as a lark, I applied to Yale. I loved UC Davis. I was friends with professors whose classes I hadn't even taken. It's a liberal arts colony in a science school, so law students looked to their classmates for social and intellectual companionship more than at some other places. Yale called me in August and said, "You're in. By the way, you were in before."

Cosslett: I can't even believe this.

Alexander: I thought, "Well, I've never been to the East Coast other than just to visit." So I went. I was a little disoriented at first. I think everybody who goes into a school like that has somewhat of an inferiority complex: "Oh, they're all way smarter than me."

But the reality was that there were only a handful of students that seemed blazingly more intelligent than all the rest of us. You didn't have a bottom in the class. In almost every other school I'd been in, there were at least a modest amount of people who weren't getting it, and maybe a handful who got everything, but they didn't seem to blaze with the light of intelligence. Yale had only one or two people in our class of one hundred fifty who weren't just right with it all the time.

After the first year, I started to think about teaching. At that time, if you wanted to teach law, you took at job at a commercial law firm over the summers and then after law school you would try to get to the Supreme Court as a clerk. After the clerkship, you would work at a nationally recognized firm for a few years and then try to write a *Law Review* article or do something to get noticed. Then you go be a low-level law professor in a place that you don't want to live in, like Nebraska. You try and excel there and try to get one step closer to the place you would be willing to live, like Houston or Atlanta. It's probably the third move where you get to live in a city that you would want to be in or a school you like, or both.

Cosslett: What was your experience at a commercial law firm?

Alexander: I had never had any exposure to a commercial law firm before the summer following my second year. My summer job after my first year at Davis was the kind of thing you do when you think you might want to teach. I was a research assistant for a professor and I did two kinds of research projects. One was running around visiting the police chiefs of various police departments in California to see how they handle stolen bicycles. I then gave them suggestions on how to improve their recordkeeping. And then I helped to write a model victim-compensation law for California. It was research. When I thought about jobs for my second summer, I thought, "Well, I like San Francisco and I like Boston," and I started interviewing with firms there. I just hated it.

Cosslett: What did you hate about it?

Alexander: Boston just scared me. They did things like municipal bonds. Because I wasn't invested in this and didn't want to work for them, I would say, "How can you stand this? This work sounds horribly boring." Most of them had very nice lives, but I just couldn't see myself doing that work.

In San Francisco, I interviewed with a guy doing admiralty and that didn't interest me, and then with someone else who did real estate development and somehow that seemed horrible. I remember one guy who lived in Marin County who had a sailboat. He was in the estates department of a law firm. He said he liked the work because there wasn't any pressure. Most of the clients were dead.

Wall Street stuff was just confusing. I couldn't figure out what they were doing and it didn't seem like something I wanted to do. Even if I had known how much more money they made than the rest of us, it wouldn't have made a difference. I've never been all that motivated by doing things that bore me, even if it makes you the most money.

After a few of the interviews, I met with the dean at Yale responsible for job placements. His name was Henry Thomas. Yale was very much like a family. It's small. They really care about you. Thomas asked, "Hey, how's the interviewing going?"

I said, "I don't think I want to be a lawyer." I told him some of these stories.

He said, "I don't think you know who you are."

I said, "Well, duh. I wouldn't be in law school if I knew who I was."

He told me that he had a theory about me. He said that I was a Western kid and, unlike East Coast kids who often knew what they wanted to do because it was what their family had done, I needed to go someplace that was a boomtown where they'd let younger people do more. After ten minutes in his office, he said, "I have an idea. If I set up some interviews for you, will you promise you'll go?"

I said, "Absolutely. I'm not doing well at this on my own."

So he set me up to meet with Arthur Greenberg, the head of Greenberg & Glusker. He said, "Go see that guy."

And I said, "Oh my God. It's in Los Angeles. It's the devil's place"—because I'd been in Berkeley and we all thought LA was a bad place.

He said, "You said you'd go." It was an on-campus interview and I realized I didn't have my suit at school for the interview. I went anyway, wearing jeans. I walked into the interview room and there's Arthur. Now, remember, I'd had very limited exposure to people who wore ties. And I'd certainly never met one who enjoyed his life.

Cosslett: A man in a tie who enjoyed his life?

Alexander: I had not been around lawyers who liked what they were doing. Arthur was different. He said, "I notice you're not wearing a suit."

I said, "Oh gee, I hadn't planned on having this interview today, so I hadn't brought my suit."

And he said, "Don't tell me that. Tell me, 'If I get a job in your place and there's a dress code, fine, I'll deal with that. But it seems kind of stupid to wear a suit for law school interviews. You know what we actually dress like here. It's cold.'"

And we talked, and he asked why I was interested in his firm, and I told him that I wasn't. I said, "Henry Thomas made me come in, he thought your firm might be a good choice for me." Arthur thought that was interesting, and fun.

Arthur invited me to visit the firm in Los Angeles. When I went in for the interview, they had a system where they'd assign you to what they called a "shepherd"—a lawyer who was in charge of you for the day. You would meet several lawyers in the morning and then they'd take you to lunch.

I had interviews in the morning, and then they took me to the Playboy Club, got me legless drunk, stole my glasses and, after lunch, had me interview with a partner wearing a full-head chimpanzee mask. Being drunk, I couldn't figure out what to do, so I didn't do anything. I said, "Hello, my name is Wayne. What kind of work do you do?"

And we had a normal interview. After we had spoken for a while, he looked at me and said, "Goddammit, you could play poker with Arabs. You didn't even blink!" I don't remember too much about the rest of the afternoon, but here was a group of lawyers who were really smart, who liked each other, and who liked the work they did. I thought, "Wow." So I went there for the summer job, and it was interesting.

Cosslett: How big a firm was it at the time?

Alexander: Twenty-five lawyers. There were three pieces to their practice. They had litigation, including some appellate work. They also represented some major real estate developers, which bored me, but I did some of the work. And then they had some entertainment industry work, which I had never been exposed to. I didn't see much of it in the summer because I was assigned litigation-type research projects.

Cosslett: When you graduated, you said, "This is where I want to go."

Alexander: I loved the place. The real estate guys liked me, and I did some shopping center finance work and that was interesting, but I was really interested in the film and TV work they did. Arthur Greenberg represented Bud Yorkin and Norman Lear. Yorkin and Lear had a company called Tandem Productions, which made *All in the Family* and the Redd Foxx show, *Sanford and Son*. They also had a program called *What's Happening?* I became the production lawyer for a couple of the TV series. I did the weekly contracts for the new writers, and if they had guest stars, I wrote their contracts. This kind of work just seemed to be more fun than what the real estate guys were doing.

The firm took on a big research project in which they represented the Edgar Rice Burroughs estate with regard to ownership of the rights to about fifty-one Tarzan movies. The estate wanted to figure out what rights they owned because they wanted to make a movie deal. So I was reading movie contracts from all different eras and it was fascinating. No one in the movie business has ever had the same clout as Edgar Rice Burroughs. The way many of his deals worked was that he'd give the producer—Saul Lesser for a number of movies—a seven-year license to make and release a movie. At the end of the seven years, Burroughs owned the movie, the copyright, the whole thing. That never happens now.

Not even John Grisham owns the movies they make out of his books. But Burroughs owned the movies. So when television came along needing content, he could license the movies. It wasn't the studios—he did it.

I was very happy at the firm, but about eighteen months after I started, I got a call from David Altschul. He had been a year or so ahead of me in law school and later went on to become one of the presidents of Warner Records. At this point, he was at a law firm called Hardee Barovick Konecky & Braun. The firm had a New York rock-and-roll presence, and they had opened a branch office in California. David Braun, who was a major record lawyer, was the head. He represented George Harrison, Bob Dylan, Neil Diamond, and The Beach Boys. There were a couple of other major record lawyers there as well: Mike Rosenfeld, who represented Keith Moon from The Who, and all of the Irving Azoff bands like Boz Scaggs, Steely Dan, and the Eagles. There was also a lawyer named Al Leonard who represented both Casablanca Records and Donna Summer and Tom Petty.

Cosslett: Why were they recruiting you?

Alexander: They needed a film and TV lawyer to work on the West Coast. Ron Konecky had a client, Smith-Hemion, that was a company that produced a number of variety specials. If you wanted to make a singing and dancing special starring someone like Shirley MacLaine or Ben Vereen, Smith-Hemion would be the one to produce it. I would work on their network deals, deals with the talent, etc.

Cosslett: Was it hard to move from Greenberg after such a short time?

Alexander: The Greenberg people were nice about it. I guess Henry Thomas was right about me: as a Westerner, I was looking for a boomtown where they'd let younger people do more. I know for some of my friends who went into Wall Street firms, it might take six or seven years before they got to lead on anything they were doing. While I loved Greenberg, Hardee Barovick was just too good an opportunity to turn down.

I remember when I went over to have lunch with the guys at Hardee Barovick, I saw Bob Dylan and Tom Petty sitting in one of the conference rooms—I think they were playing poker, waiting for a meeting with one of the lawyers. I just thought, "Oh God, I have to come here."

Unfortunately, it turned out to be something of an unstable environment because record lawyers didn't seem to like each other as much as film lawyers did. They were always having wars over who should get credit for signing which client, and if one of them signed a client, another would come in and say, "You've got to accept the fact that the only reason you could sign, whoever it was, is that I'm here and they know I'll fix what you can't." This didn't affect me too much because I was a film guy and they were nice to me because I had a service that they needed for their clients. They didn't feel the need to belittle me in front of their clients. The junior record lawyers were not treated as well.

Cosslett: That's unfortunate.

Alexander: The film and TV bar was moderately small in those days, and I knew a lot of the people over at Pollock, Bloom & Dekom and I liked them a lot. Tom Pollock called and said they needed somebody. Tom, at that time, was one of the top two or three movie lawyers practicing. He was a really nice guy and he only owned one suit, which I thought was good. He had a tux because he had a lot of premieres and events to go to.

Cosslett: You appear to have an issue with suits and ties. Didn't you wear a suit to work?

Alexander: You had to wear a suit when you were in a meeting or if it bothered people that you weren't wearing a suit, but you could usually wear jeans. Clients didn't care that lawyers didn't wear suits. This was a talent firm—it wasn't so much a company firm, although we did some company business. The clients tended to be actors and writers and directors, and a lot of them were hippie filmmakers like George Lucas and David Lynch and Ivan Reitman.

Cosslett: It's such a different culture than the East Coast.

Alexander: Well, it's tightened up a little since then. I loved Pollock, Bloom & Dekom, but I started worrying about having a future. Tom Pollock was so famous that even my own clients would sometimes ask that he make the calls to the studio heads instead of me, and that worried me. And sometimes if you asked my clients who their lawyer was, they'd say Tom.

I did service work for some of his big clients. For example, I did all of Sissy Spacek's acting deals at the point where she was one of the first women to make a million dollars for *Coal Miner's Daughter*, *The Missing*, and *The River*. She was a really big deal. I worked on Ivan Reitman's deals for *Ghostbusters*. I also had a handful of my own clients. Some of them were a big deal, some weren't. Peter Bogdanovich was a big deal at the time. But we're not together anymore.

Cosslett: What was the nature of the work you did for Peter Bogdanovich?

Alexander: I made his directing deals. I started working with him back at Hardee Barovick. I was introduced to him by a young hustler producer type who was working as his protégé. When I met Peter, he said, "I don't like my current lawyer."

I said, "Look, if you go to one of the big guys, they'll just give you somebody like me anyway."

He said, "That's true. Okay, I'll go with you, but I have to be clear that if I need someone big, you've got them."

I introduced him to David Braun, who was then at Hardee Barovick, and he liked David, and then we had him talk to the other name partners in New York, I think Dick Barovick or Ron Konecky, both of whom had done film/TV work. He said, "Okay, that will work."

Cosslett: So you were selling yourself, but you were also selling the law firm as a full-service provider for this client?

Alexander: Yes, in case he needed someone who had clout. When I moved over to Pollock, Bloom & Dekom, Peter knew Tom and was fine with that. I did ninety-nine percent of whatever there was to do for Peter, but when we needed a studio head call, and he said, "I want Tom to do it," Tom would call in with me.

Cosslett: The client thought that Tom would negotiate a bigger fee for him because he was a heavy hitter?

Alexander: No, it's more a question of whether you are someone the studio talks to a lot. If a studio lawyer talks to a lawyer he knows, that lawyer is going to get things he wouldn't get if he were someone they didn't know. Part of the process is knowing what you can get and what you can't, because overreaching will get you zero. You have to know what range you can push into.

I had a lot of fun working at Pollock Bloom. Tom gave me Don Simpson, who was president of Paramount, and then moved over to start the company that became Simpson-Bruckheimer Productions and made movies like *Flashdance* and *Beverly Hills Cop*. Don was great and I did very high-level work for him, like the deal between his company and Paramount.

While the work was great, I started to worry that we didn't make as much money as some other law firms. Tom would work for love, whereas our competitors were much more money-oriented. It's not that the firm didn't do well, but they did nowhere near as well as some other firms at the time.

Tom loved the movie business and would do things that weren't only motivated by, "I'm going to make the maximum amount of money." Now, he clearly had some major clients. He had George Lucas, who certainly made a lot of money, and he had Dino Di Laurentis, and he had some very, very high-paying clients, but that wasn't why he was a lawyer. He just loved the creative process and the people.

I left there in '84 to go to Manatt, Phelps & Phillips, not because Manatt seemed all that wonderful a fit for my practice at the time, but it was not under Tom's shadow. I figured I needed to start building up my own practice. Enough business moved with me that it was okay.

Cosslett: When you made the move, was it was the same conversation with your clients that you had with Bogdanovich: "You get me, plus you get the support services"?

Alexander: They didn't care. I'd been a lawyer for about eight years. There was not too much that I needed help with, at least in the entertainment field. If a TV series had their financing go bankrupt during production, I would need help with

Chapter 10 | Wayne Alexander: Entertainment

that, but as far as deals in the film and TV industry, I knew about as much as a lawyer was going to know.

Cosslett: Moving as a partner in New York generally requires a specific expertise or a significant book of portable business.

Alexander: You didn't need a million dollars, but if you were trying to move in as a partner somewhere, you either needed to have a particular skill set that the firm needed or you needed to have clients. In the case of entertainment lawyers, you generally have clients, and I had enough. I was not the highest business-getter by any means at Manatt, but I was holding my own. And I wasn't working for someone else, which I enjoyed. My clients, however, generally weren't the kind of people who were used to being at a firm like Manatt. They were there for me as opposed to being there because of the firm.

Cosslett: The reason being that the firm had lawyers wearing suits and ties?

Alexander: It was not the atmosphere my clients were used to, although I liked many of the lawyers. While there was a disconnect with my clients, there was a bigger contrast with the rock-and-roll crowd. The firm had a very big musical practice. Peter Paterno, for example, represented Guns N' Roses. It was always fun to see the Guns N' Roses guys sitting in the tenth-floor lobby. The tenth floor had the music lawyers, the film lawyers, and some of the high-level bank lawyers. So you'd see clients there for bank meetings sitting across from Axl Rose. And they'd be looking at each other, and they'd each be thinking, "Who the heck is this guy on the other side of the couch?"

Manatt is a very good firm, but it became clear that their specialties weren't specialized in the direction that I needed them to be. In my present firm, we only do work in the entertainment industry—so when a client needs a litigator, I'll help them find someone who's specialized in the field that they need and I don't have the pressure to feed the firm's litigation practice.

Cosslett: So, rather than looking for another firm, you decided to go on your own?

Alexander: I just stumbled into a situation. I joined up with Mark Halloran and Jay Shanker, and we started our firm and fumbled our way along. You worry at first. "Are we going to bring in enough to survive?" And we did. No one was getting really rich at first, but we stayed open.

We were originally three partners and there have been occasional personnel changes. The firm was bigger at one point when there was more business from independent producers, but as the financing of television and film has evolved over the last twenty years or so, there are less and less standalone indie production companies that can do things like make TV movies or TV series. My former partner, Rob Nau, for example, represented about half of the Aaron Spelling work, and there were several TV series he worked on. Spelling was bought by Paramount and then disappeared, for example.

Cosslett: How many big names are there at the level of Paramount in the film and TV industry now?

Alexander: There are six studios. There's Columbia, which is Sony, and then Paramount. Universal Pictures is big. Warner is big, and Disney. DreamWorks is a little smaller. MGM is not big anymore. That's about it. They've absorbed what used to be independent production, and it doesn't work as well.

Take for instance the TV movie: there aren't as many now, but that was something that used to work really well in independent production. Bob Papazian and Jim Hirsch had a company in the eighties and nineties that made a lot of TV movies—maybe fifty or so. So the economics were this: they'd make a movie for X amount of money. The networks would pay them a license fee. It didn't cover quite all of it, but most of it, and then they could sell the distribution rights for the rest of it, the parts the network didn't take, to a syndication company and come away with a fair amount of money.

But when the TV industry changed, the financial interest rule changed and the networks were now allowed to own pieces of the shows. Beforehand, the financial interest rule didn't allow the networks to own profit interests in outside productions. So that made a big difference, and it allowed indie companies like Aaron Spelling's to build up a catalog.

Cosslett: If you don't have relationships with these major studios, is it hard to maintain a practice?

Alexander: It depends what you do. I do more work with studios than some of my partners. They do more independent production. I also do some independent production, and I go through phases where, if my clients are doing it, I do a lot.

One type of work we have done in this area is piecing together a financing package for an independent movie that has a coproduction element with another country, and bank loans against distribution contracts, and deals with investors in a couple of different countries. There is some of that, but generally there's less independent production of that kind than there used to be. Part of it is just the audience. If you had a movie like *Sideways* come out now, it probably wouldn't be the hit it was when it came out.

Cosslett: Why is that?

Alexander: People don't go to small movies as much as they used to. If you're a studio, now you'll make three or four tentpole movies that cost a couple of hundred million dollars. A tentpole movie is something like *Avengers, Battleship, Cowboys & Aliens*—the really big ones. James Bond movies, things like that. They'll make three or four of those, and they'll make two or three things trying to hit a niche audience like the romantic comedies, for instance, and they're all trying to do things that will turn out to be something like *The Hangover*.

But if you're trying to get a movie made like *All the Presidents' Men* now, it would be awfully hard. Adult drama about serious subjects, it's hard. There's just less of it. The audiences don't go as much. And the business done by foreign movies in the States is usually much smaller now than it was, so some of the film business that was more prominent a while ago is less prominent now. These movies are still around, though—look at *The Girl with the Dragon Tattoo*. The first one did about $10 million at the US box office here, but then the remake that David Fincher made did a lot more.

The studios have become much more about marketing and branding. They look to exploit franchises like Marvel Comics or Batman or Superman. If they can come up with another one of those, they'll do that over making something original.

Cosslett: Let's talk about your practice specifically. I know you do a lot of work with authors. Can you describe what that work involves?

Alexander: I do more work with authors than most other West Coast–based lawyers. The first really big deal I did was as Vince Bugliosi's lawyer. He wrote a book called *And the Sea Will Tell*, which became a miniseries, and he got a whole lot of money for that. It was actually both a good book and a good miniseries. I like books. I read a lot. I get along with literary agents. My clients who are writers have either come to me directly or through their agents. There are two kinds of book agents. One kind usually deals with the publishers, and the other takes books and sells them to movies and television. I have a handful of agents in both categories that I do a fair amount of work with, and we send each other business back and forth.

Cosslett: When an author or an agent comes to you wanting to sell a book, what do you do?

Alexander: While I usually don't help to find the buyer, I help to make the deal once a buyer is found. More of my work is in making film and TV deals from books than it is in dealing with the publishers, although we do get involved in publishing contracts as well. It depends when I got the client and how. If, for example, a book agent brings me in when they're also bringing in a film-to-TV agent, the part I'm working on specifically will be the film and TV sales, although I may look over their shoulders a little bit as they deal with the publishers. I'll consult with the agents, and we'll all trade notes about what to go for. It varies about who talks to whom, but I'll be involved in the early negotiations, and then when it comes to the contract drafting process, I'll have the heavier load and those can go on for months, depending on what you're dealing with.

One of the main gratifications I find in being an entertainment lawyer is that I am able to help someone whose stories and writings or work I admire get their stuff done. A real estate lawyer might look back and think, "Okay, that building is there because I was part of it, and there's a mark on the world even though nobody knows I did it." I can look back over TV series or movies or books, and it feels good even though I didn't write them or direct them. It's nice to know you helped those things happen.

Cosslett: Why does negotiating the contract take such a long time?

Alexander: If you close a deal for, let's say, a movie based on a book, you've negotiated maybe twenty or twenty-five different things, and some of them will be in the contract when you get the first round, and some won't. This is where experience matters. You need reference points to know, "What are they not giving me that I could get?" And if you ask for the wrong things, you can't get them, but if you ask for the right things, you can. But they rarely will give you a contract that has everything you can get. They'll start from scratch. And you have to say, "Wait, wait. In this area, you've given me this stock clause. I want this one." And you go back and forth—some places will make you go through six or seven rounds, which can take months.

Cosslett: They don't ever show their hand? They make you ask for everything?

Alexander: Well, it depends. Once in a while, you'll say, "Look, we just did that deal with you last month for this book over here. How about using that contract as a model?" Sometimes you can get them to do that. It depends. And various studios will do it different ways. Some always play the game very hard, where they start with, "We assume you're very naïve. We're giving you a first draft, and hope you don't know anything."

There are some that start from that point every time, and others that will give you a partially negotiated contract. Some play the game harder than others, and even when you have a fairly friendly place, it's usually two or three rounds of negotiation at least. They send out a contract, you send them notes back, you have meetings about it, and you do it again. It's usually takes several rounds to get a signable agreement in a friendly place. It can be five, six, seven rounds at places that play harder.

Also, you'll have certain things that you know from long experience are just the way things are done. But then a studio will get a new legal department or a new business affairs policy and say, "Well, we're not going to do that anymore." If you have enough clout and enough other options, you might get it anyway, but if you don't, you won't. Also, there will be sticking points where the process can take a long time.

There are some studios and networks at which the legal and business affairs philosophy is that they will dig in on certain things and you can't get it from them, and you try and get these points narrowed down to a small list and eventually go over their heads to the creative people. That's the way they have institutionalized the process and how they want it to happen.

Cosslett: So it is the creative people who determine the terms of the agreement?

Alexander: They will come down and say, "We really do have to give them all of this." The process becomes somewhat scripted. There might be ten things that you need to get for your client, but you can only get three of them because you can't get the creative people to have that deep an attention span. Ultimately, on some of these points, it is clear that the endgame of the studio is to give the artist or the writer less, so you really have to have the stamina to just hold out to get what you want for your client.

The process is probably about the same for film and TV writers. If you're negotiating a deal to be a staff writer or a producer on a TV series, that process is about the same. I'll work with the agents in kicking ideas back and forth about what to go ask for and who should do the asking. Sometimes I make the call to the studio. Sometimes the agents will. Sometimes it's joint. And when it gets real detailed, it's kicked over to the lawyers.

Cosslett: Do book authors have more credibility in Hollywood than other writers because they've actually produced a book?

Alexander: Sometimes. If you can demonstrate that the book has become a brand—the word "brand" is used a lot—and it has a large audience who bought it, and it has a picture on the cover that people identify with, and it's got a preassembled demographic that they can look at and recognize, "Oh, girls from this age to this age buy this book."

Cosslett: So it's the bookness of it and the brandness of it that makes it attractive. Now, what about representing directors?

Alexander: To some degree, it's the same process, although it depends on what the directors are working on. Sometimes, you will have a straightforward situation where a director will be making a deal with a studio to direct a movie, and this is just employment negotiation where you talk about credit and money and back end, and whether your client gets final cut or not, and whether he gets a trailer. And then there are other situations where they are trying to organize and invent movies: "Let's go option this book"—and then it is like representing an independent producer, where they're looking around for independent financing and those sorts of things.

Cosslett: I never knew what producing was.

Alexander: Producing can be a lot of things. But, in the classic sense, producers identify a story and decide to option it, or convince the studio to option it for them. Or they find a writer who's written something they think would work, or they have an idea, or they hear an idea, and they say, "Let's either get you hired by the studio to write that script or let me find money to have it written."

You have to work from a script, and once you have that, it's, "Okay, who can we get to direct and act?" And then you have to get within a studio and assemble a potential group of people: "Gee, let's think about getting this director and that actor, and working with this script based on this novel."

Cosslett: They're putting together the whole production?

Alexander: Yes. "Can we get you to Universal here? Will you take domestic rights if we get someone to go get foreign sales?" But producers organize movies and they don't get paid until movies happen, usually. They're spending money. They're optioning things. They're hiring writers or convincing others to. They're making alliances.

Screenwriters either write on spec or are paid because someone has hired them to write. Directors, if they're sticking to just the directing thing, get paid for directing. Producers get producing fees out of movies, but only when they get made. To be a producer, you have to be wealthy or somehow be able to survive for many years until you get stuff done. Things don't happen quickly.

Cosslett: Another practice area in which you have expertise is special effects.

Alexander: There are two aspects. One is representing the companies. A company can have a contract for just certain scenes or certain kinds of work on a movie or TV series, or they can have a contract to do the whole thing. It's usually one of those two things. As lawyer for the company, your job is making sure the work is defined clearly enough: Who insures what? Is it a flat fee? Is it cost-plus-materials? When do they get extra money? What if the production company wants more changes than you're budgeted for?

And it's pretty easy when everybody knows how it works. But it can be pretty difficult and it leads into a lot of problems when, say, an effects company is working on something and the people that they're delivering their stuff to don't really know how to ask for what they want—they say, "Well, that isn't it." And then there's a whole discussion about who has to pay for what.

The other visual effects work is individual effects supervisors. Studio movies and big indie movies that are going to have a lot of visual effects may hire a person in charge of visual effects to help the director figure out how to accomplish the visual effects he wants. It's a very big job. They have to stand next to the director while they shoot, to make sure they're shooting in a way that leaves room for the effects to happen. So it's a very-long-hours job because they have to be with the director all day and then several hours before or after in order to deal with the effects suppliers to make sure they're getting what they want.

I have a handful of clients in this area. They're either freelance supervisors, who are hired by a studio or production company for a single picture, or people who work at big effects houses, which may be Sony Image Works or Industrial Light & Magic. For the company supervisors, I'll negotiate their executive contracts:

X number of years? What is the salary? What is the bonus component? How does their credit work? What is their insurance? ILM[1] has between six and ten big effects supervisors who do much the same work on individual pictures as freelance supervisors would, but their contracts are with their employer.

Cosslett: Clearly, everything revolves around contract negotiation and in order to successfully negotiate terms, you really have to know how the world there operates.

Alexander: I've done this a long time, and it's the one thing that seems to matter. I know how most things work in areas I practice in, and it helps. If you don't know how the business is done, it's hard to know what you should be concerned with or asking for. Experience is basically either having screwed up or having seen somebody else screw up over and over. "Oh, when this happens, that happens. So don't do that."

Cosslett: It pays to have a depth of experience.

Alexander: It can. I'm one of those people who tend not to take things on that I haven't done, so I believe I can do a really good job. I know there are lawyers who think, "I can do anything." Well, maybe I could, but I don't like to. I think for me to be valuable to my clients, I should work on things where I know what I'm doing.

Cosslett: What sort of work do you do for agents and managers?

Alexander: I have a handful of clients who are agents or managers in smaller companies, which don't have in-house legal staffs, and I act as the deal consultant for them. They'll call up and say, "Hey, we're doing this. What do you think about this?" Or, "Have you done business with Lionsgate Television? Can we get this?" Or, "This issue has come up. What do we do?" I'm their in-house business affairs consultant.

Cosslett: What sort of work do you do for producers?

Alexander: I do less of this sort of work now than I used to, but at one time, certain production companies were using us in lieu of in-house lawyers and business affairs people. They'd have us hire the writers. They'd have us do the negotiations for optioning a book. They have us do change-of-title clearance. Actually, we just worked on a change-of-title issue that came up in connection with the sale of rights in a novel. The situation was this: we sold the rights to an old novel in a bidding war for a whole lot of money, and it turned out that the author had died before the copyright renewal, so his widow owned the rights to the novel. The widow was English and we had to hire estate and copyright detectives to go look all over England for the author's family in order to clear the title. We had to figure out how the English laws played off against the US

---

[1] Industrial Light & Magic (ILM) is the motion picture visual effects division of Lucasfilm Ltd.

copyright law and hunt down heirs who didn't know they owned things and show them that they had something to sell, and then convince a bunch of them they should get along and band together. It was fun, although really time-consuming and annoying at the same time.

We also help producers to deal with the guilds because, when you've done this for a while, you know how the Writers Guild, Directors Guild, and Screen Actors Guild work. They don't work the way you think they would, certainly from the outside. They have a lot of quirks about how credits work, and how you have to behave, and what form contracts have to take, and whether you can hire someone to do one writing step and not have them do others. They're very specific about how they work and there's an oral history that overlays their rules. You have to know what they mean by certain things and how they interpret them. A lot of it's the result of arbitration decisions that aren't published. You learn how it works over time.

Cosslett: I can't imagine walking fresh into this business.

Alexander: Well, you can. You just end up over in one little corner and, over time, you gradually gain confidence as you do a wider range of things.

Cosslett: Is there a category of client that you find particularly fun and interesting to work with?

Alexander: Emotionally, it's the writers and directors. There's just something about working with the creators that is very gratifying. As far as the complexity, it's probably the producers. Producers rely more on their lawyers than, say, real estate developers would. Real estate developers know where they're going to get their financing. They know how it works. They know which lawyers they're going to hire. And they use the lawyers more to do the papers.

A producer will say, "Hey, I just read this cool book. Go figure out if the rights are available." And then, if they are, it's, "Okay, what do you think we can offer for it?" Lawyers have a greater role in the process.

Cosslett: Is there a category of client that you find particularly difficult to work for?

Alexander: I tend to be happier with clients who are rational. Long-term we get along better. In an artistic business, there are people who are more and people who are less rational. That's not to say they are bad people, but they are people who don't really look at things logically.

People gravitate to lawyers who behave the way they want. There are clients who want bullies. I'm not really that kind of lawyer usually. That's not to say I don't ever get very firm when we need something, especially when my sense of justice is being offended—where someone's decided to behave in a way that doesn't feel either fair or right. I'm not really happy about unfair contracts. But there are people who want their lawyers to be bullies. I tend not to be the right lawyer for those people. I have turned down clients who I can tell early on want someone to go after what they want whether it's right or not. Or at least whether it feels right to me. And we just tend not to have long-term relationships when that happens.

Cosslett: I notice that you don't identify too many actors as clients.

Alexander: Some of that's just dumb luck as to who I've dealt with, but probably some of it is constitutional. Writers, directors: we get along and we think in similar ways. There are clearly actors that I would get along with, but I just don't find working on acting deals to be that interesting. They're being hired to do this job, and you negotiate that. And then they're hired to do another job. That's fine, but the work that I tend to love is often a little more complex.

Cosslett: In terms of client development, you are a named partner in your own firm. Is there a social component in terms of attracting clients?

Alexander: There is some. I do less of that than some people do. I'm not out at industry parties all the time. One of my clients called me to relate a conversation. His friend had called him to say, "Gee, I met this great lawyer. He's always at the right parties." My client replied, "Why would you want that in a lawyer? I want my lawyer to be right about deals. I don't want him to be at parties." I'm not saying there's anything wrong with that. I'm just not one of those people who spends a giant amount of time socializing.

Cosslett: How does the reality of being an entertainment lawyer compare to what most people think it's like?

Alexander: There are so many different kinds of entertainment lawyers. I do a broader range of work than some. There are a number of entertainment lawyers who just work with talent. They mostly represent actors and maybe directors, and most of their dealings are directly with the studios and networks on behalf those clients. That's both simpler and probably more lucrative than most other areas in entertainment if they can develop high-profile clients. A lot of this work is done on a percentage-of-income basis, and if you represent actors who are box-office stars, they work way more often than writers and directors, because actors can do more than one picture a year. The big ones also make more money than writers or directors, every time they work.

Cosslett: Do entertainment lawyers work on a percentage in areas other than talent?

Alexander: For producers who develop material, there's nothing to take a percentage of. If your client is a producer in the classic sense, where they identify a book or a screenplay and say, "Hey, that would make a movie," they have to pay somebody to get the rights, and then pay a screenwriter to write something, and then go hunting around for other elements. Nobody's paying them for any of this.

And then, in the true indie-type model, once they've got enough of the elements together, they have to go find the money. And, again, no one is paying them for that. They have to see if they can do coproduction deals or get distributors or find individual investors who are silly enough to think that it makes sense to invest in movies or TV shows. It's like representing a real estate developer. No one's paying them to do it. You have to be overhead. So you have to have some kind of basis where they're paying you to be their business office as producers—that's often on a straight hourly basis.

When you get into an individual movie—I don't do too much of this, but some of my partners do a fair amount more—there's a production legal line in the budget. So it's usually a flat-fee discussion: "We're making this movie and we need you to do our financing and distribution deals with these six people and the actor contracts, director contracts, writer contracts, clear up our chain of title, get our insurance coverages in place"—that sort of stuff. That's a negotiated fee based on the scope of the work and what the budget is and time pressure and all that.

Cosslett: So it's not a billable-hours relationship either?

Alexander: It can be, but it usually isn't—at least for movies in production, or TV series, or TV movies in production. Where they need a lawyer to be the production lawyer for the show, legal fees are usually a negotiated budgeted expense. It's most often a flat fee of some kind.

Cosslett: Where do you see the industry heading? Do you think that it's going to change in terms of the medium?

Alexander: I know people like escapism and they like stories. One trend I see is the diminishment of documentaries, and nonfiction, and news. I presume recent trends will continue as far as the feature films that get into theaters, and there will be a continued emphasis on brand. So it's likely we'll see another sequel to *Spiderman*.

In this regard, being a novelist can be a good thing if a novelist has developed a following. Studios look at *Twilight* or *Hunger Games* or *Harry Potter* and think, "Oh, my! If I make this movie and it works, I not only get to make three or four more movies with the same general cast, but then I might also get a theme park attraction out of it, and toys and video games." They like the cross-selling.

Also, technology changes everything. I just don't know how it will change. In fact, I know that I don't know. There are so many outlets now. Certainly, younger people are willing to watch TV shows and movies on whatever device happens to be handy. I have a Netflix account where if I start watching something and I get interrupted, I can pick it up on my iPad and, if I get interrupted again, I can pick it up on the phone. The Netflix app knows where you were in the show and goes right back to it.

Cosslett: Are there issues of professional responsibility that come up that are specific to an entertainment practice?

Alexander: One thing that comes up for entertainment lawyers of all types is that if you're good at it, you're going to get clients working together or your client will bring in somebody as a partner on something, and you'll end up being their lawyer too.

There can be a conflict of interest that arises when two people are doing something and their interests aren't exactly the same. The rules say you have to get permission, and we do that. Most of the time it's okay, but now and again you'll have a problem. For example, let's say you represent client numbers one and two, who write a screenplay together. It doesn't get sold right then. Client number two then goes off and works with person number three, who has written a hit movie, and doesn't tell number one. A year later, because of number three's participation and name, the screenplay can be sold. Clients number one and two start feuding. You try and mediate: it's clear to everyone that you can't take sides in the dispute. You can lose clients over these types of situations.

Another conflict could present itself when you represent a producer who has made an independent movie, and you also represent the distributor that is going to buy it. That comes up with us now and then. When everybody is professional, issues tend not to arise. People understand they can disagree about deal points without needing to sue their lawyer. But as an entertainment lawyer, you have to be very conscious of these potential conflicts, and stay on top of things, and make sure you don't try to represent both sides if there is any indication of a real dispute.

If you're good at what you do, it is not uncommon to represent both a buyer and a seller in a deal, because you know the bottom line for both sides. If people are mature enough, and aware enough of the business, usually it's not a problem. That's not to say everybody always agrees on everything. When things turn into real disputes, we have to step back and let everybody get different representatives.

That doesn't happen all that often in our lives. But, again, you have to be careful who you represent, and what you say to them, and what their expectations are. If you get someone who says, "Yes, yes, I know they're your client, but you need to be on my side and not tell them that"—that's going to be a problem. You certainly can't keep secrets, and the conflict-of-interest waiver letters tell them that there isn't attorney-client privilege between clients who have the same lawyer.

Cosslett: I've talked to so many lawyers who tell me they want to get into entertainment law. How hard is it to break into the practice?

Alexander: There are certainly not thousands of jobs doing what I do right now, but a lawyer wanting to get into this business should look at the bigger law firms with entertainment practices and work there for a while, or at a studio, network, or big agency. He or she can always move on. It depends what someone wants to do ultimately. There is a need for people to do this kind of work, but there certainly aren't as many opportunities now as thirty years ago or maybe ten or twenty years from now. The industry is regrouping, there's less production now at studios, and less scripted television production now than at other times, but things always change.

There are too many lawyers now who are doing it already. It's certainly not as easy and open as it was in the seventies when I stumbled in, because a lot of the people that I stumbled in with are still there. And I'm way better at this now than I was in 1979.

Computers and e-mail have affected what kind of work I do, and how fast it happens, and how much support I need. I do a lot more dealing directly with contract negotiations than I would have fifteen years ago, when we would have had more associates and more time. So efficiency has increased, and the need for support lawyers has decreased, at least in the kind of work I do. If you're in a production or distribution environment, where you have multiple projects and the work has some kind of structure and routine to it—like inside a studio legal department, for instance—it makes sense to have several layers of lawyers, and that can be a good training ground.

Usually, my clients want me for what I know, and I do such a wide range of stuff that, at this point, it's very difficult for me to have anybody as a second.

Cosslett: So it's an industry where seniority and longevity are actually rewarded?

Alexander: It can be, if you have clients who don't need someone who's particularly good at parties.

Cosslett: Who's going to provide your annuity when you want to go and lie on the beach and play your guitar full-time?

Alexander: I don't think people like me retire.

CHAPTER 11

Sean Delany

Executive Director
Lawyers Alliance for New York

Lawyers are quick to say that they love their clients. But when your clients don't pay and you continue to love them, it must be true love. **Sean Delany** truly loves his clients. As the executive director of Lawyers Alliance for New York, Delany leads the largest provider of pro bono business and transactional legal services to community development and other nonprofit groups in the United States. Through a staff of in-house attorneys and a corps of more than 1,400 volunteer lawyers from more than 100 leading law firms and corporations, Lawyers Alliance provides business legal services each year to almost 700 community-based organizations.

In this interview, Delany shares what a career on the side of the angels looks like and how he has been able to leverage his outreach from one lawyer helping one client at a time in a tiny office in the Bronx to thousands of lawyers helping hundreds of nonprofits every year. His enthusiasm and pride in the good work done by Lawyers Alliance are palpable, yet he is all too conscious of the grinding realities and hazards that lawyers face in undertaking a career in public service for the indigent: low pay, repetitiveness, corruption, and cynicism. He is also acutely aware at present of the problems that arise from public legal service providers' dependence on a shrinking supply of pro bono associates during a period of law firm downsizing. Notwithstanding the drawbacks, Delany derives deep satisfaction from his work and affirms his career choice. For prospective public service lawyers, he describes the prerequisite preparation and temperament.

Delany serves on the board of advisors for the Frances L. & Edwin L. Cummings Memorial Fund and as an advisor on the American Law Institute's Principles of the Law of Nonprofit Organizations. He is an adjunct professor of clinical law at the New York University School of Law. He served on the Advisory Committee for Tax Exempt and Government Entities, a group that advises the Internal Revenue Service on issues involving tax-exempt organizations. He was president of the National Association of State

Charities Officials. From 1999 to 2010, he served as the board chair for BronxWorks, Inc., formerly named Citizen's Advice Bureau, a settlement house serving residents of the Bronx. Delany received a JD from the University of Virginia School of Law and a BA from Hamilton College.

Clare Cosslett: Were you raised with a sense of public service?

Sean Delany: Perhaps surprisingly, I would say not. I came to my passion for public service later in life, after I had left home, and, in fact, after I had graduated from college. I grew up in Stamford, Connecticut, the eldest of three children. My family had for several generations operated a small business in Brooklyn manufacturing plumbing fixtures. We moved to Virginia in 1968. One of my sisters is now in show business, and the other is an interior designer. Perhaps my sense of public service was always a part of me and I did not recognize it. That might be so. But, in any event, it didn't emerge until I graduated from Hamilton College in upstate New York in 1975, without a clue as to what I was going to do. I had a friend who had graduated a year earlier who had chosen to become a VISTA volunteer at a legal services program here in New York. He encouraged me to consider the opportunity and I did.

I can remember sitting in the job interview on the Lower East Side in a typical legal services office with the managing attorney of the program and being asked, "What makes you want to do this paralegal work?" And I spoke a little bit about my own career path and what I hoped to learn from the experience. And when I answered the question along very personal lines, this fellow took me to task and said, "This isn't really about you." I pointed out the window—and it was a pretty desolate view out the window—and said: "It seems like an inappropriate time and place for foolish optimism, but I am interested in making a difference as well." He wanted to make sure that I had the necessary fire in my belly in order to stick it out under difficult conditions.

I can't say that I did at that moment, but somehow it developed. And I spent two years working on the West Side of Manhattan helping individual poor people and families with government benefit problems: Social Security, disability, and welfare problems. This was in a somewhat heady period in the mid-seventies. The welfare rights movement in New York and around the country was in full force, and there was a lot of excitement about whether poor people would become a viable political force in this country. That really never happened, but the theory abounded at the time about whether it could. And so it seemed like I was part of something that was growing and that mattered. But there was a frustration. And the frustration was watching my colleagues who had "Esquire" at the end of their names be able to go to court to challenge decisions that had been made by the government and the other forces that controlled poor people's lives and to have a judge adjudicate those decisions. As a lowly paralegal, I could argue across the desk in a welfare office, but I didn't have the power to do more than that. Which led me to law school.

I applied to law school and was accepted at the University of Virginia. I decided to attend there because it was far and away the least expensive form of legal education that I could possibly have embraced. Being technically an in-state resident at a state school enabled me to pay less than $3,000 a semester. And it was just for that reason that I went to Virginia. Once I arrived, I realized quite quickly that I was a fish out of water. All of my classmates, with very few exceptions, were there because they intended to go to work for large law firms and they were interested in taking courses that would prepare them to do so. They had little, if any, understanding, let alone affinity, for the public interest motivations that made me want to be a lawyer.

Cosslett: So there were no clinics or relevant course work available there?

Delany: The year I arrived, the University of Virginia hired its very first clinical faculty member, revealing a recognition that this might be necessary, but on a very small level. There were extracurricular activities. There was a student legal aid society, which I became very involved in and spent most of my time working with, and there was a core group of students who were interested in that, but they were a tiny minority at the school. And certainly when it came time to decide where one would go after graduation, the school was completely oriented towards interviewing and placement at large law firms, mostly in Washington and New York City. There was a smattering of the most talented students who went on to judicial clerkships, but those who went to public interest jobs could be counted on the fingers of one hand, possibly two, in a fairly sizable graduating class.

Cosslett: Do you think this push towards the law firms was because it was the early eighties when Wall Street and the law firms were booming?

Delany: Well, I think it's due to a variety of factors. First of all, the University of Virginia was, and to a great extent still is, a very conservative institution and its mission certainly was heavily tilted towards the world of large law firms. Even among other institutions at that time, it was particularly conservative. Also at that time law schools were not very good at connecting with public interest organizations for placement. And public interest organizations were not very good at connecting with law schools. There's still a good deal of valid criticism of public interest organizations that they don't develop and sustain relationships with law schools as they should for hiring purposes in many places around the country—but it's far improved over the way it was in the early 1980s.

Cosslett: Why do you think they don't reach into the law schools?

Delany: Because the hiring of public interest organizations is sporadic. They aren't prepared in most instances—there are exceptions—to consume on an annual basis a sufficient number of new hires to be able to set up the apparatus that can be sustainable year in and year out. Now, there are exceptions. The Legal Aid Society here in New York will hire one hundred–plus new young lawyers every year. But that's the exception to the rule. Most public interest organizations aren't hiring on that scale and, for them, the cost-benefit equation of having an interviewing and placement program at law schools, particularly in multiple law schools that are geographically far away, is still not perceived as being worthwhile.

Cosslett: They also need to have the infrastructure to educate a young lawyer as to what practicing public interest law is actually all about, because you can be wonderful in law school and come into the real world, and it's different.

Delany: It's very different. To a great extent, the growth of clinical programs in law schools in the last thirty years has made that a proposition less daunting than it used to be, but clinical programs are not a substitute for actual practice. To some extent students can now benefit from law schools and public interest employers now collaborating to offer summer opportunities to students by subsidizing their placement at public interest organizations, as we do here at Lawyers Alliance and many other places I know. That's an important introduction to that work for those students.

Cosslett: Clearly, you knew from the time you went into law school that you were going to go into the public sector. How did you choose Bronx Legal Services?

Delany: It was serendipitous. Because I had worked in a legal services office in Manhattan, MFY Legal Services, as a paralegal before I went to law school, I was familiar with the legal services community in New York City. I returned to New York looking for a job. I didn't have one when I graduated. I volunteered for some period, a month or two, in my old office. Then an opening came up at Bronx Legal Services for an attorney because one of their lawyers went on maternity leave, so I was hired in a temporary capacity to work there. At the end of that maternity leave, that lawyer returned but they decided to keep me on as a permanent staff member, so I ended up working at Bronx Legal Services. It was exactly what I had aspired to do when I went to law school. I was doing public benefits litigation on behalf of individuals and families in the Bronx. I did that work for three years before moving on to the Attorney General's office.

Cosslett: Over the years I have met with many young lawyers who spent time working in criminal defense, and they said, almost to a one, that they had every good intention going in, that they loved the work, that it was very challenging, but that they met with hostility from both sides: they were viewed as a clog in the system by the courts, and their clients viewed them as part of the problem rather than the solution. Did you have that sense in the Bronx?

Delany: I think that sense is more common to criminal defense work. I think the assembly-line nature of that work—and I've never done any criminal defense work, but I have friends who have—can make it feel that not only is it a routine for those who represent, but that the defendants perceive you as part of the system that's oppressing them and not as part of the solution. I think that if you do the kind of work that I did, which is to help people get the benefits to which they're entitled—and I did some consumer work as well—there's a greater level of appreciation because there's an outcome that they otherwise wouldn't have achieved. Not that you're able to be successful for everyone, not that there aren't any disappointments . . . there certainly are. But if you are successful, you're not perceived as part of an oppressive system necessarily, so it's a different kind of thing.

Cosslett: How did it feel to see case after case come up that were similar?

Delany: Eventually, the endless stream of identical problems became a little numbing. And also the sense of trying to empty the ocean into a hole in the beach. It never seemed to have the impact that one would hope. You know, I think it's God's work, and I think that lawyers, young lawyers and particularly those who sustain it later into their careers, are to be put on a pedestal and held in awe, frankly.

I wasn't able to do it on a sustained basis—even the impact litigation that I was involved with in federal court involving arcane calculations of welfare benefits seemed to move the needle only so much. And it was a difficult time in the South Bronx. The crack epidemic was in full flower in the early 1980s. It was a tough place to work. The legal services office where I worked had its own internal problems. Certainly there were conflicts between the attorney staff and the support staff, which could get difficult at times. So there were other strains as well. But ultimately, the sameness of it and the feeling that I wasn't making as much of a difference as I could is what drove me out of the place.

I went to the Attorney General's office, hired by a very progressive attorney general, Bob Abrams, who felt that you could use the power of that office to do good and, in my opinion, he did. I was hired to do consumer protection work, where I could have an impact on thousands of people on a regular basis, not just individuals. The work ranged across any kind of consumer work that you can imagine that the office would do. I spent a good deal of time, for example, defending New York's Lemon Law for automobile sales, which at that time was new and subject to constitutional challenges by automobile dealers and manufacturers. That's just an example, but it affected a lot of people. And certainly it was satisfying to have the power of the State of New York behind you when you got to court.

Cosslett: That must have been nice, coming out of a small office where you were representing one person at a time.

Delany: Well, I can tell you that the first time I went to court in that capacity and the judge or the court officer said, "Who's here representing the government?" I looked around to see who he might be referring to before realizing it was me.

Cosslett: When you were in law school, you said, "I'm never going to represent the government. That's not me."

Delany: I went to law school to sue the government, not to represent the government.

Cosslett: Little did you know that sometimes the government was on the side of the angels. So you had two years in consumer fraud and then moved into the Charities Bureau?

Delany: A supervisory position in the Charities Bureau opened up and I immediately jumped on it—and I'll tell you why. In my final year working at Bronx Legal Services, the managing attorney in the office where I was working suggested that I take on a new client, an organizational client rather than an individual or a family. He said, "You might enjoy this. It's a small community group here in the Bronx that doesn't have a lawyer. I've been helping them out, but I'd like to transition this to someone else. So why don't you work for this organization?"

The organization, called the Citizens Advice Bureau, did its work out of a single site on the Grand Concourse in the Bronx, with a budget of between two and three hundred thousand dollars and a staff of approximately a dozen. I began working with them and enjoyed it, and when I went to the Consumer Protection Bureau in the Attorney General's Office, I asked for permission to continue to do that work on a pro bono basis. When I moved over to the Charities Bureau, I again asked for permission to continue to do that work, and it was granted—to my surprise, since the Charities Bureau regulates nonprofit organizations in the State of New York. As long as I didn't make any appearances before the office in any capacity of representing the organization, it was approved.

My work with the Citizens Advice Bureau continued for the next decade as I worked in the Charities Bureau. Now, if you work in the Charities Bureau, you can get a skewed view of what the nonprofit sector looks like. Fraud and waste are the focus of many of the investigations that you conduct: charities misrepresenting themselves when raising money, charities wasting funds in their operations, miscreants misappropriating funds—that sort of thing. That's your job: to focus on correcting those wrongs. If that had been my only picture of the nonprofit sector, through my time at the Attorney General's office, I might have become a pretty cynical guy, but I had this work that I continued to do as outside counsel to the board of the Citizens Advice Bureau. The organization grew and grew, merged with another large nonprofit and took over their facilities in the Bronx, and continued to add programs and funding streams until by the time I left the Charities Bureau in 1997, it was a $25 million operation with services for thousands of people at twenty sites in the Bronx.

Cosslett: You were with the Charities Bureau for over ten years. How did your job grow during that period? Did you have a mentor there?

Delany: I supervised litigation for the first eight years that I was there, and then when there was a vacancy, I was appointed to be the bureau chief, so I was running the operation for the Attorney General. The person who hired me was a mentor. Pamela Mann was the bureau chief in the Charities Bureau and supervised me for the first eight years that was I there. She was the one who taught me how to be a nonprofit lawyer and who really enabled me to grow to the point where I was qualified to be the bureau chief when that time came.

Cosslett: Mentoring for lawyers is hugely important.

Delany: In this age at large law firms, where attorney development has become so much more of a focus than even it once was, there's beginning to be a recognition about how important mentoring can be to that whole process. But for too many years it's been neglected, I agree. If you're lucky enough to find an individual who will mentor you successfully, you really have a big advantage over those who do not.

Cosslett: You've been with Lawyers Alliance for New York for almost fifteen years. Can you tell me about your position and the work of Lawyers Alliance?

Delany: When I first arrived, I was hired to be the legal director here, and I was in that role for two years before becoming executive director. At Lawyers Alliance, we provide high-quality, affordable, business law services to nonprofit groups that are working to improve the quality of life in low-income communities here in New York City. So we're working with groups developing low-income housing, stimulating economic development, and providing social services to children and young people, the elderly, new immigrants, community arts programs—any kind of an organization that might have a program presence that is intended to make life a little bit easier in New York City neighborhoods.

Last year we worked with almost seven hundred nonprofit groups so, over our forty-three-year history, we have reached many thousands. We provide corporate tax, real estate, employment law services—any business law need that our nonprofit clients might have. We don't do litigation, as there are other agencies in New York that will do litigation for nonprofit groups. But we will provide almost any other legal service that they might need, and we're able to do so on the scale that we do because we put more than fourteen hundred volunteers to work each year from a network of more than one hundred law firms and corporations. The work of these volunteers ranges from a consultation that may take no more than an hour, to a commitment to a large development project—typically with a team of lawyers—that may take years and hundreds of hours. And everything in between.

Cosslett: The ABA Model Rules provide that every lawyer has a professional responsibility to provide legal services to those unable to pay, and that a lawyer should aspire to provide at least fifty hours of *pro bono publico* services per year. So there's an *ethical requirement* that lawyers do good. There's a *desire* on the part of law firms and associates to do good, and they also want to *appear* to do good. Pro bono work is a good thing, and law firms want to do it. So my question to you is: how do law firms strike a balance between a billable hours requirement for associates with wanting their associates to go out and do good, so that everyone gets the benefit of looking good as well?

Delany: Let's distinguish between individual lawyers and law firms. Individual lawyers are subject to the ethical precepts that you've just outlined. Law firms, as institutions, are not. Individual lawyers are expected, if not required, to perform pro bono service, and the form that that pro bono service takes is prescribed here in New York State by the Office of Court Administration with a very carefully worded set of guidelines about what kind of work qualifies. And the motivations that those individual attorneys have to do that work vary widely. Yes, their ethical obligations certainly are part of it, but it certainly doesn't stop there. They're very interested in doing something different than what they have to do every day for their paying clients. They're interested in acquiring skills that they might not otherwise acquire. They're interested in exploring other ways of being a lawyer that might lead to a different sort of career path if, perhaps, they're interested in choosing a different career path.

So their motivations are many. They're also interested in pleasing their institutions when they do pro bono work, to the extent their institutions care about such things. And these days, and for many years now, their institutions have cared about these things. Not because they're technically subject to the same ethical precepts, but because they understand that it is the right thing for them to do and that it is in their business interests to do it. And their business interest is extremely important.

If we talk about the growth, we might even say "explosion," in the world of pro bono in the last ten to fifteen years, we're talking about a trajectory that closely tracks the growth in the business of large law firms. That's not coincidental. The fact of the matter is their pro bono programs have grown because it is in their business interests to have those programs. It enables them to brand themselves and, in particular, to brand themselves to the brightest and the best young associates from the top law schools who these days—certainly since the early 1990s, with the dawn of the internet—have much more access to much more information than lawyers of another generation ever did about what distinguishes one institution from another. And that more refined information has required law firms to position themselves much more carefully, to brand themselves much more carefully, in order to distinguish themselves—pardon the expression—from that other sweatshop down the street. And as a result, they've had to compete, and their pro bono programs have grown as a result because that's one of the measures of institutional quality.

Additionally, these are institutions that are human enterprises run by individual lawyers who understand in their heart that it's also the right thing to do. But they have an obligation to their partners, as limited liability partnerships, to promote the interests of the partnership. And if it were not in the interests of the partnership, it would certainly be harder for them to do it.

And we'll talk about what that means in the current era, too, because we may be experiencing another day. But I'll stick with the golden age for now. All of this came to a new level of attention when the legal press—particularly *American*

Lawyer magazine—began to rate law firms in 2002 by creating the A list each year of the top twenty institutions in the country, using a scale that involved four different criteria: profitability, pro bono service, associate satisfaction, and diversity. But the first two are weighted twice as heavily as the second two. And, therefore, you don't get on that list and stay on that list unless you have a very active pro bono program. Now, some would say that this has not always had positive effects, because it's an hours-counting game, and the *American Lawyer* editors measure the pro bono performance by the number of hours that their lawyers from reporting institutions are putting in. Nevertheless, it has certainly driven the growth in pro bono services and the cultivation and promotion of pro bono programs at large law firms to a level that they would not have otherwise achieved.

So that brings us to Lawyers Alliance's place in this cosmology. During that same period of time, as large law firms grew exponentially, they grew in a somewhat lopsided way. The number of nonlitigators, business lawyers, deal lawyers, and so on grew out of proportion to the number of litigators in most large institutions here in New York City. It's not the case in every place around the country, and it's certainly not the case if you look at patterns of growth today. But during that period of time between the late 1990s to 2008, when the bottom fell out of everything, we're talking about growth in business law practice to a greater extent than anything else.

At that point, more than seventy-five percent of the lawyers in many large law firms in their New York offices were not litigators but business lawyers. What does that mean to the pro bono programs in those institutions? Well, it meant that finding pro bono work that those lawyers could do and at the same time be able to bill two thousand, twenty-two hundred, or twenty-four hundred billable hours every year was a challenge. Those lawyers don't have time to go to the bathroom, let alone do much pro bono work, and any kind of pro bono work that requires a long learning curve is a problem. These attorneys might have been perfectly willing to learn how to go to Landlord-Tenant Court and represent people who were being evicted, but they'd never been to court before and it would be a stretch to get them there and feeling comfortable. However, they can certainly update bylaws or handle a corporate structuring project or advise a nonprofit on an employment problem without having to learn very much that's new. And so our dance card was really very full during this period of explosive growth in the pro bono world. We were quite spoiled.

That brings us to the great recession in 2008 when everything may have changed. We'll see what the future holds and whether the uncertainty in the practice of law in large law firms leads to enduring changes in their business model or not—and whether those changes are consistent across the practice of law and the business of managing large law firms or not. For a pro bono organization, like Lawyers Alliance, that operates at a certain scale, staffing requirements are, as you can imagine, extremely important. We've been the beneficiaries of the billable-hours model to an extent that we cannot overestimate. The law firm practice of having armies of young lawyers—and, indeed, even mid-level and senior lawyers—on hand to throw at any paying client's project, whenever necessary, meant that there was often excess capacity available in terms of the numbers for pro bono work that might not otherwise have been there.

Cosslett: Are associates' pro bono hours counted towards their billable-hour requirement at the firm?

Delany: A simple question with a complex answer. So I'll be a bit cynical by saying that with the growth of the internet and with the access to increased information by those who are considering going to work for a large law firm, the questions of law firm policies toward pro bono have become increasingly intricate and byzantine. The fact of the matter is that all will declare that their pro bono hours are counted and in most instances that's true. However, there are very few, if any, institutions—I know of none—in which those hours are counted on a truly blind basis when compared with billable hours. Nor would one expect them to be, which means that the variations along the spectrum of how they are treated can be quite miniscule. Above the line, below the line. Caps, no caps. The processes for approval. The differences between individual practice groups versus firm-wide policies. The unwritten rules versus written rules. It presents a complexity that's frankly quite bewildering.

Cosslett: Now you said that you had benefited from the billable-hour requirement and the significant staffing in the corporate areas. I'm a little confused by that because if you have associates billing twenty-four hundred hours, it shows that the firm is very busy and that there is more of a disincentive to send your lawyers out to do pro bono.

Delany: We don't benefit from the billable-hour requirements as it applies to individual lawyers. We do benefit from the billable-hour model, in which law firms charge their clients by the hour because, when they're able to charge by the hour, they have the luxury of having a greater staffing on hand because they are not required to be as cost-conscious as they would be if they were billing on a specific project fee basis, or on any of the alternative fee arrangements that are now becoming popular, at least in some institutions.

Cosslett: So your concern going forward is that that billable-hour model will be changed because the nature of legal practice will change.

Delany: At many institutions it's already changing. Let's face it. The largest cost center in any large law firm is personnel and the most expensive part of that cost center is the lawyers. If firms are being pressured, if their clients are refusing to pay for the billable-hour model at all or refusing to pay for the billables by anything less experienced than a third-year lawyer, that suppresses staffing levels and lower staffing levels are not good for pro bono programs.

Cosslett: So we need to keep our fingers crossed that there's full employment for all lawyers on Wall Street again. Could you give me an example of a firm or a group of volunteer associates that took on a task that became much more onerous or complex than they originally anticipated?

Delany: I can talk about a project and I'll use an extreme example, but there are others. For a decade, Lawyers Alliance has been representing a community group in the northwest Bronx that has been pushing for the redevelopment of the largest vacant space in the Bronx, a former state armory building on Kingsbridge Avenue. It's been the subject of many press accounts here in New York City. And a year ago, the City of New York and this community group fought to a draw over what would happen with this space, and the city withdrew its proposal for the approval of the development of this space. It's now been revived and the project is back on the radar screen, and we're beginning our work again with that community group.

Over the course of that project, ten years, four different law firms worked on it, in sequence, never at the same time. One would begin work as long as it could, leave the project, or become not the best candidate to continue working on the project because the nature of the legal needs changed.

In the early phases, there was a lot of land-use planning and land-use lawyers were required. Later on there were other kinds of deal-making skills that were required and other law firms were brought in to handle that. There were real estate needs throughout the project, but they changed at least in nuance over time and the law firms over time either had, in some instances, put in more hours than they could continue to put in or became unable to keep on with the long horizon of the project and needed to step out, and Lawyers Alliance would find another set of lawyers. We were able to make this work because we have expert attorneys on our own staff. We have an attorney—who formerly worked as a partner in a firm and does our economic development work—who has been the primary contact, and he and other lawyers here at Lawyers Alliance have co-counseled the project because we co-counsel all our projects and have picked up whenever the law firms have been unable to continue carrying the ball. So that's an example of a project that's still not over after a decade in which the law firms for one reason or another, after doing yeoman service in every case, have fallen out and been replaced.

Cosslett: On the flip side, have you had lawyers or law firms who over-lawyer? There are firms in New York who do outstanding work for Fortune 500 companies in large transactions, and perhaps your transactions are not quite as large, but the firm comes in with a team of lawyers. Has that happened and have you had to say, "Step back a little bit"?

Delany: It's interesting. The phenomenon of over-lawyering I think is overstated, and it's often confused with a different phenomenon. Sometimes our clients come to us with a concern before they are placed with volunteers that the matter is going to be over-lawyered. And what they're really concerned about, it turns out, is that the process will be dragged out beyond a point that will be productive for them. It's not so much about the nature of the work that's being done. It's about how long it takes that I find to be the most common translation, when you really get down to it, of over-lawyering.

And there's certainly a role that Lawyers Alliance plays in working on pro bono work with our clients. And when I say "working," I mean both in preparing clients to receive services if they haven't worked with pro bono counsel before and in working with pro bono counsel once they get started. There is a certain function that we perform that's like an English-to-English translation: we help lawyers who have never worked with nonprofit groups to understand how their businesses work and we help nonprofit managers understand what it means to work with a pro bono lawyer from a large law firm. These are two species that don't interact in any other context and don't necessarily understand each other.

One of the phenomena, for example, that we see all the time is that nobody wants to complain. The nonprofit manager might think, "Who am I to complain that a lawyer who's giving their time and free services isn't returning my phone calls?" And the law firm lawyer might think, "Well, who am I to complain that this busy, busy person doing God's work out there hasn't reviewed the draft I sent over?" And so it's our job to make sure they communicate with each other and that they indeed complain to each other when they should.

Cosslett: And, in fact, the relationship is as any lawyer–client relationship should be.

Delany: Right. But it's more than that because we, in the process of co-counseling the cases, bring an expertise on matters that our pro bono lawyers might not have. They're expert corporate tax, real estate, and employment lawyers, but they don't know anything, nor should they, about financing affordable housing, about the implications of business ventures for tax-exempt organizations, about the regulation of lobbying and political activities for charities, et cetera, et cetera. And that's what our staffing comes down to. So, as to the danger of over-lawyering, some of that is certainly addressed by the expertise that we can bring to the table to cut to the chase. There's less chasing of tails going on in here by our volunteers as a result of that. And the other thing is that our volunteers need to understand that in many ways nonprofits are no different from their paying clients—they are businesses. They are mission-driven businesses and they're interested in getting a project done on a certain timetable and not making a fetish out of it. When our volunteers understand that, then the danger of over-lawyering is reduced, because it's really about timeliness and getting the project done: understanding that every project has a beginning, a middle, and—yes—an end.

Cosslett: Junior associates in big firms are rarely asked to understand a business or to figure out a way to further a particular business objective. They are more often asked to draft documents and negotiate terms for deals that have already been structured.

Delany: And it's a shame. Putting on my faculty hat for a moment—it is a shame that business lawyers are not being trained at an earlier point in time to understand the importance and the connection between lawyering and business advice. You can't really be a successful business lawyer unless you have a full and rich understanding of the way your client's business operates.

Cosslett: I have to ask you about the case involving pro bono representation and the mailroom mix-up at Sullivan & Cromwell. As you know, the case involved two associates who took on an appeal from a death-row inmate. They subsequently left the firm but didn't advise the mailroom, the client, or the court that they were leaving. A ruling denying postconviction relief addressed to the lawyers and sent to the law firm was returned to the sender. As a result, no appeal was filed within the deadline. The case ended up in the Supreme Court, where it was decided that these attorneys had actually abandoned the client. This was a good decision for the client because, had it been decided otherwise, he would have been one step closer to execution. Do you have any thoughts on that case specifically or generally as to how so many things could have gone wrong?

Delany: I won't comment on that case specifically except to say what might be the obvious. Lawyering involves deadlines. Lawyering of all kinds involves deadlines that are often externally imposed and often have very significant consequences if they're not observed. This is certainly true in litigation—not only in high-stakes litigation involving human life, but in all other kinds of litigation and indeed in transactional work as well. There are deadlines by which things need to happen or the project won't be financed, the deal won't be possible—whatever it might be. Therefore, in any large institution, the importance of having every part of the internal machinery operating as efficiently and carefully can't be overstated.

I'm not sure that this story is especially about pro bono work, although a lot of people think it is. It's about a failure in the mailroom. I dare say failures in the mailroom occur to the detriment of paying clients as well. This became an extremely publicized matter, understandably, because a human being's life was at stake, the highest of stakes possible. So I think that the story also says something about the practice of law in a time of extraordinary turbulence. And I think this is an effect of the management of large law firms, including but not limited to their pro bono work.

We picked up the newspaper this morning and read what many of us already knew about: significant cuts at one very large law firm here in New York City, not only among their attorney staff but also among the support staff of all kinds. With that kind of turnover going on in so many institutions in the last few years, it's almost remarkable you don't hear about stories like this more often, frankly. Things are very much in turbulence and turmoil in a lot of institutions these days, and that makes it harder to manage these institutions. So it's a real challenge for the people who lead those institutions and the folks who manage the sometimes unglamorous machinery that makes things happen on time. It's been a tough time to run a large law firm, and I think that this story says more about that than it does about pro bono work in particular.

Cosslett: Let's talk a little about salary. Unfortunately students often graduate law school burdened with such a huge amount of law school debt that their choice of practice is circumscribed.

Delany: Here at Lawyers Alliance, there are two reasons why we do not hire students who are less than two or three years out of law school. The first of those reasons is that the work we do here requires a certain base of experience. We have rotating externs from four different law firms who essentially serve as our junior staff. They're not necessarily junior lawyers, but they're new to what we do. And, if we did not have them, we would have to hire very junior associates. Therefore, when we're hiring our own staff, they are two to three years out at least.

The other reason is that we find students who are less than two or three years out of law school, and sometimes even later, just haven't had the opportunity yet to pay down those enormous debts that they've graduated with and they can't afford to take the eighty-percent pay cut that they'd have to take to come and work here. So that's one example of how important debt is in the equation of whether you can afford to work in a public interest legal organization.

Cosslett: Eighty percent . . . ouch! How long do the externs work at Lawyers Alliance and do they stay on law firm salary?

Delany: For four months and they remain on law firm salary. They get an opportunity to come here and do work that they're passionate about, or at least interested in. The law firms sponsor these programs for a variety of reasons. But the best of those reasons is to increase their pro bono commitment, to create a base of knowledge in the kind of work we do, which the externs can then take back to the firm and share with others, so that they'll be able to do more easily the kind of pro bono work that we do. They acquire practice skills coming here that they might not otherwise acquire. Certainly, we put them to work with greater levels of responsibility and client contact than they might get in their earliest years at the firm. So there are a variety of reasons why it works for both of us: for the law firms and for Lawyers Alliance.

Cosslett: What would you tell undergraduates considering law school about public interest law? And what would you tell practicing lawyers who might be considering changing their practice area about being a public interest lawyer?

Delany: Law students who think that they want to do this work have a number of options before them. Demonstrating some sort of interest in it early on is certainly important. Through the clinical courses they choose to take. Through how they spend their summers, and certainly through the volunteer activities they get involved in during the school year that demonstrate a public interest affinity. It is not necessary for them to plot a career course that immediately begins at a public interest law firm, institution, or organization.

Here at Lawyers Alliance we typically hire lawyers who have worked at large law firms. I am one of maybe two lawyers here who have never worked at a large law firm. All the other lawyers have. That's because we're looking for the corporate tax, real estate, employment law, and business law skills they've acquired at a large law firm. Those attorneys may have gone right out of law school to those firms, but they also may have, along the way, demonstrated an interest in what we do, either in law school or by doing pro bono work when they're at the firm, or both.

Cosslett: If that law firm path is unavailable now because of the market, is there a second path for law students to take?

Delany: I'm going to speak more generally, and then I'll speak about Lawyers Alliance because we're a bit different from some public interest legal organizations. Certainly the organizations whose focus is litigation are looking for lawyers who have acquired litigation skills. So if you're able to go to work, for example, in the government in a litigation capacity of one kind or another, you will make yourself valuable and will be able to make that transition later on. Even if large firms are foreclosed to you and you go to a smaller firm but are able to acquire litigation skills there, those will make you valuable to a public interest legal organization whose focus is litigation.

Similarly, many public interest legal organizations need lawyers with transactional skills who have acquired those skills. There are public interest legal organizations that specialize in immigration law, to take just one example. Here at Lawyers Alliance, we'll hire attorneys from the Charities Bureau because they've worked on the regulatory side, which we need. We'll hire lawyers who have done transactional work even in smaller firms, depending on the quality of that experience. But at the end of the day, because we rely so much on the work of volunteers from large law firms, we do have a strong preference for candidates who have worked in those institutions.

Cosslett: Is there a particular skill set that you think is useful for a public interest lawyer?

Delany: The practice of public interest law is so varied now that it really depends on what kind of work you're going to want to do. It's a specialized field, and you have to go and get the experience to make yourself attractive to that kind of a public interest legal organization. So those who want to work in the public interest need to think harder about what kind of public interest work they want to do in order to pursue the appropriate skills.

Cosslett: What continues to motivate you as a public interest lawyer?

Delany: Well, there are several things that continue to motivate me. First of all, in terms of Lawyers Alliance's mission, what continues to motivate me is what has motivated me since 1984 when I first started working for the Citizens Advice Bureau and I was at Bronx Legal Services—and it's what motivates everybody who works here at Lawyers Alliance and is willing to accept the admittedly inadequate compensation that we're able to pay to them—and that's a real admiration, if not awe, for what our clients can achieve. We are, every day, excited by the creative, entrepreneurial, and persistent work that our clients do to make a difference in the communities in which they work. That's what gets us up in the morning, and that's what makes all of us want to continue to do this work day in and day out. You know, lawyers who talk about their paying clients often say that they love their clients, and that's why they do their work. But we really mean it here. We really do love our clients, and they don't pay us very much, if at all, and therefore it's true love. So that's number one.

Secondly, I'd be remiss if I didn't talk about the Lawyers Alliance itself and the enormous privilege I've had in arriving at this organization just at a time when it was entering a period of enormous growth. I owe a great deal to my predecessor for being the conceptual father of what we've become, but I'm also enormously proud of having been able to grow the organization significantly: to double in size, double our volunteer pool, double the number of clients that we work with, triple the operating budget, and to become a leader of a network of organizations around the country and in dozens of different cities that do what we do. That's all highly gratifying.

And we realize that with that scale comes greater impact. If we believe, as we do here, that nonprofit organizations—not lawyers, but nonprofit organizations—are going to make a difference in the quality of life for those who are less well-off in this country and that we bask in their reflected glory, then our ability to help more of those organizations do better and better work has an exponentially greater impact. The leveraging effect of being able to represent an organization that helps hundreds of thousands of people as opposed to an individual client is something that we think about all the time. The impact that comes from that leveraging is a very gratifying motivation.

Finally, one of the things that currently excites me about being a public interest lawyer is teaching. In my role as adjunct professor at NYU Law School teaching a business law transactions clinic, I have the privilege of engaging in a process by which young people learn to represent organizational clients. They learn what it means to work with an organization having varied internal and external stakeholders and needs that are very much business needs but, in the case of the clinic's clients, are also mission-driven. And, not coincidentally, my business law students learn what the joys of pro bono service on behalf of nonprofit organizations might look like.

To me, that's a very, very gratifying process to be involved in.

CHAPTER 12

David Whedbee

Associate
MacDonald Hoague & Bayless

Bonaventure wrote: "An artisan is one who aims to produce a work that is beautiful, useful, and enduring; and only when it preserves these three qualities is the work acceptable."

In an era dominated by the rise and fall of biglaw and big lawsuits, **David J. Whedbee** aims to practice civil rights law as an artisan. He selects his cases less by calculating the odds of a profitable outcome than by Bonaventure's three criteria for acceptable work. Whedbee looks for legal beauty in the intricacy and strategy of a case and for moral beauty in its potential to vindicate violated rights. He looks for the usefulness of a case in the ability of a successful suit to empower the impotent, defend the disenfranchised, and speak for the voiceless. And he looks for cases that will endure in their beneficial effects on the lives of his clients and on developing precedent to restrain the abuse of power.

Whedbee's practice in civil rights, criminal defense, and personal injury at MacDonald Hoague & Bayless in Seattle focuses on cases of police misconduct, wrongful incarceration, First Amendment claims, and unlawful discrimination based on race and disability. Between judicial clerkships to the Honorable Helen G. Berrigan, Eastern District of Louisiana, and to the Honorable Ronald M. Gould, Ninth Circuit Court of Appeals, he worked as a contract attorney for Gordon Thomas Honeywell, litigating clergy sex abuse claims, and he served as a Special Assistant to the General Counsel of Governor Christine O. Gregoire. He is a board member of the ACLU of Washington and a member of the Innocence Project Northwest and the National Police Accountability Project. He took his JD from the University of Washington, MSc from The London School of Economics and Political Science (LSE), and BA magna cum laude from Pomona College, where he was awarded an NCAA postgraduate scholarship.

Cosslett: Where did you grow up?

Whedbee: I grew up in Southern California. My parents were educators. My mother was a principal in the public schools and my father was a college professor and Old Testament scholar. I had a stepdad who was a history teacher and some stepsiblings, but my mother and her second husband got divorced. We all remain a more or less happy, extended family. It's very Californian.

Cosslett: Why did you go to Pomona for undergrad? Did you have a career plan?

Whedbee: My dad taught at Pomona, so it was a good deal financially. I really liked the seminar atmosphere and had a fantastic academic experience there. At the time, I was interested in literary criticism and historiography and, for better or worse, was exposed to a lot of the postmodern, poststructuralist thinkers. I was considering either going into academics or some kind of journalism.

Cosslett: You took some time off between college and law school. What did you do right after college?

Whedbee: I moved to Seattle and was a DJ for an alternative music station up here. Then I got into teaching English as a second language and the teaching experience sparked my interest in the political/social dimensions of immigration. I was exposed to Ukrainians and Brazilians and Laotians, and I became more interested in their stories—of why they came to America and the difficulties they faced—than in teaching English grammar. For a short time, I went to work for a congressman up here, focusing on immigration issues. Then I spent a little time in DC working for a congressman from Los Angeles doing the same sort of thing, and then I went to work as a paralegal with an immigration attorney named Bart Klein and started to concentrate on asylum claims.

Cosslett: When you worked as a paralegal, were you thinking that ultimately you would go to law school?

Whedbee: It was more of an opportunity to work substantively with immigration issues. It was fortuitous that I got involved with asylum cases. I spoke French, and one day a guy from Senegal or Mauritania came in wanting to seek asylum. Nobody could speak with him because he only spoke French. I went over and we started talking, and that was it. A wave of Francophone/West African petitioners followed and the law office developed a large clientele among that population. I was quite proud to help many of them get asylum in the United States. In my three years there, I think we prevailed on over thirty claims.

Cosslett: Am I right in thinking that a petitioner in an asylum case must establish a well-founded fear of persecution if they are made to return to their home country?

Whedbee: They also have to identify that their fear is based on something specific, such as an association with a political, social, or religious group. In 1991 there was a widespread political shift in Africa, and dictatorships were giving way to nominally democratic governments. The result was that groups that had previously been disenfranchised were allowed to participate in the democratic process, at least on a theoretical basis.

Of course, the transition did not happen overnight, so there were still many instances of voter abuse and intimidation. That's why we had this spate of West African asylum claims: there was a group of people who had either been a product of the old regime or who were vying for power and were being repressed. I studied the politics of the situation, and I was able to communicate, from a political standpoint, what was happening to these people. They came in and their stories were inchoate before they got to us. I was able to frame their stories into the right kind of claim.

Cosslett: You were taking their stories and framing them within a context that became a legal cause of action. Funnily enough, isn't that what lawyers are supposed to do?

Whedbee: Funny because I was naïve. I wasn't a lawyer, which actually might have been the reason behind some of the success. It wasn't couched. I've seen later asylum claims, and there's lots of legalese.

Cosslett: After two years you went to The London School of Economics?

Whedbee: I was still undecided about what I wanted to do. I was ambivalent between something like the law, which would be more practice-oriented, and something like history, which would be more academic, and I could never really make up my mind. I had received a one-year fellowship from the NCAA for playing soccer in college and it gave me a year of postgraduate studies. London School of Economics had a year program, so I got to go for free, and I did that to test the waters of academia.

What I had found in talking to the immigrants seeking asylum was that I was really interested in the process of decolonization in Africa and in other countries. I was interested in how the current political situation in Africa had evolved from the process of decolonization, and I wanted to go look at the entire immigration phenomenon from a historical perspective, which is what I did at the LSE.

Cosslett: But you didn't get involved as a lawyer in an international practice?

Whedbee: No. I wrote my thesis on a politician from the Ivory Coast, and then I had an accident about two weeks later and that derailed me for a couple of years. Ultimately, I decided from a purely practical perspective that I didn't want to go to graduate school in history because I was not sure that I wanted to spend my time trying to chase down some tenure track position in God knows where, and I really felt that I needed to be in Seattle. I decided to go to law school because I wanted to be an immigration lawyer. I was around all these people who were doing it, and I thought, "Well, I can do this, too."

Cosslett: You went to the University of Washington at Seattle. Did you enjoy the law school process?

Whedbee: I loved law school. As I said, I thought I'd want to do immigration cases and to represent immigrants as a criminal defense attorney because I had seen how marginalized they could be by the legal system. They tell you when you go to law school to suspend all your preconceived ideas and to keep your mind open, which is what I did. Within three weeks, I realized that I had finally discovered the vocation I had always yearned for because it combined history, politics, textual interpretation, and rhetoric—all applied in real, everyday life to assist people. It was an incredible epiphany.

People thought I was crazy, but I just delved into American jurisprudence and became really interested in constitutional law, which explains my shift away from international issues to domestic issues. Even though I spent a lot of time in my life traveling around the world, and living in Germany, and living in France and England, now I'm here and I think about American issues for the most part. It's kind of ironic.

Cosslett: So constitutional law was one of your favorite classes. Was it one of the most challenging?

Whedbee: Federal Courts was described to me as the crown jewel of con law, and that class was both challenging and incredibly rewarding. Trying to negotiate our system of dual sovereignties is just fascinating. That was my favorite class. I also took Equal Protection and First Amendment and your standard intro Con Law, in addition to Criminal Procedures and all the Fourth, Fifth, and Sixth Amendment issues. I like the idea that there are concepts which are elastic and which change with various interpretations as dictated by precedent. I like trying to put all that together in an argument. I found it to be intellectually very challenging and rewarding.

Cosslett: What internships did you take over the summers?

Whedbee: The first summer, I was accepted in a diversity program and was placed randomly at a primarily defense-oriented firm here in Seattle. It had a very active asbestos defense practice, but luckily, I didn't have to do any of that, and I ended up working with the one criminal defense attorney there. That's where I was introduced to criminal defense issues.

Cosslett: Did you go into a clerkship after law school?

Whedbee: As soon as I got to law school, I was completely transfixed with the idea of becoming a clerk. When I graduated, I went into the Eastern District of Louisiana, which is right in New Orleans, and I clerked for the then-chief judge, Helen Berrigan.

Federal judges, like professors, are amongst the few people in our society who have genuine intellectual independence because they have a kind of tenure. Unlike state court judges, who are elected, federal judges shouldn't have to pander to any kind of populism, and they can feel free to interpret doctrine the way they think is right. Of course, they are constrained by precedent and the appellate courts can always overturn them, but within that context, they enjoy intellectual freedom. That idea always fascinated me, so I really wanted to clerk.

I used a scattergun approach and applied all over the country. I got three interviews, all in the South, which I welcomed. Then I got the job in Louisiana. The one thing that's better than clerking for a year is clerking for a year in New Orleans.

Cosslett: What was Judge Berrigan like?

Whedbee: She was awesome. She was a very early Clinton appointment. She was the board president of the ACLU of Louisiana, which would probably disqualify her from being appointed now. Prior to becoming a judge, she had been a criminal defense attorney and had done a lot of death penalty work. We were involved in a really interesting case in which two local cops were being investigated by the FBI for giving protection to people running cocaine in and out of New Orleans. The police were alleged to have roughed up a couple of kids, and the mother or the aunt did something unthinkable and complained to the authorities. Unbeknownst to them, the cops were being taped by the FBI, and over the course of a number of phone calls with a local ruffian, the cops were heard to order a hit on the woman who had complained.

The hit was carried out. This case went between the district court and the Fifth Circuit for a number of years and was back in front of Judge Berrigan for sentencing. It was unbelievable. We had the actual sentencing trial to determine whether this policeman, Len Davis, should be put to death or not. The jury deliberated for about forty-five minutes and found that he should. Judge Berrigan was a death penalty opponent, although of course she was unbiased. There was a huge strain on her to make sure that there were no irregularities in the proceedings. It was a three-week process and super-stressful, but also really fascinating. That was something I got to work on that was probably pretty extraordinary for a clerk.

Cosslett: After that clerkship, you moved on to a clerkship with Judge Ronald Gould at the circuit court level. How different is clerking at a court of appeals from clerking at a district court?

Whedbee: In a district court clerkship, you are insulated with your judge and all the decision making is taking place within chambers. When you're working for an appellate judge, there are panels that are formed every month. Sometimes your judge is on a panel and sometimes he or she isn't, but each time a panel is formed and the Ninth Circuit is "convened," you're working with two other judges and their respective clerks.

There's a lot more behind-the-scenes politicking that goes into fashioning rulings in such a way as to garner the support of the other two judges. I hadn't really thought about that beforehand, but one of the most pronounced things that clerks did was to craft memos and communications in such a way as to convince other judges to come on board with their judge's views. The process of drafting opinions becomes much more collaborative—in spite of the judges sometimes. I drafted about ten or eleven opinions for Judge Gould that later became published. It was an incredible experience and definitely some of the hardest work I've had to do.

There was an added challenge to being a clerk for an appellate judge. Young lawyers, and clerks in particular, often have a self-imposed burden that they must get everything "right," and that they must deliver the judge the "answer" they think he or she is looking for. Before Judge Gould would hear oral argument on cases, he would meet with his clerks to discuss the cases, and he would grind away at us. At the time I remember being disappointed in myself, and even a bit terrified, when I couldn't provide that acceptable or "correct" answer. But in thinking about the experience later, I realized it wasn't at all about my bruised ego. Rather, that grinding away was the judge's process of refining his response to the legal problem presented and a dialectic at work as new law was formed. It had nothing to do with me.

Cosslett: Were the three judges coming from the same conceptual legal perspective?

Whedbee: Each month there would be a different panel, so your judge would sit with Judges A and B in November, and then maybe in December or January, your judge would sit with Judges G and H. The panels were formed randomly so you always encountered different judges. Sometimes the judges would sit by designation, and you would get some crazy Reagan appointee from the East Coast and it would be completely different than the Ninth Circuit is used to. It's pretty bizarre.

Cosslett: Between the two clerkships, you did some work involving clergy sex abuse litigation. Was there a particularly large group of plaintiffs in Seattle at the time? I assume you were not representing the clergy.

Whedbee: We represented the plaintiffs. Washington had a history of problems with various dioceses since the sixties and seventies. The challenge that you regularly confronted in these cases was that while there was often no question that the priest or church employee had committed the offense, many times the plaintiff didn't come forward until much later, so there were statute of limitation issues. Often the defendants would argue that the plaintiff should have brought the case earlier: "You knew about this years ago. You should have brought it, and you didn't." In cases where you were suing the diocese either instead of or in addition to the priest himself, questions inevitably revolved around what the diocese knew about the activity and when did they know it.

Cosslett: What happens with the statute of limitations in delayed discovery abuse cases? Like when blocked memories of sex abuse are discovered in therapy?

Whedbee: In Washington, the statute of limitations begins to run either from the date that the repressed memories are discovered or—and this is the more common event—from the date of discovery of a causal relationship between sexual abuse and an injury. The injury from abuse suffered in childhood might only become apparent in adulthood, as in intimacy or parenting issues. Washington's discovery rules turn on facts that are specific to the plaintiff's personal history, such as whether and when he sought counseling. And the rules apply to negligent third parties as well as to the abuser.

Cosslett: You wanted to impute knowledge to the diocese because you would have access to a deeper pocket?

Whedbee: That would be one strategic consideration, yes. But at the same time, it has been well documented that these people were abusing their parishioners and the powers-that-be did nothing, or would reassign the malefactor to a different parish. It was the institution's fault because this conduct was tolerated and hidden.

Cosslett: Can you describe the legal practice in Seattle generally? How big are the firms? What drives the practice there?

Whedbee: There's one big firm in town that was founded here and now has offices worldwide called Perkins Coie. They are counsel to Boeing and represent big companies. They have over eight hundred lawyers nationally. There are a few other big firms, like K&L Gates, which used to be a local bigger firm, and they do a lot of intellectual property. There are a few medium-sized firms, around fifty lawyers or so, which handle run-of-the-mill commercial litigation, tort litigation, contracts, that sort of thing. There are a number of what they call "full-service firms" that do everything from wills and estates to intellectual property to criminal defense to toxic torts.

Cosslett: On the East Coast, we have seen a lot of consolidation amongst smaller firms. It's hard to find a mid-sized general practice in New York these days. Are you seeing that out West at all?

Whedbee: We are seeing medium-sized firms that are imploding. You'll find a firm that used to take up four floors of a big building now down to three lawyers. This has happened to a number of firms just since I've been practicing.

I think there are two things happening here. On the one hand, it's expensive to hire lawyers, and in a contracting economy, lawyers get shut out. Secondly, if there's a lot of fat going around, these medium-sized firms can maintain a pretty high overhead. If times are leaner, and these firms are accustomed to this overhead, it becomes an albatross. That's what's happening. These firms have staffing, and IT, and paralegals, and data/word processors, and all these things that big firms apparently need to operate, and the work's not coming in.

Cosslett: Tell me about the practice and history of MacDonald Hoague & Bayless.

Whedbee: The firm was founded by three partners in the early 1950s—Ken MacDonald, Fran Hoague, and Alec Bayless. All three had served in World War II. Ken is from a blue-blood family in Boston and served in the infantry in Italy. He was a genuine war hero. After the war, when he came back to this country, he wanted to right many of the civil wrongs that he saw going on in the United States, including racial and other inequities. He came out to Seattle, and got together with Alec and Fran.

Ken's first claim to fame was that he represented professors at the University of Washington who were being forced to take loyalty oaths. At the time, the House Un-American Activities Committee was something of a band on the road. The committee would show up in different cities, convene, and call people in front of them to establish that they were properly American. Ken would represent people who were called in front of this and other, similar committees. He became famous for that. He also represented Paul Robeson when he came to Seattle. Robeson was banned from performing because of his left-wing background. The firm also partnered with other attorneys in representing the Seattle Seven, which was a Vietnam-era group. Since then, the firm has ridden the zeitgeist of civil rights litigation in representing plaintiffs in political, racial, and gender discrimination cases.

In the 1980s, Tim Ford joined the firm. He is one of the premier death penalty lawyers in the United States and also does a lot of police misconduct work. He is one of my mentors. I joined the firm in 2007. Ken is ninety-four and still comes into the office once a week.

The practice of the firm is split fairly evenly between immigration and litigation. It was one of the first immigration law firms in the Northwest and, over the last decades, their immigration practice has blossomed and has become nationally recognized. The litigation practice incorporates civil rights, criminal defense, catastrophic injuries, employment law, and fair housing. Then there are subspecialties, like wage and hour litigation, and prison litigation. On the litigation side, there are six partners, and I'm the only associate. There are about the same number on the immigration side, and we have two new immigration associates.

Cosslett: It's unusual these days to see a firm driven by a political ideology. Because the firm is fairly small, does it confine itself to fairly straightforward cases?

Whedbee: Quite the opposite. One thing about MacDonald Hoague & Bayless is that, foolishly or not, we take cases despite their complexity or difficulty, and we are often referred cases by other firms in which we are expected to pull a rabbit out of a hat—and often do. That's the reputation of the firm around town, for better or worse, because sometimes we really do get dog cases and we take them anyway.

One thing about the firm that I came to realize after I began to work here is that it has a great reputation for being very scrupulous. It is not uncommon to question a litigant's characterization of the facts. But I have heard from judges and mediators that, because of the strength of the firm's reputation, nobody questions our recitation of the facts.

Cosslett: You have described your firm's practice as artisanal. What do you mean by that?

Whedbee: When I say the firm's practice is artisanal, I mean that we have very close relationships with our clients, because often they've gone through really horrific or trying experiences, and you have to build a rapport with them to be an effective counselor at law. Our job is to help them outside of the legal issues, but also to be able to convey what they've gone through in a way that's persuasive and ideally cathartic for them. We try to take a holistic approach to what this person has gone through and vindicate on many levels those rights that have been violated. That's what I mean by an artisanal law firm. Each case we take presents different difficulties, complexities, and special issues. We tailor our representation accordingly.

We take hard cases, we work them up thoroughly, we produce fine work products for our clients, and we enjoy a strong reputation for honesty in the legal community. Tim once said to me, "When you're doing your work, you have to always make the right decision. And the most important decisions are those you make when you're at your office late at night by yourself, and it's only you who will know if your decision is right or wrong."

Cosslett: In the litigation department of a large firm, you might find junior associates in the library doing research, midlevel associates helping to draft briefs, and partners in the courtroom. How does your firm's structure compare?

Whedbee: Thankfully, it's not like that at all. We have a mentorship program and you're writing briefs right out of the gate. I had been here for two months and I was drafting summary judgment responses in a police misconduct case. I've argued two cases in front of the Ninth Circuit as an associate.

As an associate, I have to be supervised by another attorney, and each partner has a different approach to that relationship. As an example, Tim Ford would say, "Well, who's driving? Are you driving or am I driving?" If he's driving the case, then he'll say, "I need you to do X and to do Y." If I'm driving, I take control of the case, and I plan the discovery, I think about strategy, and, of course, I consult with him. It's a role reversal, and I'll say, "Tim, can you do this? Can you do that?"

Mel Crawford, another mentor of mine, has a superb command of the facts of each case. And when I work with him, I am often tasked with finding the law to buttress our position. We then put our heads together in hammering out our legal arguments and divide up the brief writing.

In either dynamic, you get used to being in a partner role.

Cosslett: It sounds very collaborative.

Whedbee: Yes, and that's how you become a better attorney. I've stayed in touch with a couple of my co-clerks from Judge Gould's chambers who went off to fancy, well-paying jobs in DC. They called me from some warehouse in Arizona where they were doing document review and I told them, "I just did my second trial of this year." So I'm really quite pleased I chose this route over that one, even though I'm probably paid fifty percent of what they are paid.

Cosslett: Tell me about your role as a litigator.

Whedbee: I didn't realize until I started to work in litigation that there really is a litigator code. There are true litigators and there are people that just do it for a while. You're not really accepted as a litigator until you've been at it for ten years, and even then your acceptance is gradual. You have a long apprenticeship because there are so many things that you need to learn. I've been at it for almost five years and I still just think, "My God. I don't know what I'm doing."

Cosslett: Don't tell your clients that.

Whedbee: No, I won't. When you do complex litigation, the chessboard has a lot of dimensions and you have to figure out how to move all the pieces. That's the fascinating part, but it's also the difficult part.

Cosslett: What kind of trial work have you done?

Whedbee: I've had two jury trials and two bench trials. I represented two different sets of clients who were Somali. Both clients had had their houses raided on the same day in a nationwide DEA[1] investigation. The DEA was looking for khat, a substance that is grown and is legal in the Horn of Africa and also in most European countries, but is not legal here in the United States. It's chewed socially by many Africans, including Somalis, and is about as strong as a double espresso.

The Bush Administration was looking for the channels of funding going back to Al Qaeda and other terrorist organizations, and they figured that if they got underneath this system of khat, they might be able to find out what the funding channels were as well. This was actually a totally misguided, fruitless undertaking. What happened was that a lot of people got swept up even though they weren't in possession of and weren't dealing khat. The government partnered with local law enforcement often using SWAT teams, and they served search warrants in the very early morning. They went in with full military regalia and all. These people had come from war-torn Somalia, and they got really scared.

They didn't let people dress themselves properly, so of course the Muslim sensibilities were offended and degraded. We handled two of these families. In one case, we settled with the United States and then we were dismissed on summary judgment against the local cops. In the other case, we went to trial and lost, unfortunately. At that point, I realized that as much as I might ardently believe that what we're doing was right, your general Joe Juror doesn't really give a shit and takes for granted that the government is acting appropriately. All the

---

[1] US Drug Enforcement Administration

government had to do was stand up and say, "This money was being channeled back to terrorists."

We took the cases to the Ninth Circuit, and I really thought we were going to win. The issue was about the entry into the house. There's something called the "knock and announce rule." If the police serve a warrant, they have to knock and identify themselves as police and give the people a chance to clothe themselves and come to the door. It's supposed to be an orderly process, unless there is genuine danger or risk of evidence destruction. The police have to have specific indications of "exigent circumstances" not to comply with the rule, and here there was nothing. We were trying to put a stop to the idea that the police can just assume people are going to be dangerous because you've heard that they're dealing khat. The plaintiffs were not drug dealers, they were just normal people. I think it's hard for a jury to accept that the police may not have complied with the law when they get up and talk about how dangerous things are generally.

Cosslett: Why did the Ninth Circuit rule against you?

Whedbee: They said that there were exigent circumstances with respect to the one case where the police didn't knock at all. And in the other case, they knocked and waited only ten seconds. The issue there was that the Seattle Police Department has a standard rule: they always wait ten seconds. The courts have said that the practice of maintaining a rigid rule like this, a bright-line wait period, is unconstitutional. So we sued both the officers and the city, but there's a doctrine in constitutional law that says if the underlying officers' actions are constitutional, then you don't reach the larger issue of municipal liability or the policy guidelines followed by the SPD. The court in that case said the ten-second wait was reasonable under these circumstances, and we never got to the larger issue.

Cosslett: I understand your firm also gets involved in Innocence Project cases.

Whedbee: Yes. I was with the Innocence Project at the University of Washington. Jacqueline McMurtrie, who's the director of the Innocence Project Northwest Clinic, has referred a couple of cases to us, and we're partnering with Peter Neufeld and Barry Scheck's firm in representing a couple of guys who were incarcerated for seventeen years for a rape that they didn't commit. The Innocence Project here locally got them exonerated. We're representing them in a civil context to see if there was liability on the part of Clark County officers.

Cosslett: Do a lot of Innocence Project cases result in successful civil trials? You would think *prima facie* that the fact of exoneration demonstrates that somebody, somewhere along the line, did something wrong.

Whedbee: That's true. But the hurdle that you run into—and this is one of the issues in civil rights litigation that's both fascinating from an intellectual standpoint, but incredibly frustrating from a practical standpoint—is that officials have all kinds of immunities. In the postconviction setting, when someone is exonerated, often the misconduct is that of the prosecutor, but prosecutors enjoy what's called "absolute immunity." There is only one narrow exception to this doctrine. Tim Ford won on this exception in a case he argued in front of the Supreme Court in 1997 called *Kalina v. Fletcher*, in which the Court declined to accord absolute immunity to a prosecutor acting in the role of a witness rather than as an advocate. But, for the most part, you can't sue prosecutors, and it's tragic because even though somebody has spent all this time in prison for a crime he didn't commit, he can't get any compensation.

There have been a few prominent cases that have come out of Orleans Parish, where the training of prosecutors in Brady issues, for instance, is nonexistent.

Cosslett: What are Brady issues?

Whedbee: Withholding exculpatory evidence. The prosecutor has a constitutional obligation to hand over any material exculpatory evidence to the defense, and if he or she doesn't, and there is a reasonable probability that the withholding changed the outcome of the trial, then a conviction is reversed.

What happens is that you'll discover down the road, after a defendant has been in jail maybe for many years, that the prosecutor sat on something that he shouldn't have. Obviously, a wrong has been done to the defendant and there's even been an obvious constitutional violation under the Sixth Amendment, but you can't sue the prosecutor because he's absolutely immune. What you try to do is to go after the police officers involved in the case, as they fall under Brady as well, but the officers themselves must have withheld information from the prosecutor for Brady to apply.

Usually, they're giving their evidence to the prosecutors, and as soon as it makes that transition, then we have immunity issues. It's very, very difficult to get in there and find out what actually happened, but there are a lot of cases where you do. Something obviously went wrong, and often you find out that many people were complicit in the wrongdoing and you can get some compensation for the victim. But it's a minefield.

Cosslett: What other practice areas are you involved in?

Whedbee: I've started to do some fair housing cases, which I like, and some criminal defense work. Sometimes the fair housing cases involve racial discrimination, but not always. I have a case now that is pretty interesting. My client runs a clean and sober halfway house in a small community. Studies have shown that taking people who are substance abusers or former substance abusers out of high-crime areas and putting them in a familial setting in residential areas is an effective method for keeping these people sober. This is what my client has done, and he has received accolades from probation officers and social workers and police, yet there's a local mayor who, for whatever reasons, doesn't want to have a halfway house in his little fiefdom, and so he's making it difficult for my client to get a business license.

Cosslett: Not in my neighborhood . . .

Whedbee: Right. So my client has potential claims under the Federal Fair Housing Act. Substance abuse or alcoholism is considered a disability. It has to be reasonably accommodated. Unless the city can show genuine hardship, they have to give these people a permit to live in a residential area, even though they're not in a single-family home. Our country over-incarcerates people to a mind-boggling extent and there is a stigma that attaches to people who have spent time in jail, for whatever reason. One of the things that we do is try to enforce people's rights to live where they want to live and where they are allowed to live. That is a central ethos of fair housing.

Cosslett: People like to think they live on Wisteria Lane, and having a halfway house down the block disturbs that image. Tell me about the work you do in the area of criminal defense.

Whedbee: We had a really great case here where some local artists were being investigated for engaging in illegal gambling. These artists were putting on a cabaret in the course of which there may have been some gambling. The Seattle PD went undercover and infiltrated this group for many, many months. They were actually monitoring the group because they thought they might be involved with extreme leftist organizations like the Animal Liberation Front or the Earth Liberation Front. They were not. The artists were politically active and may have even taken radical stances, but nobody was a domestic terrorist.

After they spent inordinate resources investigating these people, teamed up with the FBI at times, the Seattle PD realized that there was nothing happening. But in order to redeem the expenditure of all this money, they decided to bring gambling charges against this group of local artists under a thirty-year-old statute that literally had to be dusted off. First, members of the group were charged with felonies, and then misdemeanor deals were offered.

My client stood his ground, and we held the prosecutor's feet to the fire for almost nine months. We conducted exhaustive discovery and went on the offensive saying: "This is domestic spying that you're engaged in, and now you're trying to use more money to justify your previous actions when you came up with nothing. And that's repugnant to us." We forced their hand and they ended up dropping all the charges against my client.

We had an unorthodox situation because the community really backed him. We had fundraisers and—for a criminal defense representation, which is usually the most discreet thing that you can imagine—it was very public. It was an inventive way of dealing with the charges against my client and, ultimately, effective. It was nice to be at a small firm that has freedom to be ballsy like that. It worked out very well.

Cosslett: Are there any other type of cases or practice areas that you've been able to enjoy by virtue of being at a smaller firm?

Whedbee: Ken MacDonald, the firm's founder, passed down a credo. Remember he is over ninety years old now, but he's still just as salty as you can imagine.

He said, "Back then, we took cases. We took them, we learned them, and we won them." I really like that approach, and I understand that in today's world of lawyering, when things are so specialized, that one of the nice things about working in a small firm is the diversity of practice. When a partner gets a case, he says, "Okay, let's do this," and all of a sudden I'm becoming an expert on labor law from the 1980s and we go to trial and we get a bunch of lumber mill workers their back pay. It's incredibly satisfying to both get that kind of result and to be able to figure out stuff from scratch, and take it on and win it.

That was a labor law case involving a bench trial. I've also been involved in working on what another partner, Mel Crawford, calls "grunt torts," where somebody dropped something and a worker gets hit in the head with a piece of steel. You have to figure out which defendants to sue. We've done some litigation out at the Hanford Nuclear Reservation in southeastern Washington, which employs numerous government contractors. The DOE[2] is cleaning up the Hanford nuclear site, which is dangerous and hard work. Hanford is something of a company town, split between many companies. You have lots of workers, and literally you'll see three generations of people who've been doing nuclear demolition work. It's crazy out there.

Cosslett: What's the kind of work that you're doing out there?

Whedbee: They were demoing a big building and somebody left a catwalk door open. The DOE conducted an investigation and found that the work safety package had been screwed up, but there were a lot of different companies involved who had provided workers, and so now we're trying to figure out who is responsible for my client's injuries. He is very badly injured and right now is only entitled to Labor & Industries—L&I—a form of worker's compensation. That means he is not allowed to sue his employer for workplace injuries. We figured out who was negligent in designing the safety program and sued the responsible parties in Massachusetts.

Cosslett: It's interesting to have a firm that's ideologically a civil rights firm also do personal injury work, which is generally considered non-ideological.

Whedbee: Sometimes it is and sometimes it isn't. What you have in these situations is powerful companies and people—workers—who are not so powerful. And that's how it is. We go up against a real deep-pocket firm and then it's just us. They have a whole team of lawyers and we've got a couple of guys. They stay at big hotels and we stay at Motel 6. There are real financial considerations for a small firm, and sometimes things get a little dicey and a little volatile, and you have to win enough cases or your firm won't survive financially. There's a balance that we're always trying to strike and restrike between taking cases that we feel are righteous, and those that we feel are going to be able to bring some money into the firm. In certain cases, we end up taking only a

---

[2]Washington State Department of Ecology

percentage of our hourly rate, which means that you just work that much harder in order to stay afloat while still taking these types of cases.

Cosslett: When you posit a personal injury case as an injured individual versus a company, it is not ideologically inconsistent with the other cases you take. It's the same mindset. In terms of your lifestyle, what kind of hours do you work?

Whedbee: Well, we're not as bad as the New York firms, but I think I'm probably at eighteen hundred billable hours. It's a lot. The other thing about our firm is that the line between firm and other life is not very clean. Because it is like a small family, sometimes it's dysfunctional and sometimes it's not. Everybody is impassioned about what they do, and it becomes an all-immersive experience. It gets a little crazy. You are there a lot or thinking about it a lot. And I find it difficult to extricate myself from work because I have a great deal of responsibility both to my clients and to the firm. In addition, I'm a relatively young lawyer and perhaps extra-cautious or extra-apprehensive about getting it right.

Cosslett: Are there issues of professional responsibility that have come up that are specific to your practice, either as a personal injury lawyer or as a civil rights litigator?

Whedbee: One issue that does come up is that when you sue the government or you sue a police department, you have to be unimpeachable in your ethics because there is a presumption that the government or police acted appropriately. For example, if your client got beat up by the cops and he is suing, the presumption is that that he deserved it.

And so we have, I think, an extra burden to be ethically unimpeachable, because as soon as anybody finds a little crack, they're going to seize on that. One thing I've learned that defense attorneys are best at is making the plaintiff, who has indeed been injured, feel like it's his fault and that somehow he is responsible for his injury. This is the one thing that just pisses me off more than anything.

You see defense counsel, in many cases, not all cases, but in many cases, belittle your client in front of you—in a deposition, for example. And they have to endure it. You and your client need to be ethically superior to the defense, because the presumption is that you're a lowlife or that you're trying to take advantage—which, of course, is not true. Or they'll take things like drug use, let's say, that has nothing to do with the actual injury, and they'll seize on that. And it's frustrating when that happens. They're trying to destroy the credibility of the victim, so you have to start out with by being ethically superior in order to withstand that attack.

Cosslett: And you also have to not let it get your goat, I would think.

Whedbee: True. And you have to make sure that your client understands what's going to happen and not let it get them, because usually there's a strategy to try to get them so upset that they'll start to talk or lash out, and all those things will be used against them later on.

Chapter 12 | *David Whedbee: Civil Rights*

Cosslett: Are you able to keep your cool in those sorts of situations? Are you levelheaded and calm? Or do you get invested?

Whedbee: I definitely get invested, but I think I'm pretty levelheaded. I'm the kind of guy who will give you the benefit of the doubt, and I go in with a spirit of cooperation. At some point, however, if they cross the line and piss me off, some other part of me comes out. Usually, I think it works really well for the case because I've been noble up to a point and then, at that point, I turn into a street fighter. It's on. And now it's justified.

Cosslett: Is there a skill set that you think is particularly useful for your practice area?

Whedbee: Empathy is important. Being able to really understand—and to convey your understanding in a way that is sincere and compelling to a fact finder—is also important. The hardest thing to do is convey that understanding within the context of a legal doctrine that you're trying to work through, and to talk to a judge or a jury in a way that avoids a lot of legalese and avoids almost anything that sounds like a lawyer. People just don't really trust lawyers. Being able to shift from one rhetoric to another is probably the most important and difficult skill of a trial lawyer, and it takes quite some time to learn because we go to law school—and all that gets taken from us.

Cosslett: What would you tell law students or undergrads considering law school about being a civil rights lawyer?

Whedbee: Be prepared for a really exhausting fight. The cases are typically uphill, and even though there might be things that you learn in law school about who has the burden of proof and what the standard of proof is, in real life, it's much higher in civil rights cases. If you're suing governments and police officers, the general social perception of these people and entities automatically puts them above you, and there are doctrines that are set up as roadblocks to prevent you from getting into court and saying what actually happened.

I like the intellectual intricacies and the complexities of these doctrines, but when you realize that you've got to run that gauntlet in every single case before you can actually go in and say what happened to your client, it can be pretty daunting. I mentor law students here each year and that's what I tell them.

On the positive side, of all the choices that law students or young lawyers have, this is one that you genuinely can feel excited and proud about almost every single day. It's rare that your work becomes drudgery or that you're doing something that seems disconnected from what's important to you. It hardly ever happens. You're always connected, and you're so tightly wound up in your work that it can be exhausting. But I would rather have that than going into a situation where I'm doing insurance defense or God knows what, and I'm just not invested at all.

Cosslett: Have you ever had to advocate for either someone or something that you just really didn't believe in?

Whedbee: I sit in a wheelchair and I've got one functioning arm, and I go to work and I work full-time, and maybe there's a little bit of me that feels that I need to work more than everybody else just to prove myself.

Sometimes I have clients who have been injured, and at some point, I'm a little less than persuaded that the injury is all that debilitating. That's the hardest thing I find. There certainly has been a wrong, and when you're working in constitutional law, the wrong you're trying to right is both concrete and abstract, because we are protecting the Constitution and there are principles we are trying to vindicate. We really are a check on the government and its power. But the way it works out practically is that you're looking at real injuries that were caused by the wrong, and that's the full form of the lawsuit. And to me sitting in the chair, I think: "Give me a break. You haven't been able to go back to work because of *what* again?" And that sort of situation I find difficult to swallow. But I think that's pretty rare, and usually the injuries are genuine and real and there's no malingering at all. That's really the only example of something I find difficult to deal with.

I don't mind representing employers and people who have a different ideological perspective than I do, although some people in our office are much more partisan. Generally, you're trying to work out some fair arrangement, and I enjoy working in a non-adversarial context where every single issue is not a fight.

Cosslett: Has your disability colored your experience as a lawyer?

Whedbee: The one thing about being in a wheelchair is that people have to do things for me a lot, and it's difficult for me to feel like I reciprocate. It would be nice, in a very mundane example, to be able to do the dishes after somebody cooks dinner. Day in and day out, I don't have that opportunity to reciprocate.

One thing I realized very early on in the law is that taking on a case and representing a client is like constructing something. It's building something. And so there's an intellectual lifting that goes on for the benefit of this person. I feel like I can reciprocate in that way, which is a way that I don't get to in ordinary life. I can actually help somebody and the disability doesn't matter. To that extent it's impacted my practice, because I feel this extra thing, whatever it is, that I've just described. The firm has been very generous with me as far as making allowances that they probably don't have to do, and everybody is very accepting of whatever deficiencies I have that a regular person might not.

Cosslett: Thank you, David.

CHAPTER 13

Shane Kelley

Partner
The Kelley Law Firm, P.L.

Shane Kelley's story presents an interesting study in contradiction. Trained by his father who was, in turn, trained by his father, Kelley joined the highly successful family trusts and estates firm in Fort Lauderdale right out of law school and has worked there ever since. Coming from a family of lawyers, some of whom practice together and all of whom have remained in close proximity to one another, the Kelley family illustrates an unusual legacy of close-knit professionalism. It is in comparing the strong ties that exemplify the Kelley family to their trusts and estates practice that the contradiction becomes apparent. The dissolution of the traditional family model is what drives much of Kelley's practice: seniors distanced from their children subjected to the predatory conduct of strangers, multiple marriages leading to distrust and alienation amongst children, corrupt fiduciaries, and philandering spouses. Add to this mix some very high-profile names and cases, such as Edna Winston and Anna Nicole Smith, and you have a good insight into the diversity and challenges posed by Kelley's practice.

Kelley graduated from the University of Colorado at Boulder. He earned his JD from Stetson University College of Law and earned an LLM in taxation from the University of Florida, College of Law-Graduate Tax Program. Kelley is board-certified by The Florida Bar as a wills, trusts and estates lawyer. He is a member and past chairman of the Probate Rules Committee of The Florida Bar. He is also a fellow of The American College of Trust and Estate Counsel, a national organization of experts in the field of estate planning and probate law.

Clare Cosslett: How did your family come to Florida?

Chapter 13 | Shane Kelley: Trusts & Estates

Shane Kelley: My family originally came from Oklahoma during the Dust Bowl. When they arrived in Florida, Fort Lauderdale was little more than a trading post. It was still part of Miami-Dade County. They put down their roots here in Fort Lauderdale and the family has been here ever since Charles Everett Farrington, my great-grandfather, became the third mayor of Fort Lauderdale. He helped to incorporate Broward County. My great-aunt, on the Farrington side, was one of the first women in the state to go to law school. Stetson Law School was the first law school in the state of Florida and she was one of the first women to graduate. My father's uncle was a judge here for a very long time, Judge Farrington. One of his children worked for Janet Reno in the Justice Department. And out of my generation, three out of five of us are now lawyers. My twin brother is a lawyer up in St. Augustine and my sister is in Tampa.

Cosslett: That's quite a family lineage. You have two generations of Kelleys currently practicing?

Kelley: My father practiced with my grandfather until he passed away in 1977, and he then continued the practice. I joined in 1995. We have two partners.

Cosslett: What is it like to practice law with a close family member?

Kelley: It's nice to be in a family business. I graduated law school in '95 and I've been practicing with my father ever since. I don't know that a law practice is any different than any other family business. When I graduated law school, the first case I worked on was the Edna Winston estate. My dad took me to every hearing and let me attend every deposition. He wasn't worried about me getting billable hours. If I had gone to a big firm, they would have said, "You need two thousand billable hours. Go get them." Billable hours didn't matter to my dad. He was trying to make me the best lawyer I could be. I got a jumpstart on being a litigation attorney. It was a great benefit to me.

Cosslett: It sounds like it is beneficial for a young lawyer to train in a smaller firm that doesn't have billable-hours requirements and perhaps has different priorities.

Kelley: I spent some time practicing with Holland & Knight here in Florida and they have some great lawyers there, but it depends on how firms are going to develop their associates. It varies firm by firm, but certainly, if you have a smaller firm where you have the freedom to focus on training, then it can be beneficial as long as you have the resources within the smaller firm to really train someone.

Cosslett: Especially when it's your dad and he has a vested interest in making sure that you learn what you need to. Has the family practice always been in trusts and estates?

Kelley: My father used to do some real estate, which was what my grandfather did, and then when he went to practice on his own, he changed it exclusively to trusts and estates law, and that's what he's been doing for twenty-five years.

Cosslett: When you were growing up, was it always assumed that you would join the family practice?

Kelley: It was always an option. I didn't always want to be an attorney. I really wanted to attend graduate school and be a professor, either English or history. When I graduated college, I had to make a decision, and I decided to attend law school. Practicing law was the family business, and it sounded interesting. I thought that was the best route to take at the time, and it's worked out great for me. I enjoy doing what I do, so I can't say I regret my decision.

Cosslett: Why did you go to Stetson?

Kelley: Well, my sister was going there and my father was a friend of the dean at the time. My twin brother went there also. It's a good law school. It's in Florida, and I wanted to come back to Florida since I was going to practice here. It was a good choice for me. I ended up going straight through and went both summers so I could graduate a semester early. At the time I thought, "I want to get out of school and get to work." Little did I know how great I had it in school! I loved law school.

While I knew I was going into trusts and estates law, I only took one class in trusts and estates because they just didn't have the classes available. Trusts and estates was a very popular class and the third-year law students were the only ones who could get into it. The only tax class I took was basic income tax, so I really wasn't exposed to trusts and estates or tax when I was in law school. I really loved constitutional law. And actually, it sounds weird, but I really liked labor law. I took advanced evidence, and trial techniques, those kinds of things.

Cosslett: Did you have any internships?

Kelley: I worked from my second year on. I always had a job. At first, I worked as a clerk at a law firm. And then I clerked for a year for a really great probate judge, Thomas Penick. He has since retired. The three of us, first my sister, then myself, and then my brother, were his clerks one after the other. He was an excellent judge. He let us sit in on all the hearings. We did research for him, and were able to discuss which way he ruled on those issues and why. He let us into the process. It was very valuable.

Because he thought it was important, the Judge took us on what they call Baker Act hearings, which is where someone is being involuntarily committed because they're a danger to themselves as a result of drug use or mental issues. He said, "It's important that you get to see that people's rights are being affected here." People could be involuntarily committed on the basis of the hearing. I received a very thorough background into every aspect of probate law. In Florida, probate courts handle guardianship and Baker Acts and those types of things.

The last semester of law school I interned with the state attorney. They have a program where students are temporarily admitted to practice law on a limited basis, and they let me handle misdemeanor cases. I think I had three DUIs and a couple of batteries. They'd have a state attorney work with you and say, "Okay, you can do the opening, you can do the direct on certain witnesses." They'd give you certain parts to do. I loved it. The only trial I lost was a domestic violence where the alleged victim didn't show up.

Cosslett: After you graduated in '95, you practiced for about three years, and then went on to get your LLM in tax at the University of Florida College of Law.

Kelley: When I began practicing, I did simple estate planning, estate trust administration, and estate trust litigation, so I was really doing the whole gamut. I was interested in doing more sophisticated estate planning and tax planning and I wanted to become more proficient in those areas. My twin brother and I went to college together at the University of Colorado, but he was an accounting major (which was a five-year degree), so he was a year behind me in law school. When he graduated, he went straight into the LLM program. When he came out, I said, "I'd like to go into the program," so he could come in and fill my spot in the office. I then went to do the LLM. It was a very intense one-year program leading to a master's degree.

Obtaining an LLM was one of the best things I've done. The experience was so beneficial to my practice. It was a different world from my law school experience. And the program at Florida is very good. NYU is the number one LLM program in the country, and then Florida is ranked number two. It's a very good experience and I would recommend it highly to anyone who wants to get involved in any type of estate planning.

Additionally, when I graduated the LLM program, I was courted—firms were flying in to hire LLMs. That was back when the big accounting companies, Ernst & Young and KPMG, were stockpiling tax attorneys because the firms were trying to become multidisciplinary firms. They wanted to do the estate planning as well as accounting. In Europe, the big accounting firms are the biggest estate planning firms because they're allowed to have a multidisciplinary practice over there. The biggest tax firms do the planning for their clients. They tried to establish that model here, but the ABA, to their credit, fought that very hard, and the accounting firms never progressed on that issue. But I remember they were just plucking people out of the LLM program in the hope that they were going to be able to do in-house estate planning.

Cosslett: On top of a large law school debt burden, adding the cost of an LLM can be prohibitive for some. Perhaps it is a good idea to do what you did, and practice a few years, trim that debt a bit, and then go out and hone your expertise.

Kelley: Yes, I went on a scholarship, but I understand. That's why people go to Florida for their LLM instead of NYU. It's a lot cheaper. The tuition at NYU and the cost of living in New York are both very expensive. Florida is a fraction of the price. While NYU is the more prestigious of the two schools, Florida is a very good program at a fraction of the cost. If you want to work in Florida, having an LLM from the University of Florida is very advantageous.

Cosslett: I notice you are board-certified. What does that mean?

Kelley: In Florida they have programs in which you can become certified in certain areas of the law and one of those areas is probate, trusts and estates. You take a certification test and, if you pass, then you can become board-certified in that area. I think other states have certifications as well, but Florida's is pretty large. Certification is supposed to signify to the public that this person has expertise in the area in which they're certified. It is a useful tool for a public who has no other way of knowing about a lawyer's field of expertise. It's like when you go to the doctor. How do you know that the orthopedist you're choosing is a good one? You have no way to judge other than what people say, referrals, and you look for board certification.

Cosslett: How has South Florida changed over the years and how is your practice different from your father's practice or your grandfather's practice?

Kelley: My practice is actually very similar to my father's in that he also does some estate planning, some administration, and some litigation. In that facet we're the same. I get more involved in some of the tax issues. It used to be that our clients were almost exclusively elderly people who came to Florida to retire and they would redo their estate plan upon becoming a Florida resident. And then we would do the estate and trust administration. These days I'm seeing a lot more people who are younger, who have either lived here for a long time or who were born here. We are also seeing more entrepreneurs. Our clients' needs are different than they used to be and, quite frankly, litigation is really what drives a practice these days. There's a lot of trust and estate litigation and I only see it increasing as we move forward.

Cosslett: What is driving that litigation?

Kelley: Especially down here in South Florida, you really don't have the nuclear family model. It's not Mom and Dad who have been married for thirty years and everyone is unified in the goals of the family. It's second, third, and fourth marriages. Families are fighting. There's also a lot of fraud when it comes to our elderly people because many of them are down here while their families are up North. No one's here to watch out for them, and there are a lot of people taking advantage of them. I'm talking about outsiders—neighbors, nurses, or anyone who understands that these people are vulnerable. They get close to elderly people and either they're getting wills or trusts done, they're outright stealing the assets, or they're establishing joint accounts—you name it. Taking advantage of the elderly is a cottage industry down here in South Florida. The Florida Department of Children and Families is supposed to look out for them, but there's a huge population and not a lot of resources.

Cosslett: Has your practice been affected at all by the roller coaster in the financial markets?

Kelley: It affects the type of cases we see and the different causes of action that people want to bring. When you have financial issues that crop up, you have more cases involving breach of fiduciary duty. Everyone wants to sue the trustee because they lost money in the stock market. Litigation is not adversely affected by the economy. If anything, it's spurred on by a bad economy because people are motivated to sue each other. You see an increase in litigation when the economy goes down.

Cosslett: Who do you generally represent? The trustee? The individual litigants? Whoever walks into your office first?

Kelley: It really depends. We'll defend the fiduciaries or we'll represent the aggrieved beneficiaries. In a will contest or a trust contest, we'll either defend the fiduciary against a challenge to a document or bring an action to challenge a document. We represent people in fiduciary litigation. We don't really choose one side or the other. It's whatever case is better and whoever comes in.

Cosslett: How big is the trusts and estates bar in South Florida?

Kelley: Very big. We are part of the RPPTL section of the bar. They call it "reptile" because it's real property, probate, and trust law. We have over ten thousand members. We're the largest and best organized section of The Florida Bar. We have an excellent organization, and our legislation is very successful. And, obviously, with a large elderly population, it's an important area of the law down here.

Cosslett: There was a period of time where you and your dad and one of the firm partners joined Holland & Knight to develop that firm's fiduciary litigation practice in South Florida. How big were they at the time, and why did you make that move?

Kelley: They were the twelfth largest firm in the country at the time and while there were several trust and estate attorneys, there were only one or two lawyers who were doing fiduciary litigation in Florida. They had a lot of planning and administration lawyers. Fiduciary litigation lawyers are a small community. There are not a lot of people that do it, and the people that do it full-time all know each other. The fiduciary litigators at Holland & Knight were great and we had been talking to them for a while and decided that we would go over there on a two-year basis and see how it worked out. We just picked up our firm and moved it over to Holland & Knight for those two years.

Cosslett: How was it to work for a larger firm?

Kelley: Obviously it was different than my experience here, but there are positives and negatives. I actually enjoyed it because I was just a lawyer there. That's all I had to worry about. I didn't have to worry about: "Is the copier working? Do I need to look at the books today? Do I need to get taxes done?" The downside of being in a small firm is you're not as productive because you have to do everything. You are running the office and being a lawyer.

At Holland & Knight, all I had to worry about was practicing law, so that was a positive for me. My practice was different because I did a lot more defense of corporate fiduciaries when they'd get sued for breach of fiduciary duty, or for some other reason. The clients I had were different and the negatives were, as with any big firm, that there was a bureaucracy that you don't have in a small firm. I have an eleven-year-old daughter. If I don't want to come to work one day, I don't come to work, and no one's asking me where I am and what I'm working on.

In a large firm, it's more structured. It's a business and they have to run it like a business. That was a lot different than what we are doing here. At the end of the two years, we decided we were more suited to being a boutique smaller firm and, because what we do is unique, I think it's very well suited to a boutique setting.

Cosslett: Are Fort Lauderdale and Miami interrelated in terms of the population and the issues that come up or are they discrete?

Kelley: We practice in all three counties: Palm Beach, Broward, and Miami-Dade. They're seamless in practice area, and I would venture to say that most people who practice in South Florida would practice in all three counties.

Cosslett: Now you mentioned that at Holland & Knight there was more corporate fiduciary work than individual representation. What is the difference in those two areas? How does a corporate fiduciary litigation present itself?

Kelley: The largest difference is that it's just not as personal. When you're representing an individual that has a lot on the line, it's a more personal experience for the litigant. That is not to say that corporate fiduciaries don't have a lot on the line in these matters as well. A damage assessment is a serious matter, but it will generally have a more significant impact on an individual than on a corporation.

Representing corporate fiduciaries is also different in that personalities really don't play into it. I came out of law school thinking, "If I have this set of facts on my side, I'm going to win this case." That's not the reality of it. The reality is that people play a large role in whether your client can ever make it to trial, whether they're going to stand tough through the whole process, or whether they're going to fold. Often the personalities of the litigants determine how your case is going to develop. That's not as true when you're doing corporate defense work.

Cosslett: A corporate fiduciary case would involve a bank as a fiduciary?

Kelley: Yes, a bank or any company with trust powers. A lot of the banks have trust powers. All the big banks do—such as Bank of America and Wells Fargo. And then a lot of the brokerage companies have trust companies such as Merrill Lynch and Morgan Stanley. And then there's the private trust companies like Northern Trust, Brown Brothers Harriman, and those types.

Cosslett: So the essence of many of those claims would be breach of fiduciary duty by inappropriate investments in risky securities?

Kelley: You have to remember that right about 2004 we were in a market decline, so a lot of the work was involving allegations of improper investments. On a technical level, the issues are very interesting but it's definitely a subspecialty. But there are often also construction actions in which people argue over document interpretation, saying that they aren't getting enough distributions or that the trustee is giving too much money to one over another. There are always those types of issues.

Cosslett: In a personal context, do you ever get tired of people being greedy?

Kelley: People always say about divorce law, "Ah, divorce law. These people are terrible." We see a lot of the same behavior in trust and estate litigation. But often these litigations aren't really about the money. They are about family disputes that have always been there: "Mom always loved you more so I'm going to get you back now." What often drives these litigations is pure, longstanding, personal spite. And people don't act rationally when you're trying to resolve these cases because it's personal to them.

With a company, the analysis is more logical: "What's the best financial outcome for this case? Is it better to settle it, or should we take a chance in litigation because the range of outcomes may be better for us?" With individuals, it can be totally illogical, irrational, and based on personal feelings. It's akin to divorce litigation because there's a pot of money out there, and everyone thinks they deserve it. Also, there's an emotional overlay if somebody has passed away. If a litigant's mother, father, sibling, or spouse has just died, it raises the stakes on an emotional level.

Cosslett: Do you find yourself being a mediator, a lawyer, and a therapist? I get a sense you're a very calm person.

Kelley: I think I'd be a pretty bad therapist, but I to do try to be calm. You can't let it get to you. You want to do the best job you can for your client, but if you get involved personally, you're going to have a lot of stress in your life.

Cosslett: You've mentioned that your practice is divided into fiduciary litigation, estate planning, and estate administration. What's involved in litigation? What's involved in estate planning? What's involved in administration?

Kelley: Fiduciary litigation tends to be the largest part of my practice because it's so time-consuming. About sixty percent of my practice is in litigation. You have the pretrial work, depositions, discovery—those kinds of things. Then you have the phase leading up to trial, the trial, and mediation. It is very specialized and in many ways, different than other types of litigation because fiduciary litigation involves a distinct area of the law.

Cosslett: At trial, are you in front of a jury or are you in front of a judge?

Kelley: We're rarely ever in front of a jury. All will and trust cases are equitable in nature, and you're only entitled to a bench trial. A fiduciary is normally subject to equity, because if you look at the way that the fiduciary holds title to property, there's a split between the equitable and the legal title. They don't really own property in the sense that if you go buy something, you own it. They're holding it for the benefit of others.

The concept goes all the way back to England, where you could not sue a trustee at law. You had to sue them in the ecclesiastical courts. And that has carried over into our law. And remember, our courts used to be divided into equity and law courts. Florida merged the two types of court into one, so our courts in Florida have both equity and law jurisdictions now, but there's still a distinction between the two.

Cosslett: What is your trial strategy in a bench trial? Do you just present the facts, or do you attempt to add a little drama, a little flair?

Kelley: It really depends. You can't answer that question until you know the judge you're in front of. Some of them strictly follow precedent and others are more influenced by the equity side of the equation. And it's always different. All judges are people, and they're affected by different things.

Cosslett: So you take your strategy from the judge that you're appearing in front of?

Kelley: Yes, and we are lucky here in Broward County. We have great judges in probate. They are appointed to the division and most of them stay there for the remainder of their career. Probate is a very desirable division in Broward County. We have three judges, and you get to know them because you're in front of them all the time. So you know what the judge is looking for and you can determine what your trial strategy is going to be from that. Of course, it's not as dramatic as being in front of a jury.

Cosslett: What is the jurisdiction of the probate court? What are all the areas that it encompasses?

Kelley: All probate matters. So anyone who passes away and has a will is involved in probate. Also, in Broward County it encompasses all trust matters, which includes trust litigation. That is pursuant to local order, so that's not always the case. At the trial level, we have county and circuit courts and small claims courts. Small claims is minor matters. County court is matters up to a certain dollar amount, and then above that you're in circuit court. All probate matters, trust matters, and guardianship matters are subject to the probate court jurisdiction. As we saw from Anna Nicole Smith, disposition of remains are also in probate court.

Cosslett: How much of your work is administration and what does administration involve?

Kelley: Probably twenty to twenty-five percent of my work is administration. When a person passes away, administration involves getting his or her property to the rightful beneficiaries. If it's through a will, it involves getting it probated, getting creditor issues resolved, and getting the tax issues resolved. It is the same on the trust side, but you're not subject to a probate proceeding. In trust administration, you're unsupervised by a court, but it's the same procedure as probate.

Cosslett: Now once you're in probate, you're under the watchful eye of the probate court, which ensures that the personal representative is doing what he needs to be doing and is not being a bad guy. Why do people say, "Avoid probate"?

Kelley: That idea was pushed a lot by people who wanted to either sell trusts or serve as trustees on trusts. In Florida, it's not that bad to go through probate, and there's actually some benefits to doing it. Right now, if you go through probate, you publish what's called a notice to creditors, and you have a three-month period where creditors can file claims, and if they don't, they're barred.

If you don't do a probate, creditors have up to four years to step forward. So a trustee could distribute all the property, have no idea about the creditors, not even check to see if there are any, and then the creditors come back after the distribution of all the property and say, "Hey, Mr. Trustee. Where's my money? I'm going to sue you because you breached your duty to me because you didn't make sure that I was taken care of."

So there are some advantages to probate. And, as you said, it's supervised. The court is going to make sure that people aren't stealing money and that everything's taken care of: the taxes are paid, the creditors are dealt with, and everything is done before they discharge that personal representative.

Now, it takes time to go through probate. It's just like any other process. If you're going to work with a government entity, it's going to take time. They're slow and they're understaffed and they're backlogged, but it's not that onerous of a process in Florida. I think a lot of states have more onerous procedures that have resulted in people saying, "I don't want to go through probate. I don't want to pay these probate attorneys. I don't want to deal with the judges." And, if you have a close family that's not fighting with each other and you have someone you trust who can administer the trust, that's fine. You don't need that oversight.

But I always say to people: "There's probably not one individual non-corporate trustee—Uncle Tom, Uncle Joe, or whoever it is—who's running the trust, that isn't doing something wrong. It's still a complicated procedure with an entire chapter under Florida law imposing duties and responsibilities and liabilities that these people are just incapable of fulfilling on their own. You still need a good attorney to bring you through the process properly."

So there are a lot of things that aren't being done in these trust administrations that should be done to protect both the fiduciary and the beneficiaries. If trusts are run properly, they're beneficial. And one of the benefits of having a trust is that they're private. If you look, for instance, at the estate of Michael Jackson, no one knows what his estate plan is because it was in a trust. Wills are filed with the courts. Any nosy neighbor can go down and look at the will. A trust is not filed with the court. It's a private administration that's not subject to court oversight unless someone invokes the court's jurisdiction.

Cosslett: Not everyone has the assets of a Michael Jackson, unfortunately, but if you want to create a dispositive instrument in which person A won't know what you're giving to person B, C, and D, then the right implement is a trust rather than a will?

Kelley: That's not the case in Florida because any beneficiary is entitled to a copy of the document. I'm talking about outsiders. Maybe you're a high-profile person and you don't want outsiders to know your business. Maybe there are other reasons you don't want anyone to see it. Personally, I don't care. If anyone wants to go look at my will after I die, let them go ahead. It doesn't matter. But some people just don't want that scrutiny.

The other benefit is that trusts are effective from the moment they're executed. That's why they are sometimes called "revocable living trusts," because they're alive while you're alive. If you become incapacitated for some reason, or can no longer manage your own assets, then the successor trustee can step in and take over for you. It's a good guardianship avoidance tool because the other way is to go into court and get a court-appointed guardian and that becomes a matter of public record. It can be humiliating to the person who is incapacitated. You pull away all their rights. You can avoid that through a trust to a large extent because the successor trustee can come in and pay all the bills and make sure the person's taken care of.

Cosslett: It sounds like a good planning tool.

Kelley: It's a good tool. A lot of people are saying, "I want a trust." But, they don't know why. They heard someone say in a seminar that they should have a trust. A lot of times you say, "Well, why do you want the trust? What's the specific purpose?" And often people don't need a trust. I always say to my clients, "I'll do a trust for you. I charge you a lot more than a will. So if it's worth it to you, then great. If not, you may want to reconsider." So I don't try to oversell trusts.

Cosslett: What are the downsides of a trust other than the fees?

Kelley: The lack of oversight. If it's not a very cohesive family unit, there's always the risk that someone is going to misappropriate those assets, and there's no real way to tell until someone starts figuring out, "Hey, where's all the money? How come I'm not getting a distribution?"

Now, you can always invoke the court's jurisdiction to say, "Hey, Judge, something's wrong here. I don't think the trustee's doing his job." But that's upon a request to the court. Otherwise, courts don't interfere with the trust administration. People are people. They steal money. They do bad stuff. And with no supervision, it can be devastating, and that's why you have corporate trustees out there. That's a different situation. They're going to do their job. They're going to presumably administer the assets properly. You don't have that same concern, but as I said, when it's Uncle Joe, who doesn't know how to manage assets, who may have a precarious financial situation himself, the temptation's there to potentially misappropriate the money.

Cosslett: I don't think I'm going to come to Florida. Between Uncle Joe stealing money and swindlers duping old people, it sounds pretty rough.

Kelley: But that's why I have a job and that's what I see. I'm called in when the kids come in later saying, "Hey, this person took $100,000 out of Mom's account." And I'm the one that's hired to deal with that for the family, so yes, that's what I'm exposed to a lot. Unfortunately, it's ripe for the taking down here because of the elderly people. Their families are often not down here to supervise. They're still up in New York or Pennsylvania, or wherever they came from. Often people come down as a couple, which is fine, and then one of them passes away and they're alone. They're looking for someone to rely on and sometimes, unfortunately, it's the wrong kind of person.

Cosslett: We talked about litigation and administration. Is estate planning all about drafting wills?

Kelley: Wills, trusts, and tax planning. At the moment, it's an unusual practice because we're in a temporary tax situation that is going to expire at the end of the year if nothing happens. We went through 2010 for most of the year with no estate tax. We had George Steinbrenner die, no estate tax. Potentially a billion dollars in assets—and no tax. It was inconceivable.

When President Obama and the Congress finally reached a compromise, it was a two-year compromise. We don't have any certainty and that makes tax planning very difficult. We don't know. Right now we have a $5 million estate and gift tax exemption, but if the government doesn't do anything, then beginning next year, it's going to be reduced to a $1 million again. There are actually a lot of opportunities because of the present law. During your lifetime, you can give away $5 million without paying any tax. It is a very good opportunity for wealthy people to disperse their wealth to younger generations.

Cosslett: Of all the areas of practice that you have that you just described, which do you enjoy the most?

Kelley: That's a tough question. I enjoy the litigation because it's always challenging and there are so many different issues that come before you. We deal with tax issues, with construction issues, with challenging documents, with breach of duty. This area of the law is very technical and very complex, and most people don't understand that. But I also enjoy the administration of trusts and estates. Unlike litigation, where it can take two or three years to reach a resolution, an administration will generally take a year from beginning to end, and there's a sense of satisfaction that you derive from having gone from point A to point B.

Cosslett: Do you have an average day?

Kelley: I'd say probably no. I do a lot of work for the bar. My whole family does—my brother, my sister, and my father. My father wrote one of the best-selling probate manuals in the state, and he donated the proceeds to the bar. He's always been very involved in education and helping other probate lawyers, and we try to do that as well. There's always something that needs to be taken care of, always an emergency. It's never average, I can tell you that. It's different than a straight transactional practice or a normal probate estate planning practice, where you meet with your estate planning clients and then do your administration. It's not like that at all when you do litigation. So I combine it all, and it's interesting.

Cosslett: You have been involved in some high-profile cases.

Kelley: The most recent case involved the remains of Anna Nicole Smith. When Anna Nicole died in Seminole Casino down here, there was a very high profile dispute over the disposition of her remains. It's an area of law that is not established at all. There's no procedure that you can use, and there's no clear answer. After the Anna Nicole Smith trial, I was the co-chair on a committee that was formed by the RPPTL section of the Florida Bar to draft a statute to address the situation. There's no good law. It's conflicting. And it's really just wide open as to what happens.

Cosslett: What is life like when you go from your daily practice, which is active and busy, but really a regional practice, to being in the national spotlight? What was your involvement with the Anna Nicole Smith case?

Kelley: That was my fifteen seconds of fame. I was sitting in my office one night, and I received a call from Judge Seidlin. The Judge was calling from his courtroom and said, "I'm appointing you as a guardian ad litem[1] in this case." And I said, "Okay, Judge. It will be my pleasure." And I added, "Well, if the other counsel wants to talk to me, here's my number." I gave my number out because I didn't know that it was on live TV. I couldn't answer my phone for three months. I can't even remember how many calls I received. My voicemail was full after two days. Crazy people were calling me and saying, "You need to call me. I know the answer. I could tell you exactly what to do," even though these people had never met Anna Nicole Smith. It was just bizarre.

And I remember around nine o'clock that night, I was still in the office, and I received a call from some guy claiming to be Howard K. Stern. I hung up the phone, and his lawyer called me back and said, "That was really him. He wants to talk to you about the case." I talked to him for about an hour and a half.

---

[1] A guardian ad litem is someone appointed by the court to represent the interests of a person or entity that is unable to adequately represent their own interests in a proceeding, such as an infant, unborn or unknown person or entity.

He had been appointed Anna Nicole Smith's personal representative and executor on her will and was proposing to have her buried in the Bahamas. As part of my duties for the court, I actually ended up interviewing all of the parties concerned, including Anna Nicole's mother. Being in that trial was a great experience, but it was very unusual.

Cosslett: At the end of the day, what was the decision?

Kelley: The decision was that she was to be buried in the Bahamas in the same plot as her son, who had died shortly before her. It was the right decision. It was funny because I had been slated that day to give my report to the court. And I'd handed out my report with the case law to all of the counsel, and I had all the case law assembled. I was ready to give my report when the father of the deceased son called. The Judge took his testimony via the telephone, and at the end of the conversation said, "All right, we're done." He walked out of the courtroom and I never gave my report. The decision was appealed and it was upheld.

I remember the Judge said to the reporters, "You can't talk to the ad litem. He's retained by the court. And you're not allowed to talk to him. He's not a party." I wasn't pushing an agenda like the parties were. And I remember walking out of the courtroom the first day and there were hundreds of reporters standing in line. And I walked around the corner, and they're all ready, and they said, "Oh, it's the ad litem. We can't talk to him." And they all turned around.

Cosslett: You also worked on a case involving the Winston family? That's a famous name.

Kelley: It was Edna Winston's estate. Harry Winston had died first, and then his wife, Edna, was the second to pass away. We represented Bankers Trust, who was a trustee on Edna Winston's trust. The dispute was between the two sons over the assets and the estate and the Winston jewelry stores.

Cosslett: Are there other cases that you've had that are particularly interesting either by virtue of the names or by virtue of the issues or the personalities?

Kelley: I think a lot of my cases are interesting. We were involved in the litigation over the rights to some of Laura Ingalls Wilder's books, *The Little House on the Prairie*. The main litigation was in Missouri where she passed away, but we had a part of the litigation in Florida. We were also involved in the Gus Boulis estate if you remember that one. He was gunned down in Fort Lauderdale under suspicious circumstances and there was extensive litigation in his estate.

Cosslett: It sounds like you have an interesting and diverse practice sprinkled with the occasional star name or particularly crazy cast of characters to keep you entertained.

Kelley: It's a great area to practice in. Most people think, "Oh, trusts and estates is so boring." But it's exactly the opposite. It's fascinating. I wouldn't want to be in any other area of the law. I think it's challenging intellectually and, on a day-to-day basis, some of the most interesting litigation.

Cosslett: What issues of professional responsibility are specific to a trusts and estates practice?

Kelley: I think the most important issue that we have to deal with is conflicts within families. You'll often represent several members of a family—husband and wife, for instance. The classic conflict scenario is one where you prepare wills for both a husband and wife, and they leave everything to each other and their family members. The husband then comes in and says, "Oh, by the way, I want to leave everything to my girlfriend, but don't tell my wife about it."

Also, if you represent multiple generations of a family, disputes break out and you have conflicts. If there's litigation, can you represent more than one beneficiary or do they have conflicts? Do they have diverging interests? Can you represent them as a fiduciary? Can you represent them in both capacities, as fiduciary and as beneficiary? Those are the kinds of issues that you have to be really careful about in trusts and estates. Potential conflicts of interest is the biggest issue that we face, and it's constant.

Cosslett: How do you deal with the husband wanting to put his girlfriend in his will?

Kelley: The bar advises that you deal with it beforehand. I always have a contract, which states, "This is a joint representation. Anything that you say to me will be disclosed to the other spouse, so there's no confidence between the three of us. If you don't want me to tell your spouse something, don't tell me. And if you're not comfortable with that, obtain your own representation."

I have never had to deal with it, but, obviously, it comes up, and that's why it's the subject of ethics opinions. In real life, these things happen and you either take care of it ahead of time or you're stuck with a problem and you've got to figure out how to handle it.

The litigation context can be more difficult. Sometimes people are aligned when you take on the representation, and their interests diverge when there's litigation. Then you have to withdraw. Sometimes you can continue to represent one party if you can obtain a waiver. Sometimes you can't. You always want to try to avoid a conflict. And to me, it's generally not worth the time trying to salvage something if I'm going to be even close to a potential conflict. I just say, "No, sorry. I can't do it."

There is another conflicts issue that also comes up with some frequency. Next week in Fort Lauderdale and Tampa, I am heading up a seminar as chair of the Trust Law Committee and one of the issues involves gifts to lawyers in wills that they have drafted. You would think that lawyers don't do that, but apparently it's happening, and it's happening frequently. People should be able to trust their lawyers and not have to worry whether he or she is angling to obtain a personal benefit.

And that leads to another issue that we face that actually hasn't been squarely addressed: attorneys who name themselves in the fiduciary position, either as the executor or the trustee. And they're entitled sometimes to significant compensation for that role.

Cosslett: You can understand why people would name their lawyer as fiduciary because they want someone who is able to deal with papers and who is very organized. Your attorney is a natural candidate to serve both of those roles.

Kelley: There's a difference between someone making a considered determination to do that and a lawyer who coincidentally ends up in a lot of the documents as the fiduciary. There's a big difference between a lawyer who says, "You should appoint me," and lobbying for the position versus a client saying, "You know what? I've considered my options and you are the best choice."

Lawyers need to discuss the options with their clients and say, "Have you considered a corporate fiduciary? Have you considered a family member or co-trustee?" And then after measured determination, they may say, "No, I think you're my best option, and I understand that you're going to be paid an additional fee. I understand that you're going to hire your own law firm to represent you in your capacity as fiduciary and you're going to be paid two fees." So there's a big difference between doing it when requested and when it's in the client's best interests, and somehow ending up on a majority of your clients' estate planning documents as the fiduciary. You should always be working for your clients' best interest and when a lawyer benefits personally it needs to be examined closely.

Cosslett: What advice would you give law students or practicing attorneys about going into trusts and estates?

Kelley: Fiduciary litigation is a great practice area, but it is hard to break into. There are not a lot of people who do it. While it's a very good practice for a boutique firm, it is not always part of a big firm practice.

It's also difficult to advise people to go into estate planning because we don't know what the future holds in terms of the tax law. That's a problem. If you want to get involved in the probate and trust area, students should try to take as many classes as possible. Students should also try to intern with trust and estate firms or in a big trust and estate office. And they should become involved with the trusts and estates section of their bar. I've been involved with the bar since the day I started because my father was. The more junior you are when you get involved, the better off you will be. You're going to meet more people. You're going to obtain more knowledge. It's going to be beneficial to you. Trusts and estates is a great area to practice in.

Cosslett: There's some talk in New York about a mandatory pro bono requirement for newly admitted lawyers. Do you think trusts and estate planning would be a good area for a pro bono practice contribution and a way for a lawyer to get his or her feet wet?

Kelley: There's always the need for that: helping out low-income people with probate issues, durable powers of attorney, guardianships, and those kinds of things. Sure, there's a lot of opportunity and there's a lot of people that need it, so that would be great.

Cosslett: It sounds like Florida might need some good lawyers to come down and help to look after your senior population.

Kelley: Well, if you eliminated your estate tax up there, more seniors would stay in New York. I met someone the other day who said, "I wish I could live in New York, but I'm not going to pay that estate tax." And you have to wonder how much money New York can bring in with its estate tax as compared to how much wealth would remain in New York if it was eliminated. It's great that Florida benefits, but the amount of money that leaves New York because people don't want to pay estate tax must be astronomical.

Cosslett: Someone needs to do a cost-benefit analysis, but that sounds like a subject for a different book.

CHAPTER 14

Arthur Feldman

Founder and Principal
The Feldman Law Firm, P.C.

What do you do if, as a junior associate in a large and respected Houston law firm, you find yourself entrusted with a high level of responsibility in a huge industrial litigation, and you know that you won't see that level of responsibility again for years? If you are a trial lawyer at heart, you take a loan from the bank and a deep breath, hang out your own shingle, and begin hustling for clients. And, if you are **Arthur S. Feldman***, you win an eleven-to-one verdict of gross negligence in your first trial as a solo practitioner and go on to build a successful practice representing clients ranging from individual plaintiffs to Fortune 500 companies in civil cases as diverse as personal injury, medical malpractice, discrimination, breach of contract, and copyright infringement. And you take pride in the fact that, while you set out to make money as a lawyer, you have also managed to do a lot of good for folks along the way.*

Feldman graduated cum laude from Duke University with a BA in political science. He earned his JD from the University of Texas at Austin School of Law (UT Law) and served as a law clerk to the Honorable Joseph T. Sneed in the Ninth Circuit Court of Appeals.

Clare Cosslett: Have you lived in Texas your whole life?

Arthur Feldman: I grew up in Houston, Texas, and have lived here my whole life, except for when I went to school. Both my parents were professionals. My dad was a physician. He's retired. And my mother was a speech pathologist. I have two brothers: a doctor and a businessman. I'm a third-generation immigrant. One side of my family came from Russia and ended up in Omaha, Nebraska. The other side came from Poland, passed through Galveston, and ended up in a small town called Shepherd, Texas. Galveston was the second-biggest port for Jewish immigration and that side of my family turned into bona fide hicks pretty quickly. They grew up eating squirrel and frog legs. I have an eclectic background for sure.

Cosslett: Are there still members of your family out there munching on roadkill?

Feldman: Well, we have a family pond still in Shepherd. And I plan to go harvest a ten-foot alligator in September. You get a dead chicken, and a big hook, and a real strong rope. You leave it there overnight, and you come back the next day, and you hope that it tried to eat the chicken, and then you shoot it. So that's it. Shoes and a handbag. After I get rid of the gator, I'm going to do some duck hunting on the pond with my dog.

Cosslett: Wow. Life sounds rough in Texas. How did you choose Duke for undergrad?

Feldman: I got in at the last minute, actually. I was on the waitlist. I had planned to go to the University of Texas like most of my high school friends, and I had a room and a roommate lined up. About three weeks before I was supposed to start school, Duke called and said a spot had opened up. I just got in my car and drove there, sight unseen. I had no idea about Atlantic Coast Conference basketball—no idea. All I knew was Southwest Conference football at the time. I learned all about basketball when I was up there. Became a big ACC basketball fan and still am.

Cosslett: Was sports a factor in your decision?

Feldman: Nope. Did not factor at all. I just wanted to get out of Texas.

Cosslett: I've talked to a few people who grew up in Texas, and what I hear is, "I wanted to get the heck out of Texas." Most of them stay out of Texas, but you came back.

Feldman: Well, it's pretty one-sided politically here—more so than it's ever been. But when I grew up it wasn't like that. I had always planned on coming back, but it was good to leave the nest for a little while.

Cosslett: When did you make the decision to go to law school?

Feldman: When I graduated from Duke with a degree in political science, I could have gone into sales or general business, I suppose, but I wanted to go ahead and get a second degree. I wanted to be a lawyer. I had wanted to be a lawyer for a long time. I was always very argumentative, so it was a natural progression.

Cosslett: Was the University of Texas a good experience? Did you enjoy UT Law?

Feldman: I would say that Texas was the first time I really tried to apply myself as a student, and I did very well my first year. In my second year, I was asked to be the managing editor of *The Texas Law Review*. So I did that, and it took a lot of time, as you might imagine. During all of my second year, most of the summer between my second and third year, and the first half of my third year, I often spent fifteen hours plus a day in the office of the law review. It was pretty demanding.

Cosslett: Were you able to keep up with your coursework when you were spending that much time at a publication?

Feldman: It dropped off, to tell you the truth, but I still did okay. I didn't have any trouble in my classes, although I wasn't getting the highest scores on my exams. I ended up graduating with a respectable GPA, but I wasn't the top of the class by any means. The law review was really a full-time job.

Cosslett: Of your courses, what do you remember enjoying the most and what do you remember not enjoying?

Feldman: I remember professors more than I do the courses. I took a procedures course from Michael Tigar that was very enjoyable. He's a very well-known criminal defense lawyer. He is now Professor Emeritus of Law at Duke. And I took some courses from Bill Powers, who became dean of UT Law and is currently the president of the University of Texas at Austin. I had a really good relationship with Charles Alan Wright, which I'm pretty proud of. He co-authored, along with Arthur Miller, the definitive fifty-four-volume treatise, *Federal Practice and Procedure*. His office was right next door to the law review, so I would see him quite a bit. He was a very interesting guy, quite a figure. I talked too much in law school, and he actually had me handcuffed and gagged at one point as part of a class on free speech. He asked the biggest guy in the room to handcuff me, and he did. I didn't talk as much in class afterwards. A year later, when I was working late on the *Review*, he asked me to witness his personal will, which I've always considered to have been quite an honor.

Cosslett: When you graduated, you clerked for a year with the Ninth Circuit. That appears to be a very popular circuit.

Feldman: There was a judge in the Ninth Circuit named Joseph Tyree Sneed III who had gone to UT and became a Nixon appointee. He always picked one clerk from Stanford and one from UT, and he traditionally picked the managing editor of the law review at UT.

He had a very famous daughter, Carly Fiorina. She was the CEO of Hewlett-Packard and unsuccessfully ran for the Senate a couple of years ago in California. She is a trailblazer as a woman in tech. They had an incredible home in Pacific Heights, and we got to go in there a couple of times. He was a very nice guy.

Cosslett: Tell me about your experience clerking.

Feldman: When you're clerking on an appellate court, it's a bit isolated. You have your judge, the judge's staff, the co-clerks that you work with, but you really don't see or interact with attorneys very much because it's not like a trial court clerkship. There were two other clerks, and a staff of two or three. It was an odd time to clerk for the Ninth Circuit in San Francisco because it was right after the Loma Prieta earthquake. The incredible Beaux-Arts building that had housed the court wasn't habitable because of the earthquake, so we had to move offices a couple of times. Eventually they were able to rehabilitate the US Court of Appeals Building and moved back in, although not until after my clerkship ended.

Cosslett: I would imagine a Nixon appointee would tend to be somewhat conservative. Did Judge Sneed look for a clerk who agreed with his worldview?

Feldman: To his credit, I don't think it ever came up, even as an interview question. He was going to rule how he was going to rule, and we were the laboring oars—we weren't steering the boat. I think he appreciated hearing many sides, so I don't think his politics were an issue when he chose his clerks. I wonder if that's less the case today, but I hope it isn't. I was sad when he passed away in 2008.

Cosslett: When you took your first job after your clerkship, you knew that you were going to sign on with the Houston firm where you had summered, Mayor, Day, Caldwell & Keeton. Why did you choose them?

Feldman: I had made some good friends there over the summer and it was a good fit. I'm still close friends with almost all of my class at Mayor Day. I see them all regularly, do business with them, refer cases to them, have cases referred by them. But, while I really liked the firm, I realized after a few big trials that I didn't want to stay. It was a fairly large-size firm, about one hundred and thirty people by the time I left.

Cosslett: Tell me about the life of a junior litigator at a big Houston firm.

Feldman: I don't think my experience was very typical. I knew I wanted to get into trial work and started as a litigator working directly under Richard Keeton, who is still practicing. I count Richard as my mentor. He was assigned immediately to a very large case and I assumed a pretty big role in it that dominated my career for the first couple of years. I'm pretty sure I took more depositions in the case than anyone else. It was a commercial fraud case involving a chemical plant. It was probably at the time one of the biggest document-production cases that there had ever been. It was a huge, huge lawsuit and it went to trial. And we lost badly.

Cosslett: Which side did you represent?

Feldman: We represented the plaintiffs. For half a billion dollars, they purchased technology and equipment to build a huge plastics plant that made ethylene, which is a principle building block in most plastics. They sued the engineering firm for fraud over the representations made concerning the capabilities of the technologies.

In hindsight, it couldn't have been a better experience for me. It was pretty tough to start out, but it was a lot of responsibility early on. The work involved a lot of depositions, briefing, work with witnesses, running around, document production, and putting evidence together—things that I continue to do to this day. I just don't think that most lawyers at my level were asked to shoulder such a high level of responsibility.

Cosslett: As a first-year?

Feldman: As a first- and second-year. There was a tremendous amount of support. There was another firm in New York that was co-counsel, but when the rubber hit the road, somehow it always ended up that I was the one taking the depositions. I took the deposition of the defendant's principal design engineer. It took a really long time—many days, as I recall.

Cosslett: How did you feel when you lost? Had you expected to win?

Feldman: It was a tough case going in, and it remained tough all the way through. We had extensive resources that were brought to bear. We had a shadow jury and a jury consultant with a video feed to the trial giving input every day.

Cosslett: What's a shadow jury?

Feldman: People picked from the public whom we paid by the hour to sit and watch the proceedings and tell us what they thought over the nine weeks of the trial. The jury consultant tried to select people who matched the actual jury in terms of age, ethnicity, and socioeconomic background.

It's too bad the shadow jury didn't get to render the verdict, because they kept telling us we were winning. In truth, I really never trusted it that much. I wasn't particularly surprised that we lost the case, but it was still disappointing.

Cosslett: Do you use shadow juries in your practice now?

Feldman: I don't. Frankly, you're molded by your early experiences. I'm probably more skeptical than most trial lawyers of jury consultants and that kind of an input. I still use them occasionally, but with a big grain of salt.

Cosslett: Did you continue to get that level of responsibility on subsequent trials at Mayor Day?

Feldman: After that case, I was still relatively junior—a third-year lawyer—and I continued to do general litigation work. It was lots of briefing, traveling, working for other attorneys, preparing materials for other attorneys. It was more traditional associate-level kind of work. I knew I wasn't going to see a trial like that again soon, if at all. And I certainly wasn't going to be before a jury or a judge for a long time in the level of responsibility that I had had before, so it ruined me for the practice of law in a big firm as a junior associate.

Cosslett: Most junior lawyers would say, "I'm going to go see what life at another firm is like. Maybe I'll get more trial work somewhere else." It's unusual to hang out a shingle.

Feldman: I had never considered moving to another firm and really still liked Mayor Day a lot. I had just decided that I wanted to do more trial work on my own and see if I could make a go of it. It was a pretty big leap of faith, and through a combination of good fortune and some favorable jury verdicts that came pretty quickly after I left, I've been able to do it ever since. I've been pretty much a solo practitioner with an employee or two here or there since 1996.

Cosslett: When you first moved into your own practice, did you have clients lined up? Or did you open a shop, look out the window, and say, "Okay, I'm here!"?

Feldman: I took a couple of cases with me and began hustling for work. A lot of those cases were injury cases and some were commercial cases. They tended to be for smaller clients.

Cosslett: How do you hustle for cases?

Feldman: I think you hustle differently now than you used to, but back then you had cards printed out, you made phone calls, you called lawyers, you told them what you were doing, and you said, "Hey, if you've got a case or two that you need help on or you want to refer, I'm available." You couldn't be very choosy. But you still had to be careful about what you took because you were putting your money into it, as you usually took it on a contingency.

So I just started getting cases, and I did have a lot of support from my colleagues. One of the first cases that was referred to me was from someone in my class at Mayor Day. His father's secretary's husband was killed in a workplace accident. The family had hired a fairly well-known lawyer, and they weren't happy with the advice that he was giving them about a settlement offer that wasn't very much and a strategy of pursuing a safety firm as opposed to going after a construction firm. I said I'd try the case. So I took the case on, tried it, and obtained a gross negligence eleven-to-one verdict against a construction company that at the time was famous for never settling. This construction company had built, literally, almost every major roadway in the Houston area.

I was able to convince a jury that there was not just negligence but gross negligence, which was required in that particular kind of case. There was something called the worker's compensation bar, so you couldn't prevail in a lawsuit against your employer unless you could establish gross negligence. The CEO of this company had given an interview a couple of months before in the *Houston Chronicle* about how he never settles. I had him on the stand explaining to me about all the money he made on his various projects, at which point the insurance adjuster asked me to speak with him during the next break. We settled right then.

Cosslett: Were you tempted to just go for it? It must have been hard to put on the brakes and say, "Okay, we'll take it."

Feldman: It was the right decision for my client, and I've had to make those decisions a number of times in my career, especially when you have children involved. The good part about that case is that I did get a jury verdict. There were two phases to the trial. So I got an eleven-to-one gross negligence vote. In Texas when you have a punitive damages case, you have to have a second trial to determine the damages. And so it was just a question of how much at that point, and there would have been some amount that would have been dragged out on appeal for a long time.

I had that verdict within five or six months of hanging out my own shingle, and so people were very happy to refer me cases after that. I've always kept up a practice of both injury work and commercial work—more commercial work just now because of the way things are in Texas.

Cosslett: When you first hung out your shingle, were you married?

Feldman: When I first hung out my shingle, I was married with children. I took on about $30,000 of debt to start my practice, and had almost no savings. It was quite a risk.

Cosslett: How did your wife feel about your starting your own practice?

Feldman: She was a lawyer and we actually worked together at the law firm. She second-chaired that case with me, and many more after. She doesn't actively practice any more, but she's got a lot more work than I do. I'll just tell you that. We have three children and a dog.

Cosslett: It's never easy to make the decision to leave a law firm and a steady income. It's a big decision when you're junior, but I imagine it gets harder the more senior you become, because you have more commitments and obligations and can be walking away from a bigger salary.

Feldman: There have been times in my career when I've thought, "Okay, I want to partner up with a few other lawyers, or a lot of other lawyers, and take a little pressure off me sometimes," because my workload and income can look like a sine wave. But I have a lot of freedom in the way I manage my time, and I don't want to give that up. And then sometimes I have no freedom, when I'm in trial.

Cosslett: Given that you have such a broad-based practice, how do you get your hands around a subject area that is completely unfamiliar?

Feldman: First of all, you have access to experts, so they help you understand the technical aspects of the case. You talk to them and talk to other people about the issues. But at the end of the day, I think you have to remember that whatever the case is about, you have to present it to either a court or a jury, and they have to understand it as well. If you can't present it at that level, then it's useless information. You can have two super-smart experts arguing over esoteric points, and it's useless in the setting of a jury trial. You have to be able to distill it.

How did I do it? How did I know as a young lawyer how to do it? I don't mean to sound like I'm tooting my own horn—because I'm not nearly the best trial lawyer in the world, but I'm not the worst either. I think that there's a set of skills that is very hard to teach and very hard to learn. You either have them or you don't: being able to master a large body of documents; being able to take those documents and apply them to what you understand to be the law; keeping in mind what the jury questions are going to be; keeping in mind evidentiary issues that are going to come up; and keeping in mind that all this has to be done in front of a jury. You can practice and you can get better, but I think there's a basic level of ability that you either have or you don't. And if you're in the first category, you're a trial lawyer. If you're not, you should do something else in the law.

Cosslett: When I think about the skill of a litigator, I think about the courtroom tactics and showmanship and in-court conduct. What is your courtroom style?

Feldman: When I think about style, I think back to an interview given by Michael Tigar and Dick DeGuerin. The two of them were representing the defendant in a high-profile criminal case, and Tigar was a huge showman, and DeGuerin was a tactician and a technician in court. They gave an interview, and when the reporter asked them a question, Tigar gave this big showmanship answer, and DeGuerin's comment was, "Well, as you can see, our styles are a little different."

They were representing the same person, and I was thinking, "At the end of the day, your style is really who you are." I am a guy who will not let you get away with even a little teeny lie. I go after it. And so I have a pretty aggressive style in court and have no problem getting up on a high horse and making a jury argument. But it's my style. It's not anybody else's style. It's who I am. You can get better and you can learn to be a trial lawyer, but the ability to be an effective one is either in you or it isn't in you. People might disagree with me, but I think that's the case.

Cosslett: Yes, I have heard from other litigators the most important thing in a courtroom is to be who you are.

Feldman: I hate the word "litigator." I don't call myself a litigator. I try to avoid it all the time. "Litigation" to me means roadblocks before a decision, either before a judge or a jury, and a lot of attorney's fees. And I tend to believe that a lot of that is for the lawyers and their billing. I like to call myself a "trial lawyer," because I'm hired to try a case, not to litigate it. "Litigator" implies a lot of things that go on from the time a lawsuit is filed, or even before, to the time it's resolved that, in my view, could be completely cut out in most cases. The word "litigator" smacks of delay, and expense, and unnecessary work. I'm usually up against litigators.

Cosslett: Can you describe the legal practice in Houston generally?

Feldman: It's probably the most varied practice in the country. We've got the oil and gas industry, and there's a massive amount of law work that's done surrounding that industry. We've got the Texas Medical Center, which is probably the premier medical center in the country, and there's a tremendous amount of health law work. There is a lot of organizational work and regulatory and research work relating to the relationships between the hospitals and the various insurance companies. We've got seven million people in Houston and we have no zoning, so there's a lot of development work as well.

There are some massive firms in Houston. Bracewell & Giuliani is a Texas-based firm. It was Bracewell & Patterson, and then they asked Mayor Giuliani to join. Vinson & Elkins is historically a very large firm. Baker Botts is one of the oldest firms in the country. And then there's usually a branch of any large New York or DC firm here, and a smattering of medium-sized firms and smaller firms. We have great trial lawyers in Texas, and Houston has become an epicenter for high-level trial work. Many of the lawyers who have practiced in Houston have really been trail blazers, such as Percy Foreman, Joe Jamail, and Rusty Hardin.

Cosslett: Do you find yourself coming up against the larger firms in your practice?

Feldman: All the time. I'm a solo practitioner, so I'm always against a firm that's bigger than me.

Cosslett: Can you describe how commercial work comes to you and how your fees are structured?

Feldman: Typically, what will happen is there will be a small- or medium-sized-business person who finds himself in a commercial dispute of some sort. He will make his way either to a business lawyer that he knows or to some larger firm that he has heard of. But it might not be the kind of a case that is justified on an hourly basis with these big firms. Law firms can bill a tremendous amount of time and legal fees that small businesses just aren't interested in stomaching. And so then I'll usually be referred the case and talk to the person about the case, and I'll either decide to take it or not.

A lot of trial lawyers that do just injury work wouldn't be very comfortable going into a copyright case or a big commercial case, but I did start out in an academic setting, both at the law review and clerking for the Court of Appeals, and then did mostly commercial work for the first four years of my practice. I'm very comfortable looking at different kinds of cases.

With regard to my fees, sometimes I will work on a blended rate, where I'll be partly compensated by the hour and partly on a contingency. Sometimes I'll finance the case entirely, or sometimes the client will partner with me in the financing of the case. And fortunately I'm in a position where I can choose from any one of those possible structures.

Cosslett: I understand that you also work for some Fortune 500 companies. What kind of work do you do for them?

Feldman: Sometimes a corporate counsel will have a certain budget and they get in disputes that are going to be very costly to litigate—that bad word again—on an hourly basis. I've been fortunate enough to be able to step in and take such cases on a contingency and do well by them. I think everybody's happy because they're not having to pay out fees that strain their annual budget in order to prosecute a lawsuit.

Cosslett: What other cases do you have on your desk?

Feldman: Well, right now I should be briefing a sovereign immunity issue in a multimillion-dollar lawsuit that we have filed in Florida against the government of Belize over telecommunications equipment that was owned by my client and leased to the government. We're suing the government of Belize in Florida federal court, and they've claimed they're immune from the suit, notwithstanding the clear language in the contract that says they aren't. I am filing that brief in a couple of days and having to work very hard on it. We'll have a hearing and I'll have to go to Florida. The trial won't take place until later, but it's a very large set of legal issues.

Did I know anything before I took this case about Belize law or the Florida sovereign immunities act? I knew generally about sovereign immunity, but I feel confident enough that I can research the law and determine, "Yes, I think we've got jurisdiction and we've got a good commercial case." I know a lot about UCC [Uniform Commercial Code] Article 2A leases, and I know that my client is owed money on the lease. So I'm going to invest in that case. There is a lot of money at stake.

I can also give you another example. One of the expert witnesses I dealt with on very first case I worked on at Mayor Day stayed in touch with me. He called me because he thought one of his customers was infringing on software that he sold him. We filed a copyright infringement case in federal court, with Vinson & Elkins on the other side in Houston. That case has been active on my docket. Additionally, I have injury cases all over the country and a slate of drug cases, which I've acquired through advertising.

Cosslett: In the drug cases, are you representing the drug manufacturer or the people injured by drugs?

Feldman: The people who have been injured by drugs. I'll put money into an advertising campaign, and I'll start fielding calls, whittling them down to meritorious cases, and determining how best to represent them.

Cosslett: Are these class actions?

Feldman: They really aren't class actions. These kinds of cases are mass actions, so they're almost always sucked up into multi-district litigations somewhere in the country.

Cosslett: You also get involved in medical malpractice cases?

Feldman: Medical malpractice was a large part of my practice for a long time, and I had an advantage there because I had a brother and a father who were doctors, so I could always get advice about whether this was a case or not a case. I was careful in the cases I took—more so than most lawyers. I wouldn't take a case unless I really, really felt strongly about it, because I don't particularly enjoy suing doctors. I don't think a doctor ever means to hurt somebody but that said, there were cases that I felt were important to take.

That work, as everyone will tell you, pretty well dried up after a series of draconian tort reforms in Texas that were supposed to do a number of things, including lower healthcare costs and make health care more accessible to the poor. It's done neither of those things, but it has pretty much made it impossible for stay-at-home parents, children, and elderly to sue for medical negligence in the state. So really, unless you have a big lost-wage claim or are hurt in such a way that the medical bills in the future are millions of dollars, those claims aren't really viable anymore. So I don't do much of that now. I still take them on, even medium-sized cases because I just feel like sometimes I need to because the client really needs it, but it's not nearly as much of my practice as it was.

Cosslett: How do you balance taking the cases you want to take on because you really believe there's been an injury or an injustice with the need to bring income into the firm?

Feldman: You try to justify some of it in your head. Any time I've taken a case that I thought, "Oh well, I can make some money on this case, but it's kind of cheap or cheesy," I've regretted it. And I just don't do it now. I told myself I would never sue an obstetrician over an injured baby, and I never have.

Those can be very lucrative cases. And to be honest, you can really wind a jury up over those cases. You can say, "Golly, you see on this readout that the blood pressure and heart rate started going up. Why didn't you do a C-section right then? Shouldn't you have done that?" You're going to find an expert to testify that the doctor should have done a C-section sooner. Those doctors are really using their best judgment. They're not trying to deliver a baby that's injured and they're not usually being careless or negligent. So I've just never taken those cases.

There have been cases where someone has come to me very seriously injured, and I won't know about the medical issue, but I'll take the time to find out about it and talk to experts about it. And I may come to the conclusion that this is just a very unfortunate set of events. And I will tell them, "I can't take this case because this is what I think happened. I don't think anybody committed malpractice. I know it sounds awful, but let me try to explain to you where I'm coming from."

And I think in many instances the clients will appreciate that and may recognize that there was no malpractice and may just move on with their lives as best as they can. I don't just take the case because there's a horrible injury, which, unfortunately, many lawyers do. It doesn't really happen as much as the tort reform bar wants you to think it happens, because the lawyers that do that go broke.

Cosslett: Because they take cases where there's not a villain?

Feldman: You could have a bad injury, but the insurance companies are going to try that case if they're solid on liability, and almost always they will win that case. So you have to have the experience to know when to say no to a case. And that's hard to learn. But it is important to learn.

Cosslett: They teach you in law school that there's not necessarily a remedy for every wrong.

Feldman: That's true.

Cosslett: Are there any areas that you find particularly interesting in your practice?

Feldman: Personally, I have a need to untie a really tight knot, and if it's a complicated case with a lot of issues that seem pretty difficult to present, I enjoy being be able to untie that knot in a way that can then be presented to a jury and hopefully won. So, for me, complexity is what gets my juices flowing: being able to take a complex transaction and distill it into, "This person did right. This person did wrong." And being able to explain that to a jury. Those are hard things to do and especially hard to do because there are a lot of legal obstacles between taking a case and getting it to a jury. So, if it's a difficult case, I like to take that challenge.

Cosslett: Are there any cases that you're particularly proud of?

Feldman: I'm particularly proud of a lot of cases. In the medical malpractice field, I think I'm the most proud of a malpractice action I brought where I represented the orphaned children of a single immigrant mother against a group of physicians at Baylor College of Medicine. The Texas Department of Child Protective Services was actually my client, because the children became wards of the state after their mother died.

I don't think the physicians meant wrong, but they made some very serious mistakes. The mother was misdiagnosed with a disease, but the medicine given to her to treat that disease allowed a parasite to fulminate, and she died of a massive hyper-infection, literally eaten from the inside out over a six- or seven-week hospital stay. It was a very contentious case. I took that case to a jury and won it. It was probably one of the hardest cases I've ever taken on. It was really a horrible, horrible case and I won it fair and square. I enjoyed that case.

There was another injury case I worked on, but it was commercial in a way. I represented a guy who had private insurance through a large carrier, and eleven months after he had bought this policy, which he had bought because he was going abroad to work, he was diagnosed with a very severe form of esophageal cancer. The insurance company rescinded his coverage, which you can't do now, under the Affordable Care Act. They rescinded his coverage because they alleged he didn't disclose a malady that he didn't even know he had. It was literally a life-and-death situation, where if he wasn't going to be able to get surgery, he was going to die. And even if he got the surgery, it wasn't clear that he was going to make it.

I was able to sue the insurance company on an emergency basis in federal court and, in short order, reverse the decision and have them pay for surgery that actually did save his life, against all odds. The survival rate for this kind of cancer, especially as advanced as his was, is usually less than a year. It's been three or four years now and he's still alive. He's able to eat food and is no longer on tubes, and, as far as he can tell, the cancer's gone.

Cosslett: He must come by your office once a week just to hug you.

Feldman: You'd be surprised. Not many people do. They move on with their lives. I hear from him every now and then. So that was a commercial case, but it also involved injury. I've also represented businesspeople whose businesses are going to go bust if they don't win this case. And I've won these cases for some of them. Those are all pretty satisfying.

Cosslett: In terms of your trial work, what percentage of your cases go to trial? Would it be fair to say that one in ten cases end in trial? One in twenty? How often do you settle?

Feldman: I try to settle all that I can because it's almost always in the best interest of my client. There is usually a lot of risk and a lot of expense involved in a trial. The client ends up paying for it at the end of the day, anyway, so it's best to settle if you can. But sometimes you don't have a choice. Because I'm just one person, the most I've done in a year is four or five trials. And then there might be a year where I do zero, and then it could go nuts again.

I would say one in ten cases get to trial, maybe less. It's hard for me to say. I don't take easy cases. There's usually a lot of money at stake, so the odds of them having to be resolved by force, with guns blazing, is higher than in a lot of cases. I don't take car-wreck cases in general—those cases settle much more often.

Cosslett: What are the pluses and minuses of being a solo practitioner?

Feldman: The pluses are the same as the minuses in my view. Your opportunity for financial reward is probably bigger than it is at a large firm. At the same time, your opportunity to lose money is there as well. Your time constraints are different. You can take three or four weeks off if you want to. I don't think you can do that at a big firm. At the same time, there are times when I can't take any time off, and I don't see my family. So it runs the gamut. So the things that are good are also the things that are bad.

Cosslett: After almost twenty years in practice, what continues to motivate you?

Feldman: Right now what continues to motivate me is three children in private school, one of whom boards, with college coming up shortly. Plus car insurance for my oldest.

Cosslett: What advice would you give law students, or practicing lawyers considering a career change, about becoming a trial lawyer and about hanging out their own shingle?

Feldman: The most important advice I can give is to be sure that you have a network of colleagues and friends that have more experience than you do about any particular case, so that you can be sure when you take a case that you have someone to talk to about it—so that you're not out there on your own. I've been fortunate enough to be able to do that. People are always very happy to help.

To the extent that you can get involved with other firms on cases, I think that's really, really important. Finance-wise, it's really pretty obvious. You need to take cases that aren't going to bust you. And you need to be able to turn down a case that you can't reasonably handle, or you should get help, either on the finance side or otherwise.

So the nature of hanging out your shingle on a plaintiff's-side firm like mine is that there's a lot of risk involved. If you can mitigate that risk by taking hourly cases, that helps. You don't need a fancy office. Even sophisticated clients really don't care too much about that. Keeping your overhead down is important starting out. Just try to mitigate your risk at all levels.

Cosslett: Are there any issues of professional responsibility that come up for you regularly in connection with your practice?

Feldman: All the time. There aren't usually the kind of conflict issues in my practice that lawyers have in big firms, because if I have a client, I'm unlikely to have a conflict with the defendant. Sometimes I do, but those are easy to figure out. When I represent injured people, though, there are a lot of professional responsibility issues because sometimes I'm representing minors, or sometimes I'm representing unsophisticated people. You have to be able to give them advice. Sometimes they don't want to hear advice about what they should be doing with money if they get it, or whether they should settle or not.

There are also professional responsibility issues involving representation of multiple clients in the same case. You have to be careful about how you allocate expenses and have everybody agree to it. I'm usually very, very careful about these sorts of issues, but they are a part of my practice.

It is also important for a solo practitioner to have somebody who knows disciplinary rules and be able to call them and ask their views on things. Not to make those decisions on your own is important. I can take a risk on the merits of a case and make a strategic decision and live or die with it on my own, but I almost never have a professional responsibility issue that I don't ask another lawyer about.

Cosslett: That's good advice for sure.

CHAPTER 15

Adam Nguyen

Entrepreneur
Ivy Link, Founder & CEO
eBrevia, Co-Founder & COO

Adam Nguyen has some good advice for lawyers thinking about leaving the law and starting a business. First, do a structured self-evaluation and understand what your strengths and weaknesses are and what is important to you. What are your goals and your interests? Are you a big-picture thinker or are you meticulous? Are you a problem solver? Do you thrive on uncertainty? Nguyen asked himself these questions as he transitioned from a career as an M&A and private equity attorney on Wall Street to become the founder and CEO of Ivy Link, a profit-for-purpose education company that specializes in one-on-one school admissions guidance, standardized test preparation, and academic coaching, as well as a co-founder and COO of eBrevia, a software company that provides technology solutions to enhance the productivity of legal and business professionals.

Nguyen's second piece of career advice is this: "The seas are rough out there—be nimble." Through a series of adverse financial and political events—the stock market crash of 2002, the defeat of the Kerry/Edwards ticket in 2004, and the financial crisis heralded by the collapse of the Bear Stearns hedge funds in 2007—he managed to ride out one downsizing after another with Candide-like optimism, always gaining additional insights into how to cultivate his own garden to yield personal growth, professional satisfaction, and civic good.

Nguyen graduated magna cum laude with a BA in economics and political science from Columbia University and earned a JD from Harvard Law School. A frequent speaker and media commentator on admissions, standardized testing, and career guidance, he has addressed such groups as The Parents League of New York, Columbia University,

Citigroup, and JPMorgan Chase & Co. He belongs to the National Association for College Admission Counseling, the State Bar of California, and the New York State Bar Association.

Clare Cosslett: Tell me about growing up in Texas.

Adam Nguyen: My parents, younger brother, and I immigrated to the US from Vietnam as political refugees in 1985, when I was ten. We settled in Houston, Texas, and I grew up in a typical suburban immigrant family: structured, sheltered, shuttling between church, school, and afterschool activities. That was my world. But I knew even then that I would leave Texas someday—and that the world was bigger than Houston.

Cosslett: How did you end up going to Columbia University for undergrad?

Nguyen: My high school did not have a very good counseling program, so I didn't go through the thoughtful process that many kids today, especially in the New York area, benefit from. A classmate had an extra application for Columbia, and he gave it to me. This was before the days of the common app and the internet, so we were still doing things by paper. The application was a light-blue book. I remember it very clearly. And I remember thinking that maybe I hadn't applied to enough schools and that I should add another one to the list. As I said, the process was not thoughtful—I considered whatever applications were coming in the mail from school recruiters after I took my SATs.

I had applied to schools like Vanderbilt, Northwestern, Chicago, and Penn—all over the place. When I looked up these schools, I realized that they were highly selective, and I thought, "Well, I better apply to a few more!" I got the application for Columbia the week before it was due, and I sent it in about ten minutes before the midnight deadline. A friend drove me to the only post office that was still open at that late hour—at the airport. On April Fools' Day, I received a call from Columbia saying, "Congratulations. You got in. Would you like to see the school?" I thought it was a joke. Columbia flew me up to see the campus and New York. I fell in love with everything I saw. When I came back home, I immediately sent in the acceptance card without even looking at the other schools.

Cosslett: How did your parents take the news that you were heading off to New York?

Nguyen: Well, I had kept them in the dark about the college process. As first generation immigrants, my parents didn't understand when students applied to college. They thought you applied or found out sometime in the summer after high school graduation. So when I told them I would be going to a college up in New York, their reaction was: "We didn't know you had applied, and why are you going so far away?" But I said, "It's a really good school." And, of course, they had never heard of Columbia. Many people in Texas hadn't heard of the highly selective schools. When I told some of my friends in high school about Columbia, they asked, "Why are you going to South America for college?"

I took charge of my education even at that age. I was the firstborn, so I had to deal with many things on my own. I knew that I wanted to go to college and that I wanted to get into a top school. I wanted to leave Texas and explore the world. I told my parents, "It's okay. Columbia is a top school." New York in the early nineties—this was pre-Giuliani—was a little edgy. I reassured my parents, "It's perfectly safe. New York is glamorous just like what you see in the movies." I sold my parents a fanciful version of New York. And that's how I ended up at Columbia.

Cosslett: And what was your major?

Nguyen: I took a double major in economics and political science. I also completed the premed program. I had a predisposition towards the sciences and math, so I started taking premed classes and performed very well in them. Before I knew it, I was taking the MCAT and thinking about going to med school.

Cosslett: What happened?

Nguyen: I took a year abroad and studied at University College London. It was the first time in my life that I was not taking any science classes. Instead, I explored subjects like political philosophy and economic philosophy. I said to myself, "Maybe this medical school thing is not the best option for me." Frankly, I hadn't considered other options besides medicine. Taking a year abroad opened up my perspective to other possibilities. In the back of my mind, however, medical school was still in the cards, so I took another year off between college and grad school to just explore options.

I ended up in DC in the honors paralegal program at the Department of Justice. I was in the mergers task force of the DOJ's antitrust division. During the late 1990s, the Microsoft antitrust case was at its height. Clinton and Congress were having a budget showdown. The Monica Lewinsky story was unfolding, and the capital was abuzz with the scandal. I remember attending the Clinton impeachment trial in the Senate. Chief Justice Rehnquist was presiding with his signature robe and its golden stripes. All of the senators were in attendance. The government basically shut down.

It was very exciting to be a twenty-two-year-old paralegal in DC during that time. Working at the DOJ with the idea of maybe medical school or maybe not, having my background in economics and political science, and being in the middle of all the historic events that were unfolding in '98 and '99 in DC made me rethink what I wanted to do. Before my time in DC, I hadn't thought about law school.

The DOJ attorneys gave paralegals a lot of responsibilities: we were doing PIs—preliminary investigations—and sending out second requests. I was traveling to Idaho and Colorado to obtain affidavits from government witnesses, declarations, and other things—work that I found out later even junior associates at law firms typically don't do. The DOJ was very leanly staffed, and the lawyers gave paralegals a lot of responsibility. I began to think that law seemed really interesting. You could do so many things and have so much influence as a lawyer.

Chapter 15 | Adam Nguyen: Corporate/Legal Technology

At that time, Joel Klein, who later became the education chancellor of New York City, was the head of the Antitrust Department. He reported to Janet Reno. I learned from their biographies that they both had graduated from Harvard Law School. I looked up to them as extremely intelligent and highly successful people, and I wanted to emulate them and the path they took to become successful. And so, on a lark, I took the LSAT and applied to law school, again very late.

Cosslett: I'm noticing a pattern here.

Nguyen: I rushed in my application to four schools: Harvard, Columbia, Yale, and Stanford.

Cosslett: As an admissions counselor now, would you advise that people apply to only four highly selective schools?

Nguyen: No. I use myself as a case study for what not to do. As it turned out, I was accepted at Columbia and Harvard. The dean of admissions from Harvard called to tell me I had been admitted, and I accepted on the telephone. I had really wanted to go to Harvard. That is not to say that the other schools were backup choices, but . . .

Cosslett: It's hard to say no to Harvard.

Nguyen: Right.

Cosslett: And so once you were there, was it like *The Paper Chase* with a John Houseman–like figure in the lecture hall terrifying first-years? Was it daunting?

Nguyen: Yes, it was extremely daunting. But perhaps a more accurate movie analogy is *Legally Blonde*. There is a scene during orientation in which the students are sitting in their advisory group, and everyone is taking turns talking about what they have accomplished. My experience with my advisory group was scarily similar. One kid in my group had started a nonprofit. Another had managed a billion-dollar portfolio at an investment firm. Another had climbed Kilimanjaro. This was in addition to the usual PhDs and people who had published books and so forth. One student in my section even had published a couple of articles in the *Penn Law Review*.

My classmates were a very, very accomplished group of people, but in hindsight, I think that underneath all the accomplishments and posturing, everybody was a bit insecure. I also think insecurity was what motivated many people to work really hard. That means you had about five hundred and fifty insecure over-achievers in each class. So, yes, there was an element of *Paper Chase*, but a lot of the pressure came from the students. Most of us had watched the movie and also read Scott Turow's *One L*. I think in our minds the school was like the one in the movie or the book, and to some extent, we made the fictional Harvard Law into a reality.

Cosslett: Did you work over the first and second summers?

Nguyen: For the first summer—shortly after the peak of the dot-com bubble in May 2000—I was lucky enough to get a job at Latham & Watkins in Washington, DC. Since I had worked in antitrust on the government side at the Justice Department, I wanted to go back to DC and experience the law-firm side of antitrust and administrative law. Of course, the compensation was a nice factor.

For the second summer, because I had worked in DC during the first summer, I wanted to check out New York and London. I had studied in London and wanted to see what it was like to work there. Shearman & Sterling, Cleary, and a few other firms that I was considering at the time had a strong international focus and offered associates opportunities to do cross-border work in M&A and project finance. Shearman & Sterling, in particular, was very serious about giving associates the opportunity to start out abroad: I could start my first year as an associate in London. They have a sizable office in London—around a hundred attorneys at the time. So my first summer was at Latham & Watkins in DC. My second summer was split between New York and London at Shearman & Sterling. Shearman also recruited very heavily at the beginning of my third year at Harvard, in fall 2001.

Cosslett: So you accepted Shearman. You'd clearly had a good summer experience there.

Nguyen: Yes. But, as you will remember, the stock market crash hit bottom in October 2002. And so the Shearman—and the legal market—that I came back to after graduation in 2002 was very different from the one I had witnessed as a summer associate in 2001. The legal environment had changed completely. Deals had dried up. As a summer associate in 2001, I was participating in capital market and M&A deals at Shearman in New York and London, but when I returned in the fall of 2002, there was very little deal work.

Firms were laying off associates left and right, and the few deals that we got to do were stop-and-go. We would spend an entire weekend, pulling all-nighters to conduct diligence for our client, and then . . . pencils down. A lot of deals just didn't happen, and it was very frustrating. Few deals got signed, and even after signing, many deals would fall apart before they got to closing.

In my first year at Shearman, I managed to work on just one deal that went through the whole process to closing. Other than that one deal, just a ton of due diligence, as well as a lot of document review to help out in the litigation department. Honestly, the experience made me question why I had pursued my law degree.

Cosslett: It's instructive to remember that there was a recession before this one. Not a lot of work at the firms, lots of lawyers being let go, and lots of unhappy legal recruiters. Looks like what's going on now.

Nguyen: Definitely. I had come to the law firm with a very open mind. I had performed my own diligence on law firm careers and knew what it took to make partner—you have to slog through and you really have to want it. The path to partnership is long, and every year the path seems to become longer. When I was starting out, it took seven or eight years to make partner. But now it seems more like nine or ten years, and increasingly there are two tiers of partners. One of the reasons I went to Shearman was that its partnership was lockstep and followed a very traditional model. After about a year of essentially just conducting due diligence, I decided that I should explore another area of law.

Litigation was an area that I had not seriously considered. I had always been a transactional-oriented lawyer. But an opportunity opened up for a federal clerkship with Judge Faith Hochberg of the US District Court for the District of New Jersey. Judge Hochberg was a Harvard alumna and the former US Attorney for the District of New Jersey. I was very lucky to get the clerkship. Very few transactional attorneys make the transition to litigation, and I was extremely fortunate to receive Judge Hochberg's offer. I jumped at it. When a federal judge makes you an offer, you don't refuse. I also thought, "M&A will still be there—or what is left of it." So I started a federal clerkship without a background in litigation.

I believe Judge Hochberg hired me with the expectation that I was smart enough to figure things out. In my first week, I had to draft an opinion for a case that was before the court. When I began to review the litigants' submissions, I had a "freak-out" moment—or rather, a series of moments. You see, the law firm environment—especially at large firms—is often very hierarchical: work product would percolate up from junior associate through senior associate and junior partner to senior partner. But in chambers, it's just the judge and me. In my first instance reporting to the judge, she asked me, "So, how should I rule?" There I was still in the frame of mind of a law firm's junior associate who expected some guidance and even micromanaging: "This is how you should write. This is what you should look at." I promptly said to my judge, "I will have to get back to you!"

Cosslett: And suddenly did you feel as though you were practicing law?

Nguyen: I felt I was doing more than practicing law. I was helping the judge to decide real cases and was being treated as an adult. Ultimately, the judge was the decider, but I certainly felt the weight of responsibilities. It was at once terrifying and very gratifying. I was thinking, "This is why I went to law school, to study these cutting-edge, leading issues that come before the court and help to decide them."

The experience offered a wonderful combination of theory and practice. Law school was mostly about spotting the issues and looking at them from different angles without having to come to a conclusion on anything because you didn't have to. In legal academia, you could explore controversial or ambiguous issues all day without having to decide. But in any court—federal court, state court—you have to make a decision at the end of the day. My judge used to say, "That's what taxpayers are paying us to do: to decide."

Cosslett: And that decision actually affects real people immediately.

Nguyen: Yes, certainly. Beyond the litigants, the cases we worked on had implications for our district or even the circuit, and we knew that they could become precedents that would be relied upon in other districts and circuits. And, of course, our work could get reviewed by the circuit court, and that added pressure to the work that I did. So I took my work very seriously.

Cosslett: Were you sad at the end of a year that you had to go?

Nguyen: I was. After about six months, that's when you really start to get the hang of it. During my orientation, another judge gave a talk to the incoming clerks, and she said—I still remember it to this day: "Judging or writing opinions is like Chinese cooking. There are four or five major ingredients, and once you know them, you can make a thousand dishes."

In my case, it turned out to be true. Once I got the hang of it, I started seeing the rhyme and reason of the process—whether it's a patent case, a habeas case, antitrust, or whatever. But at first, the experience was overwhelming.

Cosslett: After you finished your one-year clerkship, you went into politics. You didn't let any grass grow.

Nguyen: I've come to believe that you have to seize an opportunity when it presents itself. I joined the opposition research team for the Kerry/Edwards presidential campaign for three-and-a-half months. Initially, I worked in DC and then transferred to Ohio to help with voter protection. The campaign thought Ohio could be a battleground state like Florida in 2000 with *Bush v. Gore*. Personally, I picked Ohio because it was closer to New York. As you may recall, things did come down to Ohio.

As a head of voter protection, I was in charge of out-of-state lawyers, bringing them into Ohio to ensure that the protocols were followed at the voting booths on the day of the election. And we know what happened to Kerry/Edwards...

I returned to New York and joined Paul Weiss. The reason I went into private equity and to Paul Weiss was that I had attended a continuing legal education luncheon at Shearman, where they covered private equities and hedge funds. It was the first time I learned about carried interest and the business model of private equity, and I thought, "That's what I want to do. What a great way to deploy capital and generate huge returns!" In particular, I learned that private equity is about deal structuring and forming funds to invest in deals.

Fund formation is great if you're someone who likes playing with puzzles and charts, juggling multiple pieces, and putting the pieces together. It's a fascinating area to be in because of the way these funds are structured both onshore and offshore for international clients as well as domestic clients. Things could be very complex, especially when you add in tax issues and employment issues.

So I decided that this would be a very cutting-edge area to go into. And private equity, at that time, was experiencing a resurgence in the marketplace.

Cosslett: Who were you representing?

Nguyen: We were representing general partners, the guys who put together the fund. We would negotiate with very sophisticated investors, such as pension funds, endowments, and foundations, who invested in our clients' funds. Paul Weiss was one of the few firms that had, and still has, a very robust private equity fund formation practice. When I made the decision to do private equity at Paul Weiss after the clerkship and after the campaign, I had a much better sense of corporate practice than when I had joined Shearman fresh out of law school. I now had a better grasp of the roles of lawyers in M&A, finance, capital markets, etc.

And I discovered this other area that few young associates knew about—that was the opposite of public capital markets: private equity and hedge funds. These funds are also selling securities, but they are in private, not public, markets, and they're not required to file with the Securities and Exchange Commission. To that end, creating them is mostly about finding safe harbors: if you qualify for the safe harbors, then you're not required to register or file certain things with the SEC. Essentially, from a regulatory standpoint, private equity funds, or more generally, private investment funds, are about staying outside of the filing requirements of the 1933 and 1934 Acts.

Traditionally, private equity firms do not market to the general public—they deal with sophisticated investors, or accredited and qualified investors. However, with the recent regulations, more and more investment funds are required to register, so the market is changing in that respect. I say "investment funds" because that includes both private equity and hedge funds, and given the way the market is headed, you have so-called hybrid funds, which combine features of hedge funds and private equity funds. There's a blurring of the lines between those two worlds. But at the end of the day, both hedge funds and private equity funds are supposed to be targeting the private market as opposed to the public market.

So, 2007 was the height of the private equity and hedge-fund world, and I was offered an associate general counsel position at a hedge fund in Greenwich, Connecticut. People were doing deals left and right. Private equity and hedge funds were going public. Blackstone and Fortress had gone public, and KKR was about to. The hedge fund that recruited me was ready to go public, as well. As a result, they expanded their legal team in anticipation of additional legal and compliance issues. Many private equity and hedge funds were looking to hire lawyers just like myself. The investment fund recruiting market was in a frenzy.

Cosslett: Was it a difficult decision to leave Paul Weiss?

Nguyen: Yes. I liked the firm and many aspects of the work that I was doing. I had a lot of responsibilities—working directly with clients, running my own deals, mentoring younger associates. But I felt that it was time to graduate, so to speak. I had learned enough as an associate. Could I have learned more? Definitely. But I had learned enough of the law firm practice side of private equity/hedge fund, and any additional time would have resulted in diminishing returns. It was time to see how the work was done from an in-house perspective.

So I went in-house, and that summer—the summer of 2007, a couple of months after my transition—the first two Bear hedge funds imploded. I don't think the market or the Fed realized the full implications of what had occurred and was about to occur. Bear bailed out their funds and said that the mess was totally contained. Ben Bernanke reassured the market that everything was okay. After all, it was only two hedge funds within a huge and profitable institution. Looking back, though, I think that the collapse of the Bear funds signaled the beginning of the economic crisis.

Not surprisingly, many IPOs, including that of my hedge fund, were delayed and eventually abandoned altogether. My fund very nicely said, "Oops." I had been there for about ten weeks, but they provided a very generous severance package.

Cosslett: Were you able to be calm about it? Did you call Paul Weiss right away?

Nguyen: I was a little shocked, but I quickly recovered. I thought it was just a little hiccup: "This particular hedge fund is not going public and that's fine. I'll just explore opportunities for the next four weeks and see what's out there before deciding to go back to a firm." Although I mentioned my situation to a partner at Paul Weiss, I didn't say that I wanted to go back. Like many at the time, I thought the market was still very strong, and going back to a firm was not something I really wanted to do. I had been talking to other private equity funds and hedge funds in New York before I took the job in Connecticut, and those options were still open at the time. I saw this as an opportunity to explore other things, and real estate had always been one of the asset classes that I was interested in.

I talked with several contacts in the real estate business and eventually met the CEO of a real estate company here in New York. It so happened that they were looking to raise a fund to invest in New York real estate. It was a perfect fit with my background. We would be seeking capital from institutions, endowments, and foundations, and buying multifamily properties in New York. They were looking for someone with my skill set, and I managed to negotiate an arrangement that was attractive, allowing me to do both the business side and the law side. I didn't want to be identified simply as a lawyer, and I saw this as a great opportunity to transition to the business side.

I found that many people have a tendency to pigeonhole others by their professions. The better lawyer you are, the more pigeonholed you become, and it's hard to shake off that label and go into the business side within a company.

Chapter 15 | Adam Nguyen: Corporate/Legal Technology

Many young attorneys think, "Oh, I can go in-house and then go on to the business side." Often, it's hard to do, and it's especially hard at a very large company where there is an emphasis on specialization.

Cosslett: You can be more valuable as a lawyer than as a businessman to a company. There are a lot of good businessmen around, but not that many great in-house lawyers.

Nguyen: Exactly—the larger companies tend to hire lawyers to specifically practice law and fill a particular niche. At the Connecticut hedge fund, there was very little chance that I could have transitioned into the business side. So, with the benefit of hindsight, the sequence of events during the summer of 2007 and the fact that I didn't remain at the hedge fund were a blessing.

The real estate company was a relatively small place with maybe a billion dollars of assets under management at the time I joined, but the AUM grew quickly in the coming months. It was an exciting place where I could use my experience to help with the fund formation and corporate legal matters, and at the same time, roll up my sleeves to do all sorts of things, big and small, related to business development, corporate development, and operations. I got to see all aspects of real estate acquisition, management, operations, leasing, and construction. I was involved, to some extent, in almost everything. Over the course of two years, I became VP of corporate development, then the chief of staff / corporate legal officer of the company.

We didn't have a COO, so my responsibilities were very similar to those of a COO and I really enjoyed it. The opportunity to do different things, attend meetings in different departments, work with people with different job responsibilities, and learn how a whole company operated really fit with my personality. I get bored sitting at my desk all day and doing one thing repeatedly.

Then, the real estate market crashed, Lehman collapsed, and everything went down the toilet with one firm after another falling like dominos.

Cosslett: Not again! This is so sad!

Nguyen: Perhaps, but very educational! One thing that attorneys looking to leave law firms should know is that the seas out there are rough. You have to be nimble and you have to roll with the punches. And the same goes for attorneys who are looking to make partner. Ultimately, a law firm is a business, and many have gone bust because they weren't nimble and didn't adjust to changing market conditions. That's something that I appreciate more and more as I become older. You have to be in tune with what's going on in the market, whether you're a partner in a law firm or a businessperson in the private equity world.

Cosslett: So you had to take a deep breath and say, "Okay, where do I want to take this?" Tell me about how you left the legal profession—how you segued from the chief of staff and corporate legal officer of a real estate investment fund to running an education consulting company.

Nguyen: I gained a lot of operational experience at the real estate company, so the transition was about leveraging my experience to the next level. As the market was going through choppy waters, I had been taking time to volunteer by tutoring and mentoring kids through New York Cares. I worked with many kids who wanted to do well, but didn't have the tools to succeed. The motivated kids were often placed with kids who didn't want to work hard and didn't have ambition. My instinct was to separate the hard-working, highly motivated kids and work with them. I thought, "Well, maybe I could start a nonprofit that focuses on high-achieving and highly motivated kids to really help them succeed."

With that in mind, I started Ivy Link. Soon people both inside and outside of the teaching profession contacted me to tell me that there was a huge demand in the New York area for private educational services, and they offered to help build the business. As I said before, be nimble. You follow what the market wants, what people are looking for. I discovered that in New York City, Westchester, and the Hamptons, there's an emphasis on education and achievement, as well as testing and admissions to highly selective colleges and private schools. So that's how Ivy Link was formed—to fill a major need in the marketplace—and the company quickly took off. It provided a great exit opportunity from real estate.

Cosslett: Tell me about Ivy Link's business.

Nguyen: We started out tutoring kids, and quickly expanded into test preparation, admissions advising, and mentoring students. Currently, we have about twenty tutors and advisors, all of whom are Ivy League graduates. For younger students, we provide enrichment tutoring in subjects ranging from math to reading and writing, as well as organization, executive function, and analytical thinking skills. Additionally, many younger students work with us to prepare for entrance exams like the ISEE and SSAT for admission to private and boarding schools.

For the older, college-bound students, we provide intensive SAT or ACT prep, as well as academic tutoring and admissions advisory services. Many of these students are already high-achieving, A-range students who are super-motivated and aiming for the best colleges, and wanting to maximize their admission chances. We act as their academic coaches—designing tutoring and test-prep programs suited to our students' abilities and goals, and guiding them through the process of selecting colleges and completing the applications.

Not all of our students are aiming for the Ivy League schools. And, as you know, not everyone should be because it's not the right fit for everyone. Of course, many of our students aim for the highly selective colleges, as well as the super-competitive private schools in New York and the boarding schools up and down the East Coast, but we always emphasize school fit, academic and life goals, and many other factors that students and parents may not think of. I always remind them that it's not simply about getting in—it's equally, if not more important, to flourish and succeed at the school where you end up.

The name "Ivy Link" came about because the people that I initially recruited from my network—namely, Columbia, Harvard, and similar schools—were all from the Ivy League. When students and parents work with us, they are being linked to Ivy League graduates for purposes of test prep, tutoring, and counseling.

Cosslett: You describe your company as a profit-for-purpose company. What does that mean?

Nguyen: After I pivoted the company toward a for-profit route, I still wanted to focus on helping underprivileged students who are high-achieving and highly motivated. The ethos of profit-for-purpose companies is that you can make a profit while still making a social impact in a positive way. To that end, we partner with private schools, public schools, and charter schools, as well as nonprofit organizations, to provide services to their constituents, living up to the nonprofit purpose that I had envisioned when starting Ivy Link, while at the same time paying bills and keeping the lights on.

Cosslett: You said earlier that you don't like to do one thing repetitively. That's reflected in the nature of your business. It's not just churning out SAT scores, it's full service.

Nguyen: Exactly. And it's a high-quality, high-end service. So our market, by its nature, is smaller. We're not Kaplan or Princeton Review. I'm looking to maintain really high-quality services and expand the company carefully. I'm not looking for massive scalability and a quick exit, although there is room to scale.

Cosslett: What are you enjoying most about the business?

Nguyen: The fun part is counseling families and figuring out how to navigate the surprisingly complex process of testing and admissions, whether it's for elementary and middle school, upper school, or college. Then we also work with students applying to graduate programs, including law school, business school, and medical school.

I've always liked advising people, and that's the aspect that I really liked the most about law. When I was practicing law, I enjoyed advising clients—solving their problems—and that's what we're doing now at Ivy Link. But I have more control over what I'm doing. I get to set the agenda and goals for the organization, and that process of figuring out how to grow the business and how to improve upon the offerings that we provide is what really gets me up in the morning. There's a constant drive to improve upon what we're doing.

Cosslett: Other than the counseling role, how do you think your background as a lawyer and your legal training have helped you to build your business?

Nguyen: I would say that the two key skills I've imported from my legal training to my business career are my ability to spot and fix weaknesses and my ability to put together complex deals.

In my business, the central challenge is to identify the strengths and weaknesses of a particular candidate or a particular plan. Before executing a plan, you have to figure out what problems might arise. There's no point in executing a bad plan well. And that's what good lawyers do, whether in a transaction or litigation: they hone right in on the weak points and figure out the steps necessary to solve them. That's a critical skill in my business, and one that we look for when we hire people.

The other skill I apply from my legal training is how to manage a lot of pieces, package them in a sound plan, and successfully execute that plan. When a student or family comes to us, they usually have a goal in mind: getting into a highly selective school. The goal is simple, but the pieces that have to be shaped and assembled to affect that goal are complex—from figuring which tests to take and when to take them, to tutoring for different subjects, to helping with the application itself.

I'm reminded of my early experience as a junior associate doing an M&A deal. I had to pull together all the pieces of information from litigation, employment and benefits, intellectual property, tax, and so on. As an M&A associate, you're the focal point of the deal and you're the one organizing everyone else. A partner used to tell me that it's like herding cats. I think cats are less challenging than your clients and other lawyers! That's a very useful skill that many lawyers have—organizing the deal or the case and pulling together all the different pieces.

Cosslett: Now that Ivy Link is up and running, I understand that you have recently launched an entirely new and different business, eBrevia.

Nguyen: eBrevia is a start-up that a law school classmate and I founded in 2011. Using artificial intelligence [AI] technology developed at Columbia University, our software has the ability to read contracts and other legal documents to extract and summarize important provisions. For instance, if you are conducting legal due diligence and looking to understand whether a contract—actually, a data room full of contracts—contains indemnification obligations and what those obligations entail, our software would quickly and accurately provide you with an abstract of the indemnity provisions.

Many technologies are available to help litigators in the e-discovery space, but there isn't anything on the transactional side. Moreover, our AI technology—specifically, natural language processing—is different from the e-discovery technologies that rely on word searches. Our software takes searching to another level because it is able to learn to recognize legal concepts like indemnification, change of control, etc., extract them, and summarize them for the users, such as lawyers, in-house counsels, or business professionals.

Cosslett: How did you procure this technology from Columbia University?

Nguyen: Columbia University is the developer and owner of numerous NLP technologies that underlie eBrevia's products. I say "products" because while our initial software focuses on legal due diligence, there are other potential applications, such as contract management and compliance. We have been working with Columbia's Technology Transfer Office, as well as its computer science department, through a sponsored research arrangement to adapt the NLP technologies to the legal space. eBrevia is the exclusive licensee of Columbia's NLP technologies as they pertain to the legal space.

Cosslett: What are the potential applications of the software?

Nguyen: Initially, I could see the software used by law firms and in-house legal departments to increase the speed of legal due diligence. I remember when I was an M&A associate conducting due diligence. It was hugely time-consuming, and I would work all-nighters to go through hundreds of legal documents. Our clients always wanted things done as quickly as possible. If I had eBrevia's software back then, my work could have been done a lot more efficiently, not to mention more accurately. I'm pretty sure that during those all-nighters, we missed something important. If you're on the buy side, you could quickly review a target's legal documents to assess its legal obligations in order to decide if you want pursue the deal.

Further along, the software could be used to help with knowledge management and document drafting. For instance, in-house attorneys have mentioned to me that they could see the software helping with their CMS, or contract management system. Further along still, there could be applications in the retail space to help individuals quickly understand material contract terms. The potential is enormous, and I'm beginning to see it as I demo our prototype to lawyers—both at law firms and in-house—and to business professionals.

Cosslett: What are the steps necessary to build a business based on this technology? What is the role of angel investors?

Nguyen: After the sponsored research and product development, a number of things have to happen: we have to get users and get funding. We have to get companies and law firms to use our product and provide us their feedback: Is the product useful? What features should be added? How would it be integrated with existing technology platforms? At the same time, we have to obtain funding to further develop and market the product, as well build the business by hiring staff, etc.

Angels are often individual investors or groups of investors who are willing to take a risk on early stage start-ups that many venture capital funds may pass on. Angels could be friends and families, or individuals who are interested in the particular space—legal technology—and are attracted to the enormous upside, and who have the means to make a calculated risk. Without angels, most start-ups would not take flight. Large venture and private equity funds' investment mandates typically do not allow investments in early-stage start-ups.

Cosslett: How do you see the current wave of new technologies that are in development transforming the practice of law over time?

Nguyen: The legal industry is undergoing seismic transformations. Clients are demanding more value and efficiency from their lawyers. Meanwhile, corporate transactions and lawsuits are becoming increasingly complex. I don't think the work is going away, but the nature of the work is certainly changing. The question that many are asking is, "How can we do more in less time and for less money?" We have witnessed a reliance on staff attorneys to cut costs on less complex tasks. Many law firms have outsourced document review to workers in developing countries—or in some cases, states with lower wages. And others are relying on technology like e-discovery tools. Even CLEs are offered virtually.

To remain competitive, lawyers must be innovative and deliver their expert knowledge in a cost- and time-efficient manner. The key word is innovative. Lawyers tend to get a bad reputation for not being innovative, given how established the legal profession is, but one could argue that good lawyers are actually very innovative if you look at how they structure complex deals or formulate novel legal arguments. I'm sure that innovative thinking could be applied to finding ways to better deliver legal services to clients. And technology is a huge part of the solution.

If you think about it, technology integration has always been a part of law practice. From the typewriter, to Microsoft Word, to black-lining software, to virtual data rooms, lawyers have been adopting new technologies along the way. That is not to say there hasn't been resistance. When I started practicing law, there were partners at my firm who refused to use the computer or e-mail! For a while, I opted not to have a Blackberry because I didn't think it was necessary. That would be unthinkable today. I believe that new technologies will make better lawyers out of good ones. They will be able to perform their tasks more efficiently and compete more effectively. As a result, you will see a consolidation at the top with good lawyers getting the lion's share of the work—and the fees.

Cosslett: Have you faced particular challenges by not having taken a more traditional path into business? By getting a JD in lieu of an MBA?

Nguyen: I think some of the things that MBA students learn can be useful in running a business, such as management skills, HR issues, accounting, and financial modeling. But now that I know what the MBA curricula are like, I think that it's more important to learn those things on the job. You could learn them in the classroom, but many, many MBA graduates don't have the necessary skills to be an entrepreneur and run a business. Many business school students tend to look down on the "soft" classes that are concerned with people and management skills—as opposed to what they call the "hard" classes that focus on finance and accounting.

But the best CEOs that I've seen are the ones who are good at the soft skills. So when we counsel our business school students or MBA applicants, we emphasize the importance of acquiring those soft skills from both the classroom and their jobs. Increasingly, I've noticed that top business schools are looking for students with those soft skills, which are deemed essential to good management and leadership.

So, going back to your question, I think that I missed out on some of the hard-skill classes like finance, accounting, and valuation, but I've picked up many of the essentials in the course of my career. You just need to take time out and learn them. I'd like to point out that often it's not about knowing something, but recognizing what you don't know and figuring out what to do about it.

A key to success at the top of an organization is to find people to support you who are more knowledgeable and talented than you are—who are good at things that you're not good at—and that's a huge thing that I've learned. Many lawyers are good at many things and will try to do everything by themselves. Not delegating is just a recipe for disaster. There are not enough hours in the day to do everything by yourself no matter how good you are, and you simply must rely on the experts and people who have the skill set that you don't have to help you out. That's what building an organization and a business is about.

Cosslett: Are there other traits characteristic of a lawyer that might hinder a successful entrepreneur? It is often said of lawyers that they are risk-averse.

Nguyen: It's not just risk aversion, but also what I'd call the "corollary" traits of risk aversion—like the tendency to be too meticulous. That's a very good trait to have in certain situations requiring perfection, but in many business situations, perfection is not necessary for success and in fact could hinder success. Lawyers like to be erudite and circumspect, dwell on an issue, and chew on it. That's a good trait in some cases, but it could be a sign of indecisiveness or the fear of making a decision. Often in the business world, you don't have the luxury of time—you just need to get things done. Others rely on you to quickly calculate risks and make decisions. Meticulousness and attention to detail are lawyerly virtues that are appropriate to some business situations, but they could be indications of risk aversion, and need to be used sparingly.

There's a business virtue that lawyers would do well to learn: understanding goals. A lot of lawyers are very good at completing complex, focused tasks, but perhaps because of the nature of legal education or legal practice, they tend not to think about the bigger picture or goal. They work very hard to complete a task, whether it's a legal brief or a due diligence memo, but few stop to ask: "Why am I doing this? Why is this important? Why am I billing the client for this? Does the client really need this for his or her business?"

I've been on the client's end, where I look at the bill and I think, "Why did the lawyer do this and charge our company for all this work when it's not really necessary or important to our business?" So, the "big picture" approach that focuses on goals is a business virtue that lawyers would benefit from adopting—for the sake of serving their clients, and operating their own firms or practices.

Cosslett: Where do you see yourself in ten years?

Nguyen: To be honest, it's hard to think beyond the next couple of years. As I've said earlier, things are always changing, and you have to be nimble. We've gotten into the habit of setting goals and planning month by month and quarter by quarter . . . but in ten years?

With respect to my businesses, I'd obviously like to see Ivy Link grow and become more innovative. I'd like to expand into the online and social media space, offering long-distance learning and bridging the geographical gap. Currently, some of our clients are in London and other locations outside of New York, and one trend is to provide educational services via online and long-distance platforms. We've started to do that by using video conferencing and online whiteboards with our students in far-flung places like the UK, Greece, India, and elsewhere. The world of education seems to be trending toward the virtual, online space. The physical space is still important, but it's just not accessible to everyone. And whether we're talking about the high-end services that Ivy Link is providing or the more mass-market services, we have to think about the role of technology, how to educate students who are more comfortable in online environments, and how to expand our reach to students who typically may not be able to afford our services.

For eBrevia, things are moving very quickly. We are developing our software, adding users, building our team, raising funds from angels and VCs. With so much happening, it's hard to see ten years out, but in four to five years, I'd like to see eBrevia's products become as prevalent as other tools, like LexisNexis or IntraLink. At the end of the day, we're offering lawyers and other professionals the technologies to do their jobs more quickly and accurately. Our company is focused on synthesizing and managing the ever-increasing amount of information that we are bombarded with in our daily jobs. And I think in the coming years, you will see a tremendous demand for so-called productivity-enhancing technologies. I expect eBrevia to occupy a major place in that market by offering really useful, innovative tools to help people perform their jobs more efficiently.

With respect to personal goals, despite my hectic work schedule, I still find time to pursue other entrepreneurial interests. In the next ten years—or even the coming year or two—I expect to have other ventures lined up. So keep an eye out for other things that are in the works. I certainly do not see myself slowing down or cashing out and retiring in ten years. I can't imagine not working to build something. While it can be frustrating at times, I really do enjoy the process of creating.

Cosslett: Do you have any career advice to give to students who aspire to be lawyers, to practicing lawyers, and to lawyers who are contemplating leaving law for business?

Nguyen: For the aspiring law student, the thing to remember is—and I learned this later on and certainly hadn't realized this when I was applying—that law school is a professional school. It's not like graduate school for English or political science. Many English majors and poli-sci/econ majors—and I include myself in that group—go to law school expecting the same sort of academic, intellectual experience they had as an undergrad, but their expectation is far from reality. Law schools train lawyers to practice law, by and large, in law firms, corporations, government, or public legal services. Lawyers in legal academia are a minority. Students need to remember that, at the end of the day, law school is a professional school.

For practicing lawyers, I've learned that you need to be honest with yourself about what you want. If you work with a career coach, a good one will advise you to take inventory of your interests, goals, and personality type. What do you care about? What do you hope to accomplish? What type of person are you? Are you an introspective person? Are you a people person? These insights will guide your decision as to what type of practice or career you want to go into. For example, an M&A attorney has a very different personality from a tax attorney. And a public interest lawyer has a very different set of goals and interests from that of a private practice lawyer.

For those who are deciding whether to leave the law or not, you should conduct the same self-assessment that someone exploring different careers within law would. For instance, are you someone who thrives on uncertainty? Then entrepreneurship might be something for you. But if you like stability, constancy, and financial security, then entrepreneurship would likely make you miserable. While entrepreneurship has a lot of pluses, it's not right for everyone. The key is to be honest with yourself. A lot of people avoid the rigorous self-assessment that is so essential to their career, so they don't know what really matters to them.

When I was figuring out whether to leave law, I went back to Columbia and talked with a career counselor there. That's a good starting point for lawyers who are thinking about what to do next. Go back to your law school or undergraduate college and take advantage of their career counseling office. When I visited Columbia, I learned about myself through a battery of tests and a series of one-on-one discussions with my career counselor. I learned what my personality is like, what makes me tick, what my strengths and weaknesses are. It was a process that took time, and it set me on the path that I am on today.

Cosslett: So, look at what you are good at and what gives you pleasure?

Nguyen: Yes. At Ivy Link, we also provide career counseling, and I have moderated discussions and workshops on career transition. For instance, we did a couple of webinars for Columbia that are on their career office's web site. One of the things I talked about was the need to conduct a self-inventory to take into account the different aspects of your personality, like priorities, aptitudes, tastes, interests, goals, and hobbies. Some people want time for hobbies. For some, money is important, or perhaps a challenging job is a must-have. For others, leisure is a high priority, even if it means having a career in a low-paying or unchallenging field. Perhaps taking care of children or loved ones trumps any traditional office job. Be honest about who you are and what you want. I know of many lawyers for whom financial security is very important. And some of those left law firms to pursue public interest work but have been miserable in their jobs, probably because they failed to appreciate the major role a high salary played in their overall job satisfaction.

Cosslett: If you could start over again, would you still go to law school?

Nguyen: I've thought about it a lot, and this is something that I think all lawyers ask themselves at some point. For me, the answer is yes, I would still go to law school, but I would do things differently. I would take different courses. I would check out the other grad schools throughout the university. At Harvard, you could cross-register at MIT, Harvard Business School, the Kennedy School, etc. I would take advantage of the resources throughout the university, not just in law school.

Importantly, I'd also start networking with alumni long before I graduated. Starting right away in my first year, I would talk to alumni with both legal and nonlegal careers and see what advice they might give. During the first year of law school, you're consumed with navigating your classes and understanding civil procedure, contracts, and so forth. The experience is overwhelming and leaves little time to reflect on the bigger picture, like why you are in law school and how to shape your legal education to realize your longer-term goals. If I could do it over again, I would start looking outside the traditional practices of law earlier, exploring what opportunities are out there, and engaging with alumni from my law school.

Overall, I think that law school was a great opportunity. I learned a lot. I met a lot of interesting, talented people. The second point may be even more important than the first. Many law students focus so much on doing well in their classes that they fail to cultivate relationships with classmates who, in the long run, would likely be lifelong resources more valuable than what you learned from your casebooks. Even though I'm no longer practicing law, my business ventures involve partnering with my law school classmates. We're helping each other, and the relationships all started thirteen years ago when we were one-Ls.

Cosslett: The lesson again is to start managing your career when in law school. Don't wait until you graduate, right?

Nguyen: Exactly. I would say also that you should at least think about your career even before going to law school. And remember to be honest with yourself.

Index

A

Adirondack Park Council, 3
Alexander, Wayne
    acting, 178
    actors identification, 188
    advice for interested lawyers, 190
    agreement terms, 184
    Altschul, David, 177
    annuity, 191
    Arthur, 175
    Axl Rose, 180
    billable-hours relationship, 189
    Bogdanovich, Peter, 178
    book authors credibility, 184
    bookness and brandness, 184
    book selling, author/agent, 182
    Braun, David, 177
    Bruch, Carol (professor), 173
    childhood and family background, 172
    commercial law firm experience, 174
    contract as model, 183
    contract negotiation time, 183
    contract terms, 186
    depth of experience, 186
    difficulty with clients, 187
    Edgar Rice Burroughs estate, 176
    firm size, 176
    Greenberg, 177
    Greyhounds, 172
    Hardee Barovick Konecky & Braun, 177
    industry heading, 189
    interesting clients, 187
    interview with admiralty student, 174
    James Bond movies, 181
    law review article, 174
    level of Paramount, 181
    Lucas, George, 179
    Manatt, 180
    marketing and branding, 182
    new business affairs policy, 183
    new legal department, 183
    other practice area, 185
    own firm, 180
    Paterno, Peter, 180
    Pollock, Tom, 178
    portable business, 180
    practice, 182
    production, 185
    professional responsibility issues, 190
    reality of entertainment lawyer, 188
    relationship with studios, 181
    representing directors, 184
    rewarded seniority and longevity, 191
    signable agreement, 183
    Simpson-Bruckheimer Productions, 179
    Smith-Hemion, 177
    social component, 188
    studio lawyer, 179
    suits and ties, 178
    tandem productions, 176
    teaching, 174
    tentpole movies, 181
    undergraduation, 172
    work on percentage, 188
    work with agents and managers, 186
    work with producers, 186
    yale Law School, 172

Index

American Jury Project, 31
Armed Forces Entrance and Examination Center (AFEEC), 20

B

Badmouthing, 166
Barnett, J.F.
    advice to students/lawyer for matrimonial law practice, 111
    bankruptcy practice, 99
    child advocacy, 96–97
    childhood, 95–96
    client as extended family, 98
    culpability relevant to divorce, 108
    divorce as happy ending, 112
    divorce law before 2010, 101
    divorce law vs. bankruptcy law, 97
    divorce lawyers bills, 112
    economic strains vs. marriages, 107
    education, 95
    equitable distribution, 103
    fault grounds for divorce in New York, 101
    financial markets and law practice, 107
    future earning power and contributions during time of marriage, 105
    joint custody, 109
    law firm, 99
    liabilities, 109
    prenuptial agreement, 102–103
    secret information gathering about spouses, 110–111
    therapist advice and divorce, 108
    University of Wisconsin, 98

C

Communication, 166
Community property, 103
Corporate fiduciary, 233

D

Dabhol Power Project, 81
Delany, Sean, 193
    appreciation and depreciation, 73
    asset and liability management, 74
    asset/liability hedging trade, 74
    bankruptcy, 74
    billable-hour requirement, 202
    Bronx Legal Services, 196
    Buffett, Warren (financial weapons of mass destruction), 72
    buy-side participant, 75
    Charities Bureau, 198
    clinics/relevant course work, 195
    contract, 73
    corporate-end users, 75
    creative and novel contract, 75
    criminal defense work, 196
    deal-making skills, 203
    definition, 73
    derivatives, (Kopelman, Ken), 68, 70
    desk set up, 73
    Dodd-Frank legislation, 73–74
    extensive number, 73
    fixed rate payment, 74
    floating-rate bond issuance, 74
    floating rate payment, 74
    government representation, 197
    individual lawyers vs. law firms, 200
    interest-rate swap, 74
    land-use planning and land-use lawyers, 203
    law firm practice, 202
    law school, 196
    law students path, 207
    lawyer–client relationship, 204
    lawyering vs. business advice, 205
    lawyers alliance work, 199
    lawyers mentor, 199
    legitimate transaction, 73
    northwest Bronx, 203
    over-lawyering, 203–204
    pro bono programs, 200–201
    public interest lawyer, 206–208
    public service, 194
    risk of interest rates, 74
    salary, 206
    sell-side participant, 75
    similar cases, 197
    Sullivan & Cromwell, mailroom mix-up, 205–206
    total return swap, 73–75

E

Edgar Rice Burroughs estate, 176
Equitable distribution, 103
Estate planning, 238, 242

F, G

Federal judge, Knoxville, 18
Federal Practice and Procedure, 247
Federal Trade Commission (FTC), 136–138
Feldman, Arthur
  Belize law/Florida sovereign immunities act, 254
  broad-based practice, 251
  class actions, 255
  clerking, 247
  commercial cases, 250
  commercial work, 253
  corporate counsel, 254
  courtroom tactics and showmanship, 252
  drug cases, 254
  Duke, 246
  federal Practice and Procedure, 247
  financial reward, 258
  Houston, Texas, 245
  hustle, 250
  injury/injustice, 255–256
  junior litigator, 248
  law firm, 251
  law school, 246
  law students/practicing lawyers, 258
  legal practice, Houston, 253
  litigators, 252
  mayor day, 248–249
  medical malpractice cases, 255
  ninth circuit, 247
  Nixon appointee, 248
  particularly proud, 256–257
  plaintiffs, 248
  private school, children, 258
  professional responsibility, 258
  publication, 247
  roadkill munching, 246
  shadow jury, 249
  shingle, 251
  sovereign immunity issue, 254
  sports, 246
  UT Law, 246
First American Trading House (FATH), 137
French vs. American law practice, 142

H

Hardee Barovick Konecky & Braun, 177
Houston Chronicle, 250

I

India's Advocates Act, 78
Indie-type model, 189

J

Johnson, Peri Lynne
  advice, 129
    code of conduct, 129
    experience, 122
    Office of Legal Affairs, 123
    representative, 129
    salaries, 122
    seniority, 122
  Arnold & Porter, 117
  attorneys, 124
  Austria, 125
    development function, 125
    Fukushima, 126
    Iran and their nuclear program, 127
    legal advisor, 128
    mandate of, 125
    non-nuclear future, 128
    nuclear disaster, 126–127
    Nuclear Nonproliferation Treaty, 126
    UN, 125
  Barack Obama, 117
  career decision, 116
  college experience, 116
  cuban refugee, 120
  dealmakers, 124
  executive board resolutions, 122
  family background, 116
  Foreign Service Exam, 121
  gender parity, 130–131
  general assembly resolutions, 122
  Guinea, 119
  Harvard, 117
  human rights work, refugee law, 119
  IAEA, 125–128

Johnson, Peri Lynne (*cont.*)
  international work, 116
  law firm background, 130
  law students, advice, 130
  legal department, 124
  National Competitive Exam, 121
  private international law, 118
  pro bono work, 118
  public international law, 118
  refugee population, 120
  Togo Constitution, 118
  UN, 122–123, 129
  UNDP, 123
  United Nations High Commissioner for Refugees, 119
  UN Legal Department, 121
  UN Office of Legal Affairs, 120
Joint custody, 109

K

Kopelman, Ken
  advice for law students/undergraduates, 76
  associates, 67
    business model/management, 68
    client sharing, 68
    movements, 67
    multifaceted job, 67
    working with colleagues, 67
  Bear Stearns, in-house counsel, 63, 70–72, 76
  Bingham McCutchen, 63
  bonus pay, 71
    compensation, 71
    competitive environment, 76
    constituencies, 72
    derivatives, 72
    equity program, 71
    general truism, 72
    high-pressure situations, 76
    regulated business, 72
    role, 71
    role during crisis, 72
    senior management, 72
  Brooklyn Law School, 63, 64
  business lawyer, 68
  characteristics, 69
    investment bank, 69
    legal issues, 70
    trading operations, 70
    transition, 69
  client relationship, corporate lawyer, 66
  corporate associate, Baer Marks & Upham, 63
  corporate generalist, Baer Marks & Upham, 68
  financial services lawyer, 63
  firm life, 66
  Fixed Income and Derivatives Legal Groups, 63
  in-house, 69–70
  internships, 65
  law firm partner, 67–68
  law school decision, 64
  lifestyle, 67
  motivation, 76
  opportunities, 65–66
  SUNY Binghamton, 63
  unpredictable market, 76
  yonkers, 64

L

Law Review article, 174

M

Marital property, 103–104
Michael Tigar and Dick DeGuerin, 252

N

National Labor Relations Act, 22
Nelivigi, Nandan
  adequate infrastructure, 90
  arbitration petition, 82
  corporate America, 84
  corporate attorneys, India, 78
  Dabhol Power Project, 81
  degree of skepticism, 94
  economic situation in Europe, 91
  energy sector., 83
  foreign lawyers, 78
  fraudulent business, 89
  fuel sources, 82
  globalization and economic reform, 91
  Harvard, 81
  Indian courts, 89
  Indian legal system, 88
  Indian regulators, 92
  India practice, 83

India's Advocates Act, 78
industry segment, 86
international firms, 79
international lawyer, 94
international lawyers' program, 81
law school, 79
law students/practicing lawyers, 94
LLM, 80
local goods and local employment, 89
M&A, 85
National Law School, 79–80
OPIC, 87
plan B frequently, 84
power project financings, 83
power sector, 90
private and public international law, 87
professional responsibility, 93
project finance, 85
real estate, 88
school structure, India, 78
secular trends, 92–93
solar project in Austin, Texas, 86
South India, 77
stream of revenue, 83
US project finance market, 84
White & Case, 81
wind farms, 86

Nguyen Adam
admissions counselor, 264
angel investors role, 274
businessmen, 270
business virtue, 276
career counseling, 278
classmates, 264
Columbia University, 273
corollary traits, 276
DOJ attorneys, 263
dot-com bubble, 265
eBrevia, 273
economics and political science, 263
e-discovery space, 273
fund, 268
graduate programs, 272
Harvard Business School, 279
hedge-fund, 268
honors paralegal program, 263
Ivy Link's business, 271
Joel Klein, 264
Judge Hochberg, 266
Judging/writing opinions, 267
Kerry/Edwards presidential campaign, 267
law firm, 265
leave law firms, 270
legal industry, 275
legally blonde, 264
legal training, 272–273
M&A deal, 273
MBA students, 275
online whiteboards, 277
operational experience, 271
Paul Weiss, 267–268
political philosophy and economic philosophy, 263
practicing law, 266
private equity firms, 268
profit-for-purpose company, 272
real estate company, 270
Securities and Exchange Commission, 268
Shearman & Sterling, Cleary, 265
software potential applications, 274
students career advice, 277
summer experience, 265
technology integration, 275
transactional-oriented lawyer, 266
undergrad, Columbia University, 262
video conferencing, 277

Nixon appointee, 248

O

Office of Policy Development, 39–40

Open source software, 167

Overseas Private Investment Corporation (OPIC), 87

P, Q

Penalty of perjury, 104

Probate, 235–237

Public Citizen Litigation Group, 4

R

Revocable living trusts, 237

Right of election, 102

Index

Romain, Kate
- advice for law students, 150
- associates, 141
- best friends network, 148
  - common law system, 147
  - contract, 149
  - corporate and litigation, 138
  - economic crisis, 141
  - family and work life balance, 144
  - French bar admission, 146
  - Germany industry issues, 145
  - legal community recognition, 148
  - lunch hour, 144
  - own books of business, 141
  - partners and associates, 138
  - partnership, 141
  - practice, 144
  - practice change over time, 149
  - professional responsibility, 148
  - relevant factor, 149
  - US-trained attorney, 138
  - women lawyers, 138
  - work hours, 143
- Bredin Prat, 138, 141, 143–149
- career paths, 134
- civil and commercial law, 147
- clerkships, 135
- culture, paris office, 139
- family background, 134
- Federal Trade Commission, 136–138
- Federal Trade Commission's Bureau of Consumer Practices, 133
- French and American attorneys, 143
- French firms, 138
- French vs. US salary structure, 140
- graduation, University of Texas School of Law, 133
- Hogan & Hartson culture, 139
- internalization, law firm talent, 146
- law school decision, 134
- law school experience, 135
- London/Paris offices, 139
- role of in-house counsel, 146
- salaried workers, 146
- undergraduation, 134
- US firms structure in France, 139
- Washington vs. New York law firms, 140
- Weiss, Paul, 139–140

S

Sanders, Jim
- AFEEC, 20
- American Jury Project, 31
- Archibald Cox–Leon Jaworski effect, 25
- bells and whistles, 30
- bet-the-ranch cases, 25
- civil cases, 32
- clerkship, 20
- corporate defense work, 35
- corporate litigation, 26
- democrat won, 18
- expensive private school, 19
- Exxon Valdez Alaskan oil spill, 23
- Exxon Valdez cases, 31
- felony possession cases, 35
- firm's practice, 21
- illegitimate plaintiffs, 28
- International Harvester, 18
- Jacksonville trial, 28
- Jim Neal, 22
- John Landis, 31
- jurors, 27
- law school, 33
- legal practice, Nashville, 33
- litigators, 29
- nashville, 21
- national/local firms, 33
- partnerships/businesses, 33
- plaintiffs' lawyers, 28
- preparedness and familiarity, 32
- professional responsibility, 34
- public defense, 21
- skill set, 34
- tennessee, 18
- trial lawyers, 23
- Twilight Zone, 22, 31
- Valdez case, 24
- Valdez disaster, 25
- Vanderbilt Law School, 19
- Vietnam and Cambodia, 20
- white-collar criminal defense practice, 21
- wind turbines and solar power, 32

Separate property, 103

Shane Kelley, 227
- advice to law students/practicing attorney, 242

Index

Anna Nicole Smith case, 239–240
board certification, 231
corporate fiduciary, 233
Edna Winston case, 240
estate planning, 238
family lineage, 228
fiduciary litigation, 232, 234
financial markets vs. father's practice, 231
Gus Boulis estate case, 240
husband's girlfriend in his will, 241
internships, 229–230
large firm, 232
law practice, 230–231
litigation attorney, 228
litigation in Florida, 231
LLM graduation, 230
probate, 235–237
pro bono, 243
profile, 227
trial, 234
trust admistration, 237
trust law committee, 241
trusts and estates, 229, 241
    class in, 229
    professional responsibility, 241
Sprigman, Christopher, 151
    academic job, 161
    administration, 158
        center of gravity, 160
        conflicts, 159
        DC-based practice, 159
        International Trade Commission (ITC), 159
        merger, 158
    antitrust case, 161
        cocktail napkin, 161
        congress, 162
        different assignment, 168
        formalities system, 161
        Golan vs. Holder, 163
        intellectual property rights, 162–163
        learning, 167
        Peter and Wolf, 162
        stand-up comedy, 165
        Stanford Law Review, 161
        trademark, 167
    antitrust division, 158
    antitrust world, 157
    appellate counsel, 152
    behavioral economics, 153
        business and economic orientation, 153
        Davis Polk, 154
        final wisdom, 154
        intellectual property, 153
        ninth circuit court of appeals, 154
        skeptic of law and economics, 153
    career, 151
    career decision, 169
    case vs. newspaper, 156
    Chicago, 153–154
    christian louboutin, 165
    comedic sanction, 165–167
    copyright, 161–163, 165, 167–168
    DC circuit, 157
    defamation law, 155
        dissertation research, 155
        full-time jobs, 156
        Michael Osborne, friend, 155
    DOJ, 157
    fashion industry, 164
    George Bush, 158–160
    intellectual property, 164
    Kal Ravstiala, 164
    law firm, 169
    law reviews, 160
    law school, 152
    Mark Popofsky, 157
    partnership, 155
    profile, 151
    public school, 168
    research professor, 151
    South Africa, 155–156
    Stanford, 160
    teaching, 161
Streeter, Jonathan, 37
    Arnold & Porter, DC, 41–42
    Arnold & Porter, DC
        junior litigator, 41–42
        public service work, 41
        work trouble, 42
    case duration, 45, 54
        case information, 52–53
        case types, 46
        chickenshit club, 57
        competitive and prestigious job, 43
        crime quality, 44
        defense strategy, 51
        drug case, 56

Index

Streeter, Jonathan (cont.)
    duane reade case, 58
    FBI agent help, 49
    federal and state level prosecution, 44–45
    federal jurisdiction, 44
    insider-trading case, 55
    investigation work, 48
    Marc Dreier case, 57
    merger/company financial performance report, 54
    money-laundering cases, 47
    narcotics cases, 46
    New York City culture, 43
    no. of cases, 49–50
    personal style, 56
    ponzi scheme case, 57–58
    Preet Bharara, 60
    Raj Rajaratnam investigation, 50–51, 53–54
    Republican appointee/Democratic appointee, 59
    Securities Fraud Task Force, 47–48
    southern district work, 43
    trial partner, 56
    trial prep, 52
    true-believer prosecutors, 61
    white-collar case, 59
    white-collar work, 46
    winnable case, 49
    witnesses deal, 55
    working time, 52
  clerkship work, 40
  dechert, 60–61
  department of Justice, 39–40
  governmental roles, 61, 62
  inspiration as litigator, 37
  local politics, 38
  moral compass, 38
  motivation, 62
  national forest work, 39
  truth and justice, 61
  US Attorney's Office, 42–61

T

Tandem Productions, 176
The Kelley Law Firm, 227
Trusts and estates, 228, 241–242
Twilight Zone, 22

U

Unimet Trading Corporation, 137
US Attorney's Office, 3
US Court of Appeals Building, 248

V

Valuation, 105
Vladeck, Anne
  Adirondack Park Council, 3
  antitrust or corporate cases, 2
  anucha Brown Sanders case, 11
  anucha's case, 10
  bells and whistles, 12
  career paths, 2
  COBRA, 6
  Columbia, 8
  Columbia Law School, 2
  contingency, 9
  courtroom, 11
  defamation, 8
  employment discrimination, 5, 7
  employment litigation, 15
  employment litigator/general litigator?, 14
  Ezold vs. Wolf Block, 7
  federal cause of action, 9
  firm's discrimination practice, 2
  flamboyant, 12
  Frankfurt Kurnit, 3
  garden case, 13
  gold digger, 13
  human nature, 14
  jurors, 10
  labor and employment law, 2
  mandatory retirement, 5
  motivation, 14
  New York–oriented practice, 5
  professional responsibility, 14
  prosecute, 12
  Public Citizen Litigation Group, 4
  reputation, litigator, 5
  sexual orientation, 8
  University of Pennsylvania, 2
  US Attorney's Office, 3
  videotape depositions, 12
  wall street, 9
  Whittlesey case, 4
  Whittlesey vs. Union Carbide, 4

W, X, Y, Z

Whedbee David, 209
- artisanal firm's practice, 217
- asylum cases, 210
- brady issues, 220
- bush administration, 218
- civil rights firm, 222
- clergy sex abuse litigation, 214
- clerkship, 212
- clients, 218
- college and law school, 210
- conceptual legal perspective, 214
- constitutional law, 225
- contracting economy, lawyers, 215
- DEA, 218
- defense counsel, 223
- defense-oriented firm, 212
- diocese, 215
- district court clerking, 213
- experience, 225
- fair housing cases, 220
- federal courts, 212
- federal fair housing act, 221
- grunt torts, 222
- houses raided, 218
- illegal gambling, 221
- immigration lawyer, 211
- innocence project cases, 219
- Judge Berrigan, 213
- Judge Gould's chambers, 217
- Ken MacDonald, 221
- law school process, 211
- law students or undergrads, 224
- legal cause, 211
- legal practice in Seattle, 215
- literary criticism and historiography, 210
- litigation department, 217
- litigation work, 218
- London School of Economics, 211
- MacDonald Hoague & Bayless practice and history, 215
- medium-sized firms, 215
- Mel Crawford, 217
- muslim sensibility, 218
- ninth circuit cases, 219
- personal injury case, 223
- plaintiffs, 214
- playing soccer, 211
- political ideology, 216
- political, social/religious group, 210
- pomona, 210
- practice civil rights law, 209
- scattergun approach, 213
- seattle police department, 219
- sex abus, 214
- skill set, 224
- Southern California, 210
- Tim Ford, 216
- unorthodox situation, 221
- voter abuse and intimidation, 211
- work safety package, 222

Whittlesey case, 4

Whittlesey vs. Union Carbide, 4

CPSIA information can be obtained at www.ICGtesting.com
Printed in the USA
LVOW120242021112
305535LV00001B/77/P